2nd Australian Edition

QuickBooks®

FOR

DUMMIES®

2nd Australian Edition

QuickBooks® FOR DUMMIES®

by Veechi Curtis

WILEY

Wiley Publishing Australia Pty Ltd

QuickBooks For Dummies®, 2nd Australian Edition

Published by
Wiley Publishing Australia Pty Ltd
42 McDougall Street
Milton, Qld 4064
www.dummies.com

Copyright © 2012 by Wiley Publishing Australia Pty Ltd

The moral rights of the author have been asserted.

National Library of Australia
Cataloguing-in-Publication data:

Author:	Curtis, Veechi.
Title:	QuickBooks For Dummies/Veechi Curtis.
Edition:	2nd Australian ed.
ISBN:	978 1 74246 896 9 (pbk.)
Notes:	Includes index.
Subjects:	QuickBooks.
	Small business — Finance — Computer programs.
	Small business — Accounting — Computer programs.
Dewey Number:	657.90420285536

Cover image: © iStockphoto.com/monkeybusinessimages

Screenshots copyright © Intuit Inc. All rights reserved.

Microsoft Excel screenshots reprinted with permission from Microsoft Corporation.

Typeset by diacriTech, Chennai, India

Printed in China by
Printplus Limited

10 9 8 7 6 5 4 3 2 1

About the Author

Veechi Curtis is passionate about Australian business and the potential that people have to realise their dreams, achieve financial independence and contribute to the society around them.

Born in Scotland, Veechi attended university in Bathurst, NSW, where she completed her degree in Accountancy and Business Management. She has been a business consultant specialising in accounting software for more than 15 years, training all kinds of businesses in how to make QuickBooks software work for them. As a journalist, she has written for many publications including *Australian PC World*, *Australian Personal Computer*, *Australian Reseller News* and *CCH Australia Limited*, and has also been a columnist for *The Sydney Morning Herald*.

Behind the scenes, Veechi's business consulting practice provides valuable insights into how best to configure accounting software and generate meaningful reports. Veechi is also author of the Australian edition of *Small Business For Dummies*, as well as co-author of the Australian edition of *Business Plans For Dummies*.

Veechi has three children and lives with her husband in the beautiful Blue Mountains of NSW.

Author's Acknowledgements

Thanks and much love to my husband John, and to my children Daniel, Isla and Finbar. Love to Mum and Dad, and to my extended family all around the globe.

I'd also like to say thanks to the team at Wiley Publishing Australia for their valuable support and editorial guidance. Also thanks to everyone at Reckon Software, particularly Gerald Chait, Dean Darke, Kevin McDermott and Samantha Stone. Last, but not least, thanks to Nathan Elcoate for his excellent leave-no-stone-unturned technical review.

Publisher's Acknowledgements

We're proud of this book; please send us your comments through our online registration form located at `http://dummies.custhelp.com`.

Some of the people who helped bring this book to market include the following:

Acquisitions, Editorial and Media Development

Project Editor: Maryanne Phillips

Acquisitions Editor: Rebecca Crisp

Editorial Manager: Hannah Bennett

Proofreader: Liz Goodman

Production

Cartoons: Glenn Lumsden

Indexer: Veechi Curtis

Contents at a Glance

Introduction 1

Part I: Preparing for the Journey 7
Chapter 1: Hit the Road, Jack! 9
Chapter 2: Lists, Lists and More Lists 29

Part II: Everyday Transactions 53
Chapter 3: Billing Your Customers 55
Chapter 4: Staying in the Black and Getting Paid 83
Chapter 5: Shelling Out the Cash 111
Chapter 6: Keeping Suppliers Sweet 133
Chapter 7: A Balancing Act 157
Chapter 8: Stocking Up 175
Chapter 9: Setting Up Opening Balances 203
Chapter 10: Understanding GST 217

Part III: Digging a Little Deeper 249
Chapter 11: Adapting QuickBooks to Fit the Bill 251
Chapter 12: Managing Payroll 271
Chapter 13: Reporting on the Situation 307
Chapter 14: Managing Profit and Growing Your Business 323
Chapter 15: Looking After Your Company File 341

Part IV: The Part of Tens 363
Chapter 16: Ten Tips for Electronic Payments.................... 365
Chapter 17: Ten Tricks for Speed....................................... 373
Chapter 18: Ten Tips for Working with Your Accountant 379
Appendix: The QuickBooks Family...................................... 387

Index 393

Table of Contents

Introduction *1*

How to Use This Book.. 1
Conventions Used in This Book.. 2
Different Products and Versions.. 3
Foolish Assumptions.. 3
How This Book is Organised 3
    Part I: Preparing for the Journey 3
    Part II: Everyday Transactions.. 4
    Part III: Digging a Little Deeper 4
    Part IV: The Part of Tens 4
Special Icons.. 4

Part I: Preparing for the Journey *7*

Chapter 1: Hit the Road, Jack! **9**

Laying the Foundations 9
    Planning for what lies ahead 10
    Gathering all the information you need.................................. 12
    Picking a start date.. 12
Waltzing Through the EasyStep Interview 13
    Creating your first company file 13
    Telling QuickBooks what you're all about 16
Getting Acquainted.. 16
    Feeling your way around.. 17
    Understanding how QuickBooks stores info 18
    Viewing tricks: Now you see it, now you don't 19
    Expressing yourself 20
    Customising your home page.. 21
    Signing up for an instant health check.................................. 22
Calling Out for Help 23
Getting In and Out 25
    Closing QuickBooks and going home...................................... 25
    Starting a new day and opening QuickBooks again.............. 25
    Registering with the powers-that-be 26

Chapter 2: Lists, Lists and More Lists **29**

Understanding Your Chart of Accounts.. 29
    Picking your account type.. 31
    Adding a new account 34

Finding your way around 35
Deleting unloved accounts 36
Sorting your accounts, every which way 36
Grouping things together.. 38
Working with Customer and Supplier Lists................................... 39
Navigating to the centre... 39
Creating a new customer 39
Viewing your Customer List in different ways 41
Creating a new supplier 43
Changing, deleting and merging... 44
Looking up stuff in lists 45
Sorting customers into groups... 46
Getting on Top of Your Item List... 48
Creating a new item 48
Picking your item type 50

Part II: Everyday Transactions *53*

Chapter 3: Billing Your Customers. **55**

Defining Your Preferences (No Holds Barred) 56
Recording Your First Sale 56
Creating an invoice, quick as a flash 57
Getting invoices where you want 'em 59
Billing for itsy-bitsy bits of time... 61
Whispering sweet nothings 62
Creating not-quite-ready-yet invoices 63
Adding discounts and subtotals 64
Keeping Within the Law... 65
Producing a Tax Invoice 66
Choosing tax codes... 66
Calculating GST backwards 68
Fixing Things Up (Nobody's Perfect, After All)........................... 69
Finding a sale after you've recorded it.................................. 69
Changing a sale (but think before you act) 70
Deleting or voiding a sale... 70
Raising credit (or adjustment) notes 71
Invoicing Tips... 73
Working faster, playing much harder 73
Memorising transactions 74
Recalling memorised transactions (what's your name again?) 76
Working with Estimates and Sales Orders................................... 77
Printing Sales Forms... 79
The simple way 79
The not-so-simple (but quite efficient) way 79
When printing blues call 80
Emailing Invoices (Anyone Can Do It!)... 80

Chapter 4: Staying in the Black and Getting Paid **83**

Seeing Who Owes You What... 83
Recording Customer Payments 85
    Understanding the mystery of undeposited funds......................... 85
    Where to go, what to do.. 86
Finetuning.. 88
    Working with sales receipts... 88
    Depositing funds into your bank account 90
Troubleshooting Payments When Things Go Wrong....................... 92
    Finding customer payments 92
    Fixing up mistakes 93
    Dealing with overpayments... 95
    Processing customer refunds... 95
    Matchmaking credits with their debits 96
Recording Payments Made in Advance 97
Recording Other Sources of Income 99
    Processing supplier refunds.. 99
    Recording interest or investment income 100
    Receiving loans or capital contributions..................................... 102
    Figuring out which account to pick... 103
    Choosing the correct tax code.. 103
Bringing in the Dough 104
    Doing the asking, reaping the rewards.. 104
    Sending letters, sweet and sour... 106
    Keeping track of who promised what 107
    Giving up, and writing it off 108

Chapter 5: Shelling Out the Cash. **111**

Recording Business Expenses... 111
    Spending money, time after time 112
    Figuring out which tax code to choose.. 114
    Working with multiple bank accounts... 114
    Picking the right expense account 116
    Splitting hairs 117
    Making electronic payments 118
    Memorising transactions 118
Transferring Funds between Accounts... 120
Finding and Changing Transactions... 121
    Checking out your Banking Register 121
    Sleuthing in the Supplier Centre 122
    Deleting your mistakes.. 122
    Changing transactions after the event 123
Playing with Plastic 123
    Owning up to your credit cards.. 123
    Confessing your spending 124
    Paying the piper... 126

A Petty Affair 126
   Giving with one hand, taking with the other 127
   Securing your cash under lock and key 128
   Getting even pettier with GST 130
Recording Bank Fees 130

Chapter 6: Keeping Suppliers Sweet 133

Deciding if You Need This in Your Life 133
Recording Purchase Orders and Supplier Bills 134
   Creating your first purchase order 135
   Receiving items when there's no bill 136
   Receiving a bill (items only) 138
   Recording bills for services, rather than items 139
Calling Up Your Purchase Records 141
Sending Purchase Orders 141
   Whipping your purchase order into shape 141
   Printing purchase orders, easy as anything 143
   Emailing purchase orders into the ether 143
Understanding GST 144
   Tax codes — a guessing game 144
   Calculating GST backwards 145
   When GST doesn't quite add up 145
Getting Everything Just Right 146
   Destroying the evidence 146
   Closing off purchase orders 146
Assessing the Damage 146
   Taking a look at reality — how much do you owe? 147
   Recording supplier payments 148
   Paying suppliers electronically 150
   Paying suppliers using your credit card 150
   Recording part-payments or discounts 151
   Letting suppliers know you've paid 'em 152
Keeping Things in Tune 153
   Recording supplier credits 153
   Applying supplier credits to outstanding bills 153
   Finding supplier payments 154
   Fixing up supplier payments 155
   Tidying up odd amounts 155

Chapter 7: A Balancing Act 157

Deciding Which Accounts to Reconcile 158
Setting Up Opening Bank Balances 158
   Step 1: List uncleared transactions 158
   Step 2: Enter the total value of uncleared transactions
      in a special account 159
   Step 3: Check your beginning balance 159

Reconciling Your Bank Account 160
Seven Sticky Situations 162
    Sticky situation number 1: Figuring out where to start 162
    Sticky situation number 2: Forgotten bank charges or interest... 163
    Sticky situation number 3: Transactions that don't show,
        but you know exist 163
    Sticky situation number 4: Transactions are definitely
        missing.. 164
    Sticky situation number 5: Transactions that are
        (sadly) wrong... 165
    Sticky situation number 6: Customer payments aren't listed 166
    Sticky situation number 7: You haven't reconciled your
        account for years 166
When Your Bank Account Just Won't Balance............................. 167
    Tricks to try before you kick the cat 167
    Tricks to try before you kick the computer 168
    Tricks to try before you kick the bucket................................. 169
Troubleshooting Beginning Balances 170
    Generating a reconciliation discrepancy report......................... 171
    Undoing the previous reconciliation....................................... 172
Deciding When to Print.. 174

Chapter 8: Stocking Up **175**
Getting Started.. 176
    Creating your first inventory item.. 176
    Telling QuickBooks where to go 178
    Drilling down on GST.. 180
    Stating your preferences.. 180
Working with Units of Measure... 181
Organising Items into Groups 183
    Playing happy families 183
    Creating groups for speedy billing 184
    Producing a new item using other items 185
    Adding detail and custom fields 186
Doing Your First Head Count.. 187
    Counting is as easy as 1, 2, 3 188
    Ensuring your inventory records tally.................................... 189
Giving Your Item List the Once-Over.. 191
    Finding items 191
    Deleting items... 191
    Hiding items (and making them inactive)............................... 192
    Merging items 193
Pricing to Sell 193
    Pricing one item at a time.. 194
    Pricing a few items at a time... 194
    Setting different price levels... 196

Digging Yourself Out of a Hole 197
    Adjusting the quantity of an item 197
    Adjusting the cost of an item 198
    Troubleshooting transactions 199
Standing Up and Counting Down 199
    Getting ready for the countdown 200
    Doing the grand reckoning 200
Balancing Your Inventory Account 201

Chapter 9: Setting Up Opening Balances 203

Customer Opening Balances 204
    Creating an item for historical data 204
    Recording historical transactions 204
    Checking your totals 206
Supplier Opening Balances 207
Inventory Opening Balances 208
Account Opening Balances 209
    Entering a few balances to get started 209
    Taxing torture — made easy 209
    Reviewing what you've done so far 211
    Recording the remaining opening balances 212
    Troubleshooting opening balances 214

Chapter 10: Understanding GST 217

It's Elemental, my dear Watson 217
Preparing QuickBooks for GST 218
    Step 1: Customise your accounts for GST 218
    Step 2: Tell the ATO where to go 219
    Step 3: Set up your Tax Item List 221
    Step 4: Set up your Tax Code List 222
    Step 5: State your preferences 225
    Step 6: Enter opening balances 226
Cracking the Code 227
    Mapping tax codes in your Chart of Accounts 227
    Keeping everything squeaky-clean 229
    Coding transactions when you don't have a clue 230
    Coding transactions even if they're not reportable 230
    Recording transactions when GST isn't 10 per cent 231
    Getting personal 232
Psyching Up to Produce Your Business Activity Statement 233
    Making sure the raw data is right 233
    Running reports, considering the results 236
Setting Up Your Business Activity Statement 236
    Configuring your BAS (hey ho, what fun) 237
    Linking items to each box (slightly scary, but essential) 238
    Saving your settings (easy, but important) 240

Lodging your Business Activity Statement 240
    Generating your first activity statement................................240
    Making sure the whole deal is spot on..................................242
    Lodging your statement with Reckon GovConnect......................243
Recording Your BAS Payment or Refund...245
    Paying the piper — when you owe them...............................245
    Claiming the dosh — when they owe you 246
    Getting PAYG to balance...247

Part III: Digging a Little Deeper 249

Chapter 11: Adapting QuickBooks to Fit the Bill 251

Imagining a Program Designed Just for You...252
    Changing what you see before you......................................252
    Getting results that are spot on 253
Working with Templates 255
    Customising your first template 255
    Adding logos..257
    Deciding which columns to display and
        which columns to print 258
Working with the Layout Designer 260
    Fooling around with fonts...260
    Adding borders and lines..261
    Deleting stuff you don't need 262
    Inserting new text 263
    Adding extra information...263
    Lining everything up 265
Copying, Creating and Importing Templates 266
    Creating a new template from scratch 266
    Taking on pre-designed templates.......................................267
    Deleting or hiding templates 268
    Sharing templates 268
Troubleshooting Blues...269

Chapter 12: Managing Payroll 271

Heading for the Centre..271
    Getting the ball rolling...272
    Turning payroll on 272
    Sweating through the interview...273
    Tweaking accounts to make things easy................................274
Getting Acquainted with Payroll Items 275
    Wages, holiday pay, sick pay and more.................................275
    Allowances, reimbursements and holiday loading....................275
    Union fees, donations and other deductions 277
    Tax, in every flavour possible 277
    Superannuation, guaranteed 278

Finalising Employee Pays and Details...280
 Grouping pays together with schedules 280
 Checking the setup for each employee...282
Processing Employee Pays 284
 Doing your first pay run...285
 Viewing pay transactions and payslips..287
 Working with timesheets 287
 Avoiding payroll hiccups 289
 Deleting or changing pays 289
Taking a Break 290
 Setting up leave...290
 Catching up on ancient history...293
 Recording leave taken 294
Reporting Super Contributions (RESC) 295
 Setting up salary sacrifice super...296
 Figuring out what to do with additional super
  paid by the employer 297
Paying Your Dues 299
 Paying employee liabilities 299
 Balancing employee liabilities..300
 Recording tax payments 301
Keeping Everything Shipshape 302
Printing Payment Summaries..303

Chapter 13: Reporting on the Situation.........................307

Creating Different Kinds of Reports 307
 Heading to the centre...308
 Creating your first report..309
 Querying individual accounts, customers or suppliers 310
 Narrowing things down...311
Getting Reports to Look Good 313
 Mucking around with columns..313
 Fitting everything in 314
 Bringing out the artist within 314
Saving and Sharing 316
 Saving reports for next time around 316
 Sharing memorised reports with others......................................317
 Downloading reports from other sources 317
Reporting to the Outside World...318
 Sending reports to Excel...319
 Emailing reports around the globe...320
 Creating a silk purse from a sow's ear 320
Battling those Printing Blues 321

Chapter 14: Managing Profit and Growing Your Business 323

Distinguishing Fool's Gold from the Real Thing 323
 Analysing transactions, reporting on profit 324
 Imposing a class system 325

Allocating classes to transactions 326
Generating reports by class (or cost centre) 326
Managing Projects and Individual Jobs 328
Adding jobs to your Customer List 328
Reporting on the profitability of every job 329
Looking at the Big Picture 330
Telling a story with your Profit & Loss 330
Taking a photo with your Balance Sheet 332
Checking business health with one click 334
Customising financial reports 336
Working to a Budget 336
Budgeting as if you mean it 336
Gazing into the future.. 339

Chapter 15: Looking After Your Company File................. 341

Getting Your Bearings 341
Backing Up to Save Yourself from Doom 342
Deciding how often to back up 343
Backing up your company file on a local drive 343
Backing up your company file online 346
Creating a portable file instead 347
Redeeming Yourself in the Nick of Time...................................... 348
Restoring your file 349
Running a rescue mission 351
Taking Care of Your Data 353
Dealing with a file that's too big for its boots 353
Cleaning up your company file.. 353
Locating your company file 355
Staying honest, keeping clean 356
Rebuilding your file.. 357
Avoiding data hiccups in the first place 358
Upgrading to Windows 7... 358
Protecting Private Information 359
Creating an administrator password............................... 359
Restricting employee access.. 360

Part IV: The Part of Tens *363*

Chapter 16: Ten Tips for Electronic Payments.................. 365

Go the Whole Hog.. 365
Be Prepared (Before Diving In) 366
Get Employees and Suppliers Up to Speed 366
Use a Clearing Account.. 367
Group Payments Together.. 368
Keep Track of ABA Files... 369
Never Enter Anything Twice 370

Share the Good News...370
Clean Out the Dead Wood...371
Guard Yourself against Online Fraud 371

Chapter 17: Ten Tricks for Speed 373

Take the Short Way Home 373
Forget That Furry Mouse...374
Get Smart When Searching...374
Work Those Fingers..375
Memorise Regular Transactions...376
Become a Copycat 376
Get Columns Just Where You Want 'Em...................................377
Stop Printing..377
Give QuickBooks a Boost...378
Add Key Reports to Your Icon Bar 378

Chapter 18: Ten Tips for Working with Your Accountant 379

Cultivate Your Inner Pedant...380
Audit Yourself (Better You than Someone Else).....................381
Create an Accountant Copy 382
Review Changes before Merging...383
Don't Jump the Gun..384
Tell Your Accountant about QuickBooks.................................384
Set a Closing Date 384
Communicate...385
Keep Track of Your Assets...386
Anticipate the Obvious 386

Appendix: The QuickBooks Family............................387

Choosing the One that's Right for You.....................................387
Moving Up the Family Tree 389
Other QuickBooks Products 390
Retail Point of Sale..390
Reckon Payroll Premier..390
Quicken Personal...391

Index 393

Introduction

As I sit writing this introduction, the sun streaks through the picture windows and the sound of kids running feral outside on the street (a couple of whom are mine) provide the background music. The phone rings from time to time — a few business calls, a couple of personal ones — and I think to myself, this balance of work and lifestyle is what small business is all about.

Most people start their own business not because they're seeking fame and fortune, but because they're seeking some kind of autonomy in their life. Luckily, by making the boring stuff like bookkeeping and tax as swift and painless as possible, QuickBooks frees you up to enjoy the more pleasurable things in life.

In *QuickBooks For Dummies*, I don't forget for a moment that QuickBooks is a means to an end, and that you want to get your books done as quickly — and, of course, as accurately — as possible. Hopefully, I can help you achieve just that.

How to Use This Book

I don't recommend that you sit down and read *QuickBooks For Dummies* avariciously from cover to cover. If I did, then my publisher would probably have to attach some kind of health warning.

However, if you're setting up QuickBooks for the first time, I suggest you read Chapter 1, 'Hit the Road, Jack!' and Chapter 2, 'Lists, Lists and More Lists', before moving on to other areas. That's because a number of the decisions you make when getting started affect everything else that follows. A clean start takes a bit of planning and, hopefully, these early chapters help you with that process.

As well as reading the first two chapters, when it's time to do your first Business Activity Statement, pour yourself a fine glass of your preferred poison and devour Chapter 10 in earnest, page by page. And if you have employees, Chapter 12 makes for a scintillating (and fairly essential) read.

After these initiation rites, pause to consider whether you'd rather have had your two front teeth knocked out.

After checking out the essential stuff, a pick 'n' mix approach is probably the best idea: Read a little here, browse another bit there, or head for the end without missing a beat. Or, pluck this book off the shelf only when something is causing you grief. If you have a specific question, look it up in the index.

Conventions Used in This Book

On occasions, I supply you with step-by-step descriptions of tasks. For each task, I highlight the action itself in bold. If you understand this process, you don't need to read the blurb underneath, meaning you can whiz through the instructions in a few minutes flat. For example:

1. Go to your Supplier Centre.

The easiest method is to click Supplier Centre on the Navigation Bar. Alternatively, select Supplier Centre from the Suppliers menu.

My point? If you already know how to get to the Supplier Centre, you don't have to plough through a long-winded description telling you how to find it.

If a step-by-step instruction consists of menus within menus, then I simplify things further:

1. Choose Customers⇨Create Estimates

This command means you need to choose the Customers menu, followed by the Create Estimates command.

You may also come across keyboard combinations such as:

Ctrl-P

This combination means you press and hold the Ctrl key, type the letter *P* and then release the Ctrl key. (If you can type, shortcut keys are a great way to speed up your work.)

Different Products and Versions

QuickBooks For Dummies covers all seven core members of the QuickBooks family: QuickBooks Accounting, QuickBooks Contractor, QuickBooks Hosted by Reckon Online, QuickBooks Pro, QuickBooks Plus, QuickBooks Premier and QuickBooks Enterprise. If you're working with one of the more junior family members, such as QuickBooks Accounting, you may come across references to features that don't exist, such as payroll. In this situation, I try to point these differences out, explaining which products have these features, and which ones don't.

Foolish Assumptions

Over the years, I've learned to assume as little as possible. However, to write this book, I did have to make two small assumptions about you, dear reader:

- ✔ Your knowledge of computers and how they work is a little more advanced than knowing where to find the on/off switch.
- ✔ You already have a copy of QuickBooks software, or you plan to purchase a copy of QuickBooks.

How This Book is Organised

This edition of *QuickBooks For Dummies* is divided into four parts:

Part I: Preparing for the Journey

The first part of this book is the stuff you need to know when you first set up QuickBooks. I talk about the initial setup interview, as well as how to set up lists for customers, suppliers, accounts and items.

Part II: Everyday Transactions

This part deals with everyday business transactions: Making sales and receiving money (the fun bit); making purchases and shelling out money (the not-so-fun bit); handling inventory; and understanding GST.

Part III: Digging a Little Deeper

This part covers a range of topics including customising templates, paying employees, customising reports and looking after your QuickBooks company file. There's also a whole chapter dedicated to understanding financial statements and analysing where you make your money (and where you don't).

Part IV: The Part of Tens

This is the list (but not last) part of the book. You discover a list of tips to help with electronic banking, a list of tips to help speed your work and a list of things to consider when working with your accountant. Sneaking into the final pages, I also include an appendix about the QuickBooks family, listing the shining characteristics and foibles of each product.

Special Icons

Throughout this book little icons in the margins flag special information sure to be helpful as you peruse a chapter. Here's a brief description outlining their functions:

Although Chapter 10 is exclusively about GST and nothing else, the truth of the matter is that GST affects almost every transaction and forms a steady theme throughout this book. Because of this, I flag any content relating to GST with this special GST icon.

Don't forget these snappy pearls of wisdom. Remember, remember, remember . . .

This icon flags tricky procedures or in-depth detail. Depending on your level of skills, you may want to ask your accountant or QuickBooks consultant for further advice on topics marked with this icon.

 Tips are the little ways to make life easier, including shortcuts and handy brainwaves.

 This icon flags new features in the latest release of QuickBooks.

 Warning icons are serious stuff. If you want to keep your accounts clean and mean, read warnings carefully and take heed.

Part I
Preparing for the Journey

Glenn Lumsden

In this part ...

1f you're new to QuickBooks, then reading the two chapters in this part is akin to fuelling your vehicle before setting off on a road trip — a necessity if you're going to last the distance. Chapter 1 runs you through the QuickBooks setup process, and Chapter 2 explains all about the four lists that make up the backbone of every transaction: Your Chart of Accounts, your Customer List, your Supplier List and — last but not least — your Item List.

If you're an old hand at QuickBooks but recently upgraded to the latest version of QuickBooks, don't be tempted to skip the fine literature that makes up Chapter 1. Marked with handy Upgrading icons throughout, this chapter points out some of the QuickBooks features that can make you divinely happy, cure you of all diseases and generally transform your life.

Chapter 1

Hit the Road, Jack!

. . . .

In This Chapter

▶ Deciding on D-Day — your financial start date

▶ Dealing with the QuickBooks EasyStep Interview

▶ Taking the QuickBooks grand tour

▶ Getting help the moment you need it

▶ Starting a new day and quitting when you're done

. . . .

*I*n the same way as one day I'll sit my daughter down and tell her everything-I-wish-I'd-known-before-I-married-and-had-three-kids, in this chapter I share with you everything-I-wish-I'd-known-before-I-stuffed-up-QuickBooks-and-mastered-how-to-use-the-software. (The only difference is that I dwell slightly less on floundering romance, sleepless nights and owner-built homes, and focus more on timing, patience and getting rich quick.)

If you're feeling in any way daunted by what lies ahead, then cast your cares to the wind. Usually, the very people who are the most unsure about QuickBooks when they begin using the software are the same people who do the best job in the end. That's because going slow and taking things step by step pays off in the long run. (Not just with QuickBooks, but with one's choice of life partner too — back to those life lessons again.)

Enough rambling. It's time to roll up your sleeves and get started.

Laying the Foundations

Brick by brick, barrow by barrow, it's time to lay the foundations for your immaculate palace.

Planning for what lies ahead

I've done hundreds of accounting software setups over the years, which can take something like 30 minutes for a simple service business to several days for a complex manufacturing business with 25 employees. For businesses that are already established (as opposed to new businesses that are just getting started) I often find that setting up QuickBooks in two stages works best: Sometime in early July, I get the client started with setting up accounts and lists and entering transactions. A few months later, when the client's accountant has finalised the tax returns for the previous year, I return to the client and fix up the opening balances.

So, bearing in mind that setting up QuickBooks can be spread over several weeks, not to mention months, here's my step-by-step guide to what's involved.

1. **Decide on a start date and organise all your paperwork.**

   If you're not sure what your start date should be, skip to the section 'Picking a start date' later in this chapter. Get all your paperwork in order up to this date (customer bills, supplier accounts and so on) and ensure that all your essential financial information is close to hand (if you're not sure what this entails, make your way to the section 'Gathering all the information you need' later in this chapter).

2. **Install QuickBooks.**

   Instructions for installing QuickBooks software are explained in your QuickBooks user guide.

3. **Follow the steps in this chapter to complete the EasyStep Interview.**

   The EasyStep Interview walks you through setting up your first QuickBooks company file, a straightforward process that only takes 15 minutes or so. See 'Waltzing Through the EasyStep Interview' later in this chapter when you're ready to start.

4. **If you're new to QuickBooks, take a moment to have a good old stickybeak.**

   In the thick of this chapter, in the section 'Getting Acquainted', I take you on a grand tour of QuickBooks.

5. **On your QuickBooks home page, go to the Company area and click on Chart of Accounts. Customise this Chart of Accounts to fit your business.**

   I always recommend tweaking your Chart of Accounts to fit your business — adding accounts, changing account names or deleting accounts that you don't need. I explain all you need to know about this process in Chapter 2.

6. **Create listings for customers, suppliers and items.**

   Again, Chapter 2 is the place to go to find out about setting up your Customer List, Supplier List and Item List. If you're in a hurry to be up and running, it's okay to enter names only for customers and suppliers — you can always complete other contact details later on. And yes, if your business buys and sells goods for resale and you need to include inventory in your Item List, motor on to Chapter 8.

7. **Have a go at entering a couple of basic transactions, such as withdrawals, deposits, sales and payments.**

   These transactions form the guts of QuickBooks — there's nothing like getting your hands dirty and leaping straight in. Chapters 3 to 9 cover everything you need to know.

8. **Think about how you can adapt QuickBooks to be even better.**

   You may be thinking that QuickBooks is pretty good so far, but there's more. You can customise not only the stuff that QuickBooks generates as final invoices, purchase orders and remittance slips, but also what you see when you enter data for sales or purchases. Chapter 11 covers all you need to know about customising templates and designing forms.

9. **Enter opening balances for customers and suppliers.**

   If you plan to use QuickBooks for invoicing and you have customers that owed you money as of your start date, then you need to set up opening balances for each one. The same deal applies if you want QuickBooks to keep track of supplier bills — you need to tell QuickBooks how much you owed each supplier at your start date. Chapter 9 explains how to enter these opening balances and make sure that everything reconciles.

10. **If you have employees, set up payroll.**

    If you're going to use payroll, do so from the very beginning of the payroll year (July). Setting up payroll can be hideously technical and time consuming, so if you're running short of time, get some help from a QuickBooks Professional Partner (for details, see 'Calling Out for Help' later in this chapter). Chapter 12 covers payroll in depth.

11. **Decide on a backup system and set it in place.**

    Backing up is important, so be sure to establish a backup system. See Chapter 15 to find out more.

12. **After the dust has settled (which could be several months in the future), whip your account opening balances into shape.**

    If your business was established before you started with QuickBooks, you have to wait until your accountant has finished last year's accounts before you can enter all of your account opening balances (a process I explain in Chapter 9). Don't worry if this takes forever. I've often had to wait until April in the following year to set up opening balances for July.

Gathering all the information you need

You wouldn't set off across the Nullarbor Plain without water or fuel, would you? Nor should you attempt to set up QuickBooks without a couple of essentials close to hand. Here's what you need:

- ✔ A computer, your QuickBooks software, this book and maybe some chocolate cake. Yes. I know I'm stating the obvious, but the chocolate cake really helps.

- ✔ Tax returns/final accounts for the most recent financial year (if you have them). Even if these reports aren't completely up to date, they come in handy, helping you remember which categories to include in your Chart of Accounts.

- ✔ Bank statements and credit card statements, plus recent cheque books if you still write cheques. These documents are your basic supplies for the trip ahead. Without these, you won't be able to get started, enter transactions or balance your bank account the first time.

- ✔ A list of who owes you money. It's always cheering when you realise that if everyone coughed up tomorrow, you'd actually be quite rich. This list should include everyone who owed you money on the day that you started recording transactions, along with the date of the original invoice and the invoice number.

- ✔ A list of everyone you owe money to. This is the serious (and sometimes scary) bit. If you intend to record supplier bills (I talk lots more about these in Chapter 6), make a list of everyone you owe money to. Include dates, amounts and invoice numbers on the list.

Picking a start date

Here's a tip I discovered the hard way. Unless you have a brand new business, the very best time of year to start with QuickBooks is the beginning of the financial year (1 July for 99 per cent of businesses). Even if it's September, December or even February by the time you purchase the software and you're ready to get started, it's still probably best to go back and enter accounts from the beginning of your financial year.

Why? If you start on the first day of a new financial year, the transition from your old accounting system to your new one is a cinch. That's because accounts are always finalised at the end of each financial year. These final accounts provide the opening balances for the following year and save you paying your accountant to draw up the interim accounts.

That's not to say that you can't start at any time of year. You may prefer to start in May and June, have a trial run and make all your mistakes when it doesn't count. Then by the time 1 July comes around, you know how to use the software, you have things under control and you're ready for a flying start. However, even if you do it this way around, you're still not starting for real until July.

Waltzing Through the EasyStep Interview

The EasyStep Interview in QuickBooks serves the purpose of finding out all your company information (name, address, phone numbers and so on) and selecting what QuickBooks refers to as *preferences*. (Preferences allow you to tell QuickBooks how you like to work — everything from whether you want to use estimates to what colour scheme you prefer.)

Although you can never return to the EasyStep Interview after you've completed it, you can always modify the choices you've made. To change a preference, go to your Preferences menu, found under the Edit menu on the top menu bar. To update your company details, select Company Information from the Company menu on the top menu bar.

Creating your first company file

Ready to hit the road? Then hop onto your climate-change-friendly bicycle and pedal away:

1. **Fire up QuickBooks and click Create a New Company File.**

   Assuming you've already installed QuickBooks, double-click the QuickBooks icon on your desktop or select QuickBooks from the Programs folder that sits below the Start button. When the Welcome window appears, select Create a New Company File. You arrive at the EasyStep Interview window, as shown in Figure 1-1.

   By the way, if you're upgrading from a previous version of QuickBooks, you don't need to create a new company file. Instead, all you need to do is run the upgrade on your existing file. For more details, see the sidebar 'Upgrading older company files' later in this chapter.

2. **When prompted, click Start Interview.**

   Actually, you see three choices here: Start Interview, Convert Data and Skip Interview. The Convert Data option is handy if you need to carry across information from Quicken, which you can do first, and then proceed with the interview process.

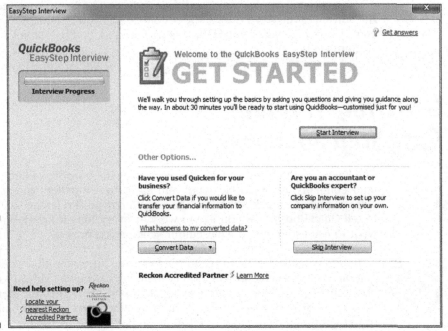

Figure 1-1:
Getting
started
with the
EasyStep
Interview.

Don't choose the Skip Interview option. This option is for QuickBooks experts only and won't save you any time at all in the long run.

3. **Divulge your innermost secrets (you know, your name, address and so on).**

   This is the easy bit. Hopefully you know your name and address by now. The only tricky bit here is dealing with some terminology: For example, when QuickBooks refers to the Tax ID, you need to enter your ABN.

4. **Select your industry, making your best bet.**

   So you're a taxidermist and can't see your industry listed? What an oversight! Don't stress, just choose the industry that's closest in nature to your own, or select Other/None. None of your choices is cast in stone at this stage — you can change everything later on.

5. **Tell QuickBooks what kind of legal structure your business has, and select the first month of your financial year.**

   If you're like 99.9 per cent of Aussie businesses, then the first month of your financial year is July.

6. Dream up a password and let QuickBooks know.

Unless you work from a home office and you're the only person who ever goes near your computer, you need an Administrator password to protect your financial information. (If more than one person is going to log into QuickBooks, you also need to set up individual users and add a password for each one. Skip to Chapter 15 for a whole load more detail on this process.)

7. Think up a name for your company file and tell QuickBooks where this file is going to live.

QuickBooks offers to name your file as per the company name you entered earlier in the interview (and adds the file extension QBW to the name as well). If you don't like this name, change it now.

When you decide where to locate your company file, consider what your current backup routines are, and ensure that your QuickBooks file isn't going to get missed. On my computer, I routinely back up all folders and files in My Documents, so I choose to locate my QuickBooks company file in a folder called Accounts, which lives inside the My Documents folder.

8. Click Next.

You did it! QuickBooks takes you to a new Customising QuickBooks window, the second stage in the EasyStep Interview. Keep on readin' to find out more.

Upgrading older company files

This book is written for the latest version of QuickBooks. The change between the most recent versions of QuickBooks (which have been written on an SQL platform) and earlier versions of QuickBooks is a big one, and just by flipping through this book you'll get a sense of the many differences.

If you're wondering whether to upgrade or not, remember that you don't need to go out and buy a whole new package. Instead, you can pay a smaller fee to purchase an upgrade. (If you haven't already received information from Reckon Software about how to upgrade, visit www.quicken.com.au or phone Customer Service on 1300 784 253.)

I sometimes come across folks who postpone upgrading because they think that upgrading involves starting with QuickBooks again from scratch. On the contrary, you don't lose a single scrap of work when you upgrade. You simply install the new software, ask to open your company file and, when QuickBooks prompts you to update this file, you click Yes. QuickBooks makes a backup, displays a few warnings and then whizzes and buzzes for a few minutes until the job is done.

Telling QuickBooks what you're all about

The next stage of the EasyStep Interview has such clear and detailed instructions at every step that I'd be double-dipping if I provided a commentary on everything. Instead, I just point out a couple of areas where confusion occasionally arises:

- ✔ **Tax tracking.** When QuickBooks asks whether you track tax, it's talking about GST, not income tax. So, if you're registered for GST, click Yes.

- ✔ **Sales receipts.** Even if you only provide credit to all your customers and never require payment at the time of making the sale, click Yes for the option to use sales receipts, because this format provides a handy way for entering things like interest income.

- ✔ **Progress invoicing (QuickBooks Pro, Premier and Enterprise only).** Usually, only builders and certain tradespeople use progress invoicing, and the whole deal is pretty complex. So only tick Yes to this option if you're really sure you need it.

- ✔ **Managing bills you owe.** Dip into Chapter 6 if you need help deciding whether to keep track of the bills you owe. (Methodically feeding all bills through a shredder instead is an alternative, of course.)

- ✔ **Selecting your start date.** If you're not sure which date to select, refer to 'Picking a start date' earlier in this chapter.

- ✔ **Entering bank account information.** When you create a new bank account, QuickBooks asks whether you opened this account on or after your start date, or before it. To make things easy for you later on, I recommend you select 'On or after', even if this bank account was opened decades ago. You find out why in Chapter 7, where I explain how to set up opening bank reconciliations.

- ✔ **Reviewing income and expense accounts.** Some of the standard charts of accounts that come with QuickBooks are nothing short of ridiculous, with lists of accounts as long as a politician's pre-election promises. Deselect any accounts you don't need. Later on, you can customise this list further to create additional accounts or change account names. (Chapter 2 explains just how.)

Getting Acquainted

Before leaping into the deep end and entering transactions, take a quick tour around QuickBooks. It helps to know how QuickBooks names things (after all, how many ordinary mortals instinctively understand the difference between a menu bar and a navigation bar?) and get a feeling for what sits where.

Feeling your way around

Ready for a whistle-stop tour? Here goes.

First stop is your *home page*, with all key activities shown on a single page. The display of this page links back to user security settings, and users only see the options that they're allowed to use. The result is a bit like a road map, as shown in Figure 1-2.

Next is the *menu bar*, which is the technical name for the list of commands that runs along the top. Not a regular three-course meal, but rather the same kind of menu you find in any Windows program (File, Edit, View, Lists and so on). Click with your mouse on each command and read the options that appear below. If an arrow appears next to an item in the list, scoot down to view the submenu (you know, the whole Russian dolls principle).

Moving right along is the *navigation bar*, the list of icons that appears immediately below the menu bar. The navigation bar is like the North, South, East and West pointers on a compass and includes one icon for each of the Customer, Supplier, Employee and Report Centres. (Because the navigation bar is so crucial, it can't be customised, although you can hide it from view.)

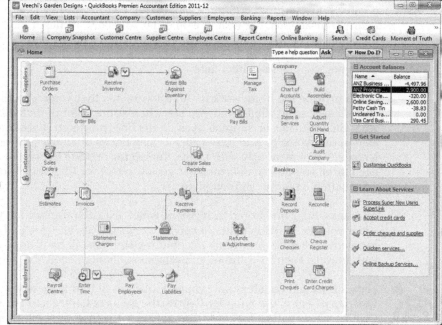

Figure 1-2: The QuickBooks home page is your central reference point.

Finally, to the right of the navigation bar is the *icon bar*, a list of shortcuts to frequently used objects, such as forms, account registers, lists or reports. The neat thing about the icon bar is that you can customise it to include the things you use most in QuickBooks, moving icons around so that they're in a sequence that makes sense to you.

The home page, menu bar, navigation bar and icon bar all exist to provide you with different ways of finding your way around QuickBooks.

Whether you get somewhere by car or by plane, via the navigation bar or the home page, it doesn't much matter. Each road leads to the same destination.

Understanding how QuickBooks stores info

QuickBooks stores information about your company in four different ways: Lists, forms, registers and centres.

Lists provide the home for storing info about customers, suppliers, inventory items and accounts. To use a more technical turn of phrase, your Customer List is essentially a customer database, just as your Item List is an inventory database. Lists form the foundations in QuickBooks, and usually come before transactions. For example, in order to record a sales transaction for a customer, you first need to set up the customer's billing details in your Customer List. (Chapter 2 explains lots more about setting up account, customer, supplier and item lists.)

Forms provide the framework for all transactions that you record in QuickBooks, controlling what you see when at the point of data entry, and what the customer or supplier sees on the final printed transaction (such as a sales invoice or purchase order). QuickBooks often uses the word *templates* synonymously with forms. Templates provide the layout for each form, so you can control what goes where. (See Chapter 11 for more information on forms and templates.)

All transactions are stored in *registers*, which list each transaction in any order you like. The Accounts Receivable register lists all sales and customer payments, whereas your Bank Account register lists all bank deposits and withdrawals. Figure 1-3 shows an example Accounts Receivable register.

Lists, forms and registers are grouped together in four main *centres* (the Customer Centre, the Supplier Centre, the Reports Centre and the Payroll Centre) where you can record transactions, view historical information or update lists. For example, you go to the Supplier Centre to view a supplier's details, look up outstanding purchase orders or record supplier bills. (In previous versions, these centres were called *navigators*.)

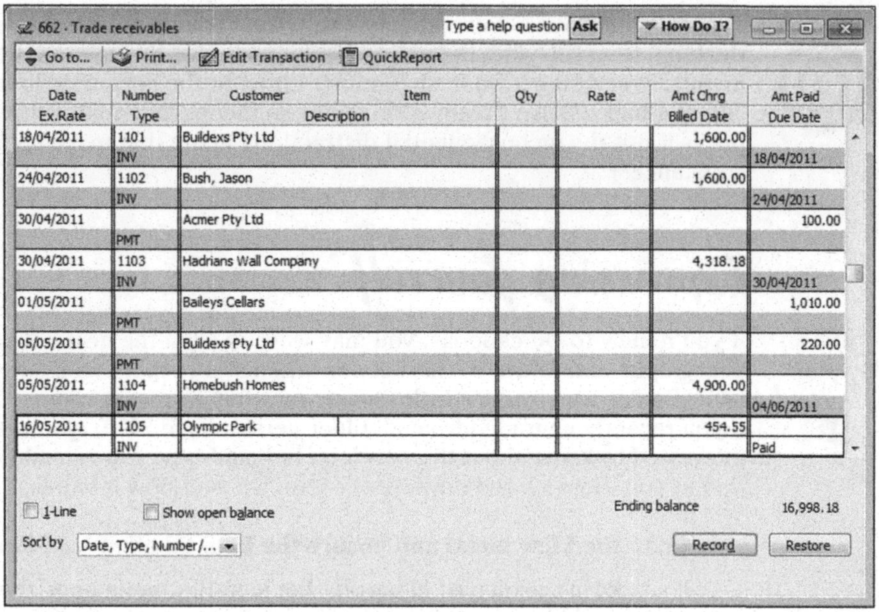
662 · Trade receivables
Type a help question Ask
How Do I?
Go to...
Print...
Edit Transaction
QuickReport
Date
Ex.Rate
Number
Type
Customer
Item
Description
Qty
Rate
Amt Chrg
Billed Date
Amt Paid
Due Date
18/04/2011 1101 Buildexs Pty Ltd 1,600.00
INV 18/04/2011
24/04/2011 1102 Bush, Jason 1,600.00
INV 24/04/2011
30/04/2011 Acmer Pty Ltd 100.00
PMT
30/04/2011 1103 Hadrians Wall Company 4,318.18
INV 30/04/2011
01/05/2011 Baileys Cellars 1,010.00
PMT
05/05/2011 Buildexs Pty Ltd 220.00
PMT
05/05/2011 1104 Homebush Homes 4,900.00
INV 04/06/2011
16/05/2011 1105 Olympic Park 454.55
INV Paid
1-Line
Show open balance
Ending balance 16,998.18
Sort by Date, Type, Number/...
Record
Restore

Figure 1-3: Your Accounts Receivable register lists all transactions relating to sales and customer payments.

Viewing tricks: Now you see it, now you don't

What you see is what you get? Not quite, for QuickBooks is a versatile and most flexible player. I suggest you try tweaking your settings to get a feel for the different ways QuickBooks can display information.

For example, from the View menu, select Open Window List. QuickBooks now displays a list of all windows currently open in a pane on the left-hand side. You can toggle this setting on and off. (By default, QuickBooks displays multiple open windows at the same time, all of which you can move, resize or minimise in standard Windows fashion. To view only one window at a time, click the View menu and select One Window.)

If you're troubleshooting, a handy trick is to have a couple of windows open at once so that you can shift easily between different views. For example, I often work with both my Bank Register and the Write Cheques windows open, so that I can quickly double-check whether a particular transaction has already been recorded, or not.

If you prefer things stripped bare — a setting I only recommend for advanced QuickBooks users — you can select either Navigation Bar or Icon bar from the View menu, and choose to hide either one or both of these bars from sight.

Try changing your colour scheme. From the View menu select Customise Desktop, then see what happens when you change the colours, which include everything from fresh Summer Linen to the corporate-looking Desert Isle. (I admit this isn't really a tip, more an inconsequential distraction, but is it not the inconsequential distractions in life that make up its very substance?)

Expressing yourself

If you're new to QuickBooks, you may want to skim the next couple of paragraphs and return to this section when you're more familiar with QuickBooks, and you're a little clearer on what you want where. However, if you recently upgraded from an older version (pre 2009), you may be interested to know about the new icon bar, and how you can add change it to suit you. Here's a run-down of the icon bar and how it works.

1. **Go to the View menu and ensure the item labelled Icon Bar is ticked.**

   If a tick isn't displayed alongside the Icon Bar menu item, the icon bar goes into hiding, and none of what I write next is going to make any sense at all.

2. **Think of a feature or report you use heaps that isn't currently on the icon bar. Open it.**

   Maybe your business uses sales receipts all the time. Or maybe you want to view your Profit & Loss report with a single-click of a button. Decide what you want and open it.

3. **From the View menu select Add to Icon Bar.**

4. **Think up a Label (that's the text that's going to appear below the icon) and a Description that makes sense to you.**

   Anything goes. A couple of pages back in Figure 1-2, I label my Profit & Loss icon 'Moment of Truth' (shown in the top right corner). Makes sense to me. Only thing is, avoid long names otherwise the icon gets too wide.

5. **Pick whatever graphic you want to use for this icon (optional).**

   I chose the pink hippopotamus symbol for my Profit & Loss icon.

   Cute.

Now that you know how to add an icon, repeat the process for every icon you need. If the icon bar isn't wide enough to display all icons, QuickBooks adds a drop-down list at the end of the icon bar. Alternatively, click on the vertical line that separates the navigation bar from the icon bar, and drag this down. Voilà The icon bar gets a whole line to itself.

Other tips? To change or delete an icon, head to the View menu, click Customise Icon Bar, highlight the icon you want to change, and either click Edit or Delete. While you're at it, you can move icons around by clicking the diamond to the left of the icon and dragging it up or down the list.

Customising your home page

Whenever you click the Home button (top left on your navigation bar), QuickBooks takes you to what's called your home page, similar to what's shown way back in Figure 1-2.

Choosing what appears on your home page

Your home page probably looks a little different from mine, because every home page depends on your choice of preferences, and how you answered questions in the EasyStep Interview.

To review what shows on your home page, go to the Edit menu on your top menu bar and select Preferences. Then select the Desktop View option, and click the Company Preferences tab (this option only appears if you're in single-user mode, so boot off anyone else who may be logged into QuickBooks at the moment). Browse through and decide what features you want to see on your home page, then ditch those you don't need. (My motto is the less unnecessary clutter, the less potential for confusion.)

Some icons can only be hidden if you switch off related preferences. For example, if you've enabled estimates in your Jobs & Estimates preferences, you won't be able to remove the Invoice icon from your home page.

Clients often ask me whether they can add other stuff to their home page, such as icons for important reports or other regular business activities. The answer is no, you can't. If you want quick access to additional features or reports, you're best to add a new icon to your icon bar (refer to 'Expressing yourself' earlier in this chapter to find out how).

Deciding whether to display account balances, or not

Notice that Figure 1-2 displays the balances of my accounts in the right-hand corner? That's fine, except that if I'm working in a busy office where lots of people are coming and going, I may not want to display this list so publicly.

Fortunately, the latest versions of QuickBooks provide you with the ability to either display or hide account balances.

To hide account balances from view, go to the Edit menu on your top menu bar and select Preferences. From here, select the Desktop View option, then click the Company Preferences tab (this tab only appears if you're in single-user mode, so boot off anyone else who may be also logged into QuickBooks at the moment). See the option in the bottom right corner to show account balances? Simply unclick this option to keep your personal finances out of view.

Setting a colour scheme to fit your mood

Another feature new to the latest versions of QuickBooks is the ability to change the colour of your home page. Yeah right. You're probably thinking that colour schemes are the product of a software developer who doesn't have enough to do. Think again ...

If you work with multiple company files, or several users access a single company file, then choosing to use different colour schemes for different companies and for different users makes a lot of sense. A visual trigger may be all that's needed to pull you up if you accidentally start working in the wrong company file; in addition to this, a specific colour scheme for users with administration rights provides an additional level of security.

Signing up for an instant health check

What is it about men? I reckon my husband would have to be half dead before he fronts up to a doctor. A pathological fear of the medical profession prevents him from enjoying the benefits of preventative medicine.

Same goes for most business people (and men more than women, I dare say). Sticking your head in the sand and pretending nothing is wrong isn't going to help your business to trade profitably.

So in the spirit of staying on top of things, make your way up to your navigation bar and click the Company Snapshot icon. You'll see something similar to Figure 1-4.

If you recently upgraded, you may not be aware that you can now customise what information appears in your Company Snapshot. You can add or remove any of the key elements and customise the snapshot for each different person who uses your company file. To find out more about this feature, skip ahead to Chapter 14.

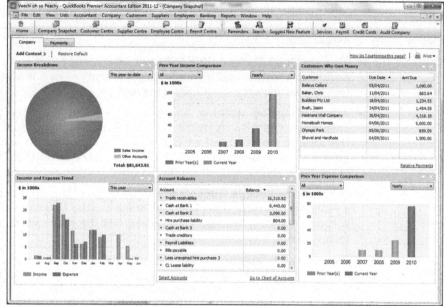

Figure 1-4:
The
Company
Snapshot
provides
an instant
financial
picture,
showing
the state
of health
of your
business.

Calling Out for Help

I don't know why you would need extra help when you're holding this trusty volume in your sticky hands, but just in case, here are a few options:

- ✔ **Inside help.** Considering that we're talking about accounting software here, the help menu in QuickBooks is amazingly forthcoming. Press F1 or click Help to view the index of QuickBooks help topics.

- ✔ **Browse the FAQs.** Still taking advantage of the help that comes with QuickBooks, if you ever see a little box called 'How Do I?' featured at the top of a QuickBooks window, click the green arrow to see a list of frequently asked questions about that topic.

- ✔ **Surf the knowledge browser.** Admittedly, the knowledge browser at www.quicken.com.au/support is a little patchy, with lots of detail about some topics and very limited content on others. Still, this resource is available 24 hours a day, 7 days a week, so it's always worth a try.

- ✔ **Get a trainer to come to you.** An onsite trainer visiting you at your business premises is one of the best ways of ensuring you get off on the right foot with QuickBooks. A couple of hours of an expert's time can save weeks of hassle. There are three types of Quicken Accredited Partners: Accountants, Bookkeepers and Consultants. You're usually best to go with a consultant for help with QuickBooks setup.

(All QuickBooks consultants need to hold a minimum of Certificate III in Financial Services, as well as Certificate IV in Workplace Training and Assessment.)

✔ **Visit my QuickBooks online forum at** www.veechicurtis.com.au. Post your question and before long, yours truly — or some other QuickBooks expert — will offer a response.

✔ **Attend classroom training.** Although the odd community college or TAFE offers QuickBooks training, most formal training is done by the QuickBooks mob themselves. Six different courses are on offer at venues around Australia. Contact Customer Service on 1300 784 253 or visit www.quicken.com.au for details.

✔ **Subscribe to Reckon Advantage.** For a couple of hundred dollars a year, membership to Reckon Advantage entitles you to the latest software updates, free upgrades throughout the year and unlimited tech support.

✔ **Pay per call telephone support.** If your budget won't stretch to a subscription for unlimited tech support, you can always choose to pay per call, at a rate of $4.90 per minute. Phone 1902 223 101.

✔ **Hop onto the official QuickBooks community forum in the United States.** Sure, the US version of QuickBooks has a few differences to our antipodean version, but this forum — shown in Figure 1-5 — is a great place to glean extra knowledge and post questions when you're in a pickle. Visit www.quickbooksgroup.com.

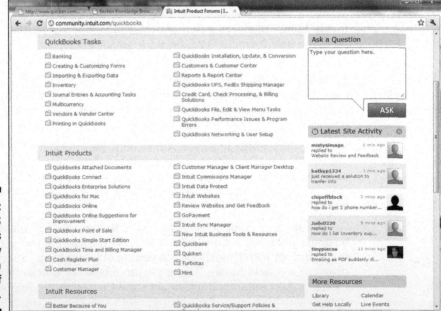

Figure 1-5:
The US QuickBooks community forum is a goldmine of information.

Getting In and Out

The most straightforward activities sometimes seem confusing when everything is new. Read on to find out how to close QuickBooks when you've had enough, open it up again when you're ready for more, and register the software to make it legal.

Closing QuickBooks and going home

Agh! You're tired and want to go home — it's time to quit.

Go to File on the top menu bar, then select Exit.

QuickBooks asks if you want to verify your data. Depending on the size of your file, verifying data can take anything from a couple of seconds to a couple of minutes. Unless you're in a tearing hurry, I recommend you always click Yes to this question.

With verification complete, QuickBooks asks if you want to back up. In almost all situations, the right thing to do is click Yes, and back up onto an external drive, such as a CD, external hard disk or flash drive. (Chapter 15 has lots more info about backing up, and how often you need to do it.)

Starting a new day and opening QuickBooks again

Want to get back into your company file? Then double click the QuickBooks icon on your desktop. Your company file opens automatically, prompting you for a password if you set one up.

If you've shifted data around or moved to a different computer, QuickBooks may open up the wrong file. If so, go to the File menu, click Open or Restore Company, and then click Open a Company File. Click Next, locate the company file you want to work with, click Open and you're done.

If you have more than one company file — maybe you have a company, a partnership and a trust as part of your business structure — an easy way to toggle between files is to go to the File menu, select Open Previous Company, and select whatever company file you're looking for from the list.

Back-to-front dates

Back-to-front dates can be one of the most confusing things: You type in a date and it's rejected. You try and try again, then suddenly it dawns on you that your dates are back to front. That is, when you type 1/7/11, QuickBooks thinks you're talking about the seventh day of the first month in 2011 — not the first day of the seventh month in 2011.

In fact, the problem isn't anything to do with QuickBooks; it's the settings in your computer's Control Panel. Quit out of QuickBooks and go to your Control Panel, then click on the Regional and Language Options icon. Under the Formats tab, select English (Australia). Click Apply. Now, open up your company file again. Hey presto, problem fixed!

Registering with the powers-that-be

You can only use QuickBooks for 30 days before you're forced to register the software. The good news? There's no charge for this process, and registration entitles you to a few benefits, such as access to technical support, the Reckon Advantage email newsletter and notification when software upgrades are released. The bad news? I can't think of any, really.

To register your software, either follow the prompts when QuickBooks offers them, or go to the Help menu and click Register QuickBooks. Select Begin Registration and follow the prompts to complete the registration process, answering all the regular stuff like your name, address and who's your cousin-twice-removed. (By the way, I suggest you make a note somewhere safe — maybe on your QuickBooks box — of the address and phone number you use for registration, because this info is essential if you ever need to re-register your copy of QuickBooks.)

If you're registering a 5-user licence, you must repeat this whole registration process on every computer that QuickBooks is being installed on.

QuickBooks no longer uses registration numbers. The *licence number* you receive when you purchase QuickBooks takes the place of what used to be known as a registration number. You can find your licence number on your QuickBooks CD sleeve, or by choosing About QuickBooks from the Help menu.

If you're not sure whether your software is 'registered' or not, press the F2 key when QuickBooks is open. In the top left, the Product Information window displays either Activated or Not Activated alongside the licence number, depending on the registration status. See Figure 1-6.

If you install QuickBooks on a new computer, you need to register again. To re-register, it's the same deal. Go to your Help menu, click Register QuickBooks and follow the prompts.

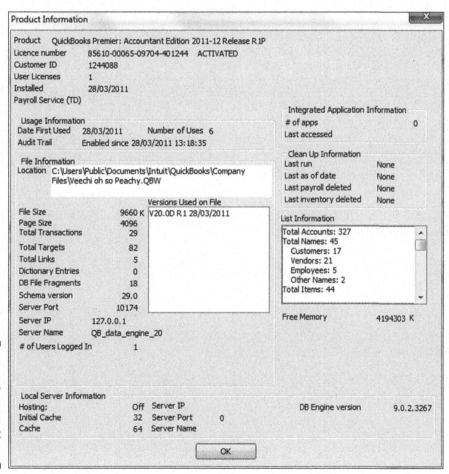

Figure 1-6: Viewing your registration details and product information.

Chapter 2

Lists, Lists and More Lists

In This Chapter

▶ Customising your Chart of Accounts

▶ Setting up lists for customers and suppliers

▶ Creating the list of items your business buys and sells

*T*his chapter is real easy, because it's all about lists. One list for accounts, one list for customers, one list for suppliers and a final list for items. Oh yes, and perhaps one very long list for all those things in life that you wish you could have right at this moment (just kidding).

These lists form the basis for every transaction you record in QuickBooks: You need to set up customer names in the customer list before you can record any customer sales, just as you need to set up supplier names in the supplier list before you enter bills.

The most important information in this chapter is in the first few pages, where I discuss how to customise your Chart of Accounts (that's your list of accounts) for your business. Your Chart of Accounts not only affects how you record transactions, but the structure of all reports in QuickBooks. With your Chart of Accounts complete, you can skim through the rest of this chapter, maybe revisiting it in a few weeks' time when you're ready to add more details. Yes, that's right, it's fine to take a few shortcuts now when setting up customers and suppliers; just enter their names to begin with and return later to complete the rest of their details if you want.

Understanding Your Chart of Accounts

The first thing I do when I set up accounting software for a client is sit down with the owners of the business and have a chat about their Chart of Accounts. That's because the Chart of Accounts affects everything else that happens, from how you record income and expenses, to the final format of Profit & Loss reports.

As you read this, go to the Lists menu and click Chart of Accounts. Here you see a list of categories describing what your business owns and what it owes, where income comes from and where money is spent.

This list varies slightly, depending on the business type you chose in the EasyStep Interview (refer to Chapter 1). Although you can often make do with this list just as it is, I recommend that you take the time to understand how you can add, change or delete accounts so that you end up with more meaningful reports.

Read through every account and figure out what it's doing there. If you don't need an account, get rid of it. If you need an extra account, add it in. And if you want to rename an account, then go right ahead. (I explain how to do all these things later in this chapter.)

One of the features in the latest version of QuickBooks is custom charts of accounts for specific industries. However, whoever designed these charts obviously never worked in small business — the number of accounts in these custom charts is ridiculous and includes lots of accounts no ordinary business will ever need. (Most businesses have 10 to 15 asset accounts, a similar number of liability accounts, 3 to 10 income accounts and about 30 expense accounts. Any more accounts than this is probably overkill.) If you have inherited a list of accounts that's too big for its own boots, don't hesitate to plunge in and delete all the accounts you think you're unlikely to need. Be brutal — you can always add a new account later if you need to.

If you like, dig out the most recent reports from your accountant and compare your accountant's accounts with those in QuickBooks. If you need to add or delete accounts to make the two match, do so.

As part of this process, it's a good idea to tweak your list of income accounts. Scroll down to the income accounts in your Chart of Accounts and look at what's listed. If you have more than five different income accounts, chances are you already have enough detail. However, if you have fewer than five income accounts, think about the different sources your earnings come from. Each major source of income needs a separate income account.

For example, maybe you're a builder who earns money from constructing new houses, as well as carrying out renovations and extensions. Maybe you're like me, and earn money from a combination of journalism, consulting and teaching (take a look at my Chart of Accounts shown in Figure 2-1). Or, maybe you run a newsagency that doubles as a post office, and is also a dry cleaning agency.

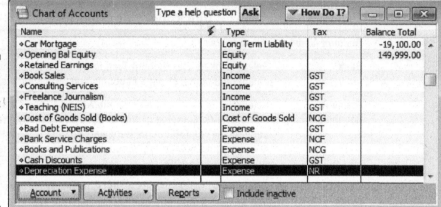

Figure 2-1:
Customising
your Chart
of Accounts
to indicate
where you
derive
income
from.

When customising your Chart of Accounts also consider how you want to set up liability accounts to track GST. As I explain in Chapter 10, I like to modify the default Chart of Accounts in QuickBooks and split Tax Collected and Tax Paid into separate liability accounts. You may want to browse through the first few pages of Chapter 10 before continuing.

Picking your account type

Whenever you do anything with your Chart of Accounts, whether you're adding, deleting or changing an account, you need to decide which *account type* you're dealing with.

I explain each account type in Table 2-1. Don't let your eyes glaze over as you read this accounting jargon. If you can drive a car or operate a DVD player, then account types are a piece of cake.

By the way, Bank, Accounts Receivable, Other Current Asset, Fixed Asset and Other Asset accounts all appear in the *assets* section of your Balance Sheet. Accounts Payable, Credit Card, Other Current Liability and Long Term Liability accounts all appear in the *liabilities* section of your Balance Sheet. Equity accounts show up in the *equity* section of your Balance Sheet report. All other Account Types (Income, Cost of Goods Sold, Expense, Other Income and Other Expense) show up on your Profit & Loss report.

Table 2-1	QuickBooks Account Types
Account Name	*When to Use*
Bank	Select Bank as the Account Type for all bank accounts, including cheque accounts, savings accounts and term deposits.
Accounts Receivable	Select Accounts Receivable as the Account Type for any account that tracks outstanding customer balances. Usually, the only account that has Accounts Receivable as the Account Type is — you guessed it — the account that goes by the name of Accounts Receivable.
Other Current Asset	Select Other Current Asset as the Account Type for any assets that are short-term or that can be converted easily to cash. Examples include employee advances, supplier prepayments, deposits paid in advance, rental or electricity bonds, shares and investments or current loans made to others.
Fixed Asset	Select Fixed Asset as the Account Type for things that you own, such as furniture, equipment, motor vehicles, computer gear or rental property improvements.
Other Asset	Select Other Asset as the Account Type for intangible assets that you can't readily convert to cash. Examples include company goodwill, formation expenses, loans to unreliable teenagers and borrowing expenses.
Accounts Payable	Select Accounts Payable as the Account Type for any account that tracks outstanding supplier balances. This usually means that the account called Accounts Payable is the only account that has Accounts Payable as the Account Type.
Credit Card	You know what a credit card is — the bane of existence for all fun-loving folk.
Other Current Liability	Select Other Current Liability as the Account Type for all funds you currently owe to anyone other than your suppliers. Examples include loans from directors, GST payable, PAYG payable and superannuation payable.
Long Term Liability	Select Long Term Liability as the Account Type for all bank loans, hire purchase debts or long-term loans from shareholders or directors.
Equity	Select Equity as the Account Type for any accounts that relate to your 'interest' in the business — the profit or loss that you have built up over time. Examples of equity accounts include drawings, capital contributions, retained earnings and share capital.

Account Name	When to Use
Income	Select Income as the Account Type for all accounts that relate to the money you earn, including everything you invoice or sell to your customers, plus freight income and bank interest.
Cost of Goods Sold	Select Cost of Goods Sold as the Account Type for all accounts that relate to the direct cost of selling goods or providing your service. Examples include purchases, freight, commissions and subcontract labour.
Expense	Select Expense as the Account Type for all accounts that relate to the day-to-day running costs of your business. Includes advertising, bank charges, rent, telephone and wages.
Other Income	Other Income is probably better described as abnormal income. This is income that's not really part of your everyday business, such as one-off capital gains, or gifts from mysterious benefactors (if only).
Other Expense	Use Other Expense for abnormal expenses that are not part of your everyday business, such as lawsuit expenses, capital losses, or entertaining aliens from outer space.

Understanding cost of goods sold

No matter what type of business you run, you probably have some outgoings that directly relate to sales. Accountants refer to these accounts as *cost of sales* accounts, and in your QuickBooks Chart of Accounts, you can see that Cost of Goods Sold appears as a choice when selecting your Account Type. The idea is that when sales go up, cost of sales goes up, and when sales go down, cost of sales goes down.

Think about your business and figure out which expenses are truly cost of sales accounts. For example, if you're a manufacturer, your cost of sales accounts probably include things like raw materials, electricity, production labour and factory rental. If you're a tradesperson, your cost of sales accounts will include materials and subcontract labour. If you're a retailer, then your cost of sales accounts are the goods that you buy to sell again, usually called purchases. On the other hand, if you're a consultant, you probably don't have any cost of sales accounts, because you're not actually producing or selling anything except your time.

Expenses that aren't cost of sales accounts include things like accounting fees, bank fees, computer gear, depreciation, electricity, interest, motor vehicle, rent, stationery and telephone. These business expenses don't change much from month to month, regardless of whether your sales go up or down.

Adding a new account

So you want to create a new account. Here's what you do:

1. **Make your way to your Chart of Accounts.**

   Go to the Lists menu and click Chart of Accounts.

2. **Click the Account button followed by New.**

   Or, for those on a fast train home, simply click Ctrl-N.

3. **Select the Account Type and click Continue.**

   Here's where you decide whether the account you want to create is an asset or a liability account, an income or an expense account, a galah or a cockatoo. If you can't see the Account Type you want, click the drop-down list next to Other Account Types to see a wider selection.

4. **Enter an Account Name.**

   You can enter a Description or Note for this account too, but to be honest, that's usually overkill. A concise Account Name is all you need.

5. **Decide whether this new account is a Subaccount, or not.**

   If your new account is to be a subaccount that belongs under another account (for example, Motor Vehicle Fuel & Oil is usually a subaccount of an account called Motor Vehicle Expenses), then click the Subaccount button and select the *header* account that this subaccount belongs to. I do this in Figure 2-2, just in case you're interested. See also 'Grouping things together' later in this chapter.

6. **Choose a Tax Code for this account.**

   Select the most appropriate default Tax Code for this account. Most income accounts should have GST as the Tax Code, unless you sell GST-free supplies which should have FRE as the Tax Code. Most expenses should have either GST or NCG as the Tax Code, except for bank charges and donations, which should have NCF or FRE as the Tax Code. (At this point, you may need to skip to Chapter 10 to tidy up both your Tax Code List and Tax Item List before continuing.)

   If you're upgrading from a much older version, be aware that the way QuickBooks manages tax codes changed substantially in 2009. Your first step is to tidy up your Tax Code and Tax Item Lists, as explained in Chapter 10, and then return to your Chart of Accounts and fix up the default Tax Codes for each account.

7. **Click Save & Close.**

   Yippee! All you need to do now is click Save & Close. You've just created your first new account.

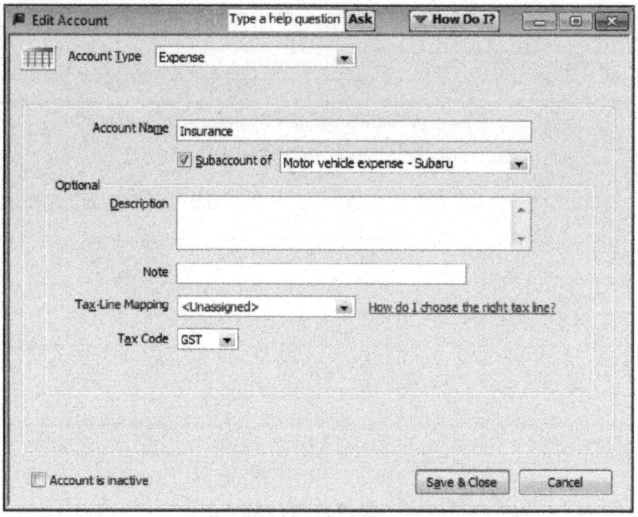

Figure 2-2:
Creating sub-accounts is a good way to organise accounts neatly.

Finding your way around

Used correctly, your Chart of Accounts is like a compass, guiding you on your way as you discover QuickBooks. Make your Chart of Accounts a starting point whenever you want to troubleshoot account balances, view account transactions or understand the figures that lie behind your financial reports.

- Click the Account button at the bottom to create a new account, delete an account, edit an account or re-sort the list.

- On Balance Sheet accounts (assets, liabilities and equity accounts), double-click to view a register of all transactions allocated to that account, along with a running balance.

- On Profit & Loss accounts (income, cost of goods sold and expense accounts), double-click to view a QuickReport of all transactions allocated to that account, as shown in Figure 2-3.

- To customise the columns that QuickBooks displays, click the Account button followed by Customise Columns. Then click any field in Available Columns or Chosen Columns, followed by the Add or Remove button.

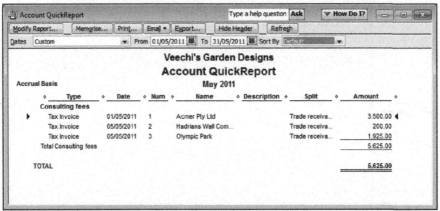

Deleting unloved accounts

Keeping accounts in your Chart of Accounts that you don't use is like living in a lounge room full of old socks. So, if there's an account that you don't need, get rid of it. You can always add it back later, if you change your mind.

To do this, go to your Chart of Accounts and highlight the account you want to delete. Click the Account button, followed by Delete Account. Pow! It's gone.

Sorting your accounts, every which way

Unless someone else has had their fingers in the pie already, your Chart of Accounts is sorted first by account type, then alphabetically by name. If an account is a subaccount of another account, it appears under that header account.

You can change the order of your accounts by clicking the headers that appear along the top. For example, if you click the Name heading at the top, the Chart of Accounts sorts by name, in alphabetical order. Or, if you click the Balance Total heading, the Chart of Accounts sorts by the balance of each account.

When you can't delete an account

If an account has transactions allocated to it or subaccounts attached to it, you won't be able to delete the account.

If you can't delete an account but you don't want it cluttering up your reports or lists, you have two choices: You can either merge the account with another account, or you can make it inactive.

To merge an unwanted account with an account you want to keep, proceed to edit the account you want to get rid of (click the Account button followed by Edit Account). Rename this unwanted account with the name of the account you want to keep. For example, to merge an old account called Transaction Fees with an existing account called Bank Fees, the aim of the game is to rename the Transaction Fees account so it becomes Bank Fees. When you try to rename this old account, a message pops up saying 'This name is already being used. Would you like to merge them?' Click Yes and let QuickBooks do its stuff.

To make an account inactive, first highlight the account. Then click the Account button and select Make Account Inactive. If you have subaccounts belonging to this account, QuickBooks automatically makes them inactive too.

By the way, when you are working with accounts, you can view or hide inactive accounts by clicking the Include Inactive button that appears at the bottom of your Chart of Accounts.

If you sort your Chart of Accounts in a different way, a little diamond-shaped icon appears in the top-left corner of your list. To return accounts to the default order, simply click on this diamond.

You can move accounts within your Chart of Accounts, so long as they stay grouped within their account type. For example, to shift your Wages Expense account so it appears first in your list of expenses, click the diamond that appears to the left of Wages and drag the account up to where you want it to be. Let go, and the deed is done. To put your accounts back into alphabetical order, click the Accounts button and select Re-sort List.

Although you can re-organise accounts, I prefer to keep accounts in alphabetical order. Not only does this make accounts much easier to find, but alphabetical order also looks best when you're presenting financial reports, such as your Profit & Loss and Balance Sheet.

Grouping things together

If you have many accounts that belong together, put them in a group in your Chart of Accounts. You might decide to group all your wages accounts together, or your motor vehicle expenses, or your marketing expenses.

The way to do this is to create *header accounts* (for example, an account called Wages) and *subaccounts* (for example, detail accounts called Admin Wages, Restaurant Wages and Sales Staff Wages).

If you're really enthusiastic, you can create groups within groups. For example, in Figure 2-4, note that I created a header account called 'Motor vehicle expense — Subaru', followed by five detail accounts to cover different kinds of expenses for the vehicle. One of these detail accounts, Insurance, drills down to show different kinds of vehicle insurance.

The great advantage of this arrangement is that I can choose, at any time, between viewing a highly detailed report (for example, a Profit & Loss report that itemises every expense), and a less detailed report that only displays subtotals of key expense groupings.

To view a Profit & Loss report at different levels of detail, first display the Profit & Loss report. Click the Collapse and Expand buttons to change the amount of detail displayed.

Figure 2-4:
Creating
groups
of similar
accounts
using
header
accounts
and
different
levels
of sub-
accounts.

Name	Type	Balance Total
◆Tyres	Expense	
◆Motor vehicle expense - Subaru	Expense	
◆Depreciation	Expense	
◆Insurance	Expense	
◆General Vehicle Insurance	Expense	
◆RTA Registration (GST Free)	Expense	
◆Petrol and oil	Expense	
◆Repairs	Expense	
◆Tyres	Expense	
◆Newspapers	Expense	
◆Night patrol	Expense	
◆Packing materials	Expense	
◆Payroll Expenses	Expense	
◆Permits, licences, fees	Expense	
◆Petty cash	Expense	
◆Plans and permits	Expense	
◆Postage	Expense	

Chart of Accounts — Type a help question [Ask] — How Do I?

Account ▼ | Activities ▼ | Reports ▼ | ☑ Include inactive

Working with Customer and Supplier Lists

One of the first things you need to discover is how to set up customer and supplier names and addresses in QuickBooks. Along the way, you'll become familiar with the Customer Centre and the Supplier Centre, both pretty smart locations that help you run your business smarter and faster.

Navigating to the centre

Because both the Customer Centre and the Supplier Centre are so important, QuickBooks offers a few different ways to get to them:

- On the top navigation bar, click either the Customer Centre or the Supplier Centre icon.
- From the top menu bar, either click the Customers menu and select Customer Centre, or click the Suppliers menu and select Supplier Centre.
- From your home page, either click the Customers button or the Suppliers button (both buttons are located on the far left).
- Or, for the fast way home, type Ctrl-J to arrive in a flash at the Customer Centre (there's no shortcut for the Supplier Centre).

Creating a new customer

So, you've made your way to the Customer Centre. Unless you've been here before, the first step is to create a new customer.

Here's the full guide to setting up a new customer:

1. **Click New Customer & Job.**

   The quick way to do this is to type Ctrl-N, but hey, not everyone is a speed maniac like I am.

2. **Fill in all the regular details — you know the drill.**

   If someone doesn't have a business name — for example, she's simply called Nicole Kidman — then don't type her name in the Company Name field. Instead, insert Kidman in the Last Name field and Nicole in the First Name field. If you don't have the time to enter phone, fax and email addresses at this point, that's okay.

You can store more than one email address for a customer using the cc field (*cc* stands for 'carbon copy'). Lots of my clients put their own admin email address in this field, so that whenever they send a customer an invoice, a copy is automatically saved in their admin email address.

3. Fill in the Address, City, State and Postcode fields.

If a customer just has one address, type this in the Bill To field. If the customer has an alternative location or shipping address that's different to the mailing address, then in the Ship To field click on Add New. You can add as many additional shipping addresses as you like.

QuickBooks doesn't ask you to separate addresses into Line 1, Line 2, City, State, Postcode and so on, but gets smart and guesses where everything goes. To check QuickBooks has guessed right, click the Edit button below the address itself.

4. If you like, go to Additional Info and dig a little deeper.

The Additional Info tab looks a little involved, and if you're just getting started, you may not want to bother with this bit yet. However, this tab is where you can group customers according to type, set up payment terms, allocate a sales rep or choose whether you want to email or snail mail invoices (see Figure 2-5 for an example of how these settings are applied).

5. Complete the Payment Info tab, but ignore the Opening Balance field.

If you like, you can allocate account numbers to each customer — although I reckon account numbers are usually more hassle than they're worth — and also dish out a credit limit.

Ignore the Opening Balance stuff here — you don't want to be entering opening balances willy-nilly as you set up customers. Instead, you're best to enter opening balances all in one hit, documenting historical invoice numbers and amounts correctly. (See Chapter 9 for more information on opening balances.)

6. Click OK.

You did it!

Earlier versions of QuickBooks had restrictions on how many customers, suppliers or items you could list. In the latest versions of QuickBooks, these list sizes have been expanded, and at the top of the range, QuickBooks Enterprise now offers unlimited list sizes. So, even if you have 100,000 customers — you wish! — you won't get in a pickle.

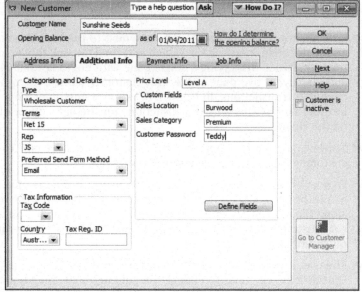

Figure 2-5:
The
Additional
Info tab on
a customer
record.

Viewing your Customer List in different ways

Many years of consulting in the business community has shown me that everyone thinks of their customer list in different ways. A sales-based business often thinks of its customers according to sales reps or location; large wholesalers often use account numbers; service-based businesses tend to think of customers simply by their name. The nifty thing about QuickBooks is that you can customise it to think in just the same way you do.

By the way, if you've recently upgraded from an older version of QuickBooks, don't assume you know all this stuff already, because a few things have changed and the latest software offers a few more special bells and whistles.

So, go to your Customer Centre and experiment with the following:

✔ Can you see an arrow on the left pane next to the View menu, just above the customers' names? Click and then unclick this arrow to toggle between displaying a single pane with customer names only and displaying two panes: One with customer names, the other with customer transactions. In Figure 2-6, I show a customer's name on the left, and I'm viewing all the transactions for the last couple of months on the right.

✔ To view customer names, click the Customers & Jobs tab. To view customer transactions, click the Transactions tab.

✔ To sort either of these 'views' (I'm talking about the list of customer names or transactions here) into a different order, click the headings along the top of the list. For example, click the Name heading to sort customers by name, or the Balance Total to sort by balances outstanding.

✔ The way lists work are particularly different in the latest versions of QuickBooks. Try this: To change the columns that QuickBooks displays, right click anywhere on the list and select Customise Columns. Then click against possible fields in either the Available Columns or Chosen Columns pane, followed by the Add or Remove buttons. You can see in Figure 2-7 how I choose to display the sales rep's name, the customer type, each customer's password and email address. I sort my list by Customer Type, but I could sort it anyway I like, toggling between different views. Pretty neat, don't you reckon?

I know that for most businesses, working with customer lists and transactions is the most crucial thing of all. However, all of the principles I explain here also apply to suppliers. Make your way to the Supplier Centre to check it out.

Figure 2-6:
A customer list with names on the left and transactions on the right.

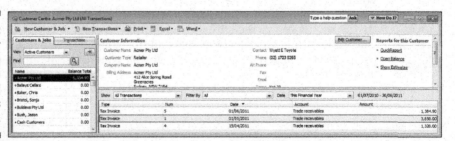

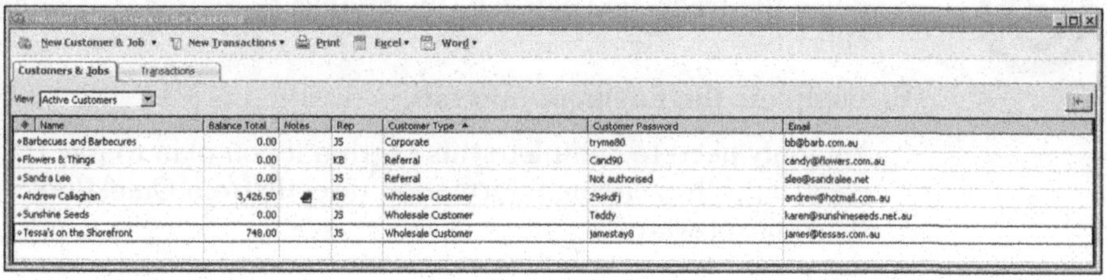

Figure 2-7:
You can
customise
which
columns
to display
when
viewing
customers.

Creating a new supplier

Sadly, running a business isn't only about receiving money. Sooner or later — usually sooner, rather than later — you need to shell out money as well. That's why it makes sense to set up suppliers' names and contact details in the Supplier Centre.

Here's the full guide to setting up a new supplier:

1. **Go to your Supplier Centre.**

   The easiest method is to click Supplier Centre from the navigation bar.

2. **Click New Supplier.**

3. **Enter the supplier's name.**

   If the supplier has a business name, enter this as the Company Name. If you want to include a specific contact name on all purchase orders and correspondence with this supplier, then include that name in the First and Last Name fields.

4. **Complete the supplier's address and contact details.**

   When you type an address, QuickBooks guesses where everything goes. If you want to check that everything is hunky-dory, and QuickBooks hasn't treated the postcode as if it's a town, click the Address Details button that appears at the bottom of the screen.

   If you don't have the time to enter phone, fax and email addresses at this point, that's okay. However, remember that the sooner you do this, the sooner QuickBooks becomes your central reference point for day-to-day business activities.

5. **Go to the Additional Info tab and complete the supplier's Terms and Tax Code.**

   You can store plenty of stuff on a supplier's additional information tab, but the really vital stuff is the supplier's credit terms and the tax status. (In QuickBooks, the term 'Tax Rego ID' means the same as 'ABN'.)

The neat thing about recording supplier's credit terms is that later down the track, you can ask QuickBooks to remind you when a bill falls due.

6. Complete the Payment Info tab.

You only need to complete this section if you plan to pay the supplier electronically, sending information directly from QuickBooks to your banking software.

7. Click OK.

When you first create a new supplier, you have the option of entering an Opening Balance. Don't. If you enter an opening balance at this point, you won't be able to track the date and amount of each outstanding bill and how much GST was included. (See Chapter 9 for more about opening balances.) In fact, unless you're an advanced QuickBooks user, avoid problems in your Balance Sheet by staying completely clear of the supplier Opening Balance field altogether, as shown in Figure 2-8.

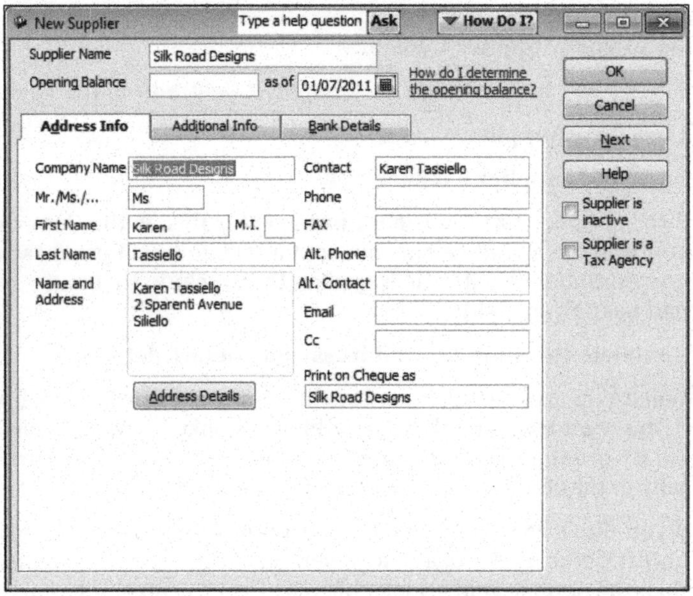

Figure 2-8:
When creating a new customer (or supplier), don't add an amount in the Opening Balance field.

Changing, deleting and merging

To change a customer or supplier details, go to the Customer or Supplier Centre and double-click on the customer's or supplier's name. Change any details that you need to and click OK.

To delete a customer or supplier completely from QuickBooks, go to the Customer or Supplier Centre and highlight the customer or supplier using your mouse by clicking only once (don't double-click because this opens the record). Then, go up to Edit on the top menu bar and select either Delete Customer: Job or Delete Supplier. Zap, it's gone. (If only getting rid of other stuff in life were as easy as this.)

If you get a message saying that the customer or supplier can't be deleted because it has a balance or transactions attached, you can choose to make the name inactive. Simply click the Make Inactive button when prompted.

If you have two names and you want to combine them — maybe you've inadvertently created duplicate records — then double-click on the name you want to get rid of and rename that customer or supplier with the name you want to keep. For example, if you have one name in your list called Saint Mary's College and another called St Mary's College (and they're both the same customer), and you want to keep the first one, then double click on St Mary's College and edit the Customer Name so it becomes Saint Mary's College. QuickBooks rather helpfully asks if you'd like to merge the two. Click Yes and the deed is done.

Looking up stuff in lists

I love the search function on my computer where I can type in any name (or word) and Windows produces a list of results showing every email, document or other kind of file that includes that name. However, my computer doesn't find data that lives inside QuickBooks itself.

I'm happy to report that new to the latest version of QuickBooks are search features, which let you look up any text that can be found in a list of names or email addresses.

Try this search feature yourself to see how it works:

Go to the Customer Centre and in the new Find field (next to the magnifying glass on the left-hand side) type in a postcode that's relevant to at least one of your customers. Click the magnifying glass and QuickBooks automatically displays only the customers with this postcode.

Similarly, you can search on any string of text that exists in a customer or supplier record. For example, if I know a customer is in the suburb of Greenacres but I can't remember the customer's name, I simply type 'Greenacres' into the Find field.

Sorting customers into groups

No matter what kind of business you run, regardless of how large or small, you can always benefit from analysing your customers and organising them into groups. Here are some different types of groups you could set up:

- **Referral source.** Many businesses group customers by how their customers found out about them (for example, by radio, newspaper or word of mouth).

- **Demographics.** I'm talking about the nitty-gritty here: Male versus female, different age groups, income brackets, profession and so on.

- **Specific groups.** I know of a vet who groups customers according to their pets (after all, the average poodle owner usually has a different perspective to that of a pig farmer). I also know of a community college that groups students according to the subjects they enrol in.

- **Location or sales territory.** Grouping customers or clients in this way is ideal for finding all clients assigned to a particular salesperson or sales territory.

QuickBooks offers two ways to organise customers into groups: The first way is to use the Customer Type list; the second way is to use Custom Fields.

To work with Customer Types, go to your Lists menu and from the Customer & Supplier Profile List, select Customer Type List. From here, click Add to set up customer groupings specific to your business. For example, to group customers according to their gender, set up two new Customer Types: One for Female, the other for Male. If there are already groupings in this list that aren't relevant to you, simply select Delete Customer Type.

With this list in place, all you have to do is double-click on each customer name, then click the Additional Info tab. Here, you can select the Customer Type that applies to that customer.

Can QuickBooks be your database?

QuickBooks is wonderfully versatile and, in most cases, is the best possible place for you to store information about customers. You won't need a separate database or a separate software program.

However, sometimes I come across a business that needs to maintain loads of very specific information about its customers. It may be a club that wants to keep a record of golf scores for each member, a vet who wants to record every animal's vaccination history, or an acupuncturist updating a client's treatment records. In these situations, you're probably best to maintain an independent database in addition to QuickBooks.

Before you do so, work out how you can best use QuickBooks in conjunction with your database. It's a breeze to export customer information (such as names, addresses and so on) from your company file into your database, or vice versa. To see how this works, go to the Customer Centre and click the Excel button, followed by Export Customer List or Import from Excel. You could also consider contracting a programmer to write a program that will perform this import or export process automatically.

To work with Custom Fields, go to the Additional Info tab and click the Define Fields button. QuickBooks then displays a window like the one shown in Figure 2-9 (except in my screen, I've already jumped in and defined a few custom fields). All you have to do is define all the possible ways you want to group customers and choose whether these groups apply to customers, suppliers, employees or all three at once.

Custom Fields work well for recording lots of detailed information about customers. However, grouping customers according to Customer Type is a little more robust, because you can select options from a drop-down list. For example, if you use the Customer Type list to store information about customer age groups, you can click a drop-down list that shows all the choices (under 25, 25–34, 35–49 and so on). If you try to store this information in a Custom Field, you have to type the data from scratch each time, and you often end up with duplicate entries or very inconsistent customer groupings.

Getting on Top of Your Item List

One of the things that some people find confusing about QuickBooks, especially at first, is the way QuickBooks talks about items. In QuickBooks, the word *items* doesn't only refer to physical things that you can buy and sell, but refers also to anything your business buys, plus anything your business sells. An item can be an hour of your time, a delivery fee from a supplier, or a standard service you provide to customers. Items can also be used to refer to invoice subtotals, discounts or even part payments.

With this in mind, one of the main tasks in getting QuickBooks up and running is to set up your Item List. In the following sections, I explain the concept of items, the different types of items that exist, and how to set up items for services. However, if your business also buys items and sells them again, you'll not only need to set up service items as described in this chapter, but you'll also need to make your way to Chapter 8, which focuses on the setup of physical inventory items.

Creating a new item

I'm going to leap straight into the thick of things and ask you to think of a service you provide to customers, such as a service fee, an hourly fee, a consulting charge, delivery fee or call-out fee. With this in mind you can then jump in and create this service as your first QuickBooks item:

1. **Go up to your List menu and select Item List.**

2. **Click Item from the bottom of the list and then click New.**

3. **Select Service as the item type.**

   You're going to select Service as the item type this time around, but when you set up more items in QuickBooks later on, you'll probably want to set up different kinds of item types. Table 2-2, later in this chapter, provides a quick run-down on different item types and what they mean.

4. **Enter an Item Name/Number for this item.**

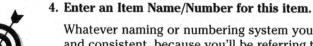

   Whatever naming or numbering system you use, make sure it's logical and consistent, because you'll be referring to the Item Name/Number every time you make a sale.

5. **Ignore the subitem, unit of measure and subcontractor settings.**

   There's no point in knowing how to do an inside double-cross triple-leap turn if you haven't mastered the basic dance steps yet. So for the moment, avoid a sprained ankle and proceed to Step 6.

6. **Enter a meaningful Description, remembering that this is what customers are going to see on their sales invoices.**

   For example, if you're setting up an item for billing your labour, the Item Name could be something simple like Consult 100, but the Description would probably be more detailed, such as 'Consulting Fees (and yes, you're-so-lucky-to-have-me) at $100 per hour'.

7. **Enter the Rate and the Tax Code.**

   The Rate is how much you charge for this service, which in Figure 2-10 is a modest $100.00. The Tax Code in my example is GST, which is what you'd expect for any GST-registered business (notable exceptions would be businesses that are exempt from charging GST, such as medical services or childcare).

   If the Rate you enter includes GST, don't forget to tick the Amts Inc Tax option.

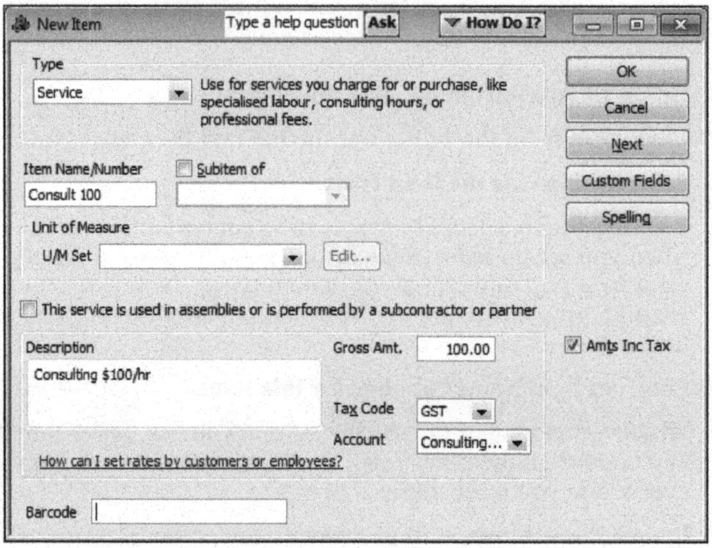

Figure 2-10:
Creating
items
for each
service you
provide (or
each item
you sell).

8. **Select an income account as the Account.**

   At the beginning of this chapter, I talk about designing your QuickBooks Chart of Accounts so that your income accounts reflect the different kinds of revenue your business generates. Now that you're setting up items, link each item to the most relevant income account, as shown in Figure 2-10.

9. **Click either Next or OK.**

   When you click Next, QuickBooks saves your new item and flips to a fresh New Item window, with the same Tax Code and Account information carried across to this new entry. This works well if you're creating lots of items that are all fairly similar. If you click OK, QuickBooks simply saves your new item and returns to your Item List.

Picking your item type

Table 2-2 explains the different item types that exist in QuickBooks. For more information regarding items, skip to Chapter 3, which explains how to use the Group item type to speed up repetitive invoicing. Also, Chapter 4 includes more details about using subtotal, discount and payment item types, and Chapter 8 shares everything you ever need to know about inventory parts and inventory assemblies.

Table 2-2	QuickBooks Item Types
Item Name	*When to Use*
Service	Use Service as the item type for anything that isn't physical. No, I'm not talking about Elle Macpherson, I'm talking about anything that you can't see, touch or smell. Examples include hourly fees, labour totals or consulting charges. (And if a client tells you that your fees are on the nose, I suggest you firmly deny the charge.)
Inventory Part	Anything you buy, keep track of and then resell. For example, I sometimes buy a few of my own books from my publisher, such as *Small Business For Dummies*, and resell these books to clients. I set up each title using Inventory Part as the item type, so I can keep track of how many books I have available for sale.
Inventory Assembly	Assembled goods you build or purchase, track as inventory, and resell.
Non-inventory Part	Select Non-inventory Part as the item type for goods that you buy but don't resell (such as office supplies or new equipment), or for consumables that you use on a job. If you like, QuickBooks can help you charge purchases of non-inventory parts back to customers.
Other Charge	I find this item type very handy, and tend to use it for miscellaneous stuff that I charge customers for, such as additional materials, delivery charges or setup fees. You can also use this item type to account for bounced cheques, late fees, prepayments or retainers.
Subtotal	Usually, you'll only have one item in your list with this item type, and that's the item called — you guessed it — Subtotal. Insert this item on any QuickBooks form and it adds up all the items above it, as far as the previous subtotal.
Group	A neat way to group items together on invoices. For example, I often sell three of my business titles together as a 'Business Bumper Pack'. All I have to type in QuickBooks is the Item Name (that's 'BBP'), and QuickBooks populates my invoice with all three books, listed one after the other. Heaps faster than two-fingered typing.
Discount	Use this item type if you want to offer customer discounts or record supplier discounts. You may only have one or two discount items in your items listing, or you could find that you don't need a discount item at all.
Payment	If you sometimes receive part-payment at the time of a sale, then you can create an item with Payment as the item type to show this part-payment on the customer's invoice.

Part II
Everyday Transactions

Glenn Lumsden

'I'm running late, darling. I still have to bill clients, order stock, pay suppliers and the tax ... so I'll be another five minutes.'

In this part . . .

Everyday business transactions are the heart and soul of any enterprise. In this part, I cover making sales and receiving money (the fun bit), making purchases and shelling out money (the not-so-fun bit), as well as working with inventory and understanding GST.

After you get into the swing of things, these everyday activities become second nature in QuickBooks, just like brushing your teeth, taking a shower or whispering sweet nothings in your loved one's ear.

Chapter 3

Billing Your Customers

In This Chapter

▶ Stating your preferences (no assertiveness training required)

▶ Creating your very first invoice

▶ Getting GST just right

▶ Finding invoices and fixing mistakes

▶ Spending more time at the beach (and getting your work done faster)

▶ Creating estimates and sales orders

▶ Printing invoices, estimates and sales orders

▶ Emailing invoices into the never-never (well, to your customers actually)

*1*s there anything better than sending out a whole swag of invoices to customers? Every invoice represents a sale, every sale represents a few dollars and every extra dollar helps keep that hungry wolf from baying at your door.

QuickBooks makes the whole sale thing pretty easy. So easy, in fact, that you may wonder why you need to read this chapter. The reason is this: In this chapter, I share lots of tips on how to make the billing process as painless as possible, including handy hints on customising templates to determine which columns show up on your screen and what to print on each customer invoice, and how to ensure you've got GST under control.

I also explain how to email invoices to your customers, to save you from dealing with piles of paper, crusty envelopes and bitter-tasting stamps. What more could you ask for?

Defining Your Preferences (No Holds Barred)

Before creating any customer invoices, take a moment to check your Sales preferences. Go to the Edit menu, select Preferences, and click Sales & Customers.

On the tab called My Preferences, you can choose whether QuickBooks automatically adds unbilled time and expenses to a customer's invoice when you enter that customer's name. For example, if you've already logged an expense against a customer and marked this expense as reimbursable, you can ask QuickBooks to automatically add this expense to the next invoice for that customer.

The Company Preferences tab within the Sales & Customers preference offers a few more options, most of which are fairly self-explanatory, but here are some pointers, just in case:

- Usually, FOB means the location you normally ship from. If you don't need to print this info on your invoices, leave the field blank.

- I like to tick the preference to receive a warning for duplicate tax invoice numbers. Consecutive invoice numbers without duplicates ensures a solid system from an audit perspective, and prevents possible confusion when receiving payments.

- Under Receive Payments, tick the option to use undeposited funds as a default deposit account if you receive more than a couple of customer payments a day. This option allows you to group cash, cheque and EFTPOS payments together in batches. These batches then appear as single amounts in your bank register, matching perfectly with your bank statement.

- Click on Use Price Levels if you want to charge different prices for different kinds of customers. For example, you may have different prices for Retail, Wholesale and Online. (*Note:* Multiple price levels are only available in QuickBooks Premier and QuickBooks Enterprise.)

Recording Your First Sale

Finding your way through your first invoice is like finding your way through a foreign city for the first time. Although it's possible to reach your destination by sheer animal instinct, it's much easier if you have a map with street directions. So, with the aim of finishing your first invoice by the shortest possible route, I suggest you provide the animal instinct and let me provide the street directions.

Creating an invoice, quick as a flash

Ready to create your first invoice? Here goes:

1. **On your home page, click Invoices.**

   Alternatively, if you're already in the Customer Centre, go to New Transactions and select Invoices.

2. **In the top-right corner, toggle between the different templates to decide which template best suits your business.**

   Standard QuickBooks templates include a Product Invoice, a Professional Invoice and a Service Invoice.

   Later in this chapter I explain how you can customise any QuickBooks template to suit your individual needs, but for the moment, pick the template that's closest to what you have in mind (so that you cut down on the amount of customising you have to do later on).

3. **Type the customer's name, and if applicable, choose a job from the Customer:Job list.**

   If the customer already exists in your list, the customer's details come up automatically. If one or more jobs belong to this customer, you can select a specific job.

   If the customer doesn't exist yet, a message appears saying this customer isn't in your list. You can either click Set Up to enter the customer's name, address and a thousand other details, or you can click Quick Add to create a new record that contains the customer's name and nothing else.

   If in doubt, refer to Chapter 2 for more on setting up customers and jobs.

4. **Accept the invoice number and check the date.**

   Most of the time, you're fine to accept whatever invoice number QuickBooks offers. (The invoice number automatically goes up one with every new invoice.) However, if you want to change the invoice number, you can do so.

5. **If the customer has a purchase order number, type this number in the P.O. No field.**

6. **Type the item's name in the Item column.**

   As I explain in Chapter 2, an item isn't necessarily something you can touch and smell. An item can be a unit of time or a service provided, similar to the invoice shown in Figure 3-1. If you need to create a new item so that you can generate this invoice, do so now. (See Chapter 2 for how to set up items for services provided, or make your way to Chapter 8 to discover how to set up items for stuff that you buy and then resell.)

7. Review the item Description and enter the quantity.

Assuming the item has a description attached to it, this description pops up automatically, but if you want to change it, you can.

8. Decide whether you're going to print or email this invoice, and check the Template settings.

Being an advocate of a paperless office, I recommend you email the invoice. All you have to do is click the box To Be Emailed, located in the bottom-left corner of the window. (Otherwise, click the box To Be Printed.)

If you always use the same template, QuickBooks defaults to the correct one each time. However, if you have more than one template, make sure you select the right one.

9. Fill in any other information, if it takes your fancy.

The other fields in an invoice are entirely optional, and pretty self-explanatory. You can change customer payment terms, add a Customer Message, apply credits or make additional notes in the Memo field (the Memo field is for internal use only and doesn't print on the invoice).

10. Click Print to print the invoice or, if you're the cautious type, click Preview (which you access from the Print menu) to have a squiz at how everything's going to look.

11. Click Save & Close when you're done.

Alternatively, click Save & New if you're keen to keep going, and create another invoice.

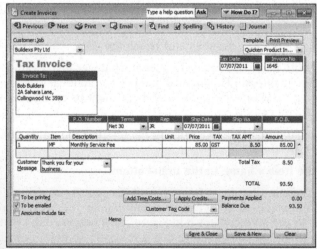

Figure 3-1:
Creating
your first
invoice.

Jack be nimble, Jack be quick

Why go on the back roads when you can take the expressway? Hop straight to Create Invoices from anywhere in the program by holding down the Ctrl key and then at the same time pressing the letter 'I'.

Getting invoices where you want 'em

One of the neat things about QuickBooks is that you can change what appears on the screen while you're creating an invoice, as well as what prints on the final invoice. You can hide columns, insert new columns, add custom fields, change the headers and rename everything and anything. Figure 3-2 gives you some idea of how extensively you can adapt each template.

Even better, you can narrow or widen the columns on any invoice — or any form, for that matter — simply by resting your mouse on the vertical line that separates each column. When the crosshair appears, drag to the left or to the right to narrow or widen the column.

Although I go into heaps more detail in Chapter 11 to help you customise screens and invoice templates, here's an overview of what to do:

1. **From the Lists menu select Templates.**

2. **Double-click the invoice template you want to customise.**

   If you're just getting started, the invoice template is probably called Custom Invoice or New Invoice Template. If you're not sure which template to customise, temporarily quit the Templates window and proceed to create a new invoice for a customer. Toggle through the different templates available from the drop-down list in the top-right corner and find the template that's closest to what you want.

3. **Click the Additional Customisation button.**

   This takes you to a window with either four or five tabs: Header, Columns, Prog Cols, Footer and Print (the Prog Cols tab is only available in QuickBooks Pro and Premier). On each tab is a series of headings. For example, under the Header tab, QuickBooks lists things such as Date, Invoice Number, Account Number and so on. Next to each of these fields are three columns: Screen, Print and Title.

4. In the Screen column, click each field that you want to see on the screen when you're preparing invoices.

Imagine you want QuickBooks to display both the billing *and* the shipping address, but you're not fussed about viewing customer payment terms or sales rep details. All you have to do is click or unclick against the relevant field in the Screen column. Repeat this process on each of the tabs.

5. Decide what you want to print on the invoice, and click in the Print column next to each field.

Usually, what you want to print on a final invoice is pretty similar to what you want to see on the screen when you're preparing the actual invoice, but sometimes you may want to add a little extra info to the printed version. For example, you may not want to view customer payment terms every time you type an invoice, but you probably want these payment terms to print on the version that the customer receives.

6. Decide what title you want to appear against each field.

For example, your business may prefer to describe sales reps as support contacts. If this is the case, go to the Header tab and under the field called REP, change the Title to Support Contact.

7. Click OK twice to save your changes.

8. Go to create an invoice, type in a few details and print a copy to see if everything looks as it should.

In practice, I find it often takes a few goes before I get everything where I want it, both on-screen and also on the final printed invoice that QuickBooks produces for the customer. For more details on working with the final design of your printed invoice, make your way to Chapter 11.

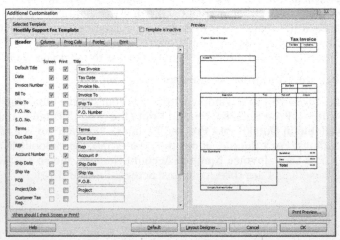

Figure 3-2:
Customising what QuickBooks displays on invoices (on-screen and in print).

Billing for itsy-bitsy bits of time

So far I've talked about billing for services provided, and billing for stuff that you buy and resell. But what if you're one of those professional types who wants to bill in detail for your working hours?

It's easy. From the Customers menu, select Enter Time, followed by Time/ Enter Single Activity. (*Note:* Time-tracking features are only available in QuickBooks Pro, Premier and Enterprise.) Here, you can note all the time spent on an activity, and include information such as which customer the time needs to be billed to, whether you want the allocated time to flow through to an employee's pay, and what description you want to appear (if any) on the customer's invoice. In Figure 3-3, for example, I've logged 45 minutes of my time, and included details on the customer, the date and the job.

It's fine to record this time in lots of little bits. For example, maybe you do an hour here, an hour there, a ten-minute phone call one evening, or a whole day visit. You can record time spent as it happens — try using the stopwatch in the Duration window — and then when you're ready, create an invoice for that customer.

When you go to bill this customer, QuickBooks knows you've been up to something. All you have to do is type in the customer's name, and QuickBooks ever so intelligently queries whether you want to add billable time to this invoice. Click OK to review all time outstanding for this customer and mark this time to be billed. (You can even ask to print selected time and costs as one invoice item, if you like.) When you click OK one more time, QuickBooks automatically populates your invoice with all the necessary details.

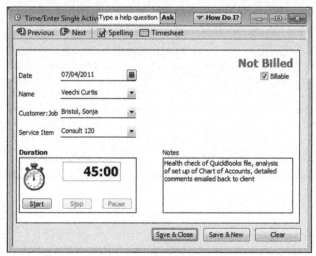

Figure 3-3: Logging time or activities.

Whispering sweet nothings

Every standard QuickBooks invoice has both a Customer Message field and a Memo field. The Customer Message field is handy for saying things like 'Thanks for the lunch' or 'Frankly my dear, I don't give a damn'. When you type text into the Customer Message field, QuickBooks adds this text to your standard messages list, making it quick and easy to use the same text on future customer invoices.

In contrast, the Memo field acts more like an internal note, and doesn't print on the customer's invoice. I use the Memo field to store special comments that are for my reference only, and which customers don't need to see, such as the reason for issuing a credit note, or why I varied the price. I also find Memos work really well for recording branch locations when the main invoice has to go to head office, because the locations print out line by line on the final statement. However, remember one thing: Although memos don't print on customer invoices, they *do* print on customer statements. (So be restrained with those 'smart' comments.)

By the way, if you want a standard message to appear on all customer invoices, all year round — for example, a standard disclaimer or a declaration that goods remain the property of your business until paid for in full — then you're best to add this message as an additional text field, using the Layout Designer (head to Chapter 11 to find out more).

Different kinds of discounts

If you create an item as a Discount type, this item appears as a negative amount whenever you use it on an invoice. You can only use discount items to subtract a percentage or a fixed amount from a total or subtotal.

In contrast, price levels let you set custom pricing for certain customers or jobs. (**Note:** Price level features are only available in QuickBooks Premier and Enterprise.) After you create a price level and associate it with a customer, each time you create an invoice for that customer, QuickBooks automatically pulls up the correct custom price. In other words, the discount is built into the price itself. (See Chapter 8 for more about price level features.)

I find that if a client sells a mix of taxable and non-taxable items (in other words, some stuff has GST on it and other stuff doesn't), discount items don't work well at all because of the need to group taxable and non-taxable items together, and to insert different subtotals and then insert discounts. In this kind of scenario, I prefer to set different price levels for different customers, building discounts into the prices.

Creating not-quite-ready-yet invoices

Sometimes you want to create an invoice in QuickBooks, but you don't want to finalise it yet. Maybe you want to prepare an invoice ahead of time for goods that are on backorder; or maybe you want to record time spent on a job in lots of little bits, and only finalise the invoice when it goes above a certain amount.

The solution in all of these situations is to create a *pending* invoice. Pending sales don't appear in registers, don't affect account balances and — with the exception of the Pending Sales report — don't affect reports.

Here's what to do: Go to create a customer invoice as normal, completing all the details that you're ready to record. Then, because you're not ready to finalise the invoice just yet, go to the Edit menu and select Mark Tax Invoice as Pending. When you choose this command, QuickBooks displays the word Pending on the form. Click Save & Close to record this pending sale.

When you're ready to convert a pending sale into a final invoice, go to your Pending Sales report, located in the Sales section of the Reports menu. Double-click the pending sale in question, go to the Edit menu and select Mark Tax Invoice as Final.

Falling in love with your Tab key

Don't rely on your mouse too much. It's fiddly and, unlike the real guys, it's slow. It also tends to make your forearm ache.

Instead, get into the swing of moving around invoices (and indeed, most areas of the program) using the Tab key. (That's the very versatile key with the arrows pointing in either direction, positioned next to the letter Q.) The Tab key, used on its own, moves you forwards.

The Shift key and the Tab key, used together, move you backwards — kind of like first gear and reverse gear, except driving QuickBooks is safer than driving your car.

Also, when you finish a transaction, you don't have to click Record with your mouse. Instead you can press the Ctrl key and the Enter key at the same time.

Adding discounts and subtotals

Adding discounts and subtotals go hand in hand with QuickBooks because, in order to add a discount to an invoice, you need a subtotal first. Read on — you'll find out why.

In order to insert a subtotal, you need to first create an item. Go to your Item List, select New Item from the Items menu, and as the Item Type select Subtotal. Enter Subtotal as both the Item Name and Description, then click OK to save your new item. To check out how this subtotal works, create a dummy invoice for a customer, type in a couple of lines and then insert a subtotal. Quick as a robber's dog, QuickBooks adds up all the invoice lines above the subtotal. Similarly, to create an item for discounts, go to your Items List, select New Item, then as the Item Type select Discount. Enter Discount as the Item Name, insert a worthy Description (for example, Student Discount), then add either an Amount or a Percentage. As the Account, I usually choose an expense account called Discounts Given.

Discounts work in a similar way to subtotals, but with one crucial difference: With percentage discounts, QuickBooks only calculates the discount on the line immediately above the Discount item. For example, if I have three lines on my invoice, with the first line coming to $100, the second line coming to $200, and the third line being a Discount item for 10 per cent, QuickBooks only calculates a discount on $200, not $300. The solution? First insert a Subtotal item — which in this example comes out as $300 — and *then* insert a Discount item.

Here's another thing to be aware of when working with percentage-based discounts: QuickBooks calculates discounts *before* GST. This means that if you sell a mix of taxable and non-taxable goods, in order for the GST on discounts to calculate correctly, you need to group all taxable items together, then insert a subtotal, and then insert a discount. Next, group all non-taxable items together, insert a subtotal, then insert a discount. See my example in Figure 3-4.

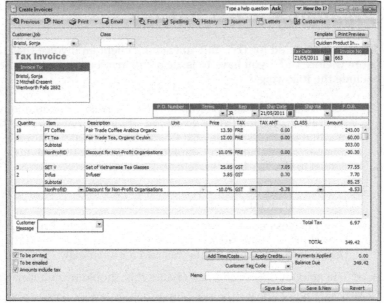

Figure 3-4:
Dealing with
discounts
if you sell a
mixture of
taxable and
non-taxable
goods.

Keeping Within the Law

Although QuickBooks handles GST perfectly, it can't guarantee that you
produce legit and perfect Tax Invoices every time. You have to complete
your part of the deal as well.

For example, QuickBooks always prints Tax Invoice at the top of the first
page, but if you don't type the description of what you're supplying in
the body of the invoice, the invoice won't meet the requirements for a
Tax Invoice. Similarly, if you sell goods that cost more than $1,000 but
forget to type in the customer's address or ABN, the invoice won't meet
requirements either.

Producing a Tax Invoice

If you're registered for GST and you send a client an invoice that's $50 or more (before GST), you have to issue a Tax Invoice. The invoice needs to include the following:

- ✔ Your Australian Business Number (ABN). This is the number that the Australian Taxation Office gives you when you register your business, or when you register for GST. (If you haven't done so already, go to the Company menu and find Company Information, then fill in your ABN details in the Tax Rego ID field.)

- ✔ The words Tax Invoice clearly in nice big letters on the first page of the invoice (the good news is, QuickBooks does this automatically).

- ✔ Your business name or trading name, and the date. Unless you've done something really weird when customising your invoice in the Layout Designer, QuickBooks prints this info automatically.

- ✔ The amount of GST charged (again, this should print automatically).

- ✔ If you give a client an invoice that comes to more than $1,000 (including GST), you need to show all the information listed above. As well as this requirement, you need to include:

  - • *Either* your customer's name and address *or* your customer's name and ABN. In other words, if you don't have the customer's ABN, you need to ensure their address details are correct.

  - • The quantity or volume of whatever it is that you're supplying. For example, the number of hours charged, or the number of units supplied.

Choosing tax codes

Instead of closing your eyes, wiggling your mouse at random and accepting whatever tax code first appears, you need to get a grip on which code to pick when. Doing so may scramble your brain at first, so here are some pointers:

- ✔ If you're registered for GST, and charge GST on your sales, select GST as your tax code.

- ✔ If your business sells GST-free goods, such as childcare or medical services, choose FRE as your tax code.

✔ If your business sells a mixture of goods, some attracting GST and some GST-free, choose the appropriate code (either GST or FRE) as your tax code.

✔ If your turnover is less than $75,000 annually, and you have chosen not to register for GST, you can ignore tax codes altogether. Just leave this column blank.

✔ If your customer is overseas, and therefore exempt from GST, select EXP (which stands for export sales) as the Customer Tax Code on the bottom of each invoice.

✔ To be really efficient, head to your Customer List, click the Additional Info tab for that customer, and select EXP as that customer's Tax Code (as shown in Figure 3-5). Now, QuickBooks defaults to the EXP tax code every time you bill this customer.

For more information on dealing with GST and tax codes, make your way to Chapter 10.

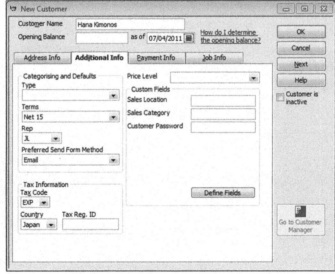

Figure 3-5: Setting up overseas customers (and selecting the right tax code).

Calculating GST backwards

I hope you realise that GST marked a major shift in our education system. Forget multiplying by two, dividing by five or understanding fractions. Cast algebra to the wind and speak not of spelling or grammar. To get by in the world of GST, all you need to master is multiplying by 10 and dividing by 11.

Fortunately, QuickBooks software can divide by 11 to calculate GST amounts sooner than you can say the words. All you have to do is click the Amounts Include Tax box, found on the bottom left of your sales invoice.

Figure 3-6 shows how this works: When Amounts Include Tax is ticked, the Price is displayed as $110 and the Amount comes to $550. Alternatively, if Amounts Include Tax is unticked, the Price displays $100 and the Amount changes to become $500. The Total remains as $550 regardless of whether Amounts Include Tax is ticked or not.

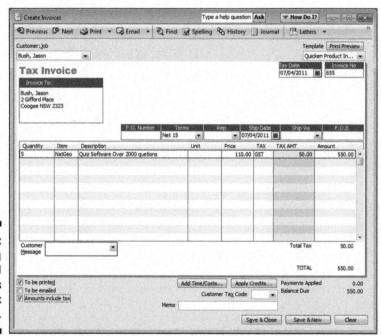

Figure 3-6: Showing Prices and Amounts as tax inclusive.

Fixing Things Up (Nobody's Perfect, After All)

No one is perfect. That's why you need to know how to fix up mistakes, delete your blunders and generate the occasional credit note.

Finding a sale after you've recorded it

To find an invoice you've already recorded, navigate to your Customer Centre, select the Customers & Jobs tab and highlight the customer's name. When you do this, QuickBooks automatically displays all transactions for this financial year for this customer in the right-hand pane, as shown in Figure 3-7. If the customer has a busy transaction history, you can narrow the selection displayed by choosing Filter By Open Invoices and Charges so that QuickBooks only displays invoices that are still unpaid or, you can narrow down the Date to a smaller range.

To view *all* invoices for any date range, rather than just invoices relating to a particular customer, select the Transactions tab in the Customer Centre. Lo and behold, on the right pane QuickBooks displays all invoices for whatever date range is currently selected.

Click on any of the headings (Type, Amount, Num and so on) to sort by that heading. For example, if I click on the Date heading, QuickBooks sorts transactions in date order, with the most recent transaction first. If I click the Date heading again, QuickBooks continues sorting transactions in date order, but with the oldest transaction first.

Figure 3-7: Viewing customer information to find invoices after you've recorded them.

Changing a sale (but think before you act)

To change a sale, all you need to do is find it in the customer's transaction register and then double-click to open it. With the sale now displayed in all its glory, you can make any changes you like. You can change amounts, insert lines (click the Edit menu and select Insert Line), delete lines (click the Edit menu and select Delete Line) or even add new items.

But wait! Before you change an invoice, pause for reflection. Have you already printed or emailed the invoice and sent it to the customer? If so, you can't change this invoice willy-nilly, because this creates a state of confusion in your accounts that can be almost impossible to unravel. Instead, you need to create a new sale that adjusts whatever was wrong with the first sale.

For example, if you accidentally overcharged on an invoice and the customer has already received this invoice, the right thing to do is create a credit note (I explain how in 'Raising credit (or adjustment) notes' later in this chapter). Or, if you accidentally undercharged, you need to raise a new invoice to cover the shortfall.

Deleting or voiding a sale

Similar to changing sales, only delete a sale if you haven't already sent the invoice to a customer. In addition, never delete an invoice to which a payment has already been applied, because this creates horrible accounting problems of a kind that can only be compared with blocked toilets.

If you're confident that neither of these situations apply — maybe you only just clicked the Record button a few seconds ago — then go right ahead and make the change. Display the sale, make your way to the Edit menu at the top and select Delete Tax Invoice. In a flash, it's gone.

If you decide you want to delete a sale that was recorded more than a couple of minutes ago, I suggest you take a different approach. As your business grows, you need to maintain internal security, one aspect of which is to ensure that you have a continuous list of consecutive invoice numbers. If an invoice number is missing, this often indicates a problem. A good alternative to deleting a sale, especially in situations where a sale was raised accidentally or more than once, is to *void* the transaction. To do this, display the invoice, navigate to your Edit menu and select Void Tax Invoice.

Raising credit (or adjustment) notes

When GST came in, what you, me and the dog next door had always called a *credit note* was suddenly renamed an *adjustment note*. After a while, the hubbub died down and everyone went back to calling them credit notes. However, QuickBooks still refers to them as adjustment notes, so that's the term I use here.

In principle, creating an adjustment note in QuickBooks is the same as creating an invoice, with a couple of minor differences:

- ✔ To create an adjustment note, simply select Adjustment Notes/Refunds from the New Transactions menu in the Customer Centre.

- ✔ Always assign the same Tax Code in the adjustment note that you used in the original invoice.

- ✔ Ensure that you add a brief explanation in the adjustment note to outline the reason for the credit, in either the Description field or the Customer Message field.

- ✔ Always date credit notes or invoice adjustments with the current date. Never date them for a previous month, even if you're fixing up a mistake for that period. The reason why? If you make changes in your accounts for a previous month, and you've already included that month's figures in your most recent Business Activity Statement, all those figures you so carefully prepared and sent to the tax office will be up the spout.

Figure 3-8 shows the Adjustment Note window, ready to roll.

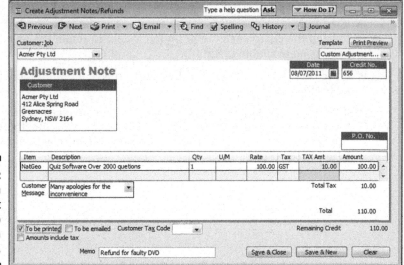

Figure 3-8: Creating an adjustment note (also known as a credit note).

Fixing up mistakes and GST

Life's a bit more serious these days, thanks to GST. Before you change or delete an invoice, always ask yourself: 'Does this invoice belong to a prior BAS period?' If it does, don't change or delete the invoice. Instead, you need to fix your mistake by issuing an *adjustment note* (the term QuickBooks uses to describe credit notes) to accompany it.

Here's an example: Jim, a mechanic, uses QuickBooks software for all his invoicing and submits his Business Activity Statement every quarter. One day in November, he looks up the list to see how much he's owed from outstanding invoices and discovers that the usually reliable Katy still owes him for work he did on her car in September. Strange, he thinks to himself. He investigates further and discovers that the reason his receivables report says that Katy still owes him money is

that in September he accidentally created two identical invoices for Katy.

In the days before GST, Jim would simply have displayed the unpaid invoice and deleted it. But if he does this now, Jim's income figures for the first quarter of the year would change — figures that he has already submitted in his last Business Activity Statement. Jim's only choice, in this scenario, is to create an adjustment note for Katy, dated November, that credits her account for the duplicate invoice. (For help on doing the same, read 'Raising credit (or adjustment) notes' in this chapter.)

So, what's the moral of this tale? Sure, it's possible to change or delete invoices when you make mistakes, but only do so if the invoice belongs to the current GST period.

When you record an adjustment note, QuickBooks displays a pop-up message asking whether to retain this note as a credit, use it to give a refund, or to apply it to a tax invoice. Here's what to do:

✔ If the customer doesn't owe you anything at the moment, but you want to keep the customer's credit on file, select to retain the adjustment note as an available credit.

✔ If the customer wants a refund, choose to give a refund (now that's a no-brainer).

✔ If the customer already owes money on other invoices, select to apply the adjustment note to a tax invoice. This takes you directly to the Apply Credits to Invoices window, where you can select an invoice to apply the credit to.

Invoicing Tips

Invoicing customers is almost the most pleasurable part of running your own business. (The most pleasurable part is when the invoice results in a quick payment to reward your hard work.) So, to help you add even more joy to the times when you sit down to run off a pile of invoices, the next few pages include some very handy hints.

Working faster, playing much harder

Want to spend more time at the beach? Then keep reading . . .

✔ If you make a one-off sale to someone you think you'll never see again, you don't have to create a new entry in your customer listing just for them. Simply create a new customer called Cash Customer and fill in the name and address details in the body of the invoice as necessary. Then grab a good book and head off into the sun.

✔ If a customer pays in full at the time of sale, you can record both the invoice and the payment in one hit by going to Create Sales Receipt, rather than using Create Invoices. That's another couple of minutes saved — just time enough to lather on some sunscreen. (See Chapter 4 for more information on creating sales receipts.)

✔ If a customer part-pays at the time of sale, you can show this payment as a minus line on the customer's invoice. The first step is to set up a new item in your Items List, selecting Payment as the Item Type and entering Payment or Part-payment in both the Item Name and Description areas. Now, all you need to do when a customer offers a part-payment is to add this item as a new line on the invoice. QuickBooks then subtracts the payment from the customer's final amount, and shows the payment as going into your undeposited funds account. (Hey, this is much quicker than recording a sale, recording a payment, then printing a receipt!)

✔ If you change an item description on an invoice, the change only affects that particular invoice. To *permanently* change an item's description, you need to change the description on the Item itself.

✔ To delete a single line from an invoice, right-click on the line and select Delete Line. This whole right-click business also works fine if you want to insert a line. (Okay, I admit you only save a few milliseconds here, but every second counts.)

✔ Do you sometimes wish you had a column to show the date? No problem. Go to your invoice template (the Professional Template is probably your best starting point), click the Additional Customisation button, followed by the Columns tab. In the Serviced Date area, click to select both the Screen and Print options and, if you like, rename the column Date or Date of Service. The result? You now have a date column in your invoice, as shown in Figure 3-9.

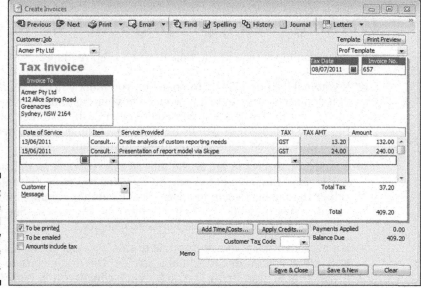

Figure 3-9:
An invoice customised to display a Date column.

Memorising transactions

Do you send some customers the same invoice month after month, or year after year? Maybe you're a music teacher and you send out tuition fees term after term, or a security firm with a set monthly fee, or an air-conditioning technician with a standard monthly service retainer.

The good news is, you can set things up so that you don't have to wear out your fingers typing the same invoice every month. Instead, you can create the invoice automatically.

The first step is to create a *memorised invoice*, just like a template that you use to produce identical products again and again.

1. **Create your customer's invoice, but instead of clicking Save & Close, go to the Edit menu and select Memorise Tax Invoice.**

2. **Give your memorised transaction a name.**

   Name your memorised sale whatever you like, as long as it's something you can recognise (the customer's name usually works pretty well).

3. **Choose between Remind Me, Don't Remind Me or Standing Order.**

   If you want to be reminded to record this sale, click Remind Me. If you want QuickBooks to record the sale automatically — something that works well for sales such as regular support agreements or monthly rent — then click Standing Order.

   If you organise memorised transactions into groups — to do so, go to Lists➪Memorised Transactions — then a fourth option appears: With Transactions in Group. This option allows you to allocate the memorised sale to a group and then record it in the same way as all other transactions in that group.

4. **Select how often the sale happens.**

   You can choose between a few options, including Daily, Weekly and Quarterly. If there's no particular pattern to this sale, simply choose Never.

5. **For standing orders, specify the Number Remaining and Days In Advance To Enter.**

   The number remaining relates to how many times you want QuickBooks to bill the customer automatically. For example, if a customer signs up for an annual agreement, paid in 12 instalments, you memorise the first transaction and, for the Number Remaining, enter 11 (as shown in Figure 3-10).

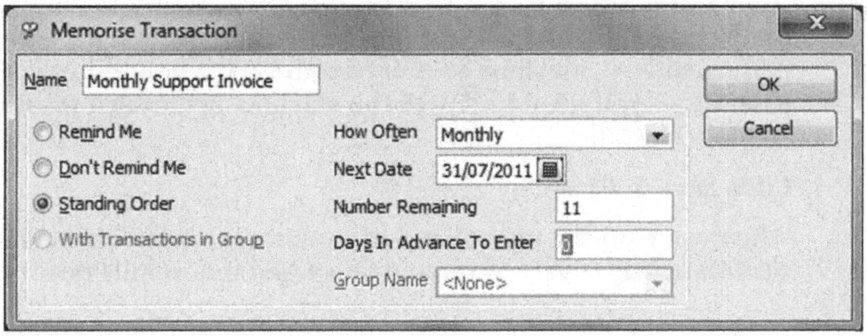

Figure 3-10:
A memorised transaction makes repetitive invoicing easy.

6. Click OK.

When you click OK, you're flicked back to your original invoice. Don't get confused and think that nothing's happened. It has. All you have to do now is click Save & Close one last time to record the sale and save the template for the next time you want to bill this customer.

Recalling memorised transactions (what's your name again?)

So you've created an invoice, saved it as a memorised transaction so that you can use it again, and you've recorded the invoice itself. Now, close your eyes and imagine time ticking by. Tick, tick, tick … Aha! You've arrived at the future, and now you're ready to bill your customer again.

Unless you saved this sale as a Standing Order, in which case QuickBooks records it automatically, here's what to do:

1. From the Lists menu, select Memorised Transaction List.

2. Double-click to open the transaction you want to record.

If you end up with lots of memorised transactions and it gets fiddly finding the transaction you're looking for, click the headers along the top to sort by columns. For example, click on the Type column to group all sales together, all withdrawals together and so on. Alternatively, try creating memorised transaction groups and edit each memorised transaction so that it belongs to a particular group.

3. Make changes if you need to.

When you select your memorised sale from the list, all the details come up exactly as they were last time you recorded this sale. If prices or descriptions or anything else has changed since the last time you used the invoice, make these alterations now.

By the way, if the details of a memorised transaction have changed permanently — maybe a sale used to be $80 a month but it's now $90 a month — you need to delete the existing memorised transaction and create a new one.

4. Click Save & Close.

When you record a memorised transaction, QuickBooks updates the Next Date field, ready to remind you when it next falls due.

Generating invoices automatically (or not)

One of the neat things that QuickBooks does is generate invoices automatically, using the Standing Orders feature. However, there's one potential hiccup: If you ask for a transaction to record automatically, but you don't work on your accounts every day, QuickBooks only records this transaction when you open your company file, dating the transaction with the system date.

For example, if you have lots of sales that you set up as memorised transactions, scheduled to be recorded on the first day of every month, but you don't open your company file on that day, then QuickBooks only records these transactions when you next open up your company file, using the system date for that day as the date of the transaction.

What this means in practice is that transaction dates go haywire if you don't work on your company file regularly and you ask for transactions to record automatically. For this reason, if you don't work on your accounts on a daily basis you may be best to set up transactions to receive reminders, rather than record automatically.

Working with Estimates and Sales Orders

The good news is, if you know how to create a customer invoice, you already know how to create an estimate or a sales order (QuickBooks uses the word *estimates* to mean quotations). To create an estimate or sales order, head to the Customer Centre and then New Transactions, then select either Sales Order or Estimate from the list. (***Note:*** Estimates and sales orders are only available in QuickBooks Pro, Premier and Enterprise.)

Sometimes novices get a little bamboozled by estimates and sales orders, so here are a few pointers to give you an extra hand:

- ✔ If estimates don't appear as an option when you go to create a new transaction, change your preferences. Go to your Edit menu, select Preferences, and click Jobs & Estimates. Under the Company Preferences tab, click Yes to the question that asks whether you want to create estimates. Similarly, if sales orders don't appear as an option, enable this feature in your Sales & Customer preferences.

- ✔ Whenever you create an estimate or sales order, QuickBooks records the transaction in a *non-posting account* (non-posting means an account that doesn't impact any financial statements). You can see this account at the very bottom of your Chart of Accounts list. To view a list of estimates or orders, simply double-click on either of these accounts.

✔ For an alternative way to see a list of all outstanding estimates or sales orders, head to the Customer Centre, click the Transactions tab on the left-hand pane, and then select either Estimates or Sales Orders below that. See Figure 3-11.

✔ If you generate the same kind of estimate again and again, you can memorise it in the same way you memorise any other kind of transaction (see 'Memorising transactions' earlier in this chapter).

✔ If you want to generate an estimate that's very similar to one you created in the past, call up the past estimate, go to your Edit menu and select Duplicate Estimate.

✔ When a customer accepts your estimate, find the estimate in the Customer Centre and double-click to open it. Next, click on the Create Invoice drop-down menu at the top of the estimate and choose between Tax Invoice, Purchase Order and Sales Order. Make any necessary changes, then click Save & Close.

✔ When the job is complete and you want to change the sales order into a Tax Invoice, first display the original order and then click the Create Invoice button. QuickBooks may then ask if you want to create an invoice for every line on the order, or just some lines. Make your choice, click OK and your order is converted into a Tax Invoice, ready for your approval. Make any final changes, then click Save & Close.

✔ To print a batch of estimates or orders — rather than print them one by one — go to either Create Sales Orders or Create Estimates. Then from the Print menu at the top, select Print Batch.

✔ QuickBooks uses special layouts for estimates and sales orders, but you may want to customise these further, possibly adding disclaimers or specifying an end date beyond which an estimate isn't valid. Go to your Lists menu, select Templates and double-click on either the Custom Estimate or Custom Sales Order template. (See Chapter 11 for lots more on creating customised templates.)

✔ Fancy the tricky stuff? You can convert estimates into orders or invoices on a percentage basis to create a sophisticated progress invoice. This feature applies to QuickBooks Pro and above only. (See your QuickBooks user guide to find out more.)

Figure 3-11: Viewing outstanding estimates or sales orders in the Customer Centre.

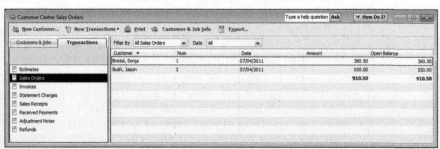

Printing Sales Forms

QuickBooks offers two ways to print invoices, estimates or sales orders: The simple way and the not-so-simple (but quite efficient) way.

The simple way

You can print an invoice, estimate or sales order simply by clicking on the Print button (this button is at the bottom of the invoice) just before you record it. No fuss, no muss. Or, if you want to abandon your mouse completely, simply type Ctrl-P.

Using the Print button to print invoices works best if you only create one or two invoices at a time and your desk is close to the printer.

The not-so-simple (but quite efficient) way

Perhaps you prefer to print invoices, estimates or sales orders in batches? When you have lots of stuff to print, you can walk away and leave your sales forms printing, one after the other, while you take a snooze, talk to your loved ones or nibble on some caramel fudge. Follow my lead:

1. **Go to the File menu, select Print Forms, followed by whatever it is you want to print (for example, select Invoices).**

   If a form doesn't appear in the Select Invoices to Print window, it means you didn't click the To Be Printed checkbox on the invoice itself. To fix this, return to the invoice and click in the box.

   By the way, if you want to print mailing labels, remember to print them before you print your invoices. Don't sweat — even if you select several invoices for the same customer, QuickBooks gets smart and knows to only print one mailing label for that customer.

2. **Mark the invoices, estimates or orders you want to print and click OK.**

   Click Select All if that's quicker.

3. **Review your print settings and click Print.**

   There's no rocket science here, but you can specify to print more than one copy, and ask QuickBooks to collate copies as well.

When printing blues call

Things are all sounding pretty easy and straightforward, aren't they? But between you, me and the gatepost, sometimes things don't go as smoothly as you expect them to. Here are some problems you may come across, along with their solutions:

- ✔ **An invoice that you changed doesn't show when you go to Print Forms.** If you printed invoices in batches, invoices that have already been printed once don't come up when you go to Print Forms. The solution? Open the invoice and click that little To Be Printed box in the bottom-left corner.

- ✔ **Credit notes didn't print.** You may think of a credit note as just another invoice, but QuickBooks doesn't. To print credit notes, you need to go to Print Forms and select Adjustment Notes.

- ✔ **Invoices print in reverse order.** Ah, you've got one of those printers that's just too clever for its boots. Go to Windows, open the Control Panel and select the Printers option. Find the printer you're using, then from the File menu select Properties. Now all you need to do is find the option that determines whether the first or the last page prints first.

- ✔ **The invoice looks like something the cat dragged in.** The fact that it's first thing in the morning after a big weekend is no excuse. You may need to customise the layout to smarten it up. Flip over to Chapter 11 to find out how to customise templates.

- ✔ **The printer isn't working.** Don't waste a moment. Grab the printer and hurl it out the window, taking care to avoid little old ladies on the footpath below. (This doesn't fix the printer, but it sure makes you feel better.)

Emailing Invoices (Anyone Can Do It!)

Did you know that you can email invoices directly from QuickBooks to your customers? No longer do you need to sacrifice forests in the name of the printed word, suffer the pace of snail mail or be revolted by the taste of envelope glue. Instead, after a couple of clicks, your customer invoices travel into the ether, arriving at their final destination within minutes.

To email an invoice to a customer, first display the sale, then click the Email button (found at the top with a white envelope icon), followed by Email Tax Invoice. Before you know it, the invoice appears in your Outbox, attached to an email that's addressed to your customer. If you're already connected to the internet, the email is sent immediately.

This blinding efficiency is all very well, but if you want to be able to review the message in your email before it gets sent, a better strategy is to select the Email button, then choose Send Batch, rather than select Email Tax Invoice. This takes you to another menu — similar to the one shown in Figure 3-12 — which displays all invoices ready to be emailed, but not yet sent. From here, you can click Edit Email to review or change messages.

If you find yourself forever changing customer messages, go to your Preferences menu and select Send Forms. Here you can change the default text and make it slightly different for each kind of form that you send.

Your customers receive your invoices in a special format called a PDF file. If they experience problems opening this format, they may not have Adobe Acrobat Reader software. Don't sweat. Simply tell them that they can download the software for free from www.adobe.com.au.

Unlike me, you probably don't set off for work in the morning without taking a quick glance in the mirror first, right? (I remember being in the middle of cutting my fringe once when the phone rang. It was only later at work that I realised I'd turned up with one side of my fringe short, and the other still long.) I reckon it's the same with your business correspondence. Check that your email invoices look good by emailing a copy to yourself first (when prompted, simply insert your own email address instead of a customer's email address). That way, you can check the appearance of your invoice in PDF format and tweak anything that's not looking 100 per cent right.

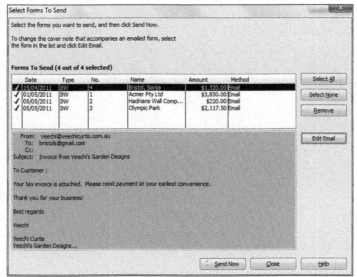

Figure 3-12:
Emailing invoices to customers.

Chapter 4

Staying in the Black and Getting Paid

In This Chapter

▶ Tracking how much money you're owed

▶ Recording customer payments

▶ Changing or deleting customer payments

▶ Fixing overpayments and generating refunds

▶ Dealing with payments made in advance

▶ Recording money that doesn't come from customers

▶ Chasing overdue accounts

You won't get far in business if you can't find out in an instant who owes you what. In this chapter, I explain everything you need to know in order to manage your customers' accounts: Record customer payments, fix up customer account queries, send customers regular statements and chase up slow payers — ever so sweetly, of course — when bills are overdue.

I reckon managing customer accounts is kind of fun. Even though I've been running my own business for years, I always feel pretty chirpy when customers pay me. You will, too, especially when you find out how easy QuickBooks makes everything seem.

Seeing Who Owes You What

For a summary of who owes you what, go to your navigation bar and click the Company Snapshot button. You should see a neat pane somewhere in this snapshot that lists each customer along with how much they owe.

Alternatively, to analyse how much you're owed in a little more detail, go to your Reports menu, navigate to the Customers & Receivables menu and click A/R Ageing Summary (A/R is short for *accounts receivable*, just in case you're wondering). A list of everyone who owes you money pops up (see Figure 4-1), grouped in columns according to how overdue the accounts are.

Like a set of Russian dolls, you can strip back layer after layer to see what lies underneath. Double-click on any amount to see the individual invoices that make up a customer's debt. Some other comments:

✔ If you use job reporting in QuickBooks, the format of this report can become a little messy. In this situation, I prefer to click the Collapse button to condense the report to one line per customer only. If I need more detail, I double-click individual details to see the job totals that make up each customer's balance.

✔ The older an account is, the less likely you'll be paid. Chase accounts as soon as they are overdue — never wait until months have passed.

✔ If a customer constantly runs overdue on an account, consider setting a Credit Limit on the customer's record in the Payment Info field. Although QuickBooks still lets you record a sale if a customer exceeds the credit limit you apply, you at least see a warning message first.

✔ As your business grows, review your Ageing Summary report every week. Make sure that the percentage of accounts that are overdue doesn't increase month after month. Don't wait until you're already strapped for cash before asking customers to cough up.

✔ If you like, you can sort your A/R Ageing Summary report to show the customers that owe you the most at the top of the list. To do this, click Modify Report, then in the Sort By field select Total. Click Descending Order and there you have it.

✔ If you bill customers weekly or fortnightly, you're probably best to click Modify Report and specify either 7 or 14 days as the number of Days Per Ageing Period. If you then select Age Through and specify 60 days, you get a report that still fits on a single page.

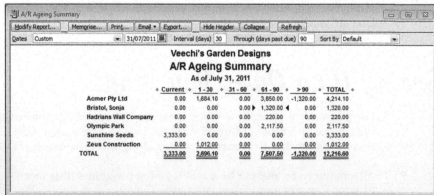

Figure 4-1: Seeing how much you're owed.

Ageing gracefully

What follows can be a bit of a brain drain so listen up: QuickBooks defaults to displaying ageing reports according to when bills are due, rather than by their transaction date. For example, if you send an invoice to a customer on 1 October and the invoice is due in 30 days, this invoice appears in the Current column on the A/R Ageing Summary report right up until 1 November. However, after this, the invoice doesn't shift to the 31–60 days column, but instead shifts to the 1–30 days column. In other words, the report displays invoices according to how many days *overdue* they are, rather than how old they are.

Some people find viewing receivable reports in this way a tad confusing. If you do, too, I suggest you navigate to the Edit menu and look for the Reports and Graphs preferences, then on the Company Preferences tab click the option to age reports from transaction date. Now, if you send out a 30-day customer account on 1 October and you view your A/R Ageing Summary report on 1 November, this bill appears in 31–60 days, rather than 1–30 days.

Recording Customer Payments

In this chapter I assume that you've already recorded a few sales using QuickBooks, but if you haven't, skip back to Chapter 3. (Why? Because unless you're paid in cash at the time of sale, you need to record customer sales before you can record customer payments.)

To deal with customer payments, the main hurdle newcomers need to overcome is to understand how undeposited funds accounts work. I explain everything you need to know about this truly scintillating topic in the following sections.

Understanding the mystery of undeposited funds

Before you start recording customer payments, think first about how they appear in your bank account. For example, if you receive payments from ten different customers in one day, this means that you record ten different transactions. However, if these payments are made by cash, cheque or EFTPOS, they only show up as one deposit on your bank statement, making it a tad confusing when you're ready to reconcile your bank account.

The ideal solution in this scenario is to use *undeposited funds*, basically a special holding account, and deposit all customer payments made by cash, cheque or EFTPOS into this account. Later, when you're ready to go to the bank or close off the EFTPOS machine for the day, you create a bank deposit to transfer the money out of undeposited funds and into your bank account. Hey presto ... the balance in the undeposited funds account returns to zero, and the deposit of all the customer payments shows up as a single amount in your bank account.

Using an undeposited funds account in QuickBooks makes sense if you receive several customer payments per day or if you tend to spend cash received from customers before banking the money (assuming you declare cash-in-hand takings, of course). However, if you only bank a couple of customer payments at a time and don't deal with much cash, then forget about setting up an undeposited funds account. Instead, simply record all customer payments directly into your bank account.

However, even in situations where I choose to use undeposited funds, I prefer to set my preferences so that I can choose which account to bank a customer payment into. That way, I can select undeposited funds for cash, cheques and EFTPOS, but select my business bank account for customers who pay direct into my bank account by electronic funds transfer. To set up my preferences in this way, I go to the Sales & Customers section of my Preferences menu, and unclick the option Use Undeposited Funds as a Default Deposit Account.

Where to go, what to do

Recording customer payments is easy. Close your eyes and take my hand:

1. **On the home page select Receive Payments.**

   Alternatively, go to Customers⇨Receive Payments.

2. **Enter the customer's name in the Customer field, fill in the Date and write the amount in the Amount field.**

3. **Select the Payment Method.**

   To add a new payment method to this list (for example, Direct Deposit), type the description in the Payment Method field, press Enter and click Set Up when prompted.

When you select a Payment Method, other fields pop up too, such as a Reference, Card No, Expiry Date and so on. Unless you're using Reckon's credit card processing service, you can usually leave all of these fields blank.

4. **Decide whether you want to deposit the payment straight into your bank account, or whether you want to use an undeposited funds account.**

   I suggest you select Undeposited Funds as the account for payments made by cash, cheque or EFTPOS, and select your business bank account for payments made direct into your bank account by funds transfer.

   I'm assuming here that your preferences are configured so you can choose between depositing customer payments into your bank account or grouping customer payments using an undeposited funds account. If you can't see an option saying 'Deposit To' to the right of the Memo field, then you may want to tweak your preferences. See 'Understanding the mystery of undeposited funds' earlier in this chapter for more info.

5. **Check that the payment has been applied correctly. If not, click Un-Apply Payment, then re-apply the payment to the correct invoice(s).**

   Although QuickBooks automatically applies customer payments to the oldest invoice first, sometimes this isn't correct. To fix up payment allocations, click Un-Apply Payment and then click against the invoices that the payment belongs to. (Alternatively, if you prefer that QuickBooks doesn't apply payments automatically, you can switch off this option in your Sales & Customers preferences.)

   By the way, if a customer pays a totally weird amount on an invoice rather than the full amount, you can click in the Payment column and adjust the amount so that it shows what the customer has paid.

6. **Click Save & Close.**

   Figure 4-2 shows the final result. Unless you want to do complicated stuff, such as apply credits or record overpayments — and if that's the case, read on to find out more — then you've discovered everything you need to know in order to record your first customer payment.

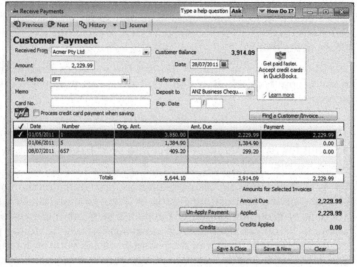

Figure 4-2:
Recording
a customer
payment.

Finetuning

After you figure out the basics of recording a customer payment, it's time to finetune the whole deal:

✔ If the way that QuickBooks allocates payments automatically sends you nuts, you can switch off this preference. Go to the Edit➪Preferences and select Sales & Customers. On the Company Preferences tab, unclick the option to automatically apply payments.

✔ If you trade regularly with a customer, you can set the customer's payment details to appear automatically. Go to the Payment Info tab for this customer and choose the preferred payment method.

✔ You can't record a customer payment against a sales order or an estimate, which can be tricky if you receive advance deposits from customers. See 'Recording Payments Made in Advance' later in this chapter for more details.

Working with sales receipts

If a customer pays you at the time of sale, the easiest approach is to record a sales receipt (much quicker than recording an invoice, then a payment, then printing out some kind of receipt). Sales receipts are also ideal if you want to record daily takings using only one transaction — maybe you're a hairdresser, restaurant or small retailer — rather than recording every individual sale that makes up your daily takings.

Accepting credit card payments

If you want to streamline customer payments so that customers can pay by credit card, check out Reckon's Credit Card Payment Service. If you subscribe to this service, you can use Receive Payments in QuickBooks, enter the customer name and amount that you want to debit and then process the card payment. After you respond to the prompt to process the payment, the customer's card is debited immediately, with the funds appearing in your bank account the next day. To assess whether this service would work well for your business, visit www.quicken.com.au and follow the link to Reckon Tools.

If customers pay in advance, then skip ahead to 'Recording Payments Made in Advance' later in this chapter. Also, note that you can't use sales receipts to record past payments. Sales receipts require full payment at the time you record the sale.

Here's the easy-step guide to generating a sales receipt:

1. **Go to your home page and select Create Sales Receipts.**

   Alternatively, go to Customers⇨Enter Sales Receipts.

2. **Enter a customer name in the Customer:Job field (optional).**

   Even if you don't want to record the customer's name, I recommend that you at least enter the payment type in the Customer:Job field. For example, a client of mine enters three sales receipts per day and has three (types of) customers — one called Cash Sales, one called EFTPOS Sales and another called AMEX Sales.

3. **Enter the Item that relates to the sale.**

   In Chapter 3, I talk more about setting up different items for each kind of income. Some businesses keep things really simple, creating an item called Sales, which in turn links to an income account called General Income. Other businesses include lots of the detail on each sales receipt, showing each item purchased.

4. **Choose a Payment Method.**

5. **If relevant, select the bank account in the bottom-left corner.**

   Depending on your sales preferences (see 'Understanding the mystery of undeposited funds' earlier in this chapter), you may see a Deposit To drop-down box in the bottom-left corner. If you record lots of cash sales, you're best to select your undeposited funds account here, storing cash separately until you're ready to deposit it into your bank account. Alternatively, if the customer has paid funds directly into your bank account, select your bank account here.

If the Deposit To drop-down box doesn't appear, which is possible depending on your Sales & Customer preferences, all sales receipts automatically go to your undeposited funds account.

6. **Memorise this transaction if you're going to use it again and again.**

   Obviously, if this is a one-off cash sale to a customer, you don't want to memorise it. However, if you're using sales receipts to record daily sales totals, chances are you want to set up a template to make data entry as swift as possible. In this case, go to Edit⇨Memorise Sales Receipt, and enter a descriptive name for the template (such as Daily Sales Summary).

7. **Click Print Preview to review your printed sales receipt. If necessary, take steps to make it look good.**

   I talk heaps more about customising templates in Chapter 11. However, the crux of the matter is that if your sales receipt doesn't look quite right, go to Lists⇨Templates, select the Custom Sales Receipt template and do your stuff using the Layout Designer.

Depositing funds into your bank account

If you use an undeposited funds account, this means you effectively record customer payments in two steps. The first step is recording the customer payment itself (a process explained earlier in this chapter). The second step involves transferring money from undeposited funds into the bank account of your choice, which I explain here:

1. **On your home page, select Record Deposits.**

   You're getting ready to transfer money out of your undeposited funds account and into your regular bank account. See Figure 4-3.

2. **Click to select the payments you want to deposit.**

   QuickBooks lists all payments currently sitting in your undeposited funds account. If all your payments are a similar type, you can simply click Select All to select all payments. However, if you receive a mixture of cash, EFTPOS, cheques and so on, then you're best to select one payment method at a time (that's because different kinds of payments show up separately on your bank statement).

3. **Click OK.**

   QuickBooks arrives at the Make Deposits window, with the payments you selected listed, one by one.

4. **Select the bank account you want to transfer the money into, along with the date of the transfer.**

   See the Deposit To box in the top-left corner of the Make Deposits window? Choose the bank account that you want to deposit funds into.

5. If you like, write a comment in the Memo field.

I recommend you say something meaningful like 'EFTPOS payments' or 'To be or not to be, that is the question'.

6. If you received any deposits other than customer payments, and there are no GST implications for these deposits, add these as additional lines on the entry.

Don't use this spot to record any kind of income that's reportable on your Business Activity Statement, because there's no column for recording tax codes. For a safer approach, see 'Recording Other Sources of Income' later in this chapter.

7. Not enough cash? Record any cash taken from the till by selecting an account from Cash Back Goes To.

The Cash Back Goes To menu only lets you select one account per transaction, so I recommend you select Petty Cash as the account here. That way, you can record how petty cash got spent in more detail later on. (See Chapter 5 for the full spiel on petty cash transactions.)

8. Click Save & Close.

When you save the deposit, the amount is transferred from your undeposited funds account to your bank account. Congratulations — you've recorded your first bank deposit.

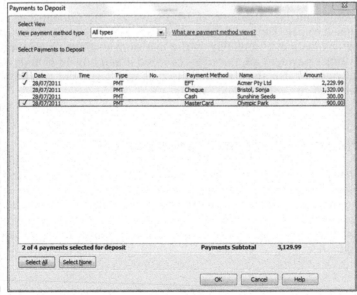

Figure 4-3: The Payments to Deposit window itemises all customer payments received, but not yet banked.

Be a pedant, it's worth it

I found out the hard way that undeposited funds accounts can be a pain in the neck if you're not careful. (I can be a pain in the neck, too, but perhaps I won't go into that right now.) The only way to keep 'em sweet is to be on the case: If a particular transaction keeps turning up in your undeposited funds account, then you need to get pedantic and find out why.

Whenever you record a deposit, QuickBooks starts by listing all the payments that are sitting in your undeposited funds account. If

there's a payment listed here that's more than a few weeks old, then look into it. For example, if a customer payment has been sitting in the Make Deposits window for several weeks, find out why it doesn't show up as being banked. Maybe you've recorded a customer payment twice, or maybe you've lost a customer's cheque on the way to banking it.

This kind of housekeeping is like brushing your teeth. A little regular attention helps avoid huge pain and big bills later on!

Troubleshooting Payments When Things Go Wrong

In the real world (as opposed to the perfect world assumed by most software manuals), customers don't always pay the amount they're supposed to pay. They may pay more, they may pay less, or they may pay the wrong amount completely. In the following sections, I explain how to find a customer payment after you've recorded it and how to change or delete the payment. I also show you how to deal with customer overpayments, underpayments, refunds and credits.

Finding customer payments

To view payments received from a particular customer, the easiest method is to go to the Customer Centre, highlight the customer's name in the left pane, and then in the right pane select Show Payments and Credits as the transaction type. Pick a suitable date range and, voilà, a list of all customer payments for that period appears on-screen, as shown in Figure 4-4.

Figure 4-4:
Finding a
customer
payment.

To view payments received from all customers, go to the Customer Centre and click the Transactions tab on the left pane (you can choose between the Customers & Jobs tab or the Transactions tab, but QuickBooks normally defaults to the former). Then select Received Payments from the list.

Fixing up mistakes

To fix up a mistake in a customer payment transaction, first find the payment and display it (refer to 'Finding customer payments' earlier in this chapter if you're not sure how). Make your changes, then click Save & Close.

Things become a little trickier if QuickBooks displays a message saying that you need to delete this payment from the deposit before you can continue. What this means is that the customer payment has already been transferred from undeposited funds into your bank account, using the Make Deposits window. In order to change the amount or customer's name on this transaction, you need to take more drastic action:

1. **Display the payment that you're having problems deleting or changing.**

2. **Click the History button to find out which deposit this payment is linked to.**

   QuickBooks first displays the invoices that this payment was applied against and, at the bottom, displays the deposit transaction that transferred this payment out of the undeposited funds account into your bank account.

3. **Highlight the Deposit line, then press the Go To button.**

   QuickBooks displays the deposit transaction that relates to the customer payment you're trying to change. If this customer payment was part of a whole batch of other payments, all the other payments will be listed as well.

4. **Click Print to print a list of the payments in this deposit.**

   Don't skip this step. Printing a record of this transaction is vital, because what you're about to do is delete the whole deposit. After you delete this deposit and fix up the mistake you made, you have to return to Make Deposits and re-enter the deposit.

5. **Without leaving the Make Deposits window, go to Banking⇨Reconcile.**

   Enter the current date as the Statement Date when prompted, and then click Continue

6. **Figure out whether you've already reconciled this deposit in your bank account.**

   If the deposit doesn't appear in the Reconcile window, this means that you've already reconciled this deposit.

7. **If the deposit *has* been reconciled, consider your options very carefully (including how important your sanity and wellbeing is).**

   If you delete a deposit that has already been reconciled in your bank account, you're going to throw your bank reconciliation out of balance. Because of this, only delete the deposit if you plan to enter another deposit for exactly the same amount.

8. **Assuming you want to do the deed, return to the offending deposit and select Delete Deposit from the Edit menu.**

9. **Now highlight the Receive Payments transaction that was wrong, and go to Edit⇨Delete Payment (or make whatever change you need to make).**

10. **Record the customer payment once more — but correctly this time! — and then record the associated deposit transaction again.**

11. **If the original deposit that you deleted had been reconciled, go immediately to your bank reconciliation and click off this new deposit, and double-check that your bank account still reconciles.**

    Go on, no backsliding now. Follow everything through to its logical end and the rewards will be many.

The moral of this rather long-winded procedure is that you can't simply delete transactions and customer payments without a second thought. In the same way that a flutter of a butterfly's wing in Patagonia can cause an earthquake in Brisbane, deleting a transaction without first engaging your brain can cause hours of accounting anguish further down the track.

Dealing with overpayments

Don't be tempted. There's no point in grabbing the loot and escaping to Tasmania. You're going to have to come clean and either send your customer a refund, or apply the credit to the customer's account.

Fortunately, QuickBooks makes this process simple. Go to Receive Payments and record the total amount paid. QuickBooks applies as much as it can to outstanding invoices and then in the bottom-left corner, displays the amount of the overpayment and asks whether you want to hold this as a credit on the customer's account or send a refund. If you select to hold the overpayment as a credit, QuickBooks stores this credit information against the customer's account. If you select to send a refund, QuickBooks automatically displays a refund window when you click Save & Close. From here, all you have to do is select the payment method, the date and in the Memo field write a meaningful note.

If a customer overpays by a very small amount, a simpler approach is to find the sale in your Customer Centre, double-click to display the transaction, and change the Amount column so that it matches what was actually paid. For example, if a customer pays $99.95 instead of $99.90 on a sale, then you simply edit the sale so that its value becomes $99.95.

Processing customer refunds

Sometimes you decide to send a customer a refund long after you've recorded the overpayment on their account. In this situation, you need to take a different approach to recording the refund:

1. **Go to Banking⇨Write Cheques.**

   You select 'Write Cheques' even if you plan to send a refund by electronic funds transfer, rather than writing a cheque.

2. **Fill in the customer's name, the date, the amount of the refund and write a brief memo.**

   Adding a note in the Memo field is optional, but I do like to write a short description to explain why this customer is receiving a refund.

3. **On the Expenses tab select Accounts Receivable as the Account. Leave everything else blank.**

   Leave the Tax Code and Tax Amount columns blank, and don't worry about entering the Customer name again on this line. (It makes no difference whether you do, or don't.)

4. **Click Save & Close.**

5. **Apply the refund against the invoices to which it belonged.**

   You need to do this in the Receive Payments window. Read on to find out all about applying credits on customer accounts.

Matchmaking credits with their debits

Often you end up with credits sitting on a customer's account, unallocated and unloved. Not far away, within this same customer's account, are a string of debits, each one looking for a mate. And you, matchmaker extraordinaire, are just the person to put a little bit of spring loving back in the air.

1. **Go to Customers⇨Receive Payments.**

2. **Enter the customer's name in the Customer:Job field, but leave the Amount at $0.00.**

   QuickBooks obligingly includes a wee note in the bottom-left, telling you that this customer has credits available, and just how much.

3. **Click the Credits button, and check how QuickBooks allocates the credits.**

   The Credits window appears, as shown in Figure 4-5. In most cases, QuickBooks instinctively matchmakes, automatically applying handsome-slightly-balding credits against intelligent-almost-blonde debits, but if you'd rather pair up credits and debits in a different way, just click and unclick on items listed till you're happy.

4. **Click Done.**

   QuickBooks returns to the Customer Payment window.

5. **Click Save & Close.**

   You're truly brilliant (not to mention under-appreciated, of course).

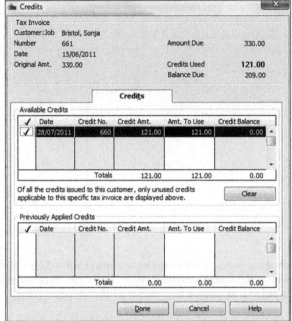

Recording Payments Made in Advance

When customers pay money in advance, before you've done the work or sent out goods, this advance becomes a liability. Why? Because an advance is money that you've received but not yet earned.

You need to allocate payments made in advance against a liability account called Customer Deposits Held. Then, when you complete the work or dispatch the goods, you transfer the value of the payment out of this liability account and into an income account. Here's how:

1. **Go to your Chart of Accounts and create a new liability account called Customer Deposits Held.**

   If you're unsure about how to create new accounts, refer to Chapter 2.

2. **Go to your Items List and create a new item called Deposit Received. Select Customer Deposits Held as the linked Account for this item.**

   Figure 4-6 shows the new item created to track customer payments.

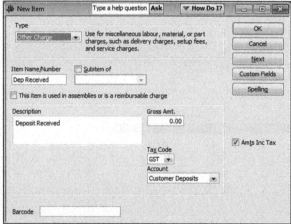

Figure 4-6:
Setting up
an item
to track
customer
payments
received in
advance.

3. **When a customer pays you in advance, generate a Sales Receipt for that customer, selecting Deposit Received as the item on this sale. As the Rate for this item, enter the value of the deposit paid.**

   When you record a sales receipt that has Deposit Received as the item, QuickBooks increases both the balance of your bank account and the balance of your Customer Deposits Held liability account.

4. **When the work is completed for this customer, or goods are shipped, go ahead and create a new invoice as normal.**

5. **At the bottom of the invoice, insert the item Deposits Received and type -1 as the Quantity, with the Rate equal to the original deposit amount or the amount of the deposit that you want to apply.**

   By typing -1 as the Quantity, you reduce the value of the invoice by the amount of deposit received from this customer. You also reduce the balance of your Customer Deposits Held liability account. Things are going well — this is just as it should be!

I recommend that you check the balance of your Customer Deposits Held account occasionally. The balance of this account should always equal the value of outstanding customer deposits. For example, imagine that you receive a $300 advance from a customer, and you later subtract this deposit from their final invoice. If you then view the register of your Customer Deposits Held account, you should see the value of this account increasing to $300, then returning to nil.

Recording Other Sources of Income

Sometimes you receive money from sources other than your customers. In the sections that follow, I explain how to deal with three different scenarios: Supplier refunds; interest or investment income; and money received from loans, capital contributions or random gifts from benevolent great-aunties.

Processing supplier refunds

Every now and then you'll receive a refund from a supplier. Maybe it's a refund for faulty goods, maybe you double-paid a previous account, or maybe you're receiving a refund for an overpayment. The process for recording supplier refunds is a little complex, I admit, but take my warm (and my not too sweaty) hand, and I'll guide you through each step.

1. **From your home page, click Enter Bills and in the top corner, click on the Credit button.**

   QuickBooks displays the regular supplier credit note window.

2. **Enter a credit note for the value of the refund.**

   You know the drill (I hope). Enter the supplier's name, the amount, and whatever expense account and tax code this supplier is normally associated with. For example, if it's a refund from Telstra, enter Telephone Expense as the expense account.

3. **Go to Record Deposits, and record the refund, selecting Accounts Payable as the Account.**

   The main trick to remember here is to enter the supplier's name in the Received From column, then select Accounts Payable (always possibly called Trade Creditors) as the Account, not the expense account normally associated with that supplier.

4. **Go to Pay Bills and highlight the refund transaction that you just entered.**

   Figure 4-7 shows what this transaction looks like — with the refund transaction showing up as if it's a bill. Click against this refund and QuickBooks displays all credits available for this supplier under Total Credits Available.

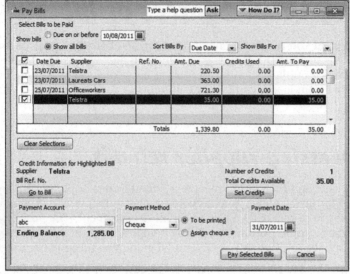

Figure 4-7:
Receiving
refund
cheques
from
suppliers.

5. Click Set Credits, followed by Done.

The Apply Credits window appears, matching the refund cheque against the credit note. When you click Done, you return to the Pay Bills window.

6. Click Pay Selected Bills.

QuickBooks displays a message confirming that the credit is settled.

Recording interest or investment income

If you recently upgraded to the latest version of QuickBooks and you make your way confidently to the bank reconciliation window in order to record interest income, then you could be justified in thinking that you've lost your marbles. And no, the solution isn't that you need to take more fish oil tablets. It's just that this feature has been removed (there was a problem with how bank fees and interest income were detailed on your Business Activity Statement when you recorded them this way).

So, whether you're new to QuickBooks or an old-timer, here's the latest-and-greatest procedure for recording interest or investment income:

1. Go to your Item List and create a new item called Interest Income, selecting Other Charge as the Item Type.

Or, you could name the new item Dividend Income, as the case may be. Hook up this item to an account called Interest and Investment Income (if you don't have this account in your Chart of Accounts, then create one now).

Select INP as the tax code for this item. This ensures that interest income comes up in the right spot when you do all the workings for your Business Activity Statement. (Skip to Chapter 10 for more about tax codes.)

2. **Go to your Customer List and create a new customer called Interest and Investment Income.**

Don't worry about adding contact details; a name is enough. (Alternatively, you can use the name of your bank or the company that's paying the dividend as the name of this new customer. Either method is fine.)

3. **Click Create Sales Receipts and record a sales receipt for the interest received.**

On your home page, see the button that says Create Sales Receipts? Click that one. Enter Interest and Investment Income as the customer name up the top, select your new item Interest and Investment Income as the Item, then slot the amount received into the Amount column. By now, your transaction should look similar to mine, shown in Figure 4-8. (In this screen, I customised my sales receipt so it doesn't include columns for the rate or for the quantity, which makes more sense for interest transactions. However, if your sales receipt has a quantity column, just enter **1** as the quantity.)

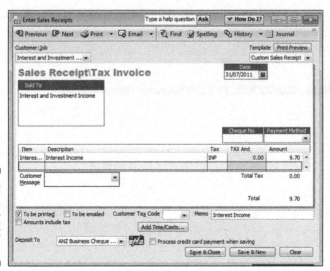

Figure 4-8: Recording interest or investment income.

When I record interest on a sales receipt, I also add a brief comment in the Memo field. This is to ensure that this transaction shows up clearly when I'm ready to do my bank reconciliation.

4. **Depending on your preference settings, select your bank account in the bottom-left corner.**

   If your preferences are set so that payments don't automatically go to your undeposited funds account, choose your bank account in the bottom-left corner, similar to how I've selected my ANZ Business Account in Figure 4-8.

5. **Click Save & Close.**

Receiving loans or capital contributions

The easiest way to record a loan or capital contribution is to go to Record Deposits (on the home page). In the top-left corner select the bank account into which the moolah is going, then type in the name of the person who's giving you the money, the account it's coming from, then the amount. Check out Figure 4-9 to see how I record a $20,000 bank loan.

Although going to Record Deposits is a quick and easy way to record money when it comes in, always ask yourself first whether this transaction needs to be reported on your Business Activity Statement. (Loans and capital contributions don't need to be reported, but other deposits, such as supplier refunds and interest income, do.)

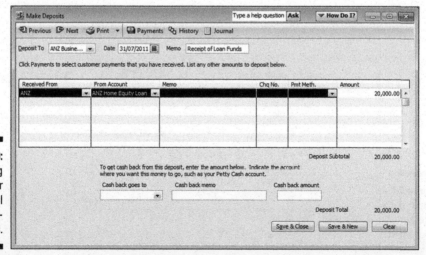

Figure 4-9: Receiving loans or capital contributions.

The rule is this: If a deposit *does* need to be reported on your Business Activity Statement, then either follow the procedure for interest income (refer to 'Recording interest or investment income' earlier in this chapter) or the procedure for supplier refunds (refer to 'Processing supplier refunds'). Otherwise, if a deposit *doesn't* need to be reported on your Business Activity Statement, Record Deposits works just fine.

Figuring out which account to pick

When recording any kind of income that doesn't come from a customer, selecting the correct account can be confusing. But, never fear, help is here:

- ✔ If you're depositing your own money into your business bank account, select either Owner's Contributions (if you're a sole trader or partnership) or Loan from Directors (if you're a company) as your allocation account.

- ✔ If you don't have the foggiest where this deposit should go, create a new account in your Chart of Accounts called Suspense, choosing Other Expense as the Account Type. Every month or so, print a report of all transactions sitting in this account and ask your accountant to help you work out the details.

- ✔ If the money is from an insurance claim or workers compensation claim, create a special income account called Insurance Recovery and use this as your allocation account. (Your accountant will be so impressed!)

- ✔ For money from bank loans, create a new liability account called Bank Loan. If you have more than one bank loan, include as much of the account number as fits in the Account Name area.

Choosing the correct tax code

Most businesses live in fear of auditors arriving at the door. Not because they're knowingly ripping off the tax office, but more because they're afraid that if they have made a mistake, they'll be up for a hefty fine. Hey, I feel the same way.

When it comes to GST, getting records right isn't actually so technical. The trick is picking the right tax code for every transaction, every time.

- ✔ If you're recording a sales receipt for income, and you know that this income attracts GST, select GST as the tax code.

- ✔ If a deposit is for interest income, investment income or for services that are input-taxed, select INP as your tax code. (I talk more about this tax code in Chapter 10.)

- ✔ Never record income that's reportable on your Business Activity Statement using Record Deposits, because this window doesn't include a column for tax codes. (If you record income in this way, QuickBooks won't report it on your Business Activity Statement reports.)

- ✔ If you're not registered for GST, you don't need to put anything in the tax code column. Lucky you. Simply leave the tax code column blank.

Bringing in the Dough

One of the first principles of successful business management is to be paid on time. If you can keep the money coming through the door, you can improve your cashflow, boost working capital, save on overdraft interest and reduce bad debts.

If you have trouble getting fired up about the idea of timely debt collection, then think of it this way: Imagine your monthly sales are $30,000 and your customers pay on average in 60 days (some pay on time, some pay pretty late). If you can reduce this average from 60 days to 45 days, then you generate an extra $15,000 of working capital, interest free!

With this in mind, the next few pages in this chapter explain how to print customer statements, see how much you're owed, fire off scary reminder letters and keep track of all those money-chasing phone calls. Last of all — and most regrettably — I explain how to write off a bad debt.

Doing the asking, reaping the rewards

Few customers will cough up without you telling them how much they owe, and there's no better method for keeping customers painfully aware of their debts than by sending regular customer statements:

1. **Go to your home page and click Statements.**

2. **Either select a Statement Period or click the option to View all Open transactions as of Statement Date.**

I usually prefer to list all open transactions because this format is so straightforward — the statement simply lists all invoices with any amounts outstanding, and doesn't include any amounts that have already been fully paid. (***Note:*** Not all versions of QuickBooks offer this choice — it may be that you're only able to select a date range.)

On the other hand, if you select a date range, the statement shows *all* transactions on a customer's account for any specified date range, starting with the opening balance outstanding, and then listing every single sale and payment.

3. **Select the customers you want to send a statement to.**

   I normally select All Customers, but if you want to pick and choose, click Multiple Customers and mark names off, one by one.

4. **Click Customise to preview the statement format and if necessary, tweak the template to suit your needs.**

   Chapter 11 explains lots more about customising forms.

5. **Experiment with the statement options, and click Preview to see what suits you best.**

   Don't be tempted to click the option 'Do not create statements with no account activity'. Just because a customer's account does not have transactions in the current statement period doesn't mean you shouldn't chase them for the money that they owe.

6. **Either click Print or Email.**

   If you click Print, your printer springs into action. If you click Email, the Select Forms to Send window opens (this process is slow, and may take quite some time). From here, you can review the text on each email and click Send Now when you're ready.

If you recently upgraded your version of QuickBooks, you may not be aware of a feature that lets you customise any invoice to include the customer's total current balance outstanding. Go to Lists⇨Templates, followed by the template you're customising. Click the Additional Customisation button and on the Footer tab, click in the Print column next to Customer Total Balance. This feature is great because it not only lets customers know how much they owe you every time you send out invoices, but gives you a quick reminder too.

Credits that hang around like a bad smell

Every now and then, head to your Reports menu and from the Customers & Receivables submenu open the A/R Ageing Detail report. Unless you're superhuman (and do let me know if you are, especially if you're tall, dark and handsome to boot), then chances are that along with a whole swag of invoices, you'll see a few customer payments and adjustment notes listed. You may even see that a customer owes $90 in one period, followed by a payment for $90 in a previous period. The total amount due is zero, but these transactions still show up on the receivables report.

Unless a customer genuinely has an account that's in credit, what you need to do is match up unallocated credits or adjustment notes against the invoices to which they belong. To do so, go to Receive Payments, enter the customer's name, highlight the invoice to which you want to apply a credit, and click the Credits button. Highlight the credit or credits that you want to apply to this invoice, then click Done.

Sending letters, sweet and sour

Go to the Customer Centre, ensure you click the Customers & Jobs tab on the left pane, and select Prepare Collection Letters from the Word menu that appears above the customer names (*Note:* This feature isn't available in QuickBooks Accounting). QuickBooks then displays a window similar to the one shown in Figure 4-10, where you can choose between active and inactive customers (or both), creating a letter for each customer.

Click Next and QuickBooks gives you a chance to sort the list by Customer or Amount. I often choose to sort by amount, so that if there's a pile of tiddly amounts at the top of the list, I can untick them — there's nothing worse for PR than sending a rude collection letter chasing your number one customer for an outstanding debt of five cents.

Click Next one more time, then choose between formal, friendly and harsh collection letters. (I reckon QuickBooks does a pretty good job with these templates, but if you like, you can click the option to Create or Edit a Letter Template, and create a new one from scratch.) Click Next again, and QuickBooks prompts you to enter your Name (that's easy) and Title ('Most Venerable Veechi' has a certain ring to it, don't you reckon?). Click Next one last time and Microsoft Word miraculously creates letter after letter, each one personalised with the customer's name, address and how much the customer owes, and signed at the bottom with your name and title.

Figure 4-10:
Using
standard
letters
to chase
money.

Just because you create letters in Word doesn't mean you have to post them using snail mail. Instead, you can generate these collection letters and then cut and paste the text of each letter into an email to the customer. You can even generate statements from QuickBooks, selecting to send these statements as emails, and cut and paste the text from your collection letter into the body text of each email. (The statement itself is sent as a PDF attachment.)

Keeping track of who promised what

One neat feature in QuickBooks is the *notepad* that's attached to every customer's record. To find this notepad, open your Customer:Job list, double-click on a customer's name, then click on the Notes button.

This notepad is ideal for keeping track of your debt collection activities. Perhaps you phone an overdue customer and the receptionist says, 'The accounts lady only comes in on Wednesdays'. You ring on Wednesday and the receptionist says, 'The accounts lady took the day off and won't be in again till next Tuesday', and on and on and on . . .

I like to click the Date Stamp button to enter the date whenever I record an entry on the notepad. Also, I like to create reminders when I need to follow something up. To do this, I click the New To Do button and write a short description such as 'Ring Sally again regarding overdue account' along with a reminder date. QuickBooks gets really smart and inserts a reminder in the To Do List, which you find on the Company menu.

Giving up, and writing it off

Although I talk lots about chasing money before it gets too overdue and how QuickBooks can help you to do this, sooner or later you'll probably come up against a customer who simply isn't going to cough up. So, in the name of pragmatism, here's how to write off a bad debt:

1. **Go to your Item List and create a new item called Bad Debt Expense, selecting Other Charge as the Item Type. Select Bad Debt Expense as the Account for this item.**

   If you don't have an account named Bad Debt Expense in your Chart of Accounts, then create one now.

   If you normally charge GST on sales, then select GST as the tax code for this item. If you don't normally charge GST, select FRE as the tax code. If you sell a mixture of taxable and non-taxable goods, then leave the tax code blank.

2. **Click Refunds & Adjustments (available from the home page), and create an adjustment note for the amount of bad debt.**

   Figure 4-11 shows an example. Note that I outline the reason for this bad debt in both the Description and the Memo fields, and I use my new Bad Debt Expense item in the Item column.

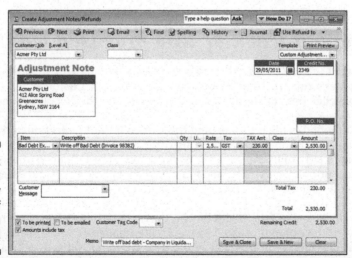

Figure 4-11: The sad and sorry business of writing off a bad debt.

The important thing to remember here is to select the same tax code on the adjustment note as you selected on the original sale. If you're writing off a bad debt that was a mixture of taxable and non-taxable goods, you need to use the Bad Debt Expense item on two lines, with GST as the tax code on the first line, and FRE as the tax code on the second line.

3. **Click Save & Close and then when prompted, click Apply to a Tax Invoice.**

   QuickBooks takes you directly to Apply Credit to Invoices. How charming.

4. **Check that QuickBooks has matched your adjustment note against the invoice that you want to write off, then click Done.**

   Breathe one last sigh of resignation, as you give up a fight well fought. Win some, lose some.

If you happen to be browsing the Reckon knowledge base or any of the US community forums, you may come across the recommendation to write off bad debts using the discount feature. Please don't: Writing off bad debts this way doesn't take GST into account and creates deep problems — many of which can take years of therapy to resolve — in your tax reporting.

Chapter 5

Shelling Out the Cash

. . . .

In This Chapter

▶ Telling QuickBooks about all the money you spent

▶ Transferring dosh from one account to another

▶ Finding stuff, fixing it up

▶ Running up credit, then owning up

▶ Looking after petty cash

▶ Dealing with bank fees

. . . .

My granny always used to say, 'Keep an eye on the pennies, and the pounds will look after themselves.' Fortunately, QuickBooks helps you to keep right on top of your expenses, so you can see how much you spend on vital outgoings, such as wages, rental expense, supplies and so on.

In this chapter, I explain how to record all your expenses in QuickBooks, including things such as working with multiple bank accounts, deciding which expense accounts to choose, dealing with credit cards and how to handle petty cash. I also provide a helping hand with a few things that tend to cause grief, offering tips on tax codes, fixing up mistakes and recording those very tiresome bank fees.

Recording Business Expenses

You record most expenses (other than employee pays and supplier payments) in the Write Cheques window. Don't be hoodwinked into thinking that this window is only for cheques — this is also the spot for recording ATM withdrawals, direct debits, EFTPOS payments and petty cash transactions. In short, the Write Cheques window is where you're going to spend a lot of your time.

Spending money, time after time

Ready to record your first business expense? Here's what to do:

1. **Go to the home page and click Write Cheques.**

   I know that most businesses don't use many cheques these days, but just ignore the terminology — Write Cheques is where you record all withdrawals from all bank accounts, whether electronic or by cheque.

2. **Select your bank account.**

   In the top-left corner, where it says Bank Account, select the correct bank account.

3. **Choose your payment method.**

   See that inconspicuous box halfway down on the right-hand side? Here's where you choose the payment method, toggling between Bank (Online), Cash/Cheque or Cheque to Print.

   Only choose Bank (Online) if you plan to use QuickBooks to generate a banking file that you then import into your banking software. If you've already made this payment online, choose Cash/Cheque as the payment method.

4. **Enter a reference number in the No. field.**

   For cheques, simply enter the cheque number. For other types of payments, such as direct debits or electronic transfers, you can ignore the number. (I used to suggest entering a brief description such as Debit, ATM or EFT, so that electronic transactions didn't get confused with cheque numbers. However, so few businesses use cheques these days that it's usually fine just to ignore the No. field altogether.)

5. **Enter the date.**

6. **Type in the name of the person or company who's being paid (or has received) the moolah and enter the Amount.**

   If you've never recorded a payment for this person or company before, QuickBooks asks if you want to add this name to your list. Click either Quick Add (that's the quick-and-dirty way) or Set Up (the more thorough approach) to record these details.

7. **Depending on your literary talents, record a brief but erudite description in the Memo field.**

   Actually, you only need to write a memo if the transaction isn't obvious. For example, if you're paying a bill to Telstra and allocating the transaction to your Telephone Expense account, you don't really need to write Telephone Bill in the Memo field. You only write a memo if there's something unusual or special about the transaction.

8. **Decide which account the expense should go to, or if you're purchasing inventory items, click the Items tab and specify what items you received.**

   Click the down arrow under the Account column to view all your accounts, or if you know the account name already, just type the first letters (QuickBooks leaps into action and fills in the rest for you). If you're not sure which is the correct expense account, see 'Picking the right expense account' later in this chapter.

9. **Double-check the tax code.**

   Make sure the tax code is correct — see the following section 'Figuring out which tax code to choose' — and that the amount of GST comes up correctly in the Tax total. Most payments either have NCG as the tax code (advertising, computer stuff, rent, telephone and so on) or NCF as the tax code (bank charges, donations, government charges and so on). If you're setting up QuickBooks from scratch, you may prefer to use the tax codes GST or FRE instead (see Chapter 10 for details).

10. **Check that the Amounts Include Tax box is selected.**

    See the little box called Amounts Include Tax? Click here if you intend to enter amounts including GST. (If you can't see this box, go to the Tax section in your Preferences and tick the option to allow tax-inclusive prices and costs to be entered.)

    By now, your payment should look similar to Figure 5-1.

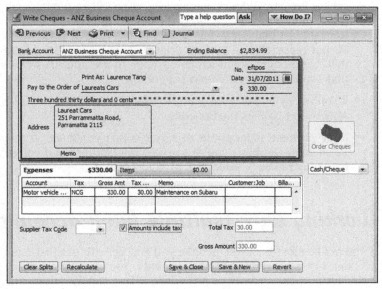

Figure 5-1: Recording your first payment.

11. **If you want to onbill a customer for these expenses or items, type the customer's name in the Customer:Job column and make sure the Billable box is ticked.**

12. **Click Save & Close.**

    Find your mouse, close your eyes, breathe deeply. You made it.

Figuring out which tax code to choose

Here's a crib sheet to keep you on the straight and narrow when deciding which tax code to use. If the following list mentions a tax code that you don't already have, see Chapter 10.

✔ If goods or services attract GST, select NCG as the tax code. (If you set up tax codes from scratch as I discuss in Chapter 10, GST is also fine as the tax code.)

✔ If goods or services are GST-free — bank fees, medical supplies, GST-free food and so on — then select NCF as the tax code.

✔ If goods are of a capital nature, such as new office equipment or tools, then select CAG as the tax code.

✔ If goods or services are of a private nature, such as groceries, kids' school fees or wild weekends away, select NR as the tax code. (Some QuickBooks consultants suggest leaving the tax code for non-taxable transactions blank instead. I prefer to use the NR code — which stands for not reportable — because that way my accountant can at least see that I've thought about which tax code to use and doesn't simply think that I've forgotten to enter a tax code.)

✔ If you're paying someone who isn't registered for GST, but who has an ABN, select NCF as the tax code.

✔ If the payment is for goods or services that you'll use to make input taxed sales (perhaps you're a residential landlord and you're paying for plumbing repairs), select INP as your tax code.

Working with multiple bank accounts

If you're like most business people, you end up with not just one bank account, but a few different bank accounts. You may have a cheque account, a savings account and even a term deposit account, not to mention a wad of credit cards and the odd loan. Make sure you set up each of these bank accounts correctly in QuickBooks, listing each one separately in your Chart of Accounts:

1. **Check all your bank accounts are listed in your Chart of Accounts.**

   All bank accounts appear as asset accounts at the top of your accounts list, with Bank as the account Type. Credit cards come near the top of your liability accounts, with Credit Card as the account Type.

   In a fit of denial, QuickBooks doesn't have any easy way to record overdraft or line of credit accounts. In order to be able to record transactions from these accounts, you need to set them up as asset accounts with Bank as the account Type. These accounts will show up as negative assets on your Balance Sheet, which is a little irritating, but that's just one of those things. (You can set up overdraft or line of credit accounts as liabilities if you set them up with Credit Card as the Account Type, but you can't generate online payment batch files from this kind of account.)

2. **If a bank account is missing, work out a suitable description for it and click New.**

   If you have lots of bank accounts, consider entering the last few digits of the account number in the Account Name, and the whole account number as the Account Description.

   Don't forget to click the Online Bank Details tab and enable the account for online access if you intend to create online payment batch files from this account in the future. (Chapter 16 talks more about online payments.)

3. **Go to Edit⇨Preferences⇨Banking, followed by Company Preferences. Select default bank accounts for payroll payments.**

   Select the account you use for paying employees, and second, select the account you use when paying superannuation or PAYG tax.

Taxing times

Set up your Chart of Accounts so that the correct tax code comes up automatically. For example, donations are almost always GST-free, so go to your Chart of Accounts, edit your Donation Expense account and enter FRE (or NCF if you've migrated from an older version of QuickBooks) as the Tax Code. That way, whenever you allocate a transaction to Donation Expense, the tax code will always be correct.

4. **Still in Banking preferences, click the tab that says My Preferences, and select default bank accounts for writing cheques, paying bills, paying tax and making deposits (as per Figure 5-2).**

Pick whatever account you use most frequently for each transaction type. That way, QuickBooks guesses the correct bank account more often than not, every time you go to record a transaction.

5. **Check your email. At the very first offer to receive US$50,000, email your account details and passwords to some unknown person in a far-flung country.**

Just kidding!

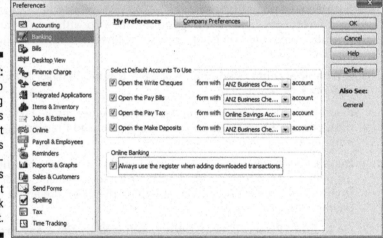

Figure 5-2:
Setting up
Banking
preferences
so that
QuickBooks
automati-
cally selects
the correct
bank
account.

Picking the right expense account

QuickBooks asks you to select an allocation account every time you record a transaction in Write Cheques. Think of this account as being the same as a heading in a ledger. All you have to do is work out which heading an expense belongs to. Is it an advertising, stationery, cleaning or insurance expense? Is it bank charges or entertainment? Or something else again?

If you sometimes get in a muddle deciding which account to choose, consider these points:

✔ **Keep personal drawings separate.** If you're a sole trader or a partnership, allocate personal drawings to a Drawings account (listed under Equity in your Chart of Accounts). If your business has a company structure, allocate anything of a private nature to a Directors Loan account (listed under Other Current Liabilities in your Chart of Accounts).

✔ **Keep separate accounts for interest expense, bank charges and merchant fees.** You need to allocate interest expense and bank charges to different expense accounts so that you can report on them separately in your tax return. Merchant fees need to be a separate account again, because they have GST on them and bank charges don't.

✔ **Make a distinction between capital acquisitions and regular expenses.** Accountants describe new bits of plant and equipment, tools, vehicles, computer gear, furniture or leasehold improvements as capital acquisitions. Allocate all capital acquisitions to a fixed asset account with a suitable name and description.

✔ **Don't allocate customer refunds to an expense account.** Customer refunds go against whatever income account the original sale went to.

✔ **Split travel expenses between Travel Expense (local) and Travel Expense (international).** I know I'm nit-picky and pedantic, but I'm making things easier for you when tax time comes around.

✔ **Allocate tax payments to liability accounts.** See Chapter 10 for more on this riveting topic.

✔ **Don't allocate superannuation or PAYG tax payments to expense accounts, but instead allocate them to the relevant liability accounts.** Assuming you're using the payroll features in QuickBooks, superannuation payments go to Superannuation Payable and PAYG goes to PAYG Tax Payable.

If you're not sure which account to choose, create a new expense account called Suspense. In the future, use this Suspense account whenever you're in doubt where a transaction belongs, then later — perhaps every month or so — ask someone more knowledgeable than yourself (I suggest your accountant) to re-allocate any transactions sitting in Suspense to their correct spot.

Splitting hairs

What happens if you want to allocate an expense to more than one account? Simply keep typing when filling in the Account and Amount details, entering one line for each type of expense.

Figure 5-3 shows how easy it is to record split expenses. In my example, a telephone bill is split between a telephone business expense account and a personal drawings account. Lovely.

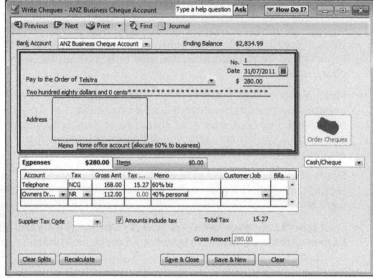

Figure 5-3:
Splitting
expenses
across more
than one
account.

Making electronic payments

When I talk about recording your first payment at the beginning of this chapter, I mention that you need to select Bank (Online) as the payment method if you want to pay someone electronically. After that, you progress to the Online Banking Centre, ready to create the file to send to your bank. What happens next and much more is covered in Chapter 16.

Memorising transactions

Do you make some payments regularly every week or every month, such as loan payments, lease payments or regular transfers?

If you're like me, you don't want to waste your precious time entering the same stuff again and again. So I'll share a handy hint: You can set things up so that QuickBooks records these transactions automatically. Here's how:

1. **Record the direct debit or regular payment in Write Cheques as normal, but instead of clicking Save & Close, go to the Edit menu and select Memorise Cheque.**

2. **Give your memorised transaction a name.**

   Call your memorised transaction whatever you like, but ensure it's something you can recognise (sometimes I include the amount as part of the name, making it easier to spot).

3. **Choose between Remind Me, Don't Remind Me or Standing Order.**

   If you want to be reminded to record this debit, click Remind Me. However, if you want QuickBooks to record this payment automatically — something that works well for regular direct debits — then click Standing Order.

4. **Select how often the payment happens.**

5. **For standing orders, specify the Number Remaining and Days In Advance to Enter.**

   The number remaining relates to how many times you want QuickBooks to record this debit. For example, if you've signed up for a five-year lease, paid in 60 instalments, you memorise the first transaction and, for the Number Remaining, enter 59.

6. **Click OK.**

   When you click OK, you're flicked back to your original transaction. Don't get confused and think that nothing has happened. It has. To record the debit or payment, click Save & Close one last time.

What happens next? If you record a standing order, then all your work is done. QuickBooks records this transaction automatically every time it falls due. If you record a memorised transaction and ask to be reminded when it falls due, QuickBooks displays a reminder in your Reminders window a certain number of days before it's due (you can specify the number of days in the Reminders section of your Preferences menu).

Names versus numbers

If you've worked with other accounting software programs in the past, you may be used to working with account numbers, rather than names. For example, instead of typing in Telephone Expense, you type in something like 62100 as the account number.

Which way works best? It kinda depends on you. If you're used to account numbers, they can be a tad faster in the long run when it comes to data entry. Also, if you use the first digit of each account number to indicate the account type (using 1 for assets, 2 for liabilities, 3 for equity and so on), then it's harder to make allocation mistakes, such as selecting Superannuation Expense instead of Superannuation Payable. On the other hand, account numbers can be fiddly, and account names are a whole lot less intimidating.

If you'd rather switch to account numbers, you can. In the Accounting section of your Preferences, on the Company tab, click the option to use account numbers.

Transferring Funds between Accounts

Figuring out how to record the transfer of funds between bank accounts can be tricky at first. However, when you know how, it's easy as pie.

1. **Go to your Banking menu and click Transfer Funds.**

   I'm talking about the Banking menu that runs along the top menu bar, rather than the Banking area of your home page (the Transfer Funds command doesn't show there).

2. **Select the account that you want to transfer money out of.**

3. **Select the account that you want to transfer money into.**

4. **Enter the Transfer Amount and, if you like, a note in the Memo.**

   That's all there is to it, as shown in Figure 5-4. If you're feeling pedantic, you could add a memo to the transaction that says something like 'Transfer of funds from business bank account to credit card account', but that's probably overkill.

5. **Click Save & Close.**

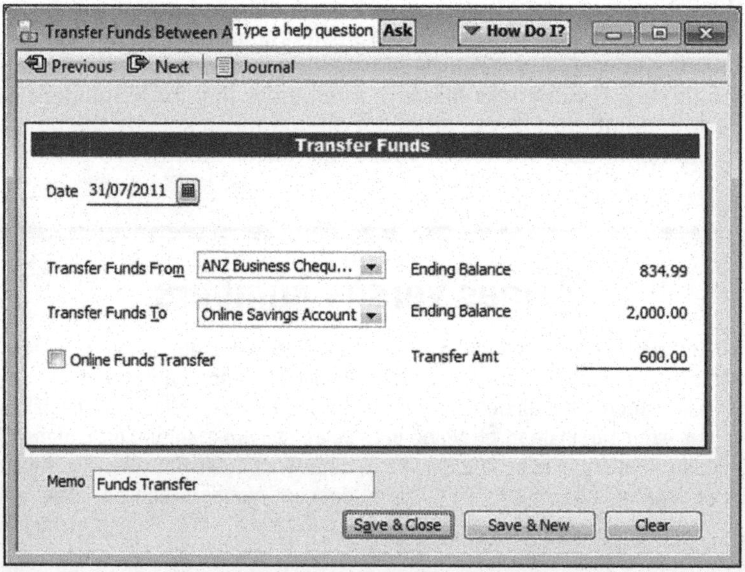

Figure 5-4:
Transferring funds from one account to another.

Finding and Changing Transactions

So, you've recorded heaps of payments and now you want to have a look at them. You can do this in your Banking Register, your Supplier Centre or via the Find menu.

Checking out your Banking Register

To view transactions that you've already recorded, go to Banking from your home page and click Use Register.

If you have more than one bank account, QuickBooks asks you to select which one you want to view. Select your bank account, click OK and QuickBooks displays a list of your most recent transactions, similar to what you can see in Figure 5-5.

If you can't find a transaction, try sorting the register using the Sort By menu that appears in the bottom-left corner. You can sort by Amount, by the Date of the transaction or by the Date that the transaction was recorded.

Although beginners often like working with the Banking Register because it's a handy way of viewing every transaction you've recorded, I find scrolling through registers a bit slow, especially if there are lots of transactions. In this situation, I prefer to hunt for transactions by supplier name. Read on to find out more . . .

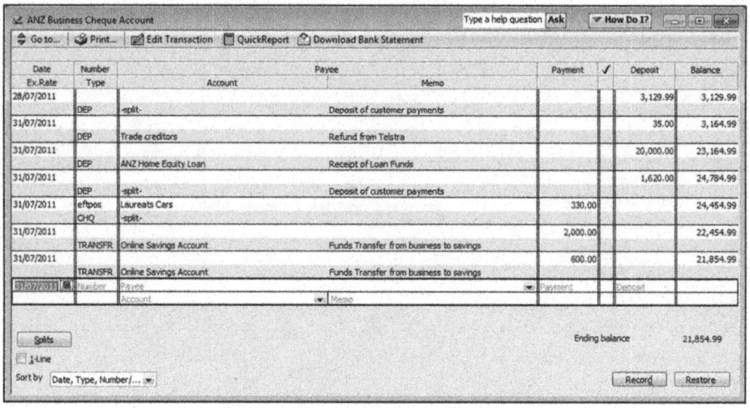

Figure 5-5:
Viewing
transactions
in your
Banking
Register.

Sleuthing in the Supplier Centre

To view all transactions for a certain supplier, click the Suppliers button on your home page. On the left pane, highlight the supplier's name, and on the right pane, select the transaction type you want to view. If lots of transactions appear, filter the date to a narrower period.

Deleting your mistakes

So, you're human after all. If you've recorded a transaction and you want to delete it, don't waste a moment. This is easy.

1. **Find the transaction in your Banking Register or via the Supplier Centre.**

2. **Double-click on the transaction to display it.**

3. **Select Edit⇨Delete Cheque.**

   The Edit command is on the top menu bar, as shown in Figure 5-6. After you select Delete Cheque, the screen flickers for a second and the transaction disappears, never to be seen again.

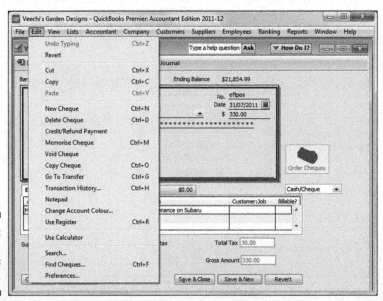

Figure 5-6:
Deleting
transactions
is easy.

Sounds easy, hey? However, there's one situation in which you shouldn't delete a transaction, even if it seems a good idea at the time, and that's if the transaction has a big CLEARED stamp printed across it. If you delete a transaction that has already been marked as cleared in your bank account, you'll throw your bank reconciliation out of balance.

Because of this, only delete a cleared transaction if you plan to enter another transaction for exactly the same amount. After recording this new transaction, make sure your bank account stays in balance by going to your bank reconciliation and marking this new transaction as cleared.

Changing transactions after the event

Sometimes you may want to change a transaction, rather than delete it. Perhaps you allocated an expense to the wrong account or entered the amount as $97 rather than $79. To make a change, first find the transaction in the Bank Register or via the Supplier Centre and double-click the transaction to display it. Then make your changes and click Save & Close.

If the transaction displays a CLEARED stamp across it, think carefully before proceeding. If a payment has been marked as cleared, you're safe to change the date, the account or the memo, but you're not safe to change the amount. Changing the amount of a cleared transaction knocks your bank reconciliation out of balance.

Playing with Plastic

However dreadful credit cards may be — I'm a serious sinner when it comes to impulse buys on credit — they're also a fact of life. If, like many smaller businesses, you use credit cards more often than regular bank accounts for business purchases, then keeping tabs on your credit card spending becomes one of the more important aspects of managing business expenses.

Owning up to your credit cards

Before recording credit card transactions in QuickBooks, the first thing you have to do is set up your credit card account correctly. To do so, head for your Chart of Accounts, scroll down to the liability accounts, and see if your credit card appears in the list — it's usually near the top somewhere.

If you can't see it, select New from the Account menu to create a new account. As the Account Type, select Credit Card, and as the Account Name, type Visa Card or American Express or whatever. If you have more than one credit card, I suggest typing the card number in the account number field, so you don't get confused about which card is which. Figure 5-7 shows an example.

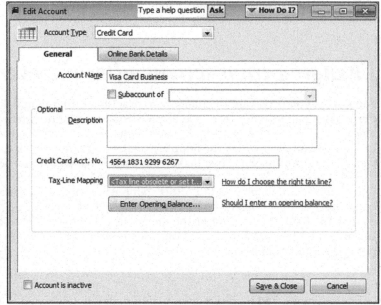

Figure 5-7:
Setting up a credit card account.

If you already have an amount outstanding on the credit card when you create its account, click Enter Opening Balance and record the balance in the Opening Balance field. See Chapter 9 for some more information on opening balances.

Confessing your spending

Human nature is indeed a gullible and vulnerable thing. Sometimes when my credit card statement arrives, it sits on my desk for a few days before I can bear to open it. Sooner or later, I face up to the inevitable, tear open the envelope and record the day-by-day testimony of my reckless habits. You need to do this, too, every time your statement arrives.

1. **From your home page, go to Banking and click Enter Credit Card Charges.**

   You see before you the Credit Card Charges window. At the top are two buttons: Purchase/Charge and Refund/Credit. QuickBooks always defaults to the first option, because you're much more likely to be entering credit card debits than refunds.

2. **Select your credit card account in the top left-hand corner.**

   If you haven't got a credit card account set up in your Accounts List already, refer to the preceding section.

3. **Enter all the details in exactly the same way as a Write Cheques transaction.**

   I explain all the details of recording regular bank transactions at the beginning of this chapter. The only difference is the Ref No. field. Although most credit card statements do print a reference number against each transaction, this number is usually very long and rather meaningless. I suggest you skip the Ref No. field and leave it blank.

   By the time you've done your stuff, the transaction should look similar to Figure 5-8.

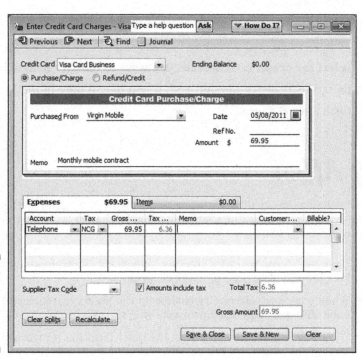

Figure 5-8: Recording credit card transactions.

4. **Click Save & New when you're done.**

5. **Record transactions for each debit on the credit card, allocating each one to an appropriate expense account.**

   Carry on recording a separate transaction for each debit on your credit card statement. Continue until you reach the end of your statement.

When a debit on the statement is for a personal purchase, choose a drawings account or director's loan account as the Account.

Paying the piper

All this spending on your credit card is very well, but before long, you're going to have to transfer some funds into the very-hungry jaws of your credit card account. Here's how to record this transfer.

1. **Go to your Banking menu and click Transfer Funds.**

   I'm talking about the Banking menu that runs along the top menu bar, rather than the Banking area of your home page (the Transfer Funds command doesn't show there).

2. **Select the account that you want to transfer money out of.**

   This is usually your business bank account.

3. **Select the credit card account you want to transfer money into.**

4. **Enter the Transfer Amount and, if you like, a note in the Memo.**

5. **Click Save & Close.**

A Petty Affair

You can find as many different ways to deal with petty cash as there are to make bolognese sauce. But a few things never change — no matter what type of business you run:

✔ Chocolate bars, roses for the beautiful girl at the train station and vet bills are not legitimate petty cash receipts.

✔ When someone takes petty cash from the tin and promises to come back with a receipt, they probably won't.

✔ When someone sticks an IOU in the petty cash tin, it means that they'd love to pay you back, but they're just not sure whether it will be this century, or the next.

✔ No matter how finicky you are, petty cash will never, ever balance.

In the next few sections, I talk about two ways to deal with petty cash. The first method is best for owner-operators paying expenses out of their own pocket. The second method is best for businesses with a few employees and a petty cash tin. Read on to see which method suits you best.

Giving with one hand, taking with the other

If you're a sole operator and you tend to pay for lots of little expenses from your own pocket, then I suggest you record petty cash expenses using this simple method:

1. **Every month or so, go on a mad Mintie hunt for receipts.**

   If you're the business owner reading this book, dig through your pockets, tip out your wallet or look under the seats in your car. If you're a bookkeeper, hassle your employer/client to find every receipt they can lay their hand on.

2. **Clear a patch on your desk and sort the receipts into categories.**

   One pile for stationery, one pile for computer supplies, one pile for postage and so on.

   At this point you only want receipts for business expenses paid for by cash or paid for out of personal accounts that aren't tracked using QuickBooks; ignore receipts for things paid for by business cheques, EFTPOS or corporate credit cards.

3. **Use a calculator to add up the total value of each pile, writing these totals down on the front of an empty envelope.**

   You end up with an envelope that reads something like:

   Total stationery receipts = $15.00

   Total postage receipts = $45.50

   Of course, if you want to type these entries into a simple spreadsheet, that's fine too.

4. **Add up the total value of all petty cash receipts and write this total on the front of the envelope.**

   Alternatively, print your spreadsheet summary and staple it to the front of the envelope.

5. **Stuff the receipts into the envelope and close it up.**

6. **Go to your Company menu and select Make General Journal Entries.**

7. Record a journal entry that debits each expense and credits Owners Drawings.

You can see a typical general journal in Figure 5-9. In this journal, I debit three expense accounts (Motor Vehicle Expenses, Postage and Newspapers), and credit the Owners Drawings account.

The only yucky thing about journal entries and QuickBooks is that you have to remember to enter all amounts before GST. Wondering how? If an amount has GST included, simply divide the total by 1.1.

The beauty of this journal is that you don't miss out on claiming out-of-pocket expenses — these expenses show up in your Profit & Loss report even if you don't physically reimburse yourself out of your business bank account.

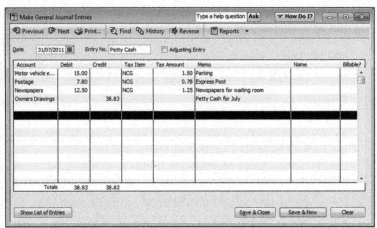

Figure 5-9: Recording a journal entry for petty cash expenses paid using owner's cash.

Securing your cash under lock and key

When your business grows, you need a more sophisticated approach to petty cash management. Here's the whole deal, from start to finish:

1. Buy a petty cash box.

It's time to liberate your cash from the biscuit tin. Instead, purchase a real petty cash box with a lock and key. I'm serious.

2. **Appoint a gatekeeper.**

   Put someone in charge of petty cash and make sure no one else knows where the key is kept. This includes you. You're not allowed to raid the petty cash tin for Indian takeaways and meat pies any more. Those days are gone.

3. **Start a float between $100 and $200.**

   Withdraw a round amount (about $100) from your business bank account and put the corresponding amount of cash in the tin. When you record this withdrawal, allocate it to an asset account called Petty Cash (if you don't already have an asset account by this name in your Chart of Accounts, then create one now).

4. **Every time anyone takes money out of the tin, tell them you need a receipt.**

   This is the part that requires a huge leap in psychology. Every time someone takes money from petty cash, they have to come back with a receipt. This is pretty radical. It works well if the gatekeeper hassles everyone mercilessly: No receipt, no cash next time!

5. **When petty cash is low, sort out the receipts.**

   When petty cash funds dwindle, tip all the receipts out and sort them into piles. Write a breakdown of the receipts on the front of an envelope (for example, $30 postage, $10 telephone, $15 chocolate biscuits and so on), and stick the receipts in the envelope. Alternatively, create a spreadsheet that summarises these receipts.

6. **Write a cheque (or make a cash withdrawal) to top petty cash up to the original value of the float.**

   Getting your head around this step is important: If you're left with $4.50 in the tin and the original float was $100, write a cash cheque (or make a cash withdrawal) for $95.50. Or, if you're left with $4.50 and the original float was $200, write a cash cheque for $195.50.

7. **Enter the withdrawal in Write Cheques, splitting it across a number of different allocation accounts.**

   Look at the front of your envelope or your spreadsheet summary for the breakdown of receipts (refer to Step 5). Enter each amount, line by line, selecting a different allocation account for each different kind of expense. When you're finished, your Write Cheques transaction should look similar to mine, shown in Figure 5-10.

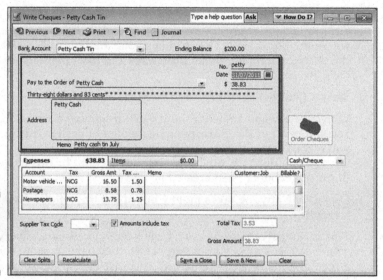

Figure 5-10:
Reimbursing
the petty
cash tin.

Getting even pettier with GST

If petty cash receipts don't show GST separately, that doesn't mean they're GST-free. A packet of staples for $2.20 includes 20 cents GST. And even if you do feel that you've got better things to do than think about such nitpicking details, you still can't afford to lose these valuable input tax credits.

To claim the GST on these petty receipts — even if the tax amount isn't shown separately — all you have to do is click the Amounts Include Tax box in the bottom left of the Write Cheques window. So long as you select the correct tax code, the GST calculates automatically.

Recording Bank Fees

Recording bank fees is easy, although exactly how you go about recording this transaction depends on what version of QuickBooks you're using.

If you recently upgraded from an older version of QuickBooks, you're probably used to recording bank fees as part of your regular bank reconciliation. But hey, that's no good anymore, because the Bank Fees & Charges window has disappeared (due to a problem with how bank fees were reported on Business Activity Statements when recorded this way).

So, in recent versions of QuickBooks, you record bank fees in the Write Cheques window, just as you record a cheque, direct debit or electronic payment. The only difference is that you override the No. field in the top right and replace it with a short memo, such as 'fee', so that you end up with a transaction that looks similar to Figure 5-11.

I usually create two accounts for bank fees, with one account called Bank Fees and another — if relevant to you — called Merchant Fees. (Your bank only charges merchant fees if you offer credit card facilities to customers.) The reason I separate transactions into two accounts is that while regular bank fees, white bread and contraception don't attract GST, EFTPOS and merchant fees do. I also create a third account called Interest Expense (interest also doesn't attract GST).

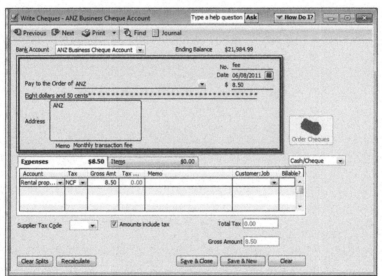

Figure 5-11:
Recording
bank fees.

Chapter 6

Keeping Suppliers Sweet

. . . .

In This Chapter

▶ Understanding whether you need to even read this chapter

▶ Dealing with purchase orders and supplier bills

▶ Receiving goods (that's the good bit) and receiving bills (ah, reality strikes)

▶ Finding your stored purchase records

▶ Generating and sending purchase orders

▶ Staying on track with tax

▶ Discovering what you owe, then coughing up your dues

▶ Tidying up your payables listing

. . . .

Many people, new to running a business, take a while to realise how important their suppliers are. Instead, they focus on building relationships with their customers. But the truth of the matter is this: Suppliers are as important as customers, because without suppliers you don't have any goods to sell.

A supplier needs to know what you want, when you want it and where you want it. They need to know when you'll pay them, and how. And guess what? In this chapter, I explain how to do all of these things, and more.

Deciding if You Need This in Your Life

Before plunging headlong into this chapter, pause for a moment. Do you actually need to record purchase orders or supplier bills? Maybe not. Probably half of all small businesses that use QuickBooks don't bother recording purchase orders and bills at all, but instead record all payments using Write Cheques.

The *benefits* of recording supplier bills in QuickBooks as you receive them, instead of simply recording supplier payments in Write Cheques when bills are settled, are:

- ✔ You can claim GST on bills that you've received, but haven't paid for yet (this only applies if you report for GST on an accruals basis).

- ✔ At the click of a button, you can see exactly how much you owe suppliers.

- ✔ You can easily see whether accounts are overdue (and by how much) before things get out of hand.

- ✔ You can see what bills you have to pay (and when) and plan your cashflow better.

- ✔ Your monthly Profit & Loss reports are more accurate, because expenses show up in the month to which they belong, rather than showing up in the month that you pay them.

- ✔ When you're ready to pay suppliers, the processing of payments is quick, easy and efficient.

The *downside* of recording supplier bills in QuickBooks as you receive them, instead of simply recording supplier payments in Write Cheques when bills are settled, are:

- ✔ Every supplier bill involves two entries instead of one. That's because you first record the invoice in Enter Bills and then the payment in Pay Bills, instead of recording the purchase and payment as one transaction in Write Cheques.

- ✔ Getting your head around supplier bills and payments can be difficult, especially if you're new to QuickBooks.

Recording Purchase Orders and Supplier Bills

The process of recording a purchase order or supplier bill varies depending on whether you're just placing an order, receipting goods or processing a final bill. Read on to find out all you ever wanted to know, and more. (*Note:* Purchase order features don't exist in QuickBooks Accounting and are only available in QuickBooks Accounting Plus, Pro and Premier.)

Creating your first purchase order

Imagine you want to create a purchase order, ready to send to a supplier. The beautiful and illustrative Figure 6-1 shows a typical purchase order, including columns for quantity, description, price and so on.

1. **From the Suppliers area on your home page click Purchase Orders.**

   If this button isn't visible, go to Items & Inventory in your preferences and click the option Inventory and Purchase Orders are Active.

2. **Fill in the supplier name.**

   If this is the first time you're using this supplier, click New or Quick Add to add the supplier's name to your list of suppliers.

3. **Verify the shipping address.**

   QuickBooks completes the shipping address automatically (see the Ship To field in the top right of the purchase order). If this address isn't correct, select Company Information from the Company menu and review your address details.

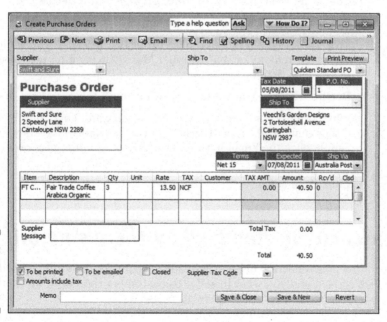

Figure 6-1:
A typical
purchase
order.

You can ask QuickBooks to ship direct to customers, if you like. To do this, simply select the Customer name from the Ship To field displayed in the middle of the purchase order, at the top. If you select a customer name here, QuickBooks automatically populates the shipping address field with the customer's shipping details.

4. **Accept the purchase order number (called P.O. No.) and check the date.**

   Unless you have a different kind of system, go with whatever purchase order number comes up (the number automatically increases by one with every new order).

5. **Enter item codes in the Item column and quantities in the Qty column.**

   To enter a purchase order for something that's not a stock item — maybe you're sending a purchase order through to a supplier for a new computer system, or some stationery — create a new item called Stationery Supplies, Computer Equipment, Cleaning Supplies or whatever, making sure to link this item to an expense account that makes sense.

6. **Check the Description and Rate. Change 'em if necessary.**

7. **Fill in any other necessary information.**

   Everything else on this purchase order is optional. If you want to add a comment, remember that Supplier Messages print on purchase orders, but Memos don't.

8. **Decide whether you want to print or email this purchase order.**

   Why not hurl yourself into the 21st century and email purchase orders rather than print them? Think of all the Tasmanian forests you'll save. Simply click the Email button at the top of the purchase order, then click Send.

9. **Click Save & Close.**

Receiving items when there's no bill

In this true-reflection-of-how-life-really-is scenario, the stuff you ordered has arrived and you want to sell it to customers right now, but the supplier hasn't sent a bill yet. Here's how to proceed:

1. **From your home page, go to Suppliers and click Receive Inventory, and then when prompted, click Receive Inventory without Bill.**

When you click Receive Inventory, QuickBooks asks if you want to Receive Inventory without Bill, or Receive Inventory with Bill. I'm assuming you don't have a bill yet, but if you do, skip to the next section 'Receiving a bill (items only)'.

2. **Enter the supplier's name and, if you already recorded a purchase order for these goods, select the relevant one.**

   If you already recorded a purchase order for these goods, QuickBooks displays a window asking you to select the order from a list. Select the relevant purchase order and click OK. The Item Receipt window appears, showing everything you ordered.

3. **Review quantities and pricing.**

   If you didn't receive the full amount of your order (maybe you ordered three items but only got two) then simply enter the quantity you received — with blinding efficiency, QuickBooks keeps track of backordered quantities. You can also add new lines to this item receipt for any goods you've received that weren't on the original order. If you start losing the plot, click the Show P.O. button at the bottom to view your original order.

4. **Click Save & Close.**

Different methods, same result

My clients fall into two camps when it comes to entering their supplier purchase orders and bills.

✔ The first camp sits down once a week or so with a pile of supplier bills and enters these into QuickBooks. As soon as they record each bill, it shows up as owing in their Payables report. That's all there is to it.

✔ The second camp records all their purchase orders using QuickBooks, faxing or emailing these orders direct to suppliers.

These purchase orders don't show up as owing in their accounts, but they do show up in the purchase order transaction listing in the Supplier Centre. When the goods arrive, they call up the original purchase order and record the receipt of goods. When the bill arrives, they fix up any details or price variations and record the goods as being received in full.

Choose whichever method suits you best. (If your suppliers like to receive purchase orders, use the second method. If not, you're better off to use the first, simpler, method.)

Receiving a bill (items only)

In this last step of the process, you record the final bill for your inventory items. If you haven't yet recorded a purchase order for these goods (maybe you placed your order over the phone), then you don't need to go through the whole rigmarole of first creating a purchase order and then receipting goods against it. Just record the final bill when it arrives.

1. **Go to the Suppliers area on your home page.**

2. **If you've already received items against this purchase order, click Enter Bills Against Inventory, and select the matching item receipt. If you haven't yet received items, click Receive Inventory with Bill. Alternatively, if you never recorded a purchase order in the first place, simply click Enter Bills.**

   Whichever action you choose (Enter Bills Against Inventory, Receive Inventory with Bill or Enter Bills) takes you to the Enter Bills window.

3. **Enter the supplier's name.**

4. **Enter the date of the bill and the supplier's invoice number (called the Ref. No.).**

   QuickBooks automatically completes the date this supplier bill is due. If this due date isn't correct, change the payment terms using the Terms menu.

5. **Enter the Amount Due.**

   Ensure you include GST and freight in this total.

6. **Check that all quantities and costs are correct.**

   By clicking the Amounts Include Tax button, you can toggle cost prices so that they show either tax-inclusive or tax-exclusive. (If you can't see this button, go to the Tax section of your Preferences and tick the option to allow tax-inclusive prices and costs.)

7. **Click on the Expenses tab and add freight or service charges, if applicable.**

   Click on the Expenses tab to add any additional charges, such as freight. (*Note:* If you prefer, you can set up a new item in your Items List called Freight, which means you can add freight charges to supplier bills as if they were just another item.)

   By now, your bill probably looks similar to mine, shown in Figure 6-2.

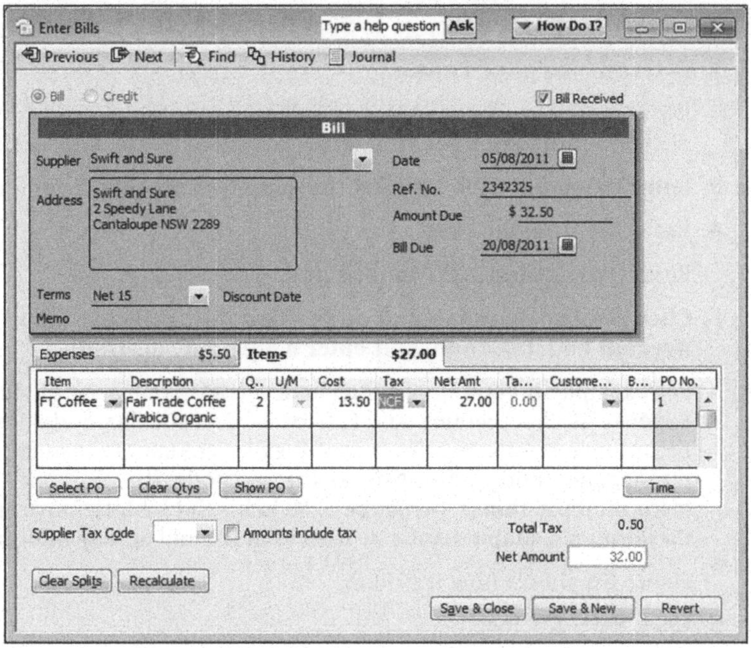

Figure 6-2:
Recording
the final bill
for goods
received.

8. Click Save & Close.

In the perfect world, QuickBooks gives a happy beep and closes the Enter Bills window. However, if a message appears saying the bill doesn't balance (meaning the total cost of items entered plus freight doesn't match the Amount Due), then don your thinking cap and go through your supplier's bill, line by line, until you identify the difference. (The difference will be there — logic always wins in the end.)

Recording bills for services, rather than items

Most businesses receive lots of different kind of bills, not just ones for inventory items. So, what do you do if you get a bill for something like advertising, consultancy fees, electricity or telephone? The answer is that you record a supplier bill, but instead of listing items on each line, you list expenses. These kinds of bills are easy to record, so I'll simply give you a quick run-down on what's important.

1. **From your home page, go to Suppliers and click Enter Bills.**

2. **Enter the supplier's name.**

   If you don't already have this supplier in your Supplier List, click Quick Add or Set Up when prompted and complete all the supplier's details.

3. **Enter the date of the bill and the supplier's invoice number.**

4. **Enter the Amount Due.**

   Ensure you include GST in this total.

5. **Click the Expenses tab and on the first line, select an appropriate Account and Tax code, and enter a Memo (if desired).**

   For example, if you're recording an electricity bill, select Electricity Expense as the Account, and GST or NCG as the Tax code. If you're recording a bill for repairs, select Repairs & Maintenance Expense as the Account, and GST or NCG as the Tax code. If a bill from a supplier is for multiple things — maybe $200 is for Rubbish Removal and $100 is for Repairs & Maintenance — then split the bill across multiple lines.

   Figure 6-3 shows how it's done.

6. **Click Save & Close.**

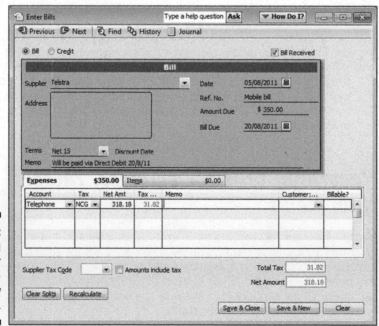

Figure 6-3:
Entering a supplier bill for non-inventory items.

Calling Up Your Purchase Records

After you've recorded a purchase order, item receipt or supplier bill, how do you find it again? Try these ways:

- ✔ **Searching by amount.** If you know the exact amount of the purchase order, go to the Edit menu and click Find Bills. Enter the amount, click Find and watch as QuickBooks does its stuff. (You can also click the Advanced button, found in the Find Bills window, to search on all transactions, not just bills.)

- ✔ **Searching by supplier name.** Go to your Supplier Centre, choose a supplier from the list on the left pane, then on the right pane, choose to show Purchase Orders, Item Receipts or Bills (the exact options that appear here depend on which version of QuickBooks you're using). Tweak the date range if necessary.

- ✔ **Searching through purchase orders.** Go to your Supplier Centre and click the Transactions tab. On the left pane, highlight Purchase Orders. On the right pane, choose to filter by either All Purchase Orders or Open Purchase Orders. Again, tweak the date range if necessary.

- ✔ **Searching through item receipts.** Go to your Supplier Centre, click the Transactions tab and on the left pane highlight Item Receipts.

- ✔ **Searching through supplier bills.** Go to your Supplier Centre and click the Transactions tab. On the left pane, highlight Bills, then on the right pane choose to filter by either All Bills, Open Bills or Overdue Bills.

Sending Purchase Orders

Recording a few purchase orders in QuickBooks is one thing, but getting them looking good and emailing them to suppliers is another. Never fear, help is here.

Whipping your purchase order into shape

It's Monday morning. You look glorious, sitting in your home office dressed in spotty pyjamas and fluffy rabbit slippers. It's time to dress up your purchase order so it looks good too.

To customise your purchase order, select Templates from your Lists menu and double-click to select the Quicken Standard PO template, followed by the Additional Customisation button. You're prompted to create a copy of this standard template — go right ahead.

I talk lots about the basic techniques for designing forms in Chapter 11, but here are a few points that apply specifically to purchase orders:

✔ The Header tab has a few handy fields that may not show up on the default purchase order, such as Expected Date, Account Number, Ship Via method and a custom field called Other2. You can use this Other2 field for anything you like, such as additional comments or delivery details.

✔ Click the Footer tab and consider whether you want to add anything to the Long Text field. In Figure 6-4, I adapted mine to state that if the order isn't delivered within five days, any deliveries may not be accepted.

✔ On the Columns tab, choose the columns you want to display and columns you want to print. To include supplier item codes as well as your own item codes on purchase orders, click in the Print column against Man. Part Num (MPN). I usually change the Title of this column from MPN — which doesn't mean much to me — to Supplier Item Code.

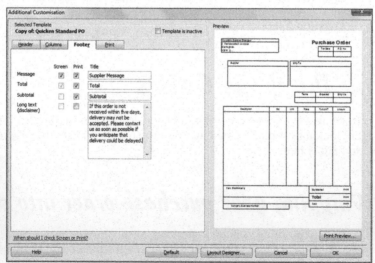

Figure 6-4:
Adding
standard
messages
to your
purchase
orders.

Printing purchase orders, easy as anything

To print a purchase order, first dance the hula-hula. Then click the Print button (you can find this button at the top of the Create Purchase Orders window) just before you record it. No fuss. Or, if you prefer to abandon your mouse completely, simply type Ctrl-P.

You can print purchase orders in batches if you prefer, as long as you've marked the To Be Printed checkbox on each order. Printing in batches works best if you have lots of stuff to print, because you can walk away and leave your orders printing while you go off and do something else. To do this, go to the File menu and select Print Forms, followed by Purchase Orders. Mark the orders you want to print, click OK and then click Print.

Emailing purchase orders into the ether

The most efficient way to send a supplier a purchase order is not to print it at all, but to email the order direct. Try it and see: First display the transaction, then click the Email button that appears on the top menu, followed by Send. Before you know it, the order appears in your Outbox, attached to an email that's addressed to your supplier. If you're already connected to the internet, the email is sent immediately.

This blinding efficiency is great, but if you want to be able to review the message in your email before it gets sent, a better strategy is to select Send Batch from the Email button, rather than to select Send. This takes you to another menu — similar to the one shown in Figure 6-5 — that displays all forms you've marked to be emailed. From here, you can click Edit Email to review the message that the supplier will receive.

If you find yourself forever changing the default email messages, go to your Preferences menu and select Send Forms. Here you can change the default text, and make it slightly different on each kind of form that you send.

Check that your emailed purchase order looks good by emailing one to yourself first (just insert your own email address instead of the supplier's email address when prompted). This allows you to check the appearance of your purchase order when it's in PDF format and tweak anything that's not looking 100 per cent right.

Select Forms To Send

Select the forms you want to send, and then click Send Now.

To change the cover note that accompanies an emailed form, select the form in the list and click Edit Email.

Forms To Send (5 out of 7 selected)

	Date	Type	No.	Name	Amount	Method
	05/05/2011	INV	2	Hadrians Wall Comp...	$220.00	Email
	05/05/2011	INV	3	Olympic Park	$2,117.50	Email
✓	15/06/2011	INV	4	Bristol, Sonja	$1,320.00	Email
✓	31/07/2011	PO	3	Carrot Teasers	-$330.00	Email
✓	31/07/2011	PO	4	Luscious Foods	-$275.00	Email
✓	31/07/2011	PO	2	Swift and Sure	-$110.00	Email

Select All
Select None
Remove

Edit Email

From: veechi@veechicurtis.com.au
To: info@carrotteasers.com.au
Cc:
Subject: Purchase Order from Veechi's Garden Designs

To Supplier :

Please review the attached Purchase Order. Feel free to contact us if you have any questions.

Thank you for your service.

Sincerely,

Veechi's Garden Designs

[Your Purchase Order will be attached to the message as a PDF file]

Send Now   Close   Help

Figure 6-5: Emailing purchase orders is easy.

Understanding GST

I'm not entirely sure why I wrote 'Understanding GST'. If senior politicians can't understand GST, how do mere mortals (like you and me) have a hope? However, the good news is that when it comes to purchases and QuickBooks, everything is pretty straightforward.

One thing though: Make sure you receive an invoice complete with an ABN for everything you buy. If a supplier doesn't provide an ABN, you're meant to withhold 48.5 per cent tax from the supplier's payment, and complete mounds of paperwork to boot. It's simply not worth it.

Tax codes — a guessing game

Every time you record a purchase you must complete the Tax column. Here are some tips in case you're not sure which code to use when:

✔ If the purchase is for goods or services that attract GST, select GST as your tax code. Or, if you've migrated from an earlier version of QuickBooks, NCG works just as well. (See Chapter 10 for more about GST and tax codes.)

✔ If the purchase is for a new piece of equipment or furniture, select CAG as your tax code (CAG is short for Capital Acquisitions). If you're eligible for small business entity tax concessions (ask your accountant if you're not sure) any new gear over $1,000 (not including GST) counts as a capital acquisition. If you're not eligible for these concessions, the threshold is $100.

✔ If the purchase is for goods or services that are GST-free (medical supplies, GST-free food and so on) select FRE as your tax code. (Or, if you've migrated from an earlier version of QuickBooks, NCF is fine, too.)

✔ If the purchase is for goods or services that are of a personal nature — takeaway dinners, exotic holidays, school fees and so on — pick NR as your tax code. This code stands for Not Reportable. (See Chapter 10 for more on setting up this tax code.)

✔ If the person you're trading with isn't registered for GST, select FRE or NCF as your tax code.

✔ If the purchase is for goods or services that you'll use to make input taxed sales (perhaps you're a residential landlord and you're paying for plumbing repairs), then select INP as your tax code.

Calculating GST backwards

If a supplier provides a bill that's tax-inclusive (meaning the supplier charges GST but the bill doesn't show how much), select Amounts Include Tax at the bottom of the Enter Bills window. Then, simply enter the tax-inclusive amount in the Rate or Amount column of the bill. Voilà! The GST calculates correctly.

When GST doesn't quite add up

Occasionally QuickBooks calculates the amount of GST on a purchase slightly differently to your supplier and the GST total differs by a cent or two. Don't tear your hair out wondering about this (although I can tell you now that it's due to the way different software packages deal with rounding cents up and down). Instead, be pragmatic and ignore the problem. Life is too short to worry about a couple of cents.

If you find that the tax is out by more than a few cents, the difference will probably be due to a mistake that you've made entering the transaction, such as the wrong price or wrong tax code. If the supplier has sold you a mix of taxable and non-taxable goods, you need to split the bill across two lines, selecting different tax codes on each line.

Getting Everything Just Right

If you're at all like me, you sometimes make mistakes. In fact, if you're anything like me, you often make mistakes. Fortunately, you can cover your tracks so that no one need ever know a thing.

Destroying the evidence

You've recorded a purchase order or bill and now you want to delete it? No problem:

1. **Locate the transaction (refer to 'Calling Up Your Purchase Records' earlier in this chapter), and double-click to display it.**

2. **From the top menu bar, choose Edit⇨Delete Bill or Edit⇨Delete Purchase Order.**

   This transaction has now gone to live in the land of ballpoint pens and odd socks, never to be seen again.

Closing off purchase orders

When you receive all the items against a purchase order, QuickBooks stamps the purchase order as RECEIVED IN FULL. However, if you don't expect to receive all the items you ordered, you can close all or part of the purchase order manually so that QuickBooks doesn't show the items as being on order. To do this, simply display the purchase order and click the Closed button at the bottom.

Assessing the Damage

The best way to pay suppliers depends on your psychological profile. If you tend to pay suppliers at random, one at a time, it works best to sit down with QuickBooks every now and then and record all the supplier payments you made in recent weeks, using your cheque book or bank statement as a reference. On the other hand, if you pay suppliers in batches, you're best to open up QuickBooks, run a report to see what's due, record the payments in QuickBooks, and then generate an electronic banking file.

Read on to find out more and to figure out which system suits you best.

Taking a look at reality — how much do you owe?

Go to your Report Centre and click the Suppliers & Payables tab on the left. Under the A/P Ageing heading, click the Summary link for a listing of all amounts owing to each supplier, grouped neatly by month and complete with totals and ageing details. Look at Figure 6-6 to get the general idea.

A/P Ageing Summary							
Modify Report...	Memorise...	Print...	Email ▾	Export...	Hide Header	Collapse	Refresh
Dates	Custom	15/08/2011	Interval (days) 30	Through (days past due) 90	Sort By Default		

Veechi's Garden Designs
A/P Ageing Summary
As of August 15, 2011

	Current	1 - 30	31 - 60	61 - 90	> 90	TOTAL
Carrot Teasers	0.00	0.00	3,010.00	0.00	0.00	3,010.00
Georgian Plywood Import Co.	0.00	0.00	0.00	850.00	0.00	850.00
Laureats Cars	0.00	363.00	0.00	0.00	0.00	363.00
Luscious Foods	0.00	0.00	925.00	0.00	0.00	925.00
Officeworkers	0.00	721.30	0.00	0.00	0.00	721.30
Swift and Sure	32.50	0.00	0.00	0.00	0.00	32.50
Telstra	350.00	220.50	0.00	0.00	0.00	570.50
TOTAL	382.50	1,304.80	3,935.00	850.00	0.00	6,472.30

Figure 6-6:
Seeing how much you owe.

Like my goldfish, the payables report is simple in nature, but hides a subtle layer of complexity:

✔ QuickBooks defaults to displaying ageing reports according to when bills are due, rather than by their transaction date. For example, if you receive a bill on 1 October and the supplier offers 60 days terms, this bill appears in the Current column on the A/P Ageing Summary report until 1 December, at which point it shifts to 1–30 days.

✔ If you like — and I certainly recommend working in this manner — you can click Modify Report and choose instead to display ageing reports according to their transaction date. In other words, if you receive a bill on 1 October and you view an A/P Ageing Summary report on 1 December, this bill appears in 61–90 days, regardless of when it's due to be paid.

✔ If you receive lots of bills from suppliers with weekly or fortnightly payment terms, you're probably best to click Modify Report and specify either 7 or 14 days as the number of Days Per Ageing Period. If you then choose to Age Through to 60 days, you'll get a report that can still fit on a single page.

✔ If you like, you can sort this report showing the suppliers that you owe the most to at the top of the list. To do this, click Modify Report and select Total in the Sort By field. Click Descending Order and there you have it.

Recording supplier payments

Ready to pay a few bills? Ready, set . . .

1. **Go to Suppliers on your home page and click Pay Bills.**

   The list of all suppliers you owe money to appears. Ah, such cheery stuff.

2. **Decide if you want to hide bills that aren't due yet by changing the due date.**

   Assuming you recorded each supplier's terms and due dates correctly when you entered bills, you can get QuickBooks to filter out bills that aren't due yet. Click the button to show bills that are due on or before the current date.

3. **Limit the bills owing to one supplier at a time, if you like.**

   If you like, you can choose to display bills for one supplier at a time. Simply select that supplier's name in the Show Bills For field.

4. **Sort these bills in a different order, if you like.**

   By changing selections in the Sort Bills By list, you can sort bills by supplier, due date, amount due and so on. I generally choose to sort bills by supplier, so I can get a sense of how much moolah each supplier is going to receive. To view the details of a bill, highlight the bill itself and click the Go to Bill button.

5. **Select the payment method.**

   In the bottom-left corner, where it says Payment Method, select whether you're paying this supplier or these suppliers by credit card, online transfer, cheque or gold bullion. Then check that the Payment Account that appears next to the Payment Method is correct.

   If you intend to pay one batch of suppliers by one method and another batch of suppliers by a different method, you need to enter a separate Pay Bills transaction for each batch.

6. **Select the Payment Account (that's your bank account) in the bottom left.**

   If you usually use a particular bank account for paying suppliers and QuickBooks doesn't default to this account when you go to Pay Bills, it's time to tweak your default settings. Go to the Banking tab of your

Preferences menu and select the account that you most often use against the Pay Bills option.

If you don't set a preference in this way, the Pay Bills window always defaults to whatever bank account you used last time.

7. **Record the Payment Date.**

   If you're paying this transaction online *and* you want to use QuickBooks to generate an online payment batch file *and* it's already after close of banking business hours, change the Payment Date to the following day. By now, your bill payment window probably looks similar to the very glamorous and sophisticated Figure 6-7.

8. **Click Pay Selected Bills.**

   Depending on the payment method selected, QuickBooks may ask you to assign cheque numbers for each payment, or if paying online to complete supplier banking details. Follow the prompts dutifully and click Done when you're ready. Don't worry if you highlight more than one bill from a particular supplier, because QuickBooks gets smart and creates only one transaction per supplier.

9. **Click either Done or Pay More Bills.**

   It's up to you. If you're a glutton for punishment, why not click Pay More Bills and carry on. Money is for sharing, after all.

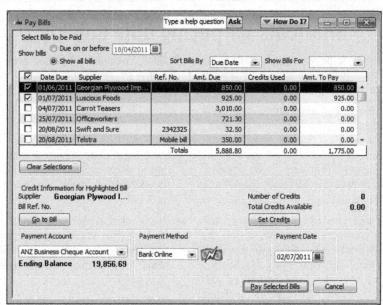

Figure 6-7:
Paying your
suppliers.

Paying suppliers electronically

A little earlier in this chapter, in the section 'Recording supplier payments', I explain that when you record a supplier payment you can select Bank Online as the Payment Method. When you work this way QuickBooks not only records the payment, but also sends a summary of the payment details to the Online Banking Centre.

When you go to Online Banking, you see a list of all transactions where you've selected Bank Online as the Payment Method. From here you can create an ABA file that summarises all supplier payments, ready to import into your banking software. Chapter 16 talks about this process in more detail.

Paying suppliers using your credit card

Sometimes you may decide to pay outstanding supplier accounts that you've already entered via Enter Bills using your credit card. No problem. Go to Pay Bills as normal, but as the Payment Method select Credit Card and as the Payment Account select your credit card account. Click Pay Selected Bills as normal and you're done.

Shortcuts for paying bills quickly

When it comes to paying suppliers, anything that saves me time and money makes me happy. Here are my favourite shortcuts:

✔ Go to the Preferences menu, select the Bills section, then click the Company Preferences tab. Click the option to warn you about duplicate bill numbers from the same supplier. That way, if you accidentally go to record a bill twice, QuickBooks displays an alert.

✔ At the end of each month, print an A/P Ageing Summary report and match the totals on this report against your suppliers' statements. This simple act of checking that you have the same figures as your suppliers means you can be confident when paying bills.

✔ Ditch cheques altogether and pay suppliers by electronic transfer, sending a payment summary file out of QuickBooks and opening this summary file in your internet banking. (See Chapter 16.)

✔ Take the time to set up payment terms for each supplier (found on the Additional Info tab in each supplier's record). That way, QuickBooks prompts you when the bill falls due.

✔ Many utility companies provide the option to debit your account automatically when the bill falls due. Why not pay the bill this way? (Hey, let them do the work, rather than you.)

✔ Don't pay your bills. This is really quick. (Just kidding.)

Recording part-payments or discounts

Sometimes, you may have a good reason not to pay a supplier's bill in full. Maybe you're making a part-payment only at this point, or maybe you're taking an early payment discount.

To pay only part of a bill now, go to Pay Bills as normal, click against the bill you want to part-pay and enter the amount you want to pay in the Amt to Pay column. Easy.

To apply a discount against a bill, the process is more complex (upgraders take note, because discounts have changed in recent editions of QuickBooks, and the Set Discount button doesn't exist anymore). In order to record a discount, you first need to create a credit note (also known as an adjustment note) for the amount of the discount, selecting an income account such as Discounts Received as the Account. After recording this credit, return to Pay Bills, highlight the bill you want to pay, click the Set Credits button and apply this credit to the bill.

One of the reasons QuickBooks canned the old discount feature was the difficulty it had in accounting for GST. If you receive a discount on a bill that had GST charged at 10 per cent, then you include GST when you record the credit for the discount. Similarly, if you receive a discount on a bill with no GST, then you don't include any GST when you record the credit for the discount. However, if you receive a discount on a bill that was a mix of taxable and non-taxable goods, then this creates a tricky scenario. The exact treatment of the tax on the discount varies in this situation, and you're best to seek advice from your accountant.

Tricks for remittance advices

Clients often ask me whether they can print remittance advices for supplier payments they record in Write Cheques, rather than Pay Bills (sometimes it's quickest recording supplier payments using Write Cheques, especially for suppliers you pay almost as soon as you get bills). The answer is yes, if you're willing to be a little creative.

The secret workaround is this: When you record the supplier payment in Write Cheques, select Cheque–To Print as the payment method.

Then, go to File➪Print Forms➪Cheques, select the payment you just recorded and click OK. Assuming you select Voucher style (in other words, a full page per cheque) in the Printer Setup for cheques, QuickBooks produces a full-page printed cheque for this transaction. The top third is the text that would normally print on a printed cheque, which you can ignore, and the bottom two-thirds acts as a remittance advice. Cut this bottom part off and there you have it: A printed remittance advice.

Letting suppliers know you've paid 'em

One of the best ways to speed up paying suppliers is to get QuickBooks to email or print remittance advices. Here's how:

1. **From the Supplier Centre, first select the Suppliers tab, then click the Email button.**

   QuickBooks displays a pop-up window asking what remittance advices you want to email. (Even though it says 'email' here, you can print from here, too. Keep reading and you'll find out how.)

2. **Select the bank account the payments were made from and the date range.**

    As long as all suppliers have an email address in the Address Info of their record, QuickBooks lists every supplier payment for that date range, so you're best to limit your selection to the date that you want to print remittance advices for, which is usually just the current date.

3. **Unclick any payments that you don't want a remittance advice for.**

4. **If you want to print remittance advices, rather than email them, click Preview, followed by Print.**

   The only time this method doesn't work is if a supplier doesn't have an email address entered in the Address Info tab of the supplier's record, in which case payments to this supplier won't appear here. You need to go to File➪Print Forms➪Remittance Advice instead.

5. **If you want to email remittance advices, close the Print Preview window, select the remittance advices you want to email, then click OK.**

   In two shakes of a lamb's tail, QuickBooks sends individual emails to your email Outbox, each one with a standard message and a remittance advice attached as a PDF (Figure 6-8 shows how this standard remittance advice looks). Quite amazing really. Oh, and one more thing. If you want to customise the standard message for remittance advice emails, you can. In Preferences, go to the Send Forms section, click the Company Preferences tab and change the default for Remittance Advices.

Clients often ask me whether they can customise remittance advices. Reluctant as I am to be the bearer of bad tidings, the answer is no. The best I can offer is the option to change fonts (go to File➪Printer Setup, select Remittance Advices as the Form Name and click the Font tab).

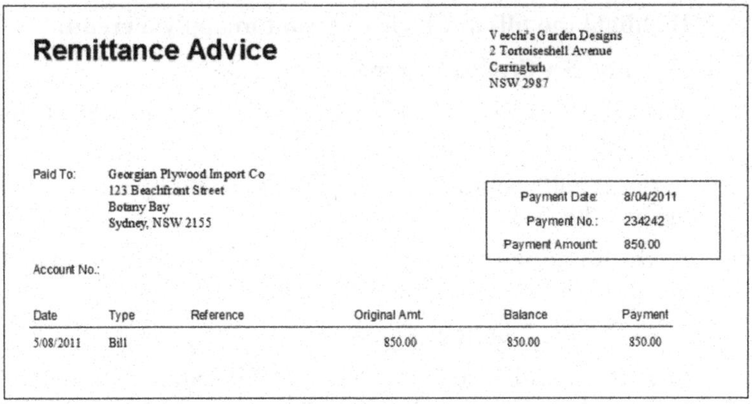

Figure 6-8:
Creating a
QuickBooks
PDF
remittance
advice,
ready to
email to
suppliers.

Remittance Advice

Veechi's Garden Designs
2 Tortoiseshell Avenue
Caringbah
NSW 2987

Paid To: Georgian Plywood Import Co
123 Beachfront Street
Botany Bay
Sydney, NSW 2155

Payment Date:	8/04/2011
Payment No.:	234242
Payment Amount:	850.00

Account No.:

Date	Type	Reference	Original Amt.	Balance	Payment
5/08/2011	Bill		850.00	850.00	850.00

Keeping Things in Tune

Keeping on top of bills in QuickBooks is a bit like keeping a car on the road — doing so requires a certain amount of maintenance. Odd amounts crop up that you can't delete, credits appear that won't go away or accounts show up as owing when you know they're not. Here's the practical mechanic's guide to a six-month service and tune.

Recording supplier credits

Recording a supplier credit is easy. When you go to Enter Bills, two buttons are displayed at the top: One called Bill, the other Credit (QuickBooks defaults to the Bill setting). To create a credit, simply click the Credit button and enter the credit note in exactly the same way as you'd enter a supplier bill.

Applying supplier credits to outstanding bills

Do you have both debits (in other words, bills) and credits sitting against one of your supplier accounts in QuickBooks? Here's how to marry one against the other:

1. **Go to the Supplier Centre and click Pay Bills.**

2. **Highlight the bill to which you want to apply a credit.**

3. **Click the Set Credits button.**

   QuickBooks opens a window listing all unallocated credits for this supplier.

4. **In the Credits window, select each credit that you want to apply against this bill.**

   By the way, if you only want to use part of a credit, change the amount in the Amt. To Use column.

5. **Click the Done button.**

6. **Back in Pay Bills, click Pay Selected Bills and click Done.**

   If you're not paying this supplier anything at this point of time, that's okay. Recording a zero value payment is fine.

Finding supplier payments

To view payments made to a particular supplier, the easiest method is to go to the Supplier Centre, highlight the supplier's name and on the right, choose to show Bill Payments as the transaction type. You then see a list of all payments to this supplier for that period, as shown in Figure 6-9. To view the details for any payment, simply double-click on it.

Understanding payment terms

You may have realised by now that a lot hinges on setting up supplier payment terms correctly in QuickBooks, including the way Payable reports present and what bills show up as being due for payment in the Pay Bills window.

To view payment terms for a supplier, go to the Supplier Centre and double-click on the supplier's name, then click the Additional Info tab. QuickBooks shows a list of default payment terms, but you may want to add your own by clicking Add New from the Terms menu. A new terms window pops up, offering a choice between Standard payment terms and Date-driven payment terms.

With Standard payment terms, bills are due a certain number of days after the date of the transaction. For example, if you receive a bill dated 15 October and the payment terms are 30 days (meaning that the bill is due by 12 November), select the Standard option and specify that the net amount is due in 30 days.

With Date-driven terms, bills are due on a set day of the month. For example, if you receive a bill dated 15 October and it's due on the 25th day of the following month, select the Date-driven option and specify that the net amount is due before the 25th, and the amount is due the next month if issued within 25 days of the due date.

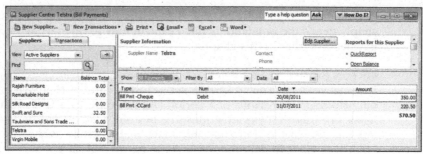

Figure 6-9:
Finding a
supplier
payment.

To view payments made to all suppliers, go to the Supplier Centre and click
the Transactions tab in the left-hand pane (you can choose between the
Suppliers tab or the Transactions tab, but QuickBooks normally defaults to
the former). Then select Bill Payments from the list underneath.

Fixing up supplier payments

To fix up a mistake in a supplier payment, first find the payment and display
it (refer to 'Finding supplier payments' earlier in this chapter). Either make
your changes, then click Save & Close, or for a fresh start go up to the Edit
menu and select Delete Bill Payment.

Before you go changing supplier payments, I have a word of caution. If,
when you zoom in on the payment, the transaction is marked CLEARED,
this means you've already marked that payment as cleared in your bank
reconciliation. For this reason, don't change the transaction amount,
because this will throw your bank reconciliation out of balance. And a sick
bank reconciliation, dear reader, is a very bad thing indeed.

Tidying up odd amounts

As the months and years roll by, leaving you with a few more grey hairs,
varicose veins and a growing sense of life's inevitability, QuickBooks
matures, too. Before you know it, your payables listing becomes rather
cluttered, with strange amounts you know you don't owe anyone,
miscellaneous credits and other minor gremlins. Here I show you how to
deal with some of them.

When you know you don't owe money but the report says you do

If your A/P Ageing Summary says you owe a certain supplier some money
and you're positive that you've paid the account, you almost certainly used
Write Cheques when recording the payment, instead of Pay Bills. Just like

putting diesel in an unleaded car, this upsets the works. To fix this problem, simply delete the outstanding bill. I explain how to do in 'Fixing up supplier payments' earlier in this chapter.

My only proviso against deleting bills is when a bill belongs to a previous financial year and you've already set a closing date for that year, or when a bill belongs to a previous GST period and you report for GST on an accruals basis. In either of these situations, the best approach is not to delete the bill, but to record a credit instead, matching this credit against the offending bill. (Remember to date this credit with the current date.)

Credits that hang around like a bad smell

Sometimes you get an amount showing up twice for a particular supplier on your Ageing Summary report — the first time as a positive amount, the next time as a minus amount. The total amount due is zero, but the Ageing Summary report keeps listing both amounts.

Change into fourth gear and head for Pay Bills. Click against the outstanding bill and then click the Set Credits button. Apply the credit, click Done and then click Pay Selected Bills to record a zero payment.

Odd amounts and fiddly stuff

No matter how meticulous you are, odd amounts inevitably creep into your supplier accounts. Here are a few maintenance tricks:

✔ If you end up with a small miscellaneous credit that sits against a supplier for years on end — maybe you overpaid a bill by two cents some time long since past — the easiest solution is to record a new bill for the amount of the credit. This complete, go to Pay Bills and set the credit against this bill.

✔ To get rid of odd little amounts (perhaps there's five cents outstanding on an account, and the supplier is never going to chase you for this money), create a credit note for the difference.

✔ To spring-clean your credits, go to your Unpaid Bills Detail report and look at every credit listed. Wherever possible, apply these credits to outstanding bills.

Chapter 7

A Balancing Act

In This Chapter

▶ Understanding which accounts to reconcile

▶ Preparing your opening balances

▶ Reconciling (it's as easy as 1, 2, 3)

▶ Overcoming tricky situations

▶ Taking action when your bank account won't balance

▶ Troubleshooting opening balances

▶ Printing reconciliation reports

*A*lthough QuickBooks makes accounting as easy as can be, and you may be the human embodiment of perfection (cough, splutter), no one is infallible.

In this chapter, I explain how the best way to ensure that your QuickBooks accounts are accurate is to check that the transactions in your company file tally with your bank statements. You tick off these entries one by one and check that you and your bank agree, down to the very last cent. This process is known as *reconciling* your bank account.

Reconciling bank accounts isn't an activity that only boring bookkeepers engage in. Instead, it's one of those necessary evils everyone has to face up to, sooner or later. Reconciling accounts is the only way to pick up mistakes, such as a payment entered as $900 instead of $90, a deposit entered twice, or a missing bank charge.

The good news is that reconciling bank accounts is surprisingly quick and easy and even kind of satisfying in a weird, nerdish kind of way. Sure, there are a few tips and tricks to learn along the way, but similar to your first stolen kiss as a teenager, some things just get easier as life goes on.

Deciding Which Accounts to Reconcile

Most businesses have lots of bank accounts, such as cheque accounts, savings accounts, term deposits, credit cards and loans. I group these accounts into three categories:

- ✔ **Accounts you have to reconcile:** As a bare minimum, always reconcile your business bank account. Unless you do this, you can't rely on any of your financial reports.

- ✔ **Accounts to reconcile if you have time:** It's a good idea to reconcile all credit card, savings and PayPal accounts, as well as your business bank account.

- ✔ **Accounts to reconcile in the ideal situation:** What's best is to reconcile all loan accounts as well. Reconciling loans can be tricky (you have to split up interest and principal on each loan repayment), but if you don't do it, your accountant will.

Setting Up Opening Bank Balances

The first time you reconcile your bank account is the hardest, because you have to allow for all unpresented payments and deposits that existed before you started using QuickBooks. Never fear, I guide you clearly through the whole kit and caboodle.

Step 1: List uncleared transactions

The first time you reconcile your bank account, you need to draw up a list of all uncleared payments and deposits as of the date you started your accounts. (By the way, you may not have any uncleared transactions at your start date. That's fine — simply skip this step.)

By *uncleared payments*, I mean any cheques you posted to suppliers before your start date, but haven't yet cleared through your bank account. By *uncleared deposits*, I mean any money received before your start date, but which you haven't banked, or which hasn't cleared. (For example, maybe you received an EFTPOS payment on 30 June which didn't appear on your bank statement until 1 July, or maybe a customer has sent you a cheque but you haven't banked it yet.)

Figure 7-1 shows an example of what your list may look like. In my example, I have two uncleared payments plus one uncleared deposit. The total value of uncleared transactions is minus $900.

Uncleared cheques	
Cheque 950 (Fastway couriers)	-200.00
Cheque 951 (Superannuation)	-1900.00
Uncleared deposits	
Credit card payments	1200.00
Total Value Uncleared Transactions	-900.00

Figure 7-1:
A list of uncleared transactions at your start date.

Step 2: Enter the total value of uncleared transactions in a special account

The next step is to record the total value of all uncleared transactions in a special account. Here goes:

1. **In your Chart of Accounts, create a new bank account called Uncleared Transactions.**

   Make sure this account sits immediately below your regular bank account in your Accounts List, and select Bank as the account type. (You only need to create this account if you have any uncleared transactions on your start date. Refer to 'Step 1: List uncleared transactions' earlier in this chapter if you're not sure.)

2. **Click the Enter Opening Balance button.**

3. **In the Statement Ending Balance field, enter the total of all uncleared transactions as of the date you started your accounts.**

   Using the example in Figure 7-1, the combined balance of uncleared transactions is minus $900.

Step 3: Check your beginning balance

The next step is to record the opening balance of your bank account. You may have already done this when you slogged through the EasyStep Interview (refer to Chapter 1), but I like to double-check that this figure is right.

Start by going to your Chart of Accounts. Highlight the bank account and then select Edit Account from the Account button. What happens next depends on whether you see a button that says Enter Opening Balance or a button that says Change Opening Balance.

If you only see an option to enter an opening balance

Find your bank statement, look up the date from which you're starting to use QuickBooks, then circle the balance on this statement at this date. Click the Enter Opening Balance button and enter this circled amount as the Statement Ending Balance. Click OK and then Save & Close.

If you only see an option to change an opening balance

If you only see an option to change an opening balance, this means that you already entered an opening balance at some point in the past. That's good! All you have to do now is check that this balance is correct:

1. Select QuickReport from the Reports menu at the bottom.

    QuickBooks displays a summary report showing all transactions that have been allocated to this bank account.

2. Check that the opening balance on your bank statement matches the first transaction on this report.

    Find your bank statement, look up the date from which you're starting to use QuickBooks, then circle the balance on this statement at this date. This balance should match the first transaction on your QuickReport. If it doesn't, double-click this transaction and change the amount.

Reconciling Your Bank Account

I'm assuming here that you've already set up your opening balances (if not, return to 'Setting Up Opening Bank Balances' earlier in this chapter), that you've already entered a few transactions, and that you have your bank statement close to hand. All done? Then you're ready to reconcile:

1. On your home page, go to the Banking area and click on Reconcile.

2. Select your bank account as the Account and enter the Statement Date.

    As the Statement Date, enter the transaction date that appears next to the last transaction on the first page of your bank statement. For example, if the first page of your bank statement runs from 1 July to 15 July, and the last transaction on this page is dated 15 July, then enter 15 July as the Statement Date. You don't need to reconcile a whole month at a time.

3. **Check that the Beginning Balance displayed in QuickBooks matches the beginning balance on the statement you're working with.**

The Beginning Balance should equal the opening balance on your bank statement. No? If this is the first time you've ever reconciled this account, then return to 'Setting Up Opening Bank Balances' earlier in this chapter and make sure you record your opening balances correctly. Alternatively, if this bank account has already been reconciled in the past, skip ahead to 'Sticky situation number 1: Figuring out where to start' for tips on starting at the right point.

4. **How much did you have in your bank account on the date that you're reconciling up to? Type this amount as the Ending Balance.**

For example, if you're reconciling up to 15 July, the Ending Balance should equal the balance of your bank account at this date.

5. **Click Continue.**

You arrive at the Reconcile window. All being well, you should see payments on one side and deposits on the other. If QuickBooks displays a whole bunch of transactions beyond the date of the statement that you're reconciling, try hiding these from view by clicking the hide transactions box in the top-right corner.

6. **Mark off all withdrawals and deposits, one by one.**

Work down your bank statement and, line by line, find each transaction in the Reconcile window. Click against it. The result should look similar to mine, shown in Figure 7-2. You can see how I've ticked off every withdrawal and every deposit with the exception of one cheque transaction which hadn't cleared yet.

When uncleared cheques or deposits that belong to the period before your start date eventually appear on your bank statement, simply record a Transfer Funds transaction that transfers the amount out of your Uncleared Transactions account and into your regular bank account (for deposits) or out of your bank account and into your Uncleared Transactions account (for cheques). (The Transfer Funds command is under Banking menu.)

7. **In the bottom-right corner, check that the Difference is $0.00.**

Hopefully the Difference is $0.00, as shown in Figure 7-2. If not, skip to 'When Your Bank Account Just Won't Balance' later in this chapter.

8. **When the Difference is $0.00, click Reconcile Now.**

Print both reports when prompted and file these away safely.

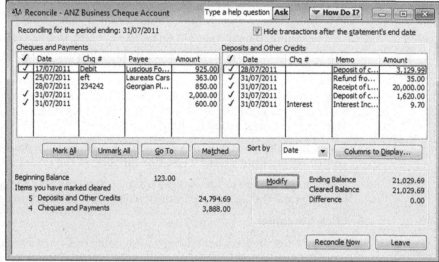

Figure 7-2:
An example bank reconciliation, with transactions marked off ready to reconcile.

Seven Sticky Situations

After you master the black art of bank reconciliations, you can progress to the more arcane areas of knowledge: How to enter missing transactions, fix up mistakes and search for particular amounts, dates or names.

Sticky situation number 1: Figuring out where to start

Every time you reconcile your bank account, you need to figure out where you finished working the last time. If you're like me and only sit down to reconcile your account every few weeks or so, it can be tricky remembering where you were up to.

Try this idea: In your Banking menu click Reconcile and select your bank account in the Begin Reconciliation window. But before you do anything else, write down the Beginning Balance as well as the date that QuickBooks says this account was last reconciled.

Rummage through your bank statements for this period, scanning the running balance column. Sooner or later (hopefully sooner), you find the amount you just wrote down when you looked at the Beginning Balance. Yippee! This is the spot you need to start from.

- ✔ I assume here that you've reconciled your bank account at least once before. If not, go back to the beginning of this chapter and start reading from 'Setting Up Opening Bank Balances'.

- ✔ You can avoid losing your reconciling place in future if you use a highlighter pen to mark the spot where you last worked on your bank statement.

Sticky situation number 2: Forgotten bank charges or interest

You're happily reconciling away and come across some bank charges, interest payments or direct debits. What should you do?

- ✔ To record a bank fee or interest charges, press Ctrl-W (that's the Ctrl key plus the letter 'w' at the same time) to hop straight to Write Cheques. For more information on recording bank fees, refer to Chapter 5.

- ✔ To record interest income, go to the Customers menu and select Enter Sales Receipts. Chapter 4 explains the details of how to record bank interest.

If you're not sure which tax code to pick, remember that most bank fees are GST-free, merchant fees and EFTPOS fees attract GST and interest income is input-taxed.

Sticky situation number 3: Transactions that don't show, but you know exist

You're 100 per cent positive that you recorded a particular transaction, yet when you go to Reconcile Accounts the darned thing won't show up on the screen. Where's it gone? Don your detective hat and try the following:

- ✔ **Check your date view selection.** In the top-right corner of the Reconcile Accounts window, check whether the option to hide transactions after the end date is selected. If this option is ticked, the transaction you're looking for won't appear if it has a later date than the Ending Date you entered.

✔ **Look to see if the missing transaction was allocated to a different bank account.** Select Find on the Edit menu and then click the Advanced tab. Select Amount as the Filter. Enter the amount of the transaction that you're looking for, then click Find. If QuickBooks displays your culprit transaction, check whether you allocated it to the correct bank account.

✔ **Sort differently.** On the bottom-right corner of the Reconcile Window, a drop-down box allows you to sort by Date, Cheque Number, Payee or Amount. Sorting transactions differently often helps locate transactions that seem to be missing, but are actually there all along.

✔ **Customise your view settings.** See the Columns to Display button in the bottom-right corner of the Reconcile Window? (Figure 7-3 shows what appears when you click this option.) Click here to display additional columns, such as the Payee as well as the Memo. Sometimes displaying this extra information helps you to identify transactions.

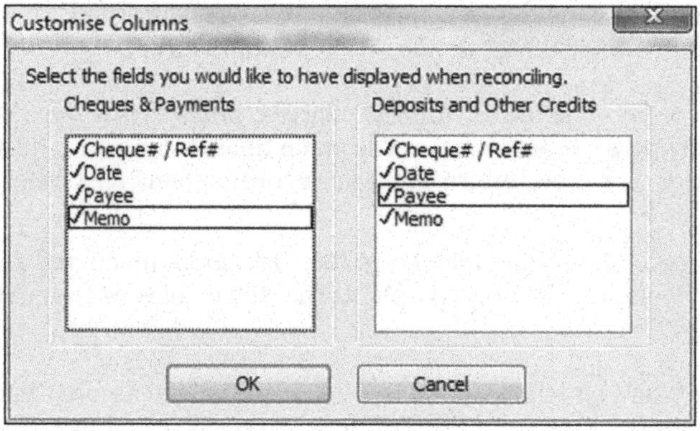

Figure 7-3:
You can customise what columns to display in your bank recon- ciliation.

Customise Columns

Select the fields you would like to have displayed when reconciling.

Cheques & Payments

✓ Cheque# / Ref#
✓ Date
✓ Payee
✓ Memo

Deposits and Other Credits

✓ Cheque# / Ref#
✓ Date
✓ Payee
✓ Memo

OK   Cancel

Sticky situation number 4: Transactions are definitely missing

If you're in the middle of reconciling and realise you've forgotten to enter a transaction, you don't need to close the Reconcile window. All you have to do is go to the top menu and navigate to where you need to be (for example, Customers followed by Receive Payments). Record your missing entry, then click Save & Close to arrive back at the Reconcile window.

If you need to stop working on your reconciliation and your bank account doesn't balance yet, don't worry. Any transactions marked as cleared will still have ticks against them when you return to the Reconcile window. In the meantime, any transactions marked as cleared, but which haven't been reconciled yet, show up in transaction registers displaying an asterisk (*) in the cleared column. This asterisk indicates that because you haven't yet finished reconciling your bank account, the transaction is still pending.

Sticky situation number 5: Transactions that are (sadly) wrong

However brilliant you are, sooner or later you'll find yourself in the middle of reconciling and discover that you've made a mistake. Perhaps you entered a payment as $800 instead of $80, or perhaps you recorded a deposit as $78 instead of $87.

To fix a mistake, highlight the transaction, then click the Go To button. You arrive at the original transaction, displayed in all its glory. Change any details that you need to, such as the date, amount or cheque number, then click Save & Close to return to your reconciliation.

If the transaction is a deposit that includes multiple lines, you need to identify which line is incorrect. For example, say you have a single deposit with five customer payments. You need to identify which one of these five payments is wrong. Then you need to delete the deposit, fix up the offending customer payment, and recreate the deposit again from scratch. Chapter 4 steps you through this process.

The bigger, the better

Reconciling accounts is much quicker and easier if you make the Reconcile window as big as possible on your screen, so that you can see lots of transactions at one time.

How? Just maximise the window by clicking on the square sitting at the top right of the Reconcile window (between the hyphen and the cross).

Sticky situation number 6: Customer payments aren't listed

So, you know for sure that you recorded all your customer payments, but not one is showing up in the list of transactions when you go to reconcile. Spooky.

Don't worry. The problem is almost certainly that you've recorded the payments, but forgotten to transfer these payments from your undeposited funds account into your regular bank account. The solution? Head to Banking⇨Record Deposits and record a deposit for each instance you did the banking. (Refer to Chapter 4 for more about preparing bank deposits.)

Sticky situation number 7: You haven't reconciled your account for years

Nobody could accuse me of not being a realist. So what do you do when you go to reconcile a bank account and it lists transactions dating back to 1998?

Start by confirming with your accountant when you last completed your tax return and what the ending balance on your bank account was for that year. With this information at hand, return to the Reconcile window in QuickBooks. As the Ending Date enter the date that your last tax return went to, then as the Ending Balance, enter the balance that your accountant used.

Mark off all the transactions up to the Ending Date, but ignore any transactions that go beyond this date. When you're done, the Cleared Balance should match your Ending Balance. If not, click Reconcile Now and when prompted, enter an adjustment for the difference. (QuickBooks allocates this difference to your Reconciliation Discrepancies account so that your accountant can review this balance when it comes time to finalise next year's accounts.)

With this step complete, it's time to move on. You may have several months of reconciliations to complete in order to finalise your accounts, but the farther back you start, the more likely it is that you will be able to unearth the dire and dastardly mistakes of the past. Don't be discouraged — several months of transactions is a more attractive proposition than several years!

TIP

Getting around without quitting

I find that when I'm reconciling bank accounts I often want to hop to somewhere else in the program without having to quit from where I am.

This is where shortcut keys are so useful. Press Ctrl-W and you arrive in an instant at Write Cheques. Record whatever transaction is missing from your statement, then click Save & Close to arrive back at your bank reconciliation. The same idea applies to customer transactions. Press Ctrl-J to arrive in

a flash at the Customer Centre from where you can record customer payments or other customer-related transactions.

You can even cycle though open windows without having to close them. To do this, while holding down the Ctrl button with one finger press Tab again and again and watch. Magic.

For a complete list of shortcuts, refer to the Cheat Sheet for this book available at www.dummies.com/cheatsheet/quickbooksau.

When Your Bank Account Just Won't Balance

It would be embarrassing if I owned up to the number of times I've had trouble reconciling a bank account. But the upside of this is that my troublesome times have taught me a few tricks. And I'm really happy to share them with you.

Tricks to try before you kick the cat

When your bank account doesn't balance, stay calm and try the following:

- ✔ **Check the beginning balance is correct.** Refer to 'Sticky situation number 1: Figuring out where to start' earlier in this chapter to find out how. If your beginning balance is wrong, skip to 'Troubleshooting Beginning Balances' later in this chapter for what to do next.

- ✔ **Check every single line.** Have you missed something on your bank statement that should have been ticked in the Reconcile window? Look at every line on the statement and check that a tick is displayed next to the corresponding entry.

✔ **Count the ticks.** Have you ticked something in the Reconcile window that isn't on your bank statement? If your eyes are going crooked looking from your bank statement to the screen and back again, try counting the number of ticks in your Reconcile window and then the number of lines on your bank statement. They should be the same!

✔ **Check that the amounts are in the correct columns.** Maybe an amount is correct but it's listed as a deposit rather than as a withdrawal (or vice versa).

✔ **Call on your mental powers.** How much are you out by? Does this amount ring a bell?

Tricks to try before you kick the computer

If you've tried all the earlier suggestions in this chapter but your account still won't reconcile, take a walk around the block and think about something totally different for a while . . . then try the following ideas:

✔ **Check your starting point.** Did you start off at the right spot in your bank statement? It's easy to accidentally skip a page or part of a page.

✔ **Match up total debits and credits.** Somewhere on your bank statement you can usually find a summary of total withdrawals and total deposits. This corresponds with the bottom of the Reconcile window, where you also see totals for deposits and withdrawals. Try comparing these totals with your bank statement's totals to see whether the problem lies with deposits or withdrawals (or both!).

✔ **Divide the difference by nine.** If the amount of the difference is a multiple of nine, look to see if you put in two numbers back to front — for example, you entered 43 instead of 34, or 685 instead of 658. (Yes, this is a curious thing, but if you turn a number back to front and subtract your result from the original number, the difference is always exactly divisible by nine.)

✔ **Divide the difference by two, and look for a transaction for this amount.** In other words, if the amount of the difference is $90, look for a transaction equalling $45. This trick helps locate transactions that have been entered the wrong way round (a debit instead of a credit, a payment instead of a deposit and so on).

✔ **Enter a minus if you're overdrawn.** If your bank account is normally in credit, but you're overdrawn, be sure to enter the Ending Balance as a minus amount.

Tricks to try before you kick the bucket

So you've tried all of the above suggestions and your account *still* doesn't balance! Don't abandon ship: Here's my sure-fire, last-resort approach, which always, always works.

1. **Check that your beginning balance is right.**

   I talk about beginning balances earlier in this chapter (refer to 'Sticky situation number 1: Figuring out where to start'). If you don't start off at the right spot, you're never going to get anything to balance. Only when you're confident your beginning balance is right, proceed to Step 2.

   If you find that your beginning balance is wrong, you need to take drastic action. Skip to 'Troubleshooting Beginning Balances' later in this chapter to find out what to do next.

2. **Click on Unmark All to go right back to the beginning.**

   When you click on Unmark All, QuickBooks removes the ticks from all marked transactions. I know this undoes all your work, but it's time for some radical action.

3. **Close the Reconcile window and then click Reconcile one more time.**

   Click on Leave to close the Reconcile window. When you click Reconcile to start all over again, you're back at the Begin Reconciliation window. Groundhog Day.

4. **Select a running balance that's only halfway down the first page of your bank statement. Enter this as the Ending Balance and click Continue.**

   By marking off only a few transactions in one hit — five or ten at the most — pinpointing the problem gets much easier.

5. **Mark off transactions as far as this running balance, then check that the Cleared Balance in the bottom-right corner now matches the Ending Balance.**

   If the Cleared Balance matches the Ending Balance, this means your account reconciles (yippee!). If it doesn't, click Unmark All one more time (as per Step 2 in this section) and start again, but this time, select an even smaller range and number of transactions.

6. **Click Reconcile Now, print a reconciliation report if you want to, then return to the Reconcile window again. Select another small date range and continue reconciling in small bite-sized chunks until the whole statement is complete.**

   My husband often refers to me as his bite-sized chunk. I'm never sure if this is a compliment or not.

Sweeping stuff under the carpet

If your bank reconciliation is out of balance, you need to track down the source of the difference. Sometimes this detective work gets pretty difficult, which is why I devote almost half of this chapter to troubleshooting techniques.

QuickBooks also realises how tricky balancing your bank account can be, which is why, if you click Reconcile Now before your Ending Balance matches with your Cleared Balance, it displays a helpful pop-up window that offers (among other things) to enter an adjustment that forces QuickBooks to match your statement.

Sounds tempting, doesn't it? But don't contemplate a forced adjustment, no matter how lily-livered you're feeling. All you're doing is postponing the inevitable. QuickBooks sends the forced adjustment to a suspense account, where it festers silently until you or your accountant has time to try to get to the bottom of the problem. Problem is, it's much harder figuring out what was wrong after the bank account has been adjusted automatically and reconciled.

To summarise: If you can't get QuickBooks to balance, try everything and anything you can, but don't ever accept the offer from QuickBooks to forcibly record an adjustment.

Troubleshooting Beginning Balances

One of the stickiest situations to resolve is if the Beginning Balance displayed in the Begin Reconciliation window doesn't match the ending balance on your bank statement from the last time you reconciled.

What this usually means is that you've inadvertently edited or deleted a transaction that had already been reconciled. For example, you've already reconciled up to October, but in a fit of creativity you decide to change a transaction belonging to September that had already been reconciled. In doing so, you made your beginning balance very sick indeed.

Want to dig yourself out this hole? Read on . . .

Generating a reconciliation discrepancy report

The most likely reason your beginning balance is out of whack is that you inadvertently edited or deleted a previously reconciled transaction. Your first port of call is to generate a reconciliation discrepancy report, a handy document that lists all changes you made to transactions that had already been reconciled since your last reconciliation.

To view this report, go to the Begin Reconciliation window, but instead of entering an Ending Balance, click the Locate Discrepancies button, followed by the Discrepancy Report button. Up pops a report like the one shown in Figure 7-4, with all your various sins listed for all to see (in my example, two transactions have been deleted after they had been reconciled, and on a third transaction, the amount has been changed by $200).

Figure 7-4:
The Dis-
crepancy
Report is a
very handy
reference.

Nine times out of ten, the total effect of the changes listed equals the amount that your beginning balance is out by.

If this report doesn't give you the answer you're looking for, you can take things one step further by regenerating reconciliation reports for previous periods and identifying when the difference first arose:

1. **In the Begin Reconciliation window click the Locate Discrepancies button, followed by the Previous Reports button.**

2. **Select Detail as the Type of Report and the most recent Statement Ending Date as the Date.**

3. **QuickBooks offers a choice between viewing transactions cleared at the time of reconciliation, and viewing transactions cleared plus any changes made since. You need both reports, so print one, then the other.**

   The first report displays as a PDF, the second report displays as a regular QuickBooks report.

4. **Compare the Beginning Balance on each report. If the Beginning Balance on each report is the same, skip to the next step. If the Beginning Balances are different, ditch both reports and generate fresh reports, going back to the next most recent Statement Date.**

   For example, if the reconciliation reports for 30 April had different beginning balances, return to the Previous Reports button and generate reports for the reconciliation for 31 March (or whatever date was most recent before 30 April). Keep going back in time until the Beginning Balances match on both reports.

5. **When you arrive at two reports where the Beginning Balances on both reports are the same but the Ending Balances are different, compare the transactions on each report, line by line. Play spot the difference until you identify the culprit transaction.**

   After you've worked out which transaction is causing the problem, you can either re-enter the transaction (if it was a cleared transaction that was later deleted) or change the transaction to what it originally was when the bank reconciled. And before you know it, you detective extraordinaire, you will have put the world to rights.

Undoing the previous reconciliation

If your beginning balance is definitely wrong, and reconciliation discrepancy reports fail to pinpoint the difference, your next course of action is to undo the previous reconciliation:

1. **Back up.**

   No ifs, no buts. After all, what you're about to do is a bit drastic. Remember to note down where QuickBooks saves this backup, just in case you need to do a restore.

2. **Go to the Reconcile window and select the bank account you're trying to reconcile.**

3. **Click Undo Last Reconciliation.**

QuickBooks displays a message suggesting that you back up, and also tells you what the beginning balance will revert to.

4. **Click Continue.**

QuickBooks tells you that any service charges, interest or balance adjustments won't be removed.

5. **Have a look to see if your bank account now reconciles with a previous statement.**

Look at the date that QuickBooks now says it was last reconciled and note down what QuickBooks says was the Beginning Balance on that day. Can you see this balance anywhere on your bank statements around that time? If so, you're cooking with gas and you can continue reconciling your bank account as normal, working forwards from that date. If not, you need to continue the undo process until they match.

 Sometimes the cause of a bank reconciliation being out of balance can be many months back. For example, it could be June now but you end up having to undo reconciliations all the way back to February. You realise that the cause of your problems is that you inadvertently deleted a February transaction that had already been reconciled. In this situation, you're best to note down the details of the offending transaction and then restore the backup that you made before undoing your reconciliation. You can then fix the problem transaction, check that your bank account reconciles and continue. (Don't forget to rename your backup file, because this will now become your current file.)

Fantastic plastic

Reconciling a credit card account is the same as reconciling any other bank account. Simply go to the Reconcile window as normal, select your credit card account as the Account and you're away. You should see the individual debits of your credit card purchases in the Charges and Cash Advances column, and your payments in the Payments and Credits column. Mark them off, one by one, and check that the closing balance on your credit card matches the Ending Balance in the Reconcile window.

Deciding When to Print

Whenever you reconcile your bank account you're given the option of either displaying or printing a reconciliation report. This report can be a summary report, a detailed report, a combination or both. What's best?

✔ If you're new to reconciling, I recommend you print a detailed bank reconciliation report at the end of every statement. When you become accustomed to the process, you can get away with printing a summary reconciliation report instead (as shown in Figure 7-5).

✔ If you get slack about printing reports, at the very least remember to print a bank reconciliation report when 30 June rolls around (or whatever the last day of your financial year is). Your accountant will love you for it.

✔ If 30 June has passed and you're cursing because you forgot to print a bank reconciliation report, you can still do it. Go to Reports⇨Banking and select Previous Reconciliation. Select the date(s) closest to 30 June and print a report for this date.

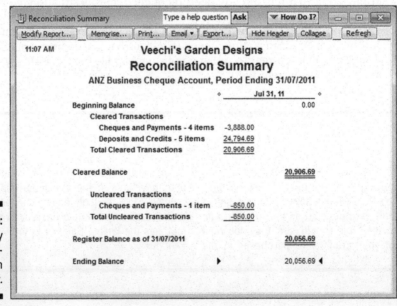

Figure 7-5:
A summary reconciliation report.

Reconciliation Summary — Type a help question [Ask] — How Do I?

Modify Report... | Memorise... | Print... | Email ▾ | Export... | Hide Header | Collapse | Refresh

11:07 AM

Veechi's Garden Designs
Reconciliation Summary
ANZ Business Cheque Account, Period Ending 31/07/2011

	Jul 31, 11
Beginning Balance	0.00
Cleared Transactions	
Cheques and Payments - 4 items	-3,888.00
Deposits and Credits - 5 items	24,794.69
Total Cleared Transactions	20,906.69
Cleared Balance	20,906.69
Uncleared Transactions	
Cheques and Payments - 1 item	-850.00
Total Uncleared Transactions	-850.00
Register Balance as of 31/07/2011	20,056.69
Ending Balance ▶	20,056.69 ◀

Chapter 8

Stocking Up

. . . .

In This Chapter

▶ Setting up inventory items in QuickBooks

▶ Creating units of measure

▶ Grouping inventory items

▶ Counting opening stock and valuing it right

▶ Managing your Item List

▶ Pricing tricks, pricing tips

▶ Understanding that you're a mere mortal, after all (oh yes, and fixing up mistakes)

▶ Fun and games at stocktake time

▶ Ensuring your Inventory Account balances

. . . .

*M*anaging inventory is one of the more complex parts of running a business. However, if you're a manufacturer, retailer or wholesaler, then you've no choice but to get a grip on the whole deal.

In this chapter, I explain everything you need to know about getting your inventory up and running in QuickBooks. I talk about how to create new items, link items to account codes, do stocktakes, change prices and make inventory adjustments. In short, you'll have more fun reading this chapter than almost anything else you could imagine.

Part of this fun can be derived from driving everyone else around you potty. Because the art of getting inventory to work well in QuickBooks lies largely in how well you do the initial setup, you can feel free to be irritatingly pedantic. Spend time pondering such life-changing matters as the design of item codes, whether costs are inclusive or exclusive of GST and whether you have 998 units in stock, or 999. The devil is in the detail, after all.

Getting Started

One of the first questions I suggest you ask yourself is whether you need to bother with inventory at all.

This question is particularly important for manufacturers, especially if you're a small manufacturer making lots of one-off items (maybe you make custom furniture, or you build some kind of custom equipment). You may find that creating inventory assemblies and monitoring manufacturing components is way too time-consuming and overly complex. In this kind of scenario, you may be better to only use inventory for recording finished products.

However, assuming that you do want to use the inventory features in QuickBooks (which is pretty likely given that you're reading this chapter), my next question is whether you have inventory *switched on* in QuickBooks. Check this now: Go to the Items & Inventory area in your Preferences menu, click the Company Preferences tab and ensure that the option Inventory and Purchase Orders Are Active is clicked.

All done? Now you're ready to create your first inventory item.

Creating your first inventory item

So, you're ready to run your first marathon — woops, I mean create your first inventory item. Follow these eloquent instructions to be on your way:

1. **Go to your List menu and select Item List.**

2. **Click Item at the bottom of the list and then click New.**

3. **Select Inventory Part as the item Type.**

4. **Enter an Item Name/Number for this item.**

   No matter what naming or numbering system you use, ensure it's logical and consistent, because you'll refer to the Item Name/Number every time you make a sale or purchase.

5. **As the Manufacturer's Part Number, record the item code that your supplier uses for this item (optional).**

   For example, if you always order your bottled olives from the same supplier, and the supplier prefers to see her own item codes on purchase orders, enter the supplier's item code here.

6. **Record the Unit of Measure.**

   If you buy and sell things in the same units, you can usually ignore the Unit of Measure field. If not, check out 'Working with Units of Measure' later in this chapter. (Units of measure work quite differently in the more recent versions of QuickBooks.)

7. **Enter text for the Description on Purchase Transactions and the Description on Sales Transactions.**

   One man's meat is another man's poison. You may want to show something on a sales invoice such as 'Luxury quilt, super-warm, queen size' but on the purchase order show the same item as 'Quilt Standard Winter 180 cm × 150 cm'.

8. **Enter the Cost (optional), Purchase Tax Code, COGS account and Preferred Supplier (optional).**

   Don't worry if you don't have accurate cost information close to hand, because QuickBooks populates this field automatically when you record your first purchase of this item. However, you need to add a Purchase Tax Code (see 'Drilling down on GST' later in this chapter) and a COGS account (see 'Telling QuickBooks where to go' in this chapter). Whether you enter the name of your preferred supplier is up to you.

9. **Enter the Sales Price, Tax Code and Income Account.**

   You're probably getting the idea of how this whole deal works by now. However, skip to 'Drilling down on GST' later in this chapter for more information on tax codes, or skip to 'Telling QuickBooks where to go' for more about income accounts.

   When you enter your Sales Price, pause for a moment to consider whether this price includes GST, or not. If you're entering the price including GST, remember to click the Amts Inc Tax button. (If you can't see this button, go to the Tax section in your Preferences and tick the option to allow tax-inclusive prices and costs to be entered.)

10. **Complete the Asset Account (that's a must) and the Reorder Point (optional).**

    The Asset Account is almost always an account called Inventory. If you can't see an account by this name, then create one now. Now your first inventory item should look similar to mine, shown in Figure 8-1.

    Ignore the On Hand and Total Value fields right now. This information relates to opening balances, which I explain a little later in this chapter. Entering opening values at this point often creates confusion and can cause QuickBooks inventory not to balance.

11. **Click either Next or OK.**

When you click Next, QuickBooks saves your new inventory item and flips to a fresh New Item window, with the same Tax Code and Account information carried across to this new entry. This works well if you're creating lots of items that are all fairly similar. If you click OK, QuickBooks simply saves your new item and returns to your Item List.

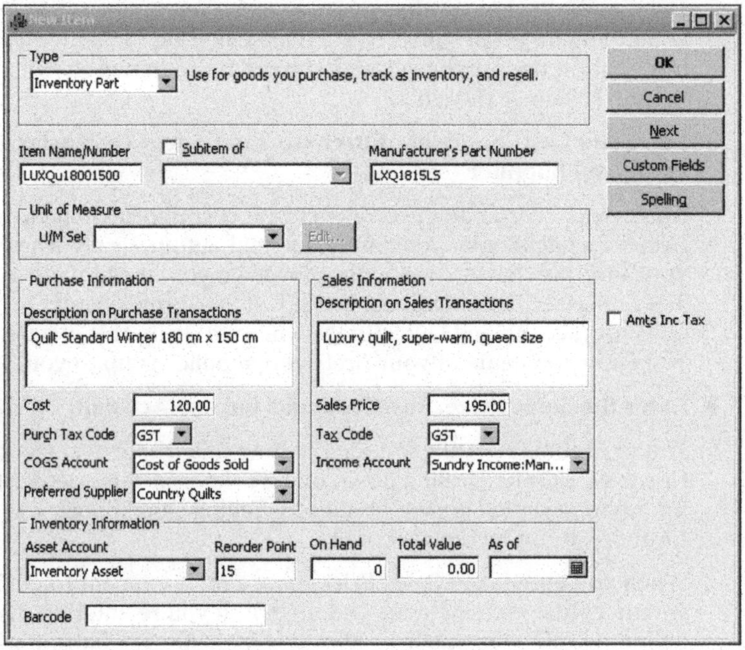

Figure 8-1:
Creating
your
first new
inventory
item.

Telling QuickBooks where to go

Whenever you create a new item, QuickBooks asks you to select the account or accounts that this item links to. Take extra care with the selection of these accounts, because they affect the format and structure of your Profit & Loss report.

Income accounts

If you select Service, Inventory Part, Inventory Assembly or Other Charge as the Item Type, QuickBooks prompts you to select an income account. Take care to select an income account that makes sense, creating a new account if an appropriate one doesn't exist already.

As I explain in Chapter 2, it usually works well to create several income accounts in your Chart of Accounts so you can track your different revenue sources. You can then mirror this arrangement by organising your items in a similar way, so that items are grouped into departments. Working in this manner allows you to see at a glance in your Profit & Loss how different product groups are performing.

Cost of goods sold and expense accounts

If you select Inventory Part, Inventory Assembly or Non-Inventory Part as the Item Type, QuickBooks prompts you to select a cost of goods sold or an expense account. For items with Inventory Part or Inventory Assembly as the Item Type, probably the simplest method is just to have one account called Cost of Goods Sold (sometimes also called Purchases).

For Non-Inventory Parts, the account you choose depends on what the item is. For example, an item called Office Supplies probably hooks up to an expense account like Office Expenses. An item for purchasing manufacturing supplies probably hooks up to a cost of sales account, such as Consumables or Manufacturing Supplies.

Inventory accounts

If you select Inventory Part or Inventory Assembly as the Item Type, QuickBooks prompts you to select an inventory account. Unlike income or cost of sales accounts, you only need one inventory account to keep track of the stock you have on hand. Surprisingly enough, this account is called Inventory or Inventory Asset, and sits in the Assets section of your Chart of Accounts.

Heaps of items? Don't retype everything

If you already have an item listing on your computer, whether in a word processor document, spreadsheet, database or another QuickBooks file, you can easily transfer all this data into QuickBooks without needing to re-key a single line. This process is called *importing data*. For more information on how to import data into your company file, refer to your QuickBooks online help.

Drilling down on GST

In Chapter 10, I focus on how best to handle tax codes and tax items in QuickBooks, and it's there that I explain how you can set up tax codes in a very simple way, with GST as the code for anything that attracts 10 per cent tax. However, if you've used QuickBooks in the past, you're probably used to using GST as the tax code on items that you sell, and NCG as the tax code on items you buy. As far as I'm concerned, either method is quite okay.

A couple more tips about GST on items:

✔ If the item is GST-free (medical supplies, GST-free food and so on), then either select FRE as the tax code in all situations, or select FRE as the tax code for sales, and NCF as the tax code for purchases. Either method is okay.

✔ It's up to you whether you enter the item Cost and item Sales Price including GST or not. If these figures include GST, then click the Amts Inc Tax option. (If you can't see this option, go to the Tax section of your Preferences and tick the option to allow tax-inclusive prices and costs to be entered.)

Stating your preferences

Now that you're focusing on how inventory works in QuickBooks, take a couple of minutes to review your inventory preferences (go to the Preferences menu and click Items & Inventory, as shown in Figure 8-2).

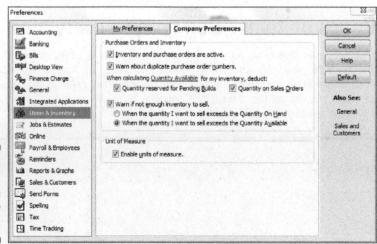

Figure 8-2:
Reviewing
your Items
& Inventory
preferences.

You can ask QuickBooks to warn you if you try to record a sale that exceeds either the Quantity on Hand or the Quantity Available. (Quantity Available means what you currently have on hand, plus what's currently outstanding on customer sales orders.) You're usually best to choose the second option, because to be forewarned is to be forearmed.

By the way, QuickBooks lets item quantities go into negative. Say you have 30 coffee tables in stock and you record a sale for 35 coffee tables. QuickBooks displays a pop-up warning but still allows you to record the sale, so that you end up with −5 coffee tables in your Item List.

Working with Units of Measure

In a typical trade-off between complexity and capacity, units of measure are more complex in the latest versions of QuickBooks, but they're also much more powerful.

The first question is whether you need *units of measure* in the first place. If you always buy and sell things in single units, and you don't need to print this unit column on customer invoices (for example, you don't need to print an Each column on invoices), then you can ignore units of measure entirely. (***Note:*** The units of measure feature is only available in QuickBooks Pro, Premier and Enterprise.)

However, if you buy and sell in different units, then you do need to enable this feature. For example, maybe you buy muesli by the sack but sell it by the kilo, or buy timber in 4.8 metres lengths but sell it by the metre. In my example that follows, I show you how to set up wine so that you buy it by the case (with a dozen bottles to each case) and sell bottles individually.

1. **When creating a new item, if the Unit of Measure field is blank, click the Enable button.**

2. **In the Unit of Measure field, click Add New.**

   QuickBooks takes you to the main Unit of Measure window. This is exciting stuff.

3. **Select a Unit of Measure Type that applies to this item, then click Next.**

   You can choose between Length, Weight, Time and so on, but in 90 per cent of cases, Count is your best bet. In my wining and dining example, I select Count as the Unit of Measure Type for my wine.

4. **Select a Base Unit of Measure, considering the smallest unit of measurement that you'll ever buy or sell for this item.**

   The temperance movement may suggest I set up a thimbleful as the base unit, but no, I'm sensible and select Each.

5. **Tell QuickBooks about any Related Units and then click Next.**

   In my example, I select Dozen as the Related Unit, because I'm buying wine by the dozen. QuickBooks defines a related unit by the number of base units it contains. For example, if the base unit is grams, the related unit could be 100 g or 1 kg.

6. **Select the Default Units of measure for both purchases and sales and then click Next.**

   For my wild and drunken example, I choose Dozen as the Purchases unit of measure and Each as the Sales unit of measure.

   You can also select a Shipping Unit of Measure, which overrides the unit of measure on sales orders when printing picking slips. This feature is handy if the packaging of an item doesn't make it obvious how many units are contained within.

7. **Finally, provide a U/M Set Name and click Finish.**

   QuickBooks offers a name for this set voluntarily, but I often change this name so that it makes more sense to me. Figure 8-3 shows the end result.

The units of measure feature in QuickBooks has been considerably refined in the latest versions of QuickBooks. If you were using units of measure in a previous version, do refer carefully to the documents that came with your upgrade to ensure that your settings carry across properly.

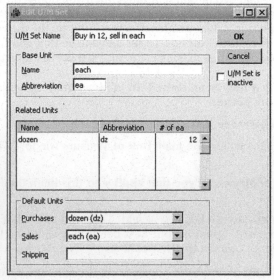

Figure 8-3:
Setting up
units of
measure
to buy and
sell items
in different
units.

Organising Items into Groups

There are four methods for grouping items in QuickBooks, which I cover in the following sections:

- ✔ **Defining a hierarchy of parent items and subitems.** See 'Playing happy families'.

- ✔ **Creating a new item that's a group.** See 'Creating groups for speedy billing'.

- ✔ **Creating a new item that's an assembly.** See 'Producing a new item using other items'.

- ✔ **Using custom fields to add additional information or subgroups for items.** See 'Adding detail and custom fields'.

Of these methods, no single method is better than another; rather it's a case of picking what's going to work best, when. Read on to find out more.

Playing happy families

Describing what makes up a family is a tricky business. I remember a few years ago, my son's kindergarten teacher asked all the kids to draw a picture of their family. She added that if the kids weren't sure who was in their family, they could just draw a picture of everyone they lived with. I was a little concerned with my son's final effort, which included all of our family but omitted his little sister, and added an entire menagerie of imaginary pets.

Fortunately, deciding what constitutes a family in QuickBooks is a decidedly easier affair. You simply create a new item, call that item a *parent*, and then decide what other items are the *subitems* that live with that parent. For example, in Figure 8-4, I created a parent item called Consulting Fees and below that, I have lots of subitems for the different kinds of consulting that I do.

To create a parent item, first create a new item, naming it as the heading you want for that group of items. When QuickBooks prompts you for an income account, choose the income account that most closely corresponds to that group of items. Leave the rate or price for this parent item at zero.

To change an item so that it becomes a subitem of a parent (I'd hate to think what my kids would think if I started calling them subitems, but that's another matter), click on the diamond to the left of that item and drag the diamond to the right. Alternatively, you can select the Subitem Of checkbox and choose the name of the parent item.

Name	Description	Type	Account	O..	U/M	Price
◇Consult Fees	Consulting Fees	Service	Consulting & Service Income			0.00
◇TAFE	TAFE Teaching	Service	Consulting & Service Income:Teaching Income			85.00
◇SoftDes	Software and Template Design	Service	Consulting & Service Income:Consulting Income			150.00
◇Month120	Monthly Support Fee	Service	Consulting & Service Income:Consulting Income			120.00
◇ConAnalysis	Initial consultation Fee and Needs Analysis	Service	Consulting & Service Income:Consulting Income			300.00
◇PhoneSupport	Phone Support Fees	Service	Consulting & Service Income:Consulting Income			120.00
◇ReportCustom	Custom Report built with Crystal Reports	Service	Consulting & Service Income:Consulting Income			350.00
◇Consult80	Consulting Fees (Offsite rate)	Service	Consulting & Service Income:Consulting Income			80.00
◇Consult110	Consulting Onsite QuickBooks Setup	Service	Consulting & Service Income:Consulting Income			110.00
◇Books		Inventory Part	Journalism and Writing Income:Income from Bo...	0		0.00
◇VTCup6	Exploring Vietnam	Inventory Part	Journalism and Writing Income:Income from Bo...	0		35.00
◇NatGeo	Quiz Software Over 2000 Questions	Inventory Part	Journalism and Writing Income:Income from Bo...	5		100.00
◇SFD	Scuba-diving for Dummies	Inventory Part	Journalism and Writing Income:Income from Bo...	0		39.95
◇FD	Flying For Dummies	Inventory Part	Journalism and Writing Income:Royalty Income ...	0		39.95
◇QBD	QuickBooks For Dummies	Inventory Part	Journalism and Writing Income:Royalty Income ...	0		39.95
◇Other Income		Other Charge	Sundry Income			0.00
◇Freight	Freight Charges	Other Charge	Sundry Income:Delivery Fees			9.95
◇Interest Income	Interest Income	Other Charge	Sundry Income:Interest and Dividend Income			0.00
◇DepRec	Deposit Received	Other Charge	Customer Deposits Held			0.00
◇Bad Debt Expense		Other Charge	Bad debt Expense			0.00
◇Subtotal		Subtotal				
◇Book Bumper Pack		Group				
◇NonProfit Discount	Discount of 10% for non-profit organisations	Discount	Discounts Given			-10.0%
◇Student Discount 10%	Student discount	Discount	Discounts Given			-10.0%

Item ▾   Activities ▾   Reports ▾   Excel ▾   ☐ Include inactive

Figure 8-4:
An Item List, showing both parent items and subitems.

The main benefit of organising your Item List into parent items and subitems is that you create an important visual cue to show how different items belong together. I find this way of working makes it easier for me to find items in my list, and I'm less likely to end up with duplicate items or inconsistent numbering systems.

Creating groups for speedy billing

The other way to organise items in QuickBooks is to create a *group* item. Group items work well if you need to track a lot of detail about your items, but also want to give your customers simple, uncluttered invoices. For example, you can set up a group item so that the printed version of an invoice reduces a group item to a single line item and one amount, yet when you view the invoice on-screen, you see a separate line entry and amount for each item in the group.

Group items are manna from heaven for speed maniacs. All you do is enter the name of the group item and in a flash, QuickBooks fills in the details for every item in the group. Here's how it works:

1. **Go to your List menu and select Item List.**

2. **Click Item from the bottom of the list and then click New.**

3. **Select Group as the item Type.**

4. **Enter an Item Name/Number for this group, as well as a Description.**

5. **If you want customers to see a list of individual items and amounts on their invoices, click the checkbox Print Items in Group.**

   Conversely, don't tick this box if you want to hide group details when the sale prints. Either way, you still see the details when you view the sale on-screen.

6. **In the Item column, select the items you want to include in the group.**

   You can include a maximum of 20 items in a group.

7. **In the Qty column, enter the quantity that you want QuickBooks to enter for each individual item when you use the group item.**

   If you don't enter quantities, QuickBooks assumes that the quantity of each item in the group is 1. You can always change the quantities when you enter a sale or purchase.

8. **Click OK.**

   Now that you've created a group item, why not go ahead and create a QuickBooks invoice using this item. That way you can check out how this smart idea works in practice.

Producing a new item using other items

A third way to create item groups in QuickBooks is to create an Inventory Assembly item, which put simply, is a new item that's made from other items. Many manufacturers use QuickBooks in this way. For example, a client of mine sells gift hampers. To account for the items she uses to assemble a gift hamper, she 'builds' the hamper using an Inventory Assembly item in QuickBooks, reducing stock levels of individual gift items and increasing the stock level of gift hampers.

Creating Inventory Assembly items works in a similar way to creating Group items (which I explain in the preceding section, 'Creating groups for speedy billing'). However, you can add more complexity, such as allowing for labour or production expenses as part of assemblies. (For lots more on this topic, see also QuickBooks Help or talk to your QuickBooks consultant.)

I used to get confused about the difference between Inventory Assembly items and Group items. Group items and Inventory Assembly items are similar in that they both let you record a group of items as a single entry. However, Group items allow you to speed up the data entry of entering a group of individual items that you often purchase or sell together. By contrast, Inventory Assembly items let you combine inventory items and assembly costs into new, separately trackable items that represent the finished goods you produce and sell.

Have you been using QuickBooks for a while, and only recently upgraded? If the assembly features weren't detailed enough for your needs in the past, I recommend you revisit this area of QuickBooks now. The ability to create bills of materials, accurately track production costs and receive alerts when assembly components fall below critical stock levels are all new to the latest version.

Adding detail and custom fields

Sometimes you need to record more information about items, maybe organising them into groups detailing colour or size, or recording additional buying information, such as serial numbers or model number codes. This is where custom fields work a treat.

In your Item List, every item has up to five custom fields. Here's how to put them to work:

1. **Double-click on any item in your Item List, followed by the Custom Fields button.**

   Unless someone has previously set up custom fields in your company file, QuickBooks displays a pop-up message prompting you to click the Define Fields button.

2. **Click the Define Fields button.**

   A table appears, showing two columns and five empty rows.

3. **In the Label column, enter a description for each item group and click in the Use column to indicate that you want to make this item group active.**

   For example, if you sell clothing and you want to categorise items according to colour and size, then enter Colour and Size as descriptions in the Label column. Or, if you sell CDs, you could enter Artist and Distribution Method in this column.

4. **Click OK to return to the Custom Fields for this item.**

5. **Enter descriptions against each label and click OK.**

   In Figure 8-5, I show you how this works. Blue is the description against the label Colour, and Medium is the description against the label Size.

6. **If necessary, customise your invoice or purchase order templates to include this custom information.**

   Chapter 11 explains how to include additional columns for each custom field.

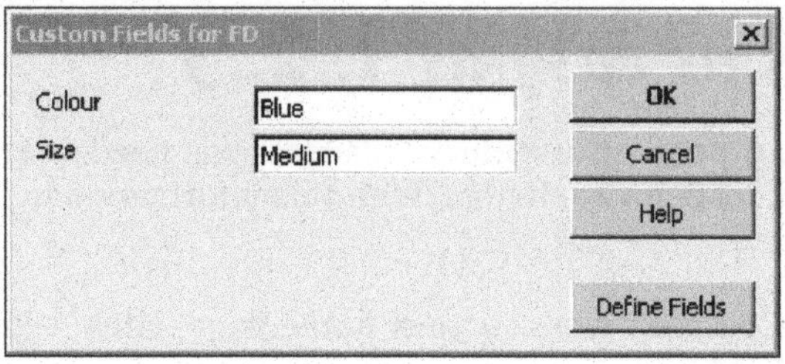

Figure 8-5: Organising items using custom fields.

Doing Your First Head Count

To get opening inventory balances up and running, first set up descriptions for all items in your Item List, as I explain earlier this chapter. When you're done, pick the starting date from which you're going to start tracking inventory. If you're new to QuickBooks, this starting date is probably 1 July, the first day of the financial year. On the other hand, if you've been using QuickBooks for a while and you're only now setting up inventory, then you're best to pick the first day of a month as your starting date.

Especially for retailers

If you're a retailer, you probably need a point-of-sale system. Chances are that you need ... drum roll ... QuickBooks' very own point-of-sale software.

As with any point-of-sale system, the idea is that you hurl your old-fashioned cash register out the window (first making sure that no dachshunds are taking a stroll underneath) and replace it with your computer. You put barcodes on all your items and replace the peaceful *tap, tap, kerchunk* of your cash register with the not-quite-so-peaceful *beep, beep, ping* of your scanner and cash drawer.

Retail Point of Sale is the core product in the QuickBooks point-of-sale range, but if you're opening a new retail business for the first time and you haven't purchased any QuickBooks software yet, then the Retail Starter Kit is probably the better deal, because it includes not only QuickBooks Plus and Retail Point of Sale, but a cash drawer, thermal receipt printer and barcode scanner as well.

One of the best things about Reckon's Retail Point of Sale product is that it speaks the same language as QuickBooks. At the end of each day or week, Retail Point of Sale automatically sends the details of every transaction into your QuickBooks company file, so that you maintain a complete record of sales, purchases and movements in inventory in your accounting system. To find out more about Reckon's point-of-sale products, visit www.quicken.com.au and follow the links for Retail and Hospitality.

Counting is as easy as 1, 2, 3

In order to enter your opening inventory balances, you need to know the opening counts and costs for each item. With this information in hand, get ready ... get set ...

1. **Go! From the Company area on your home page, click Adjust Quantity On Hand.**

   You see a list of all inventory items and descriptions in the first two columns, along with current quantities on hand in the next column.

2. **As the Adjustment Date, select the last day of the previous financial year (if you're starting from 1 July) or the last day of the previous month (if you're starting from the first day of a month).**

   Be pedantic — dates are important from a beancounter's perspective.

3. **Accept the reference number that QuickBooks offers, then select Inventory Asset account as the Adjustment Account.**

   You may receive a warning saying that adjustments normally go to an expense account. That's true, but because on this occasion you're setting up inventory balances, the correct account is indeed your Inventory Asset account.

4. **Tick the Value Adjustment checkbox in the bottom-left corner.**

   QuickBooks displays two new columns: Current Value and New Value.

5. **In the New Qty column, enter stock counts for the first 20 or so items in your list.**

   If you have lots of items, I recommend you enter opening inventory counts in short batches, rather than all at once. That way, if you accidentally press Cancel or there's a system crash, you won't lose a whole heap of work.

6. **Complete the New Value column for each item.**

   One by one, complete the New Value, at cost, for each item. *Note:* QuickBooks is looking for the *total* value at cost, not an item's *individual* value. For example, if you have 10 fridges that cost $300 each, you need to enter $3,000 in the New Value column, not $300. Also, remember that you're entering costs, not selling prices, and that these cost prices should be tax-exclusive, before GST.

   At this point, your window looks similar to Figure 8-6 (assuming you're doing a roaring trade in books and wine, of course).

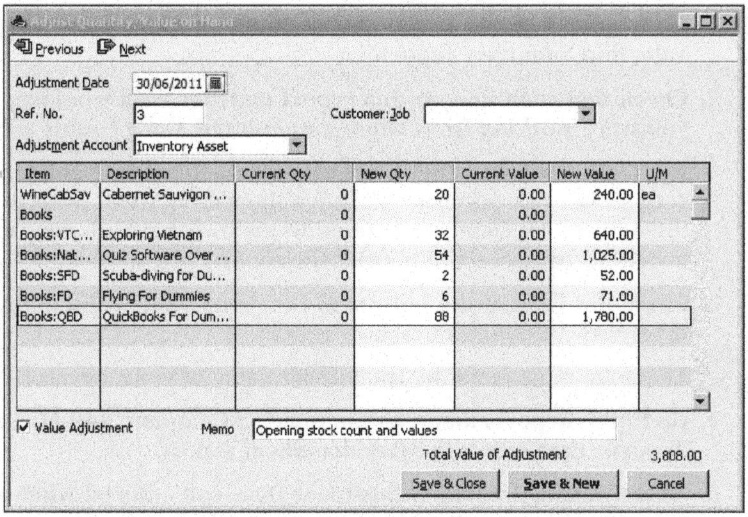

Figure 8-6:
Recording
opening
counts
and costs
for each
inventory
item.

7. **Type 'Opening stock count and values' in the Memo field.**

8. **Click Save & Close.**

   After you click Save & Close, repeat the entire process again and again, in batches of 20 or so items, until you've entered opening quantities and costs for all your items.

If you go to view the details of an item after recording opening balances, you may be surprised to see that the Cost field shows up as zero. Don't worry — further down under Inventory Information you can see the Average Cost, which should be the cost price that you entered when doing the opening stock count.

Ensuring your inventory records tally

As you know by now, entering inventory counts and unit costs is a fairly involved process. That's why it's a good idea to check your work before recording any sales or purchases. At this point, I become unashamedly technical. After all, there's a limit to how much you can simplify quantum physics.

1. **Go to your Reports menu, choose Inventory and print the Inventory Valuation Summary report.**

2. **Check that each line on this report matches with whatever records you were working from when you entered stock counts and costs.**

   If you already have other inventory transactions in QuickBooks, such as sales or purchases, change the date in the top-left to match the Adjustment Date you entered when you recorded your opening inventory balances and re-print the report.

3. **Circle the Total at the bottom of the Asset Value column on your Inventory Valuation Summary report.**

   This total represents the total dollar value of your inventory.

4. **Go to the Reports menu again, head to Company and Financial Reports, then select the Balance Sheet report.**

5. **As the date, select the Adjustment Date you entered when recording your opening inventory balances, then click Refresh.**

6. **Look at the balance of Inventory in your Balance Sheet and check that this matches the total on your Inventory Valuation Summary report.**

   Find the balance of your Inventory account on the Balance Sheet. Then pick up the Inventory Valuation Summary report you printed in Step 1 and look at the total circled at the bottom.

7. **If the two balances match, yell yippee! You're truly brilliant.**

8. **If the two balances don't match, dig a little deeper.**

   If the balance of your Inventory account shows as nil in your Balance Sheet, then I suspect you haven't set up your opening balances yet. Skip ahead to Chapter 9 to discover how to set up your trial balance and get everything perfect.

   If your Inventory account balance isn't nil, but differs from your Inventory Valuation Summary report, then you need to figure out the reason why. You've either entered a wrong quantity or cost in your opening inventory journals, or the opening balance of inventory is wrong. It's probably time to talk to your accountant and ask for some help.

Giving Your Item List the Once-Over

Regardless of whether your Item List is short or long, spotted or striped, it needs a certain amount of tender loving care. Read on for the ultimate set of care and feeding instructions.

Finding items

After you find the item you need, you can do with it what you will. But first, some pointers:

- When you go to your Item List, can you see the labels (Name, Description, Type and so on) along the top? Click on any one of these labels to sort by that criterion. For example, if I want to sort a list by Description, I click the Description header and QuickBooks sorts my Item List by each item's description, ordered A–Z.

- To sort according to a criterion that isn't currently displayed, go to the View menu and select Customise Columns. In the list of Available Columns highlight the criterion you want to sort by, then click the Add button. Voilà.

- A sure-fire method for finding items quickly, as well as always grouping apples with apples, is to start the Item Number/Name with a letter that indicates its product group. For example, a mail-order business that sells hats might start all hat Item Numbers with the letter H, all sloppy joes with the letters SJ and all T-shirts with the letters TS.

- If you have a large Item List, finding individual items gets much easier if you use parent items and subitems to organise items into groups. Refer to 'Playing happy families' earlier in this chapter to find out more about how this works.

Deleting items

To delete an item, first highlight it in your Item List. Then go to the Edit menu on the top menu bar (as shown in Figure 8-7) and choose Delete Item.

This works fine, unless you have current invoices or purchase orders for this item still in the system. In this case, a warning appears stating that you can't delete the item yet. If this happens, your best bet is to make this item inactive (I show you how in the following section).

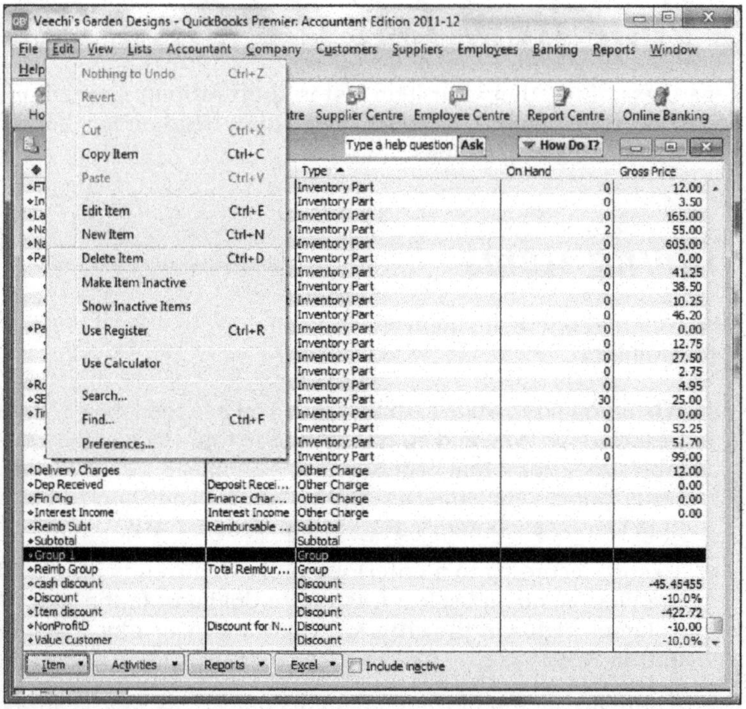

Figure 8-7:
Deleting old items when they've done their dash.

Hiding items (and making them inactive)

When it's time to spring-clean my Item List, I often find that hiding items from view is a good compromise, especially considering that QuickBooks won't let you delete items if sales or purchases transactions are on file. By hiding an item — or to use the nerdy term, making it *inactive* — this item completely disappears from view (ah, if only I could do that to the mess in my kitchen).

To make an item inactive, first highlight the item in your list, then in the Edit menu select Make Item Inactive. Quick as a flash, this item drops off your Item List. To display inactive items again, click the Include Inactive option that appears at the bottom of this list.

When you make an item inactive, QuickBooks keeps the information associated with that item — displaying this information on relevant reports — but hides the item both on the Item List and from any drop-down lists. You don't need to change or delete transactions that use the item and, if you start to use the item again, you can make it active again.

Merging items

If you end up with two items that are essentially the same — maybe you created one item called James Taylor Greatest Hits and somewhere along the line you created a similar item called Greatest Hits James Taylor — then you can combine the two into one.

1. **If more than one person is currently logged on in your QuickBooks company file, boot them off and switch to single-user mode.**

   Not sure how to change mode? Simply go to the File menu and click Switch to Single-User Mode.

2. **Go to the Lists menu and choose Item List.**

3. **Right-click the item you want to get rid of, then click Edit Item.**

4. **In the Edit Item window, change the item name to the same name as the item you're combining it with.**

   For example, change the name of Greatest Hits James Taylor to James Taylor Greatest Hits.

5. **Click OK, and then Yes to confirm.**

   QuickBooks asks if you want to merge the two. So much easier than finding a soulmate, simply click Yes to combine the two individuals as one.

Pricing to Sell

It's time to price your goods. Whether you're setting a market price, standard price, retail price, wholesale price, flat charge or some other exotic beast, the time has come to do the deed. So, in order of complexity, I explain how to price a single item, how to price a few items, then how to price a whole lot of items at once.

Smoke and mirrors

When you view an item in QuickBooks (by double-clicking on any item in your Item List), you see two different costs. The Avg. Cost field appears under Inventory Information and the Cost field appears under Purchase Information (this latter field may display as Gross Cost if the Amounts Include Tax option is clicked).

The Cost field (or Gross Cost field, depending on your tax settings) relates to the supplier cost price you set in QuickBooks. This may or may not be the last cost price you paid (when you enter a purchase order or bill, QuickBooks prompts you to update the cost, but you have the choice to click No in response to this prompt).

The Avg. Cost field relates to average cost. QuickBooks calculates average cost by dividing the total dollar value for an item by the quantity on hand, which fortunately for you and me, is the correct stock valuation method according to antipodean accounting standards. Average cost never includes GST, regardless of whether the Amts Inc Tax option is selected or not, whereas the Cost field changes when you select this option.

Be careful if referring to either of these costs when setting your prices. Remember that QuickBooks doesn't reflect any additional on-costs in either of these cost prices, such as freight, shipping fees or customs duty.

Pricing one item at a time

Want to change the price on something? Double-click the item in your Item List and change the Sales Price. Blindingly easy or what?

Pricing a few items at a time

To update prices on a few items at once, go to Customers⇨Change Item Prices. Choose the Item Type of whatever you're adjusting (for example, Service, Inventory Part or Inventory Assembly). Scroll down to find the items you want to change and fix up the price in the New Price column. You can also get QuickBooks to calculate new item prices by selecting certain items, requesting a percentage or dollar amount change and then clicking the Adjust button (see Figure 8-8).

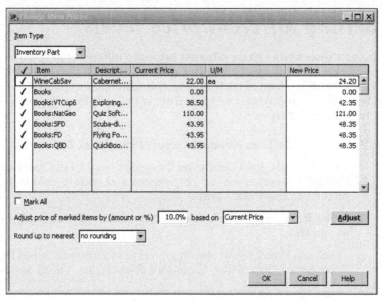

Figure 8-8:
Adjusting
pricing, a
few items at
a time.

Pricing for the perfect fit

I have a client who manufactures furniture. He sells some furniture at retail prices from his shopfront, some at wholesale prices and some at bulk prices.

My client has two price levels in QuickBooks: Wholesale and Bulk. His Item List uses retail prices as the Sales Price, and QuickBooks defaults to this price for all regular sales.

Wholesale customers are set at the Wholesale price level, which deducts 30 per cent from retail prices. A select few customers are set

at the Bulk price level, which details special prices for each item.

Occasionally, my client makes a deal with someone, say offering an additional discount for an order over $10,000. He invoices this customer using the Wholesale price level as normal, but at the bottom of the invoice he inserts a subtotal followed by an item called Discount that deducts the promised percentage from the subtotal.

Setting different price levels

Do you sometimes charge different prices to different folk? Maybe you have one price for retail customers, one price for staff and another price for ex-lovers. In the face of such variety, QuickBooks is nothing if not versatile. (*Note:* The multiple price levels feature is only available in QuickBooks Premier and Enterprise.)

1. **Head for the Lists menu and select Price Level List.**

   If Price Levels don't appear on this menu, skip to the Sales and Customers section in your Preferences and click to enable the preference Use Price Levels.

2. **In the Price Level window, click New and create as many price levels as you like.**

   Check out Figure 8-9 to view my pricing system, which has five levels: Outrageously Expensive, Expensive, Reasonable, Cheap and It Must Be Love (just kidding).

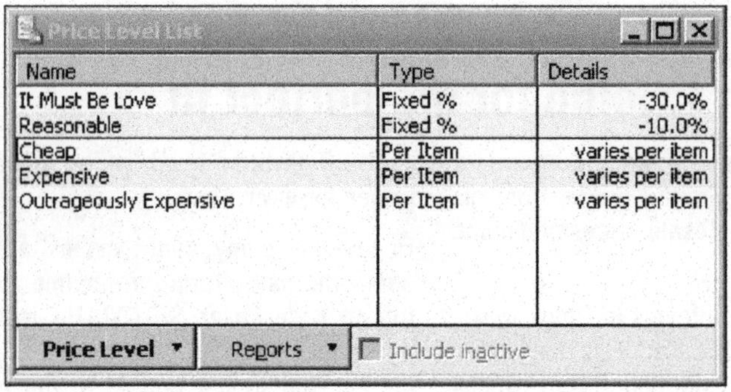

Figure 8-9:
Setting
different
price levels.

Name	Type	Details
It Must Be Love	Fixed %	-30.0%
Reasonable	Fixed %	-10.0%
Cheap	Per Item	varies per item
Expensive	Per Item	varies per item
Outrageously Expensive	Per Item	varies per item

Price Level ▾   Reports ▾   ☐ Include inactive

3. **For each price level, decide whether you want this price level to be a fixed percentage or a specified price per item.**

   If you choose fixed percentage, you can increase or decrease prices on all items by any percentage you specify. If you choose per item, you can set a different price for each item at each price level.

4. **To allocate a price level to each customer, click the Additional Info tab for each customer in your Customer List and select the relevant level.**

   Most people work this way. Remember though, if you're just going to charge the standard Sales Price for a customer, you don't need to set them up with a price level.

5. **To allocate a price level to different items on a particular invoice, first add this item to the customer's invoice. Then click the drop list next to the Price of this item and select the price level.**

This method means that you're able to select a different price level for each line of the invoice, depending on what items you're selling.

Digging Yourself Out of a Hole

Put together, computers and humans open up endless possibilities for disaster. It's hardly surprising that inventory costs and counts often go completely troppo, requiring a firm hand and serious inventory adjustments.

Adjusting the quantity of an item

What do you do if you know you have three stuffed bears on the shelf but your Item List says you have four? Or, perhaps you can see that you've completely sold out of lemonade but your Item List says you have 50 crates left? Follow these steps:

1. **Go to Adjust Quantity on Hand.**

   You find this command in the Company area on your home page.

2. **Pause and consider the Adjustment Date, changing it if necessary to reflect when the cause of the difference took place.**

   For example, if you know that the difference was due to a bunch of samples that left the warehouse last week, then enter last week's date as the Adjustment Date.

3. **Select an Adjustment Account, such as Inventory Adjustments or Cost of Sales.**

   You best bet is to choose your cost of sales account that this item normally goes to. Alternatively, if you have a particular reason why you're adjusting inventory, and you have a specific account to cater for this, select that account as the Adjustment Account. (In Figure 8-10, I select Promotional Expense as my Adjustment Account because the difference was due to giving away samples.)

   Never select your Inventory Asset account as the Adjustment Account, because this throws your inventory out of balance.

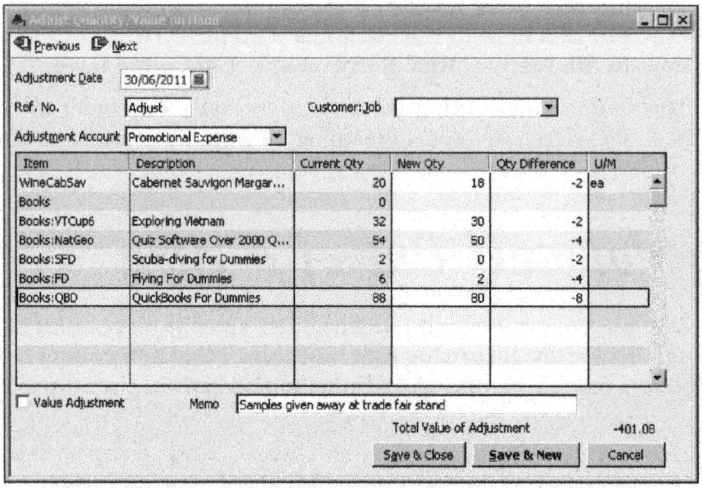

Figure 8-10:
Adjusting
item
quantities is
easy.

4. **Scroll down to the item that you want to adjust and enter the correct count in the New Qty column.**

    When you enter a figure in the New Qty column, QuickBooks automatically calculates the difference in the Qty Difference column. Alternatively, you can enter the difference in the Qty Difference column and watch as QuickBooks calculates the New Qty.

5. **Type a brief note in the Memo field to describe why this adjustment is taking place.**

6. **Click Save & Close to record your adjustment.**

Adjusting the cost of an item

Occasionally, it isn't the quantity of an item that goes awry, but the unit cost. One way to fix unit costs is to generate a QuickReport for this item and double-check the cost price on every purchase for that item. Hopefully, you can spot the mistake and apply first-aid.

A more practical approach — especially if you have a long list of purchases — is simply to fix the average cost so that it's correct. To do this, follow the same procedure as for adjusting the quantity of an item — which I explain in the preceding section — but this time click the little box in the bottom-left corner that says Value Adjustment.

Multiply the quantity of items you have on hand by the correct unit cost, then enter this figure in the New Value column (for example, if I know a coffee table costs $300 and I have four of them in stock, then I enter $1,200 as the New Value). Leave the quantity untouched. Click Save & Close to record your adjustment and then hop straight to your Item List, double-clicking to see the item in question and check that the Avg. Cost is now correct.

Troubleshooting transactions

To view all transactions relating to a particular item, go to your Item List and select QuickReport from the Reports menu (as shown in Figure 8-11). You can then double-click on any transaction to view it in all its glory.

Figure 8-11: QuickReport displays all transactions relating to a particular item.

Standing Up and Counting Down

I've done oodles of stocktakes over the years. The one I remember best was years ago in a huge warehouse when the stocktake took about ten hours, with eight staff counting all day. Then the manager and I stayed up till 2 am, typing the counts into the computer one by one.

Things seemed fine until two days later when the computer crashed. Stay calm, I declared, we can restore the information from our backup. This we did, except that our most recent backup was done the day before the stocktake. Never mind, I said, we'll just type in the stock counts from the stocktake sheets one more time.

This is where we hit trouble. We looked high and low, far and wide, but the stocktake sheets had disappeared forever — through the shredder, I suspect. And so we did the stocktake all over again. What a way to spend a weekend!

Getting ready for the countdown

Before you start your stocktake, make your way to the Inventory section in your Reports menu and print a Stock Take Worksheet report. Use this worksheet to complete your stocktake. As you go, keep an eye open for any item counts that look odd, or where they're significantly different from what you should have — you can see how much you should have by referring to the On Hand column.

Avoid complete bamboozlement by making sure that no stock leaves and no stock arrives until the count is complete.

Doing the grand reckoning

On the face of it, entering stock counts is pretty simple. Go to Adjust Quantity on Hand (found on your home page in the Company area), enter the counts from the stock worksheet in the New Qty column, then click Save & Close to record your adjustment.

Here are a few pointers to ensure your stocktake goes swimmingly:

- ✔ Don't enter any item sales or item purchases until you've completed your stocktake, entered the count and checked your work.

- ✔ Only enter counts for 10 or 20 items at a time. It's easier to see what you're doing this way, and if you (or your computer) does something silly, you won't lose too much work.

- ✔ As the Adjustment Account, pick whatever cost of sales account the items you're adjusting normally go to.

✔ Alternatively, to see the dollar effect of stocktakes separately in your Profit & Loss report (perhaps you do stocktakes every month and you want to see if counts are always under and by how much), create a new cost of sales account called Stocktake Adjustments. Select this as the Adjustment Account.

✔ Never, ever, ever select your Inventory Asset account as the Adjustment Account. If you do, you'll throw everything out of balance and make your accountant catatonic.

✔ Get the date right. If you do a stocktake on 30 June, date the adjusting transaction 30 June. (Even if you enter the stock counts a week later, you must use the earlier date, otherwise nothing makes sense in your financial reports.)

✔ When you're done, print an Inventory Valuation Summary report and compare final counts with your stock count worksheets. Check everything matches up.

Balancing Your Inventory Account

In the perfect world, the total cost value of items in your Item List needs to balance with the value of your Inventory Asset account in your Balance Sheet. For example, if you only had two items in stock — a marble fountain that cost $700 and a concrete fountain that cost $300 — then the value of your Inventory Asset account should be $1,000.

Of course, the world is not always perfect, and nor are you probably, and so every now and then you need to take the test:

1. **On your Reports menu, go to the Inventory section, select the Inventory Valuation Summary report and then click Print.**

   Before you print, ensure you select the current date as the date for this report.

2. **On your Reports menu, go to the Company & Financial section, select the Balance Sheet report, and then click Print.**

   Ensure your Balance Sheet has the same date as the Inventory Valuation Summary report.

3. **Compare the value of inventory on your Balance Sheet against the final total of the Asset Value column in your Inventory Valuation Summary report.**

   The two amounts should equal one another. If they don't, read on.

4. **If the values on the two reports don't match, go back month by month until you find the point when the two values last matched.**

   Go back to the first day of the month just gone and compare the Inventory Valuation Summary report with your Balance Sheet as of that date. If the values still didn't match then, keep going back one month at a time until you find the point that the two reports *did* match.

5. **Now work forwards, narrowing down the date range, and identify the date when the discrepancy first arose.**

   For example, if inventory balanced on 1 Aug but didn't on 1 Sept, run the two reports for 5 Aug, 10 Aug, 15 Aug and so on, and using a process of elimination, identify the date when the discrepancy first arose.

6. **Zoom in on the culprit transaction and fix it.**

   The most likely cause of the problem is that you allocated an inventory adjustment or transaction to your Inventory Asset account. Assuming this is the case, all you have to do is change the adjustment account to something more sensible. Refer to 'Digging Yourself Out of a Hole' earlier in this chapter for more details.

Chapter 9

Setting Up Opening Balances

In This Chapter

▶ Setting up opening balances for customers

▶ Doing the same thing for your suppliers

▶ Making sure inventory opening balances are okay

▶ Sorting out account opening balances

*I*n this chapter, I explain how to record opening balances for customers, suppliers and inventory. I also explain how to set up opening balances for all your asset, liability and equity accounts. Some of these activities may seem a little daunting if you don't have bookkeeping experience, but never fear; I walk you through each stage, step by step.

You may be wondering why a chapter about opening balances is tucked away deep in the heart of this fine tome, rather than being given pride of place as Chapter 1. The reason is this: If you start QuickBooks on 1 July, as most businesses do, you probably won't finalise your accounts for the previous year until much later. You almost certainly have to wait several months until your accountant provides you with all the opening balances you need for QuickBooks. In the meantime, you need to get on with entering transactions in QuickBooks, and become accustomed to how everything works.

By the way, you only need to read this chapter if your business was already up and running before you started using QuickBooks. If your business is new and you're using QuickBooks right from the word 'go', then you don't have any opening balances to carry forward. You can happily ignore this entire chapter.

Customer Opening Balances

In the first part of this chapter, the aim of the game is to tell QuickBooks about all the customers who owed you money at the point you started using QuickBooks, which for most businesses will be the first day of the current financial year. By entering opening balances you stay on top of who owes you money, and just how much, from that point on.

As you read through this chapter you may wonder why I suggest recording historical transactions for each customer, rather than simply whacking in an opening balance against each customer's name (QuickBooks displays an opening balance field every time you create a new customer). I prefer historical transactions for two reasons: First, *historical transactions* are the only way to record GST accurately, something that's vital for most Australian businesses; second, historical transactions provide an accurate and logical record of your opening balances, making it easier for you or your accountant to debug things later on if questions arise.

Creating an item for historical data

In order to create a historical sales transaction for invoices that were outstanding when you started using QuickBooks, you first need to create a new item in your Item List. Here's how:

1. **Select Item List from the Lists menu.**

2. **Select New from the Item menu at the bottom.**

3. **As the item Type, select Service.**

4. **As the Item Name, type Historical Balance.**

5. **As the Tax Code, select GST, and as the Account select Opening Balance Equity.**

6. **Leave all other details blank, then click OK.**

Recording historical transactions

Start by getting together a list of all customers who owed you money as of your start date. For example, if your start date for QuickBooks is 1 July 2011, make a list of which customers owed you money, and how much, on 30 June 2011. Make sure this list includes invoice numbers, invoice amounts and total GST for each invoice. Then, with this list in your sticky hand, go to the Create Invoices window in QuickBooks to record the details of the first invoice in your list.

Date each entry with the original date of the sale, stick the invoice number in the Invoice No field and write a comment such as 'Opening customer balance' in the Memo field. As the Item, select Historical Balance, then enter the total value of the outstanding invoice in the Price column.

If the invoice was for a mix of taxable and non-taxable goods, split the invoice over two lines as I show in Figure 9-1, but use FRE as the tax code on the second line. Check that the right amount of GST comes up in Total Tax at the bottom of each invoice. Getting tax totals accurate is important, especially if you report GST on a cash basis.

Repeat this over and over again until all outstanding amounts are recorded.

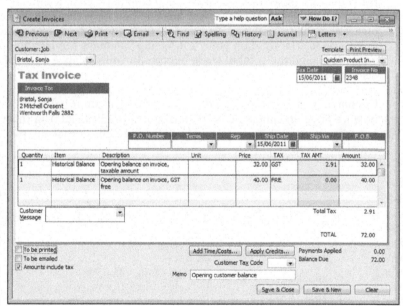

Figure 9-1: Entering a historical sale for amounts owing.

Checking your totals

After you enter all historical sales from your list, go to the Customers &
Receivables section of your Reports menu and generate an A/R Ageing
Summary report, as shown in Figure 9-2. As the Date, enter the last day
of the previous financial year (assuming you started using QuickBooks
on the first day of the financial year). For example, if your start date for
QuickBooks is 1 July 2011, generate a report for 30 June 2011. Check that
the grand total on this report matches the total that you had on the list you
were working from when entering historical transactions.

If the two totals don't match, stay cool. Compare your A/R Ageing Summary
report with your original list of outstanding invoices, line by line, and play
spot the difference. You should be able to get to the bottom of the problem.

Your A/R Ageing Summary report total should also match the total of
trade debtors (sometimes also called accounts receivable) in your opening
account balances. In other words, imagine you have three customers who
owe you money: Customer A owes $50, Customer B owes $80 and Customer
C owes $130. The total on your A/R Ageing Summary report should
equal $260, and the total of trade debtors in your Balance Sheet should
also be $260.

Of course, you may not have entered opening account balances yet for your
Balance Sheet in QuickBooks (I talk about this a little later in this chapter),
but when you reach this stage, you do need to check that the two amounts
equal one another.

Figure 9-2:
Generating
an A/R
Ageing
Summary
report to
double-
check
opening
customer
balances.

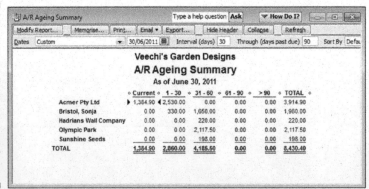

Entering opening balances on the fly

Whenever you create a new customer or supplier in QuickBooks, you have the choice of entering an opening balance at the same time. However, if you enter balances in this way, QuickBooks doesn't have a record of the date of the opening balance, which invoices or bills were owing or how much GST was outstanding. This lack of information can create a great deal of confusion from an accounting

perspective, and potentially means that you miss out on either declaring or claiming GST.

The most accurate way to enter opening balances is to use the procedure I outline in this chapter, creating either historical sales or historical bills, then recording dates, amounts, invoice numbers and tax totals.

Supplier Opening Balances

Similar to setting up customer opening balances, the idea of setting up supplier opening balances is that you have a record of how much you owe your suppliers, right from the start of the new financial year. However, one proviso here: If you want to keep things really simple, you don't actually need to enter supplier opening balances at all. You may decide to record all supplier transactions using the Write Cheques feature in QuickBooks, rather than using Enter Bills followed by Pay Bills. Chapter 6 talks more about this decision.

If you decide that you do want to set up supplier opening balances, apply the same principles you used when you set up customer opening balances. The only difference is that you record historical purchases using Enter Bills, rather than Create Invoices. You can still use the same Historical Balance item that you used when setting up customer opening balances. For example, in Figure 9-3, I record a bill that I still owed to a supplier on the day I started using QuickBooks.

Similar to dealing with customers, after you enter all historical bills from your list, go to the Suppliers & Payables section of your Reports menu and generate an A/P Ageing Summary report. As the Date, enter the last day of your previous financial year. Now, ensure that the grand total on this report matches the total that you had on the list that you were working from when telling QuickBooks how much you owed to suppliers.

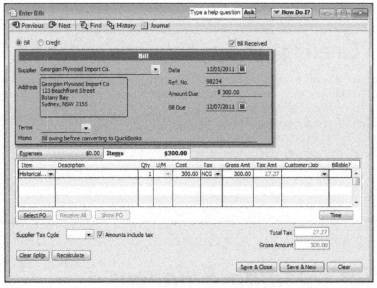

Figure 9-3:
Entering a
historical
bill for each
supplier
you owed
money to
at the date
you started
using
QuickBooks.

As well as getting these reports to match, the total of your A/P Ageing Summary report needs to match the total of trade creditors (sometimes also called accounts payable) in your opening account balances. In other words, imagine you have three suppliers who you owe money to: Supplier A is owed $50, Supplier B is owed $80, and Supplier C is owed $130. The total on your A/P Ageing Summary report should equal $260, and the total of trade creditors in your Balance Sheet should also be $260.

Even though you may not have entered opening account balances yet (I show you how a little later in this chapter), when you do reach this stage, you need to check that the two amounts equal one another.

Inventory Opening Balances

If you buy goods for resale and want to use QuickBooks to keep track of inventory costs and quantities, then you need to set up your Item List, along with opening quantities and costs for each item. The concept here is that the total cost value of items in your Item List should equal the total value of the Inventory Asset account in your Balance Sheet.

Chapter 8 explains in detail how to set up opening quantities and costs for inventory. At this point, you need to check that your inventory balances: See the section 'Ensuring your inventory records tally' in Chapter 8 for more details.

Account Opening Balances

If your accountant has already finalised last year's accounts, ask for your closing Balance Sheet report as at 30 June. This report is the perfect reference for entering your opening balances, and means that you can skip to the section 'Reviewing what you've done so far' a little later in this chapter. However, if you don't have a complete Balance Sheet report for the previous financial year, read on . . .

Entering a few balances to get started

If your accountant *hasn't* finished last year's accounts yet, you can afford to wait a while, setting up opening balances for the bare minimum as follows:

- ✔ **Customers.** Record historical sales for all customers who owed you money on your start date, as explained earlier in this chapter.

- ✔ **Suppliers.** If you want to use QuickBooks to track how much you owe suppliers, record historical purchases for all suppliers that you owed money to on your start date, also explained earlier in this chapter.

- ✔ **Inventory.** If you plan to use QuickBooks to track inventory quantities and costs, set up the value of your opening inventory count, as explained in Chapter 8.

- ✔ **Bank accounts.** In Chapter 7, I explain that you need to reconcile every bank account that you use regularly, and I show you how to set up bank account opening balances.

- ✔ **GST.** When you're ready to enter opening balances for GST, see 'Taxing torture — made easy' next in this chapter.

Taxing torture — made easy

Unless you're just starting out in your business, chances are that on the day you start entering transactions, you already owe some GST to the tax office. For example, if you start entering transactions from 1 July, you almost certainly owe GST for the month of June, if not April, May and June (depending on whether you report monthly or quarterly).

Entering opening balances for GST is tricky, but there's no getting out of it (unless you can find or hire someone else to do it for you). No squirming now . . . here's what to do:

If you report for GST on an accruals basis, here's what to do:

1. **Ensure your customer and supplier opening balances have been entered, complete with all GST amounts for each invoice or bill.**

   You may want to check out 'Customer Opening Balances' or 'Supplier Opening Balances' earlier in this chapter.

2. **Look up the amounts you declared for GST Collected and GST Paid in your most recent Business Activity Statement.**

   Confused? You want to check out boxes 1A and 1B on your Activity Statement.

3. **Print a Balance Sheet for the last day of the reporting period on your most recent Business Activity Statement.**

   For example, if your most recent Business Activity Statement was for the month of June, then print a Balance Sheet dated 30 June. You find this report under Reports in the Company & Financial section.

4. **On your Balance Sheet, look at the balance of your GST Collected and GST Paid accounts, or your GST Payable account.**

   You may have two liability accounts — one called GST Collected and another called GST Paid — or you may have a single GST liability account called GST Payable.

5. **Compare the figures from Step 2 against the figures from Step 4. Calculate the difference between the two.**

   In Figure 9-4 you can see a spreadsheet where I show how to calculate this difference.

	A	B	C
1		**GST Opening Balances, Accruals Basis, Separate GST accounts**	
2			
3		GST Collected	
4		GST Collected shown on Business Activity Statement as at June 30	$2,805.00
5		Balance of GST Collected as per QuickBooks Balance Sheet as at June 30, after entering opening customer balances	$2,700.00
6		*Adjusting Journal for GST Collected on Sales in QuickBooks should be*	$ 105.00
7			
8		GST Paid	
9		GST Paid shown on Business Activity Statement as at June 30	$2,600.00
10		Balance of GST Paid as per QuickBooks Balance Sheet as at June 30, after entering opening supplier balances	$1,900.00
11		*Adjusting Journal for GST Paid on Purchases in QuickBooks should be*	$ 700.00
12			
13		**GST Opening Balances, Accruals Basis, Combined GST account**	
14			
15		Adjusting Journal for GST Collected should be	$ 105.00
16		Adjusting Journal for GST Paid on Purchases should be	$ 700.00
17		*Adjusting Journal required to GST Payable in QuickBooks should be*	-$ 595.00
18			

Figure 9-4: Calculating opening balances for GST.

6. **Go to Make General Journal Entries from the Company menu and record a journal that adjusts your GST liability account or accounts. To make this journal balance, allocate the other side of the journal to Opening Balance Equity.**

I show how this is done in Figure 9-5. In my example, I'm adjusting a single combined liability account. However, if you have two separate liability accounts for GST, then you need to adjust each one.

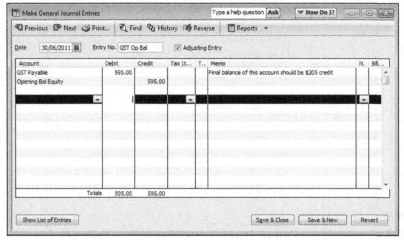

Figure 9-5:
Adjusting opening balances for GST.

The explanation I provide in this chapter for setting up opening balances for GST is based on a business that reports for GST on an accruals basis. Things get a little more complicated if you report for GST on a cash basis, and in this situation I recommend you ask your accountant for help in setting up your opening balances for GST. Alternatively, if you want to dig a little deeper in understanding how GST accounts work, check out *Bookkeeping For Dummies,* published by Wiley Publishing Australia and written by yours truly.

Reviewing what you've done so far

At this point, I'm assuming that you've already set up customer opening balances, supplier opening balances (optional) and inventory opening balances (also optional, and only applies if you buy goods for resale). Depending on how keen and bean-counterish you are, maybe you've also entered opening balances for GST as well. And depending on how you answered the prompts in the QuickBooks setup interview (refer to Chapter 1), you may have an opening balance for your bank account. The next step is to review what you've done so far and fill in the missing blanks.

On your Reports menu, go to the Company & Financial section and display a Balance Sheet for the last day of the previous financial year. For example, if your start date for QuickBooks is 1 July 2011, ask for a Balance Sheet dated 30 June 2011. Figure 9-6 shows an example barebones report.

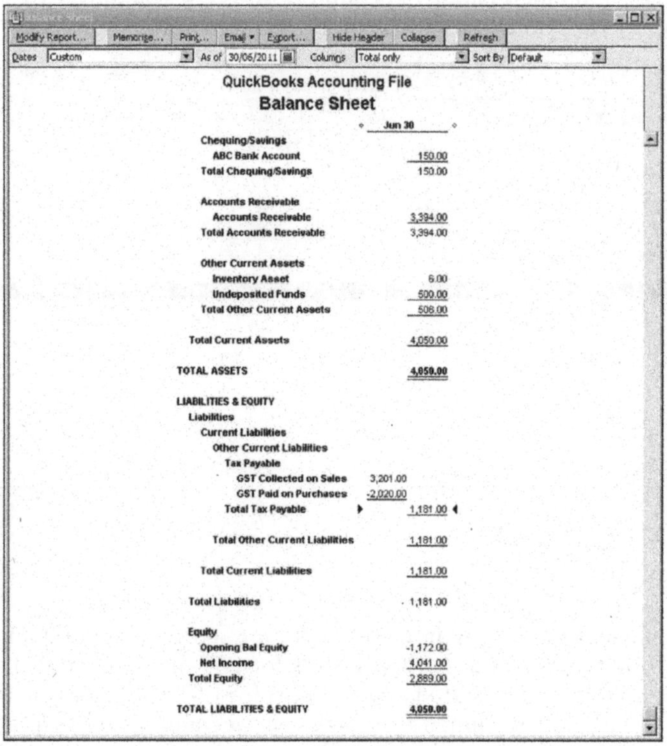

Figure 9-6: A Balance Sheet report showing a few opening balances.

Recording the remaining opening balances

After you enter your basic opening balances, your next job is to record the totals for the remaining accounts as a single journal entry, dated as the last day of the previous year. The goal here is to end up with a Balance Sheet in QuickBooks that matches, cent for cent, the Balance Sheet that your accountant created after finalising the previous year's accounts. (*Note:* If you prefer, you can also record these opening balances one by one by editing each account in your Accounts List and clicking the Enter Opening Balance button.)

When entering opening balances, remember that you don't have to worry about historical Profit & Loss figures for the previous year. Profit & Loss reports start from scratch at the beginning of every year, so historical figures are irrelevant. You only need to worry about setting up opening balances for asset, liability and equity accounts, which are all the accounts that appear on your Balance Sheet.

To record a general journal, go to your Company menu and select Make General Journal Entries. On each line, select the account that you want to enter an opening balance for, as I do in Figure 9-7. When you're done, click Save & Close and regenerate a Balance Sheet for the last day of the previous year, checking that all opening balances are now correct.

Here are some tips to help you with this journal:

✔ Enter all assets in the Debit column, and all liabilities in the Credit column. The exception to this rule is if the balance of an asset or liability shows as a minus on the Balance Sheet, in which case you enter the asset or the liability the other way around. For example, accumulated depreciation always shows on your Balance Sheet as a minus amount, so you need to enter this figure in the Credit column.

✔ If you want to include an additional explanation on an opening balance, you can, in the same way as I do in Figure 9-7.

✔ Ignore the Tax Item and Tax Amount columns completely. There should be no GST in this transaction.

✔ When you get to the bottom, your debits won't equal your credits. Figure out the difference between these two and allocate that difference to Opening Balance Equity. That way you'll be able to record the journal (QuickBooks doesn't let you record a general journal unless it balances).

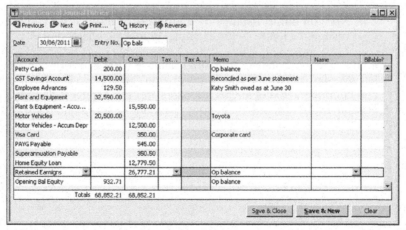

Figure 9-7:
Creating
a journal
for your
remaining
opening
balances.

✔ Earlier in this chapter, I explain in the section 'Taxing torture — made easy' how to calculate opening balances for GST. If your accountant's final balance sheet has different figures for GST from what you calculated, ask your accountant to explain why this is, and whether you need to make any further adjustments.

Troubleshooting opening balances

One of the satisfying things about accounting work is that everything has to balance. And, when it balances, you know you've got it right.

In the same way that your accountant's final Balance Sheet for the previous year balances — in other words, Total Assets on the Balance Sheet were equal to Total Liabilities plus Total Equity — so too should your opening Balance Sheet in QuickBooks balance. The two Balance Sheets should match each other, line for line, and the balance of your Opening Balance Equity account in QuickBooks should return to zero. (To print your QuickBooks Balance Sheet, go to the Company & Financial section on your Reports menu.)

If you're finding this state of nirvana hard to achieve, then check the following:

✔ **Are your minus figures minus?** Anything appearing as a negative amount on your accountant's closing Balance Sheet should appear in QuickBooks as negative amounts too. If they aren't, then you've got your debits and credits muddled in your opening balance journal entry.

✔ **Are you missing any accounts?** Count the number of accounts on your accountant's Balance Sheet and then count the accounts listed on your QuickBooks Balance Sheet.

✔ **Are you out of balance by a multiple of nine?** If so, you have probably reversed a figure — for example, typing $43 instead of $34.

If your opening balances still don't balance (that is, there's an amount left over in Opening Balance Equity), don't worry too much. You can still continue working in QuickBooks. Later on, I suggest you ask your accountant to have a look at your QuickBooks setup, and help you get to the bottom of the problem.

The Mystery of your Opening Balance Equity Account

Whenever you create a new company file, QuickBooks automatically creates two equity accounts: Opening Balance Equity and Retained Earnings.

Your Opening Balance Equity account acts like a holding account for setting up new balances, or storing out-of-balance amounts.

For example, if you record opening balances for bank accounts or if you use the opening balance feature for customers and suppliers (an activity that I warn against, incidentally), QuickBooks dumps the other side of this transaction into your Opening Balance Equity Account. Similarly, if you force a bank account to reconcile (another nefarious activity that's best avoided), then once more, the other side

of this transaction ends up in Opening Balance Equity.

In a healthy file where all the opening balances have been set up correctly, the balance of Opening Balance Equity should always be $0.00. If your Opening Balance Equity account doesn't have a zero balance, then you can be sure that either your opening balances are incomplete, or you've made a mistake somewhere.

Incidentally, the other equity account — the one called Retained Earnings — is a special balancing account that keeps a running tally of the net profit or loss that you make each year.

Chapter 10

Understanding GST

In This Chapter

▶ Getting your head around tax items and tax codes (and how they hang together)

▶ Persuading QuickBooks to second-guess tax codes

▶ Getting a grip on how QuickBooks handles Business Activity Statements

▶ Configuring your Business Activity Statement

▶ Finalising your BAS — printing the form in less than 10 seconds (well, maybe)

▶ Uploading your BAS to the tax office with GovConnect

▶ Recording your BAS payment

*F*or one brief moment, put yourself in my shoes. Here I am, a warm-blooded, relatively normal member of the human race (although my family may disagree with the 'normal' part), writing books about accounting software. Sounds tough? It certainly has its moments.

Now picture my situation in a little more detail. Late at night, James Taylor is crooning away in the background, and I'm trying to come up with a chirpy, Dummies-kind-of-style introduction to this chapter about working with GST in QuickBooks. Is it possible to make GST sound fun? And if I did, what sensible Aussie would ever believe me?

No more ramblings (after all, it is late). I'm going to ditch this whole cheerful introductory business and leap in.

It's Elemental, my dear Watson

A few definitions about GST to pave the way:

- ✔ **Taxable supplies:** Taxable supplies are any goods or services that attract GST. Examples include computers, consultancy fees, electrical goods and clothes.

- **GST-free supplies:** GST-free supplies are goods or services that are GST-free. Examples include fresh food, many medical services and products, many educational courses, childcare, exports and a range of religious supplies.

- **Input-taxed supplies:** Input-taxed supplies are supplies that don't have GST added to the final selling price. Examples include bank charges and residential rents. If your business sells an input-taxed supply (maybe you're a landlord of residential property), then you can't claim input tax credits for related expenses.

Preparing QuickBooks for GST

Like the perfect beef bourguignon (no prizes for spotting the influence of *MasterChef* here), the art of managing GST using QuickBooks lies in the preparation. So grab a wooden spoon, don your apron and get cooking . . .

Step 1: Customise your accounts for GST

By default, QuickBooks comes with only one account for tracking tax, called Tax Payable. However, one of the neat things about the latest versions of QuickBooks is the way you can create subaccounts to track GST Collected and GST Paid separately. I love working in this way, because the separate accounts make troubleshooting much easier.

Unfortunately, the moment you record your first transaction in QuickBooks, the default tax settings are locked in. In other words, if you've already been working in QuickBooks and you've only just arrived at this chapter, you're already too late to set up subaccounts for tracking GST. Never mind. You can skip this step and instead, jump ahead to 'Step 2: Tell the ATO where to go' later in this chapter.

So, with this preamble in mind, here's how to set up subaccounts for tracking GST:

1. **From the Account button in your Chart of Accounts, click New.**

   QuickBooks opens a window displaying a list of account types.

2. **As the Account Type, select Other Account Types, followed by Other Current Liability.**

3. **As the Account Name, type GST Collected on Sales, and as the Subaccount Of, select your Tax Payable account.**

   You can ignore the other guff in this window, such as the Description and Account No. fields.

4. **Click Save & New, then create another account called GST Paid on Purchases. Make this account a Subaccount of Tax Payable as well.**

5. **Click Save & Close.**

   When you click Save & Close, you return to your Chart of Accounts. Now, the GST accounts within the liability section of your Chart of Accounts should look similar to Figure 10-1.

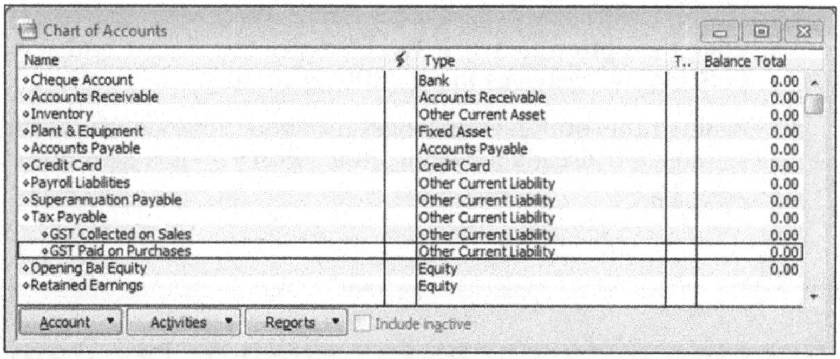

Figure 10-1:
Setting up separate GST Collected and GST Paid accounts.

Step 2: Tell the ATO where to go

By default, QuickBooks always creates a supplier called Australian Taxation Office. This is fabulous, but you have a little more tweaking to do:

1. **Select Australian Taxation Office from your Supplier List, then click the Tax Agency Info tab.**

2. **If you haven't done so already, enter your ABN as the Tax Rego ID.**

3. **As the Reporting Period, select Monthly or Quarterly.**

   Which option you choose here depends on how often you lodge Business Activity Statements.

4. **If possible, click the option to Track Tax On Purchases Separately and select GST Paid on Purchases as the liability account.**

   Hopefully, you've already created an account called GST Paid on Purchases (see 'Step 1: Customise your accounts for GST' earlier in this chapter.)

   Unfortunately, you may find that this option is no longer available: As soon as you record your first transaction in QuickBooks, the default tax settings are locked in. Unless you tweak your tax settings *before* recording your first transaction, you end up with the QuickBooks' default, meaning that both GST Paid and GST Collected are combined in a single Tax Payable account. To my mind this way of working isn't ideal, but on the other hand you need to be pragmatic: It's certainly not worth starting QuickBooks again from scratch in order to change this setting.

5. **Click the option to Track Tax On Sales Separately and select GST Collected on Sales as the liability account.**

   Again, if this option is no longer available to you because the default settings are already locked in, don't worry — just skip this step.

6. **Click OK.**

Spot the difference: Tax code or tax item?

In the latest versions of QuickBooks, every transaction requires a *tax code*. This tax code indicates whether the transaction is GST-free, input-taxed or taxable, and whether or not it's a capital acquisition. Each of these tax codes hooks back to *tax items*. Tax items also indicate whether a transaction is GST-free, input-taxed or taxable, but the difference with tax items is that for each one, you have to specify whether this item is used for sales or purchase transactions.

For example, you almost certainly already have a tax code called FRE. In the latest version of QuickBooks, you can use this tax code both for sales that are GST-free, and for purchases that are GST-free. Behind the scenes, this tax code hooks back to two separate tax items: FRE and NCF. The FRE tax item relates to sales that are GST-free and the NCF item relates to purchases that are GST-free.

Tax items come into their own when it's time to produce your BAS (Business Activity Statement), because it's on this statement that you need to differentiate between sales and purchase transactions. Tax items hook back to each box on the BAS, producing a statement that not only makes perfect sense, but is accurate to boot.

If you find this rather academic distinction between tax codes and tax items a tad confusing, don't sweat: 99 per cent of the time you only have to worry about tax codes. The only occasions you have to worry about tax items is early on when you first set up QuickBooks and then later, when you produce your first Business Activity Statement.

Step 3: Set up your Tax Item List

The next step is configuring GST in QuickBooks is to review your Tax Item List. To do this, go to Lists and select Tax Item List.

The standard Tax Item List in QuickBooks includes a motser of pretty obscure taxes (how many businesses do you know that calculate wine equalisation tax or combined cellar door tax?). With this in mind, one of your first tasks is to give this list a good old spring-clean. Most businesses can chop this list down from a whopping 18 different tax items to a relatively modest — and much easier to follow — five.

In Figure 10-2, I show the five items that make up my suggested Tax Item List. Each of these items already exists in the default Tax Item List that comes with QuickBooks, but it's worth double-clicking on each one in turn, and then checking these three points: First, that the Australian Taxation Office is the Tax Agency; second, that the Tax Rate is correct; and third, that the tax item is linked correctly to either sales or purchases.

Figure 10-2:
Culling the
Tax Item
List — most
businesses
need only
five tax
items.

Name	Description	Type	Account
CAG	Cap. Acq. - Inc GST	Tax Item	Tax Payable:GST Paid on Purchases
GST	10% GST	Tax Item	Tax Payable:GST Collected on Sales
INP	Input Taxed Sales	Tax Item	Tax Payable:GST Collected on Sales
NCF	Non-Cap. Acq. - GST Free	Tax Item	Tax Payable:GST Paid on Purchases
NCG	Non-Cap. Acq. - Inc GST	Tax Item	Tax Payable:GST Paid on Purchases

Item ▾   Activities ▾   Excel ▾   ☐ Include inactive

Here's a wee explanation on the five suggested tax items:

- ✔ **CAG.** This tax item stands for *capital acquisitions*, meaning capital purchases such as new equipment, new motor vehicles and so on. Check that the Tax Rate is 10 per cent and that the option to Use This Item In Purchase Transactions is selected.

- ✔ **GST.** This tax item relates to GST on sales. If your business charges GST on anything that it sells, then you need this code. Check that the Tax Rate is 10 per cent and that the option to Use This Item In Sales Transactions is selected.

- ✔ **INP.** This tax item relates to all input-taxed sales, such as interest or residential rental income. Check that the Tax Rate is 0 per cent and that the option to Use This Item In Purchase Transactions is selected.

✔ **NCF.** This tax item relates to all purchases that are GST-free, such as bank fees, interest expense, coffee and tea and medical supplies. Check that the Tax Rate is 0 per cent and that the option to Use This Item In Purchase Transactions is selected.

✔ **NCG.** This tax item relates to all purchases that have GST on them, which sadly includes most things. Check that the Tax Rate is 10 per cent and that the option to Use This Item In Purchase Transactions is selected.

After you have these five tax items in place, I suggest you plunge in and delete all the other tax items that QuickBooks includes as standard, but that — in my humble opinion, at any rate — you don't really need. However, before you hit that red-hot Delete button, check that none of the following situations apply to you:

✔ If you make sales that are GST-free (maybe you're a childcare or medical services provider, for example), then don't delete the tax item called FRE (this tax item should have a rate of 0 per cent and be linked to sales transactions).

✔ If you sell stuff overseas, don't delete the tax item called EXP (this item should have a rate of 0 per cent and be linked to sales transactions).

✔ If you have residential real estate properties, don't delete the tax items CAI and NCI, both which should have rates of 0 per cent and be linked to purchase transactions.

✔ If you sell liquor, ask your accountant before deleting the tax items CDG, CDS, WC, WET or WGST.

By the way, to delete a tax item, simply highlight it in the list, then from the Tax Item List select Delete. If QuickBooks tells you that you can't delete these tax item, choose to edit this item instead and make the item inactive.

Step 4: Set up your Tax Code List

If you haven't recorded any transactions in QuickBooks yet, and you're still at the setup stage, then I recommend you keep your setup real simple. However, if you've already recorded transactions in QuickBooks, the default tax settings will be locked in and your options are slightly different. I cover both scenarios below.

New to the game? Creating four tax codes, lean and mean

If you're new to QuickBooks and haven't entered any transactions yet, I recommend an elegant sufficiency of just four tax codes, as featured in Figure 10-3:

- ✔ **CAG.** Use this tax code for capital acquisitions, such as new equipment, furniture and motor vehicles. Ensure this tax code is linked to CAG as the Purchase Tax item, but leave the Sales Tax Item blank (you only ever use the CAG tax code on purchase transactions).

- ✔ **FRE.** My preference, for simplicity's sake, is to use the FRE code for both sales and purchases. I simply link this tax code to NCF as the Purchase Tax item, and FRE as the Sales Tax Item. (If you don't make any sales that are GST-free, you can leave the Sales Tax Item blank.)

- ✔ **GST.** No prizes for guessing — use this tax code for anything that has GST on it, regardless of whether it's a sale or a purchase. The Purchase Tax Item should be NCG and the Sales Tax Item should be GST.

- ✔ **INP.** Use this tax code for any transaction that's input-taxed. For most people, the only regular transaction that falls into this category is interest income, which is always part of a sales transaction. For this reason, you can leave the Purchase Tax Item blank, and select INP as the Sales Tax Item. (However, if you receive income from residential real estate, don't leave the Purchase Tax Item blank. Select NCI instead.)

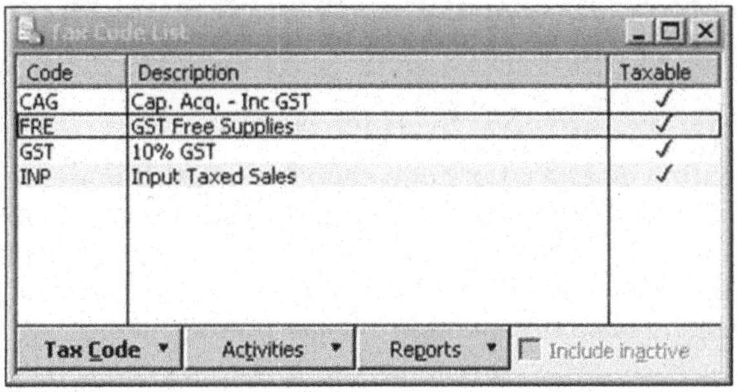

Figure 10-3:
Streamlining your Tax Code List — you may be able to get by with only four tax codes.

Code	Description	Taxable
CAG	Cap. Acq. - Inc GST	✓
FRE	GST Free Supplies	✓
GST	10% GST	✓
INP	Input Taxed Sales	✓

Tax Code ▾   Activities ▾   Reports ▾   ☐ Include inactive

Been around a while? You need a couple more ...

If you've already recorded transactions in QuickBooks, you won't be able to link the NCF tax item to the FRE tax code, nor will you be able to link the NCG tax item to the GST tax code. Instead, you need to run with the following:

- ✔ **CAG.** Use this tax code for capital acquisitions, such as new equipment, furniture and motor vehicles. Ensure this tax code is linked to CAG as the Purchase Tax item, but leave the Sales Tax Item blank (you only ever use the CAG tax code on purchase transactions).

- ✔ **FRE.** You only need this code if you make any sales that are GST-free. Select FRE as the Sales Tax Item and leave the Purchase Tax Item blank.

- ✔ **GST.** This code is for taxable sales. Select GST as the Sales Tax Item and leave the Purchase Tax Item blank.

- ✔ **INP.** Use this tax code for any transaction that's input-taxed. For most people, the only regular transaction that falls into this category is interest income, which is always part of a sales transaction. For this reason, you can leave the Purchase Tax Item blank, and select INP as the Sales Tax Item. (However, if you receive income from residential real estate, don't leave the Purchase Tax Item blank. Select NCI instead.)

- ✔ **NCF.** Use this code for all GST-free purchases. Select NCF as the Purchase Tax Item and leave the Sales Tax Item blank.

- ✔ **NCG.** Use this code for all purchases that attract GST. Select NCG as the Purchases Tax Item and leave the Sales Tax Item blank.

Adding a code for non-taxable transactions

I recommend creating an extra tax code called NR, with the description Not Reportable. The distinction between tax codes that are GST-free (such as the FRE tax code or the NCF tax code) and the NR tax code is that transactions coded FRE or NCF are reported on your Business Activity Statement, whereas transactions coded NR are not.

Figure 10-4 shows how to set up this tax code: Simply type 'NR' as the Tax Code and 'Not Reportable' as the Description. You can leave the Purchase Tax Item and Sales Tax Item blank.

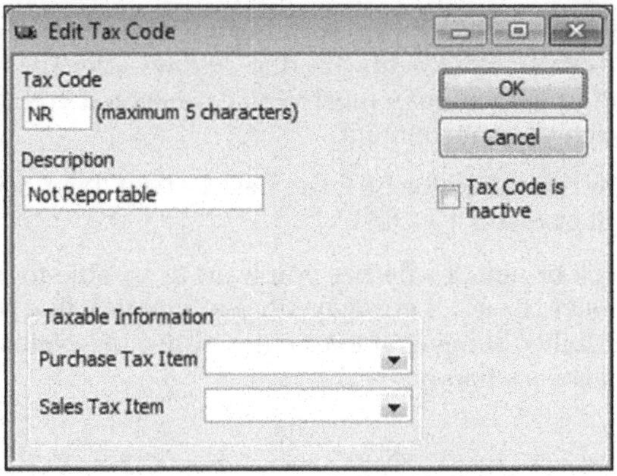

Figure 10-4:
The NR
tax code is
handy for
identifying
transactions
that aren't
reportable
on your
BAS.

Edit Tax Code

Tax Code
NR (maximum 5 characters)

OK

Cancel

Description
Not Reportable

☐ Tax Code is
   inactive

Taxable Information

Purchase Tax Item [▼]

Sales Tax Item [▼]

Deleting the tax codes you can do without

QuickBooks comes with a whole swag of additional tax codes you can probably do without, such as ADJ, CAI, CDC, CDG, WC and more. I suggest you get rid of these extra codes, unless any of the following situations apply:

✔ If you export goods overseas, don't delete the tax code called EXP.

✔ If you have residential real estate investments, don't delete the tax codes CAI and NCI.

✔ If you sell liquor, you may want to retain the tax codes CDC, CDG, CDS, WC, WET or WGST (ask your accountant for details).

Step 5: State your preferences

To get QuickBooks playing along in tune, a little groundwork is in order.

Navigate to Preferences, go to the Tax section and click the Company Preferences tab. Work through the following:

✔ Assuming that you are registered for GST, answer Yes to the question that asks whether you track tax.

✔ Select either Accrual or Cash as your Tax Reporting Basis (if you're not sure which one to choose, either ask your accountant or look at the front page of your most recent Business Activity Statement).

✔ With Sales figures, you're usually best to report them Net (exclusive of GST).

✔ QuickBooks also asks when your return is due. If you report quarterly, your Business Activity Statements are due 28 days after the end of each quarter, although you may receive an extension if you lodge your statement through your accountant.

✔ Assuming you're registered for GST, the best Default Tax Code to choose is — you guessed it — GST.

✔ Finally, either tick or untick whether you want to be able to enter prices Tax Inclusive, or not. I strongly suggest you tick this preference, because the flexibility of being able to enter either tax-exclusive or tax-inclusive prices is very handy.

Step 6: Enter opening balances

I explain how to enter opening balances for GST accounts back in Chapter 9 (refer to the section 'Taxing torture — made easy'). If you don't have time to enter opening balances right now, that's okay, but I do suggest you enter this information in QuickBooks before you do your first Business Activity Statement.

One code for both sales and purchases

In older versions, QuickBooks used tax codes not only to identify the tax status of all transactions, but also to indicate what went where on your Business Activity Statement. The problem with this system was that when it came to producing a Business Activity Statement, QuickBooks had no way of knowing whether a transaction was a sale or a purchase. This meant that you had to use a different tax code for GST on a sale (usually the tax code GST) and on a purchase (usually the tax code NCG).

Sounds okay, but in practice people got confused, and often used the code GST on purchase or expense transactions (meaning that these transactions were reported incorrectly as negative sales on their Business Activity Statements). To put an end to this confusion, the newer versions of QuickBooks take a different approach.

You still require a tax code for every transaction, and this code indicates whether the transaction is GST-free or taxable. Each tax code then hooks back to one *tax item* (notice the word 'tax item' not 'tax code') for sales, and another tax item for purchases.

The outcome — so long as you set up a QuickBooks company file from scratch — is that you can simplify things a whole lot. For example, instead of using GST for taxable sales and NCG for taxable purchases, you can use GST as the tax code on both sales and purchases. (Behind the scenes, this GST *tax code* links to the *tax items* GST and NCG, which link to the correct boxes on your Business Activity Statement.)

Cracking the Code

The secret to producing an accurate Business Activity Statement is to ensure that the tax codes are right on every transaction. Fortunately, this is pretty easy when you know how.

Mapping tax codes in your Chart of Accounts

Every income, cost of sales and expense account in your Chart of Accounts links to a tax code. Take a look: Go to your Chart of Accounts, highlight any income account and select Edit Account from the Edit menu. This Tax Code column comes up every time you select an account on a transaction. For example, if the tax code for your Advertising Expense account is NCG, then every time you allocate a transaction to Advertising Expense, NCG is inserted automatically in the Tax Code field.

If you set up the correct tax code on every income, cost of goods sold and expense account in your Chart of Accounts, as I do in Figure 10-5, you're almost guaranteed to code all transactions correctly, every time. Perfection and nirvana are but moments away. Here's an indication of which codes to use for each account, although I suggest you check all of these settings with your accountant before you begin.

Income accounts

Use GST as the tax code for all income accounts that relate to taxable services or items, and use FRE as the tax code for all income accounts that relate to GST-free services or items. Use INP as the tax code for interest income or income from residential real estate investments.

Cost of goods sold accounts

Unless you have a simplified GST configuration (refer to 'New to the game? Creating four tax codes, lean and mean' earlier in this chapter for more details), use NCG as the tax code for all cost of goods sold accounts that are taxable, and use NCF as the tax code for all services or items that are GST-free.

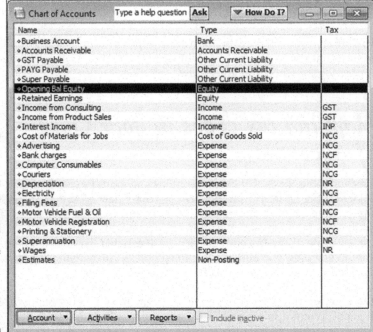

Figure 10-5:
Checking
your Chart
of Accounts
to see
that every
income,
cost of
sales and
expense
account has
a tax code.

Expense accounts

Unless you have a simplified GST configuration (refer to 'New to the game? Creating four tax codes, lean and mean' earlier in this chapter for more details), use the following tax codes as your defaults:

- Use NCG as the tax code for all expense accounts that are taxable. Most regular business purchases are taxable — in other words, they attract GST —including things such as advertising, computer expenses, electricity, office stationery, rent and telephone.

- Use NCF as the tax code for all expense accounts that don't attract GST. Typically, expenses that don't attract GST include bank charges (with the exception of merchant fees), government charges, interest expense, medical supplies, motor vehicle registration, rates and stamp duty.

- Use NR as the tax code for expenses that are non-reportable in the main part of your Business Activity Statement. Usually, superannuation and wages are the only accounts that fall into this category.

You may have expense accounts in your Chart of Accounts that sometimes attract GST, and sometimes don't. Staff Amenities is an expense like this: You don't pay GST on tea and coffee, but you do on biscuits and loo paper. Hire Purchase Expense, Insurance Expense and Subcontractor Expense are additional examples of expenses that don't always attract GST. I suggest you use QUE as the default tax code for these kinds of accounts. This way, whenever you see the tax code QUE appear against a transaction, you'll be prompted to double-check the correct GST treatment with your accountant or supplier. (For more information on setting up and using this code, see 'Coding transactions when you don't have a clue' later in this chapter.)

Keeping everything squeaky-clean

Here's a summary of the most common coding mistakes. And guess what? Because they're so common, these are the mistakes that the ATO watches out for in any audit.

- **Bank fees and merchant fees.** Although merchant fees (for credit cards and hire of EFTPOS machines) have GST on them, regular bank fees don't.

- **Government charges.** Council rates, filing fees, land tax, motor vehicle rego and stamp duty are all GST-free. So don't be tempted to claim back 10 per cent!

- **Insurance.** Insurance is tricky because almost every insurance policy is a mixture of taxable and GST-free components (stamp duty doesn't have GST on it). Don't get caught out. Instead, check the exact amount of GST on every single insurance payment.

- **Overseas travel.** Overseas travel is GST-free.

- **Personal stuff.** You can't claim the full amount of GST on expenses that are partly personal — motor vehicle and home office expenses are the obvious culprits. See 'Getting personal' a little later in this chapter for hints on coding personal transactions.

- **Petty cash.** Another trap for the unwary, petty cash is usually a mixed bag. Coffee and tea are GST-free, postage and sticky tape aren't.

- **Small suppliers.** Watch out for small suppliers who have an ABN, but aren't registered for GST. Record these purchases as GST-free.

Coding transactions when you don't have a clue

When you don't know the right tax code for something, it gets tempting just to pick any old code and ignore the problem. However, you're best to use a special query code called QUE instead. When you use this code you can still record the transaction and continue working on your accounts, but later on, you can review all transactions that have this code, and ask your accountant to help you fix them up.

Here's how to create the QUE tax code:

1. **From the top menu bar, choose Lists⇨Tax Code List.**

2. **From the Edit menu, select New Tax Code.**

3. **Enter QUE as the Tax Code and as the Description enter Don't Know.**

4. **Select NCF as the Purchase Tax Item and FRE as the Sales Tax Item.**

   Relate this code to tax-free items, because it's better to under-claim GST, rather than over-claim. You can always make an adjustment later if this query ends up attracting GST.

5. **Click OK to save your tax code.**

Coding transactions even if they're not reportable

If you started reading this chapter from the beginning, you probably noticed that I recommend creating an extra tax code called NR, with the description Not Reportable. The distinction between tax codes that are GST-free (such as the FRE tax code or the NCF tax code) and the NR tax code is that transactions coded FRE or NCF are reported on your Business Activity Statement, whereas transactions coded NR are not.

Use NR as the tax code for any transactions you allocate to an asset, liability or equity account — such as tax payments, loan settlements, private drawings or transfers between bank accounts. (The only exception to this rule relates to assets: When you purchase new capital items, you need to use the CAG code, as I explain earlier in this chapter.)

Also, if your version of QuickBooks doesn't include payroll, use NR as the tax code for all wages and superannuation payments. (Although you report wages on your Business Activity Statement, they appear separately from other expenses.)

Recording transactions when GST isn't 10 per cent

Let me get one thing straight: GST is *always* 10 per cent. That's the rate set by Australia's wonderful federal government. However, sometimes you come across a transaction where it seems GST *isn't* 10 per cent. When you look closer, you find that the transaction is actually a combination of taxable items (which are 10 per cent) and GST-free items (which are 0 per cent).

An example may help. Say you get an insurance bill for $550 and you enter the payment. QuickBooks calculates the GST to be $50 but when you look at the bill, you notice that GST is actually $49.09. That's because there's $10 stamp duty included in the bill.

Getting QuickBooks to do the right thing

Did you know that you can assign default tax codes to both customers and suppliers? When invoicing a customer or recording a bill from a supplier, this default tax code overrides whatever the tax code is for the item or account. This feature is really handy if you sell to customers or buy from suppliers who are located overseas, or if you buy from suppliers who aren't registered for GST.

For example, in my Chart of Accounts, I have NCG selected as the tax code for Repairs & Maintenance. However, one of my suppliers isn't registered for GST and so I select NCF as the tax code for this supplier. What this means is that when I record a payment to this supplier, even though I allocate the payment to Repairs & Maintenance, QuickBooks knows to select NCF rather than NCG as the tax code.

Another example is when I sell to customers overseas. Even though all the book titles that I sell have GST as the tax code, whenever I create a new overseas customer in QuickBooks, I select EXP as the tax code on the Additional Info tab of the customer's record. Then, whenever I invoice this customer, QuickBooks knows to select EXP (standing for export sales) as the tax code, rather than GST.

The solution is this: Record the insurance bill as normal, but split the transaction over two lines. With the insurance example (assuming you've ticked the Amounts Include Tax button), you'd allocate $540 to Insurance Expense with NCG as the tax code, and then allocate $10 to Insurance Expense with NCF as the tax code. Clear as mud? The illuminating Figure 10-6 shows how this works.

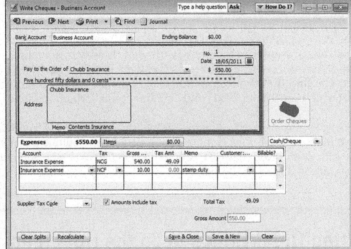

Figure 10-6: Dealing with payments when GST doesn't equal 10 per cent.

Getting personal

If your business purchases goods or services that you use partly for private purposes, then be careful not to claim the GST on the private component.

For example, if you run your car through your business but your log book shows 20 per cent personal use, it works best if you only claim 80 per cent of the GST when recording the transaction. Check out Figure 10-7, which shows that I'm paying for motor vehicle repairs on my Mercedes sports car (ha ha). The total bill comes to $1,000 but I allocate $800 to Motor Vehicle Repairs, then the remaining $200 to Personal Drawings.

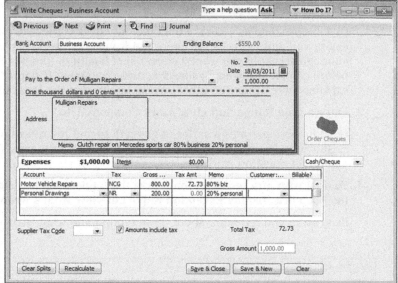

Figure 10-7:
Dealing
with GST
on personal
expenses.

Psyching Up to Produce Your Business Activity Statement

Before plunging into the ugly business of producing your Business Activity Statement (BAS for short) for the Australian Taxation Office, take a few moments to check that everything is sweet.

Making sure the raw data is right

Before cooking up a Business Activity Statement, check that your figures and tax codes are as perfect as a ripe mango in mid-summer. To help you in this quest, QuickBooks comes with its very own auditor, ready to spot every single mistake:

1. **From the Company area of your home page, select Audit Company.**

   Sounds kinda scary, but you're better off auditing your own stuff, rather than some anonymous pale-faced chap from the tax office. The Audit Company File window appears on-screen and on the left-hand side you see four menus: Company File Information, Company File Actions, Account Reconciliation Summary and Data Auditor.

2. **Click the Data Auditor menu.**

   QuickBooks displays a list of ten different checks. The sixth, seventh, eighth and ninth checks are important from a GST perspective, although arguably you want a clean bill of health on the whole deal before completing your Business Activity Statement (Chapter 18 explains more about the other checks involved in the Data Auditor).

3. **Enter a Date Range and click Audit Company File.**

   QuickBooks generates a series of green ticks and red question marks, as shown in Figure 10-8. Your mission is to address the very scary number of question marks.

4. **To deal with any red question marks that appear against an item in the list, click Display Exception Report to view what's wrong.**

   Read on to find out more about these reports and what they mean.

Figure 10-8:
The Data Auditor is an excellent tool for checking your work.

Tax reporting basis different from default reporting basis

The Data Auditor marks an alert if your tax reporting preferences are inconsistent.

The first possible alert is if your Reports & Graphs preferences and your Tax preferences don't match (that is, you select Accrual for one, and Cash for the other). I usually don't worry about this alert. Like many businesses, I report for GST and income tax on a cash basis but prefer to generate financial reports on an accruals basis, because accrual reporting is more accurate from a management perspective.

Cash is king

Lots of people ask me whether they can use accrual accounting for their finances, but cash accounting for GST. The answer is yes, no problem. It's fine to set your Reports preferences to report on an Accrual basis but at the same time set your Tax preferences to report for GST on a Cash basis.

How does this work? Imagine you only had two transactions during a quarter, one being a sale to a customer and other being a bill from a supplier, and that by the end of the quarter,

the customer still hasn't paid, nor have you paid the supplier. On your Profit & Loss report, QuickBooks still shows both the income and the expense (in other words, reporting on an accrual basis). However, your Business Activity Statement comes up blank, because this statement (assuming you've selected to report for GST on a Cash basis) only includes transactions when your customers pay you or you pay your suppliers.

The second alert occurs if you select Net reporting for Sales figures in your Tax preferences, but select Gross reporting for Tax figures in your Reporting preferences. This alert is of concern. Unless your accountant advises you otherwise, reports make most sense on a Net basis, and you're best to select Net reporting in all areas of your preferences.

Sales or purchase tax amount exceptions

This exception report identifies if you (or anyone else) have edited the tax calculations on any transactions (a mistake that's no longer possible to do in the latest versions of QuickBooks). If any transactions recorded prior to upgrading come up with tax amount variances, zoom in and fix 'em up. This may mean splitting the transaction across two lines: One line for the taxable bit and another line for the tax-free bit (to do this, refer to the section 'Recording transactions when GST isn't 10 per cent' earlier in this chapter).

Tax code exceptions

The Tax Code Exception report picks up any transactions in which the default tax code for an account differs from the code on the transaction. For example, if you have NCG as the tax code for Telephone Expense, but you record the payment of a telephone bill with the NCF code, then this transaction is flagged on your Tax Code Exceptions report.

Obviously, just because something appears on a Tax Code Exceptions report that doesn't mean to say you've made a mistake. For example, you may have GST as the tax code for Staff Amenities Expense and most staff amenities really do attract GST. However, every now and then you buy coffee and tea, and these beverages, being defined by the powers-that-be as a *necessity* (how wise for once), are GST-free. The fact that you allocated this purchase to Staff Amenities and it's GST-free doesn't mean you got it wrong.

Alternatively, the problem may be that the tax code for the account is wrong in your Chart of Accounts. To fix this up, go to your Chart of Accounts and edit the offending account.

Running reports, considering the results

Before printing your GST reports and Business Activity Statement, don't forget to reconcile your bank account right up to the last day of the period for which you're reporting. Your accountant is the best person to ask about printing reports for your Business Activity Statement, but here are the reports I suggest you print, along with why they're important:

- ✔ **Tax Summary report (go to Reports⇨Tax).** Print this report for the quarter that you're doing the BAS on. (In the top-left corner, QuickBooks states whether this report has been generated on an Accrual Basis or Cash Basis. If this basis isn't correct, skip to the Tax area of your Preferences menu and fix up your tax reporting basis.)

- ✔ **Profit & Loss Standard report (go to Reports⇨Company & Financial).** Your Profit & Loss is a vital reference. Read this report and ensure it makes sense!

- ✔ **Balance Sheet report (go to Reports⇨Company & Financial).** Your Balance Sheet is the litmus test for whether your GST accounts reconcile. See 'Making sure the whole deal is spot on' later in this chapter for more details on reconciling these accounts.

- ✔ **Payroll Summary report (go to Reports⇨Employees & Payroll).** This report is important because it provides a check for Questions W1 (total wages) and W2 (total PAYG tax) on your Business Activity Statement.

Setting Up Your Business Activity Statement

Set up correctly, QuickBooks generates a report that looks almost identical to the pink Business Activity Statement form you receive from the ATO (except that your version comes complete with the correct figures, of course).

If you recently upgraded from an earlier version of QuickBooks, you may need to 'reconfigure' your Business Activity Statement. See the next section to find out how.

Configuring your BAS (hey ho, what fun)

The first step in preparing your Business Activity Statement is to tell QuickBooks what kind of taxes you pay on your statement — every business is a little different — and also how often you report to the ATO. If you're not sure about any settings in the BAS Configuration window, look carefully at your most recent Business Activity Statement (you know, the pink form that the ATO sends you every month or quarter), or, if in real doubt, ask your accountant.

1. **Go to Reports⇨Tax⇨Simplified BAS/IAS.**

   If QuickBooks displays a message about preparing Instalment Activity Statements, click OK to skip to the Simplified BAS window.

2. **Click the Config button and review the settings on the GST Configuration tab, as shown in Figure 10-9.**

   As your BAS Reporting Period, select Annually, Quarterly or Monthly (most businesses report for GST quarterly).

   Also, tell QuickBooks whether, aside from GST and PAYG, you normally pay any other taxes on your BAS. For example, if WET, LCT, FBT or FTC taxes apply to you, click the relevant boxes.

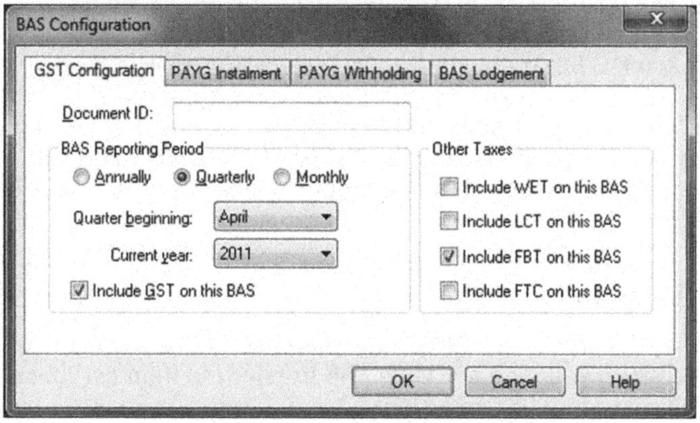

Figure 10-9: Configuring your Business Activity Statement in QuickBooks.

BAS Configuration
GST Configuration | PAYG Instalment | PAYG Withholding | BAS Lodgement
Document ID:
BAS Reporting Period / **Other Taxes**
○ Annually ● Quarterly ○ Monthly / ☐ Include WET on this BAS
Quarter beginning: April ▾ / ☐ Include LCT on this BAS
Current year: 2011 ▾ / ☑ Include FBT on this BAS
☑ Include GST on this BAS / ☐ Include FTC on this BAS
OK   Cancel   Help

3. **Still in the BAS Configuration window, review the settings on the PAYG Instalment and PAYG Withholding tabs, then click OK.**

   Again, choose between Annually and Quarterly and select your starting month. If you're not sure whether your Accounting Basis is Cash or Accrual, ask your accountant.

Linking items to each box (slightly scary, but essential)

When you open your Simplified BAS/IAS report (found on your Reports menu in the Tax section), the report divides into three tabs:

- ✔ Supplies & Acquisitions
- ✔ Taxes & Amounts Withheld
- ✔ Debits & Credits

Your job is to work through each tab, linking tax items and accounts to every grey box (the ones that say G1, G2, G3 and so on). This rite of passage gets a tad technical, but be comforted that you only need to endure it once.

Supplies and Acquisitions

When you click the Supplies and Acquisitions tab on your Business Activity Statement, you see three reporting options (Option 1, Option 2 and Option 3). Depending on which option you pick — ask your accountant if you're not sure — you either have to set up G1 only, or G1, G2, G3, G10 and G11. You do this by clicking the grey button itself (for example, G1) and then selecting the tax items from whatever list QuickBooks offers.

Here are some G-force tips on what to select and where:

- ✔ **G1.** You report all sales in this question, so select every tax item you ever use for sales. Usually, this is simply FRE, GST and INP, but if you export goods overseas or sell liquor wholesale, you also require the EXP or WET items.

- ✔ **G2.** You report all export sales here, so EXP is the item you need (if this applies to you).

- ✔ **G3.** You report all GST-free sales here, so FRE is the name of the game (of course, you may not have FRE in your tax item list, because you don't make any GST-free sales).

✔ **G10.** You report all capital acquisitions here. CAG is usually the one and only item to select. (The rare exception is if you make capital acquisitions that are GST-free or bought for the purpose of making input-taxed sales, in which case you need the CAF or CAI codes as well.)

✔ **G11.** You report all other expenses (with the exception of capital acquisitions) here. Select every tax item other than CAG that you use for purchases and expenses (usually just NCF and NCG).

Taxes and Amounts Withheld

The next tab along on your BAS is the Taxes and Amounts Withheld tab. This is where you have to specify the total value of employee wages and PAYG Withholding tax, as well as details regarding PAYG Instalment tax and FBT.

✔ **W1.** Select all payroll items that relate to wages (typically Gross Payments, Allowances and Lump Sums).

✔ **W2.** Select your Payroll Liabilities: PAYG Withholding tax account. Early in Chapter 12, I recommend you split your payroll liabilities into two accounts so that you can report for superannuation and PAYG Withholding separately. If you haven't made this change yet, I suggest you do so now.

✔ **W3.** You can usually ignore this box, unless you withhold tax from distributions made to investors.

✔ **W4.** Again, ignore this box. If a supplier can't provide you with an ABN, don't bother going through the hoo-haa of withholding tax from them. Just don't give them any business. (Remember that a supplier can choose not to be registered for GST; however, they must have either an ABN or a hobby exemption certificate.)

You also need to choose whether you pay PAYG Instalment tax as a set amount every time, or as a percentage of income. (Check the printed Activity Statement that the ATO sends you if you're not sure.) If you pay a set amount, enter this figure in T7. If you pay a percentage of income, click the T1 button, select every income account, then enter the rate from your BAS in T2.

If you don't pay any PAYG Instalment tax at all, something that's quite possible if your business is new or you're a partnership, then click the Config button and under the PAYG Instalment tab, unclick the option to include PAYG on this BAS.

Finally, complete any FBT obligations by typing the amount that you're due to pay in F1.

Debits and Credits

The last tab in your Business Activity Statement is the Debits and Credits tab. Again, click each of the grey boxes in turn and tell QuickBooks which tax items belong where.

- ✔ **1A.** Click against any tax items that relate to GST you've collected (normally simply the GST tax item code).

- ✔ **1B.** Click against any tax items that relate to GST you've paid (normally CAG and NCG).

- ✔ **1C and 1D.** Only select tax items here if you pay or collect Wine Equalisation Tax.

Saving your settings (easy, but important)

To save your settings, click the Save button and when prompted, save your Activity Statement in a logical folder (for my business, I have a folder called Activity Statements that lives inside a folder called My Accounts).

Lodging your Business Activity Statement

After you've endured the brutal initiation rite of configuring your Business Activity Statement (thankfully, a one-off process), you're ready to print your statement, check everything balances and then either lodge your statement electronically, or send it by post to the Australian Taxation Office.

Generating your first activity statement

With the configuration of your Business Activity Statement complete, you're ready to print the beastly thing, a process that's surprisingly painless:

1. **Go to Reports➪Tax➪Simplified BAS/IAS.**

   If QuickBooks displays a message about preparing Instalment Activity Statements, click OK to skip to the Simplified BAS window, as shown in Figure 10-10.

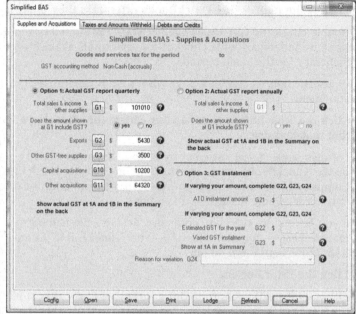

Figure 10-10:
The BAS report in QuickBooks looks similar to your regular Business Activity Statement.

2. **Click the Config button and check that all your date settings are correct.**

   Make sure that QuickBooks has selected the first month of your reporting period correctly. (That is, if you're reporting for the period July to September, ensure July is selected.) Also, check that the Current Year is correct (QuickBooks refers to calendar years, not financial years).

   Review all the settings on the GST Configuration, PAYG Instalment and PAYG Withholding tabs, checking details with your accountant if you're not sure about what options to choose.

   Also, click on the BAS Lodgement tab. Choose the ATO Business Portal Lodgement option if you intend to send your Business Activity Statement by post or if you want your accountant to lodge it for you. Alternatively, choose the Standard Business Reporting option if you have an AUSkey and want to lodge your Business Activity Statement electronically.

3. **Review the figures that QuickBooks offers. Do they make sense?**

   Double-check the GST totals against your Tax Summary report for the same period, and double-check the wages totals against your Payroll Summary for the same period.

   Check the figures on every page (that's each separate tab) of the statement.

4. **Click the Save button to save your statement, choosing a filename that makes sense.**

   I always suggest you save a copy of your Business Activity Statement on file. QuickBooks stores this backup on your hard disk in your Company Files folder, but if you want to make an additional backup onto a removable disk, then do so now.

   If you have more than one company, devise a file naming system that makes sense — for example, BAS_Trust_June11, BAS_Company_June11, BAS_Trust_Sep11 and so on.

5. **Click the Print button.**

   Although QuickBooks prints out a form that looks almost identical to the Business Activity Statement, you can't actually use this form for lodgement purposes. Unless you intend to use electronic lodgement, copy the figures (using black ink only) onto the Business Activity Statement form that the Australian Taxation Office sends you.

6. **Click Cancel to close the statement.**

   Always ensure you keep a copy of your BAS, because you need a record of what figures you lodged with the ATO.

Making sure the whole deal is spot on

Getting accounts to balance is a cinch if you report for GST on an accruals basis. Simply print a Balance Sheet for the last day of the reporting period printed on your BAS, and look at the balance of your Tax Payable account, or the balances of your GST Collected from Sales and GST Paid on Purchases accounts. In the perfect world (hey, who said it wasn't?), whatever amounts appear here should be the amounts that appear on your BAS for the same period.

Things get a little trickier if you report on a cash basis, because you have to allow for the GST that you haven't paid on outstanding customer invoices, or you haven't claimed from outstanding supplier bills. In this situation, you first print the following three reports for the last day of your reporting period:

1. A/R Ageing Detail report, modified to include the Tax Amount and to show Split Detail.

2. A/P Ageing Detail report, modified in the same manner.

3. Balance Sheet report.

The amounts for GST Collected and GST Paid on your Balance Sheet, *less* the total of the Tax Amount column on the Receivables and Payables reports, should equal the amounts that appear on your BAS for the same period.

I talk more about balancing GST in *Bookkeeping For Dummies*, also published by Wiley Publishing Australia, and which offers some of the best bedtime reading ever.

Lodging your statement with Reckon GovConnect

Until recently, the only way to lodge your Business Activity Statement was to first print the statement out of QuickBooks, and then either copy the figures onto the form that the ATO sends you and post this form, or go online and re-key each figure, one by one.

One neat thing about the latest release of QuickBooks is that you can connect QuickBooks with the ATO AUSkey portal so that your Business Activity Statement populates automatically.

To get this whole deal to work, you must first do three things:

1. Register for an *AUSkey* at the ATO portal (www.ato.gov.au). (An AUSkey is a single logon and password that enables you to access multiple government online services.)

2. Subscribe to Reckon Advantage (the support plan that goes with QuickBooks).

3. Go to Reports⇨Tax⇨Simplified BAS/IAS, click the Config button and then go to the BAS Lodgement tab. Select the Standard Business Reporting option.

With these three things in place, you're ready to get QuickBooks and the ATO to play a sweet duet. Follow these instructions to lodge your Business Activity Statement online, without rekeying a single figure:

1. **Generate your Business Activity Statement as normal, checking that all the figures are correct.**

   For more details, refer to 'Generating your first activity statement' earlier in this chapter.

2. **When you're confident all the information is correct, click the Lodge button.**

   QuickBooks automatically saves your statement information and then transports you to the Reckon GovConnect welcome window.

3. **Enter your AUSkey location, along with your AUSkey password.**

   You may also be prompted for your QuickBooks Customer ID and PIN number if this is the first time you're using the GovConnect service.

4. **If you are lodging your own BAS, select Reporting Party as your Identity. If you're a BAS Agent lodging a BAS on behalf of a client, select Intermediary as your Identity.**

5. **Enter the dates when prompted, click Current Obligations as your Search Criteria, and click OK to view the BAS that you're due to lodge.**

6. **Click Prefill.**

   If the ATO has any messages waiting for you — and don't you just hang out for those little sweet nothings? — you'll see these now.

7. **Select Import from the top menu.**

   Rather miraculously, you arrive at the folder where you saved the electronic version of your BAS earlier in this process.

8. **Highlight your BAS data file and click Open.**

   Your entire Business Activity Statement now populates automatically, without you having to rekey a single digit. I suggest you have one last check of this info and ensure you're happy with these figures.

9. **Click Send PreLodge from the top menu, then click Next.**

10. **Click Lodge BAS and when prompted, click Commit.**

    Do you suspect that the process of clicking the Commit button means that 50 per cent of the population will proceed no further?

11. **Click Logout.**

    The deed is done.

Recording Your BAS Payment or Refund

One of the trickier transactions to record in QuickBooks is your Business Activity Statement payment or, if you're lucky, refund. This is because when you lodge your BAS, you report on a whole range of taxes — GST Collected, GST Paid, PAYG Withholding tax and PAYG Instalment tax, to name but a few. Therefore, when you pay your tax (or receive a refund), you need to allocate your payment or deposit to all the different tax accounts.

I can't be definitive about how to record this transaction, because each business has a different combination of taxes to pay, but I can give a few pointers about how to proceed.

Paying the piper — when you owe them

If you owe money on your Business Activity Statement, then you record the payment by going to Suppliers⇨Tax Activities⇨Pay Tax.

If you have a single account for GST called Tax Payable, allocate the net amount of GST (that's the amount from 1A less the amount from 1B) to Tax Payable. (In tax speak, 1A is where you report GST Collected, and 1B is where you report GST Paid.)

If you have separate accounts for GST Collected and GST Paid, then you record the GST part of your payment using two transaction lines: On the first line of the transaction, enter the amount from 1A against your GST Collected on Sales account as a *positive* figure; on the second line of the transaction, enter the amount from 1B against your GST Paid on Purchases account as a *negative* figure.

Last, if you're remitting PAYG Withholding tax as part of this payment, enter the amount from W2 — as a *positive* figure — to an account called Payroll Clearing. (Skip ahead to 'Getting PAYG to balance' later in this chapter for more info about this Payroll Clearing account.)

Figure 10-11 shows how this transaction looks.

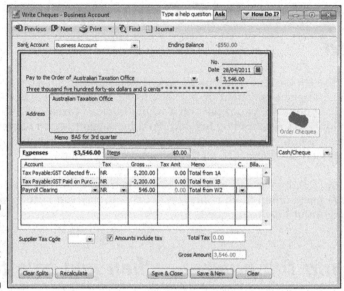

Figure 10-11:
Recording
the payment
of GST.

Even if everything balances, you'll always end up with a few stray cents, because the BAS rounds every field to the nearest dollar. Simply allocate these few cents to Bank Charges and everything will be just fine.

Claiming the dosh — when they owe you

Recording a refund on your Business Activity Statement is similar to recording a payment, except that the whole equation is flipped on its head:

1. **Go to Suppliers⇨Tax Activities⇨Manage Tax, and click the Receive Refund button.**

2. **Click OK to arrive unscathed (hopefully) at the Make Deposits window.**

3. **Enter 'Australian Taxation Office' in the Received From column.**

4. **If you have a single account for GST called Tax Payable, allocate the net amount of GST (that's the amount from 1A less the amount from 1B) to Tax Payable.**

   Or

If you have separate accounts for GST Collected and GST Paid, then record the GST part of your payment using two transaction lines, as per Figure 10-12.

On the first line of the transaction, enter the amount from 1B against your GST Paid on Purchases account as a *positive* figure; on the second line of the transaction, enter the amount from 1A against your GST Collected on Sales account as a *negative* figure;

5. **Allocate any PAYG Withholding tax by entering the amount from W2 as a minus figure to an account called Payroll Clearing.**

   Skip ahead to 'Getting PAYG to balance' next in this chapter for more about this Payroll Clearing account.

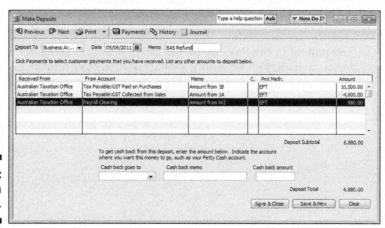

Figure 10-12: Recording a BAS refund.

Getting PAYG to balance

QuickBooks expects you to record PAYG Withholding tax in the Create Custom Liability Payments window. That's okay, but things become tricky when you have PAYG Withholding tax as part of your Business Activity Statement.

The trick to getting everything to come out clean in the wash is to create a special account called Payroll Clearing, and use this account as your bank account to record the payment of PAYG Withholding tax. Here's how:

1. **Go to your Chart of Accounts and create a new asset account called Payroll Clearing, selecting Bank as the Account Type.**

2. **When you record your BAS payment or refund, allocate the PAYG Withholding tax component to this new Payroll Clearing Account.**

   I show how this is applied in Figures 10-11 and 10-12.

3. **Go to Create Custom Liability Payments and record the PAYG Withholding tax part of your BAS payment as if you're paying it a second time, but as the Bank Account select your new Payroll Clearing Account.**

   Hopefully, if you select your payroll dates carefully, QuickBooks should come up with exactly the same Amount to Pay for PAYG Tax as what you actually paid on the BAS.

4. **Go to your Payroll Clearing Account in your Chart of Accounts and check that this account now has a $0.00 balance.**

   The idea is that when you record your BAS payment, you *credit* this clearing account. When you record paying the PAYG Withholding tax component in the Pay Payroll Liabilities account, you *debit* this clearing account. If all goes smoothly, this account always returns to zero.

Part III
Digging a Little Deeper

Glenn Lumsden

'Sometimes it's good to just sit back, relax and enjoy the view.'

In this part ...

After you master the basics of how to enter key transactions (sales, purchases, bills and so on), it's time to dig a little deeper, exploring the more interesting parts of QuickBooks.

In the next few chapters I discuss customising templates and forms, setting up payroll for employees and looking after your QuickBooks files. I also talk about all the different reports included in QuickBooks, identifying which reports are the most important for your business and how to understand them.

Chapter 11

Adapting QuickBooks to Fit the Bill

In This Chapter

▶ Deciding on the design you want, then calling the shots

▶ Understanding what templates are all about

▶ Using the Layout Designer to include borders and backgrounds

▶ Managing templates — copying, deleting and importing more

▶ Fixing template glitches

*F*or every activity in your business, QuickBooks offers a corresponding template. Adapting these templates to fit the individual needs of your business is the key to setting up QuickBooks successfully.

The possibilities are endless. Maybe you prefer to call Tax Invoices something like Record of Services Provided. Maybe you aren't registered for GST and don't want to display tax columns when entering data. Or, maybe you need to add an extra column to all purchase orders. Whatever change you seek, chances are, it's possible. Simply open the relevant template and customise it.

One of the things I like best about templates is that I can adapt them to see one thing when I'm entering data but see something altogether different on the final printed form. For example, I've customised QuickBooks so that when I go to bill a client, I simply enter a service code called CS and QuickBooks automatically fills in a long blurb about my consulting services. On the final invoice, however, the service code doesn't print at all, and only the description is displayed.

This chapter is about adapting QuickBooks so that it fits *your* business like a glove. In a way, this chapter is the most exciting and powerful of the whole book, because not only is it about you, it's about getting this software to work the way you do.

Imagining a Program Designed Just for You

Imagine for one brief moment that you don't own QuickBooks at all. In fact, you're a multi-millionaire and you're delivering a brief to a dazzlingly brilliant (not to mention rather gorgeous) software developer. This brief details exactly what you want to see when you go to generate an invoice for a customer, and what you want to see when you create a purchase order for suppliers.

I often ask my clients to do this exercise, writing down what they'd like to get out of their accounting software if the sky was the limit. Usually, they're pleasantly surprised when I tell them that the software of their dreams is what's already loaded on their computer — namely QuickBooks — and all that they need to do is a little tweaking here and there to get what they want.

Changing what you see before you

When you go to create a customer invoice in QuickBooks, pretty much everything that you see in the Create Invoices window is flexible. You can choose to display certain columns but hide others, add extra columns for dates or custom information, add extra headings or footers, and change the title of any row or column. For example, if your business doesn't use the term 'sales rep' but instead refers to 'account managers' you can ditch the original and put this heading on your invoice. This principle applies to all QuickBooks templates, including sales estimates, quotes, customer statements and purchase orders.

Take a look at Figure 11-1 to see what you can do. In this example, a specialist medical practice is using a QuickBooks invoice to record client appointments and medical receipts. You can see that the words Tax Invoice have been replaced by the words Medical Appointment, the Date is now Appointment Date, the Invoice Number now reads as Claim Number and so on. This medical practice even logs appointments into QuickBooks in the form of Sales Estimates, so that when the patient attends, all the receptionist has to do is call up the estimate and convert it to a finalised appointment (or, in accounting terms, an invoice).

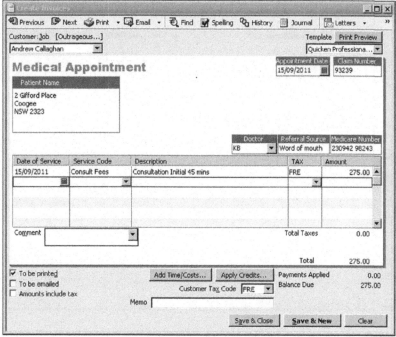

Figure 11-1:
The
QuickBooks
Create
Invoices
window,
customised
by a
business
to suit its
specific
needs.

Getting results that are spot on

You can see from Figure 11-1 that it's possible to mould QuickBooks to your
every desire, but what do your customers see? The answer is exactly what
you want them to see.

When you go to customise a template in QuickBooks, not only can you
control what you see on-screen during data entry, but you can also control
what prints out at the end. Figure 11-2 shows the final receipt that the
medical practice prints out for its patients — a receipt that includes details
such as the doctor's provider number, a mug shot of the doctor and a map
showing the location of the practice.

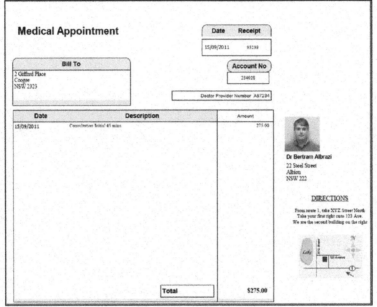

Figure 11-2:
A
QuickBooks
receipt,
customised
by a
business
for its
customers.

The rest of this chapter focuses on the practicalities of template customisation, but here are some ideas to give you some scope on just how adaptable QuickBooks is:

✔ **Create different versions of a template for different situations.** For example, if you ship goods with a packing slip, you can create an invoice template that has the title Packing Slip instead of Invoice. Alternatively, you can create different versions of a template for different kinds of customers — for example, creating one template for export customers and another for local customers.

✔ **Add new columns and fields (or delete ones you don't need).** For example, if you've created custom fields for your inventory, such as colour, size, serial number or supplier product code, you can add these fields as additional columns to your sales invoices and purchase orders.

✔ **Hide certain fields or columns when you're entering data, but show them on the final printed form.** For example, you could hide the supplier item code when you're filling out a purchase order — just referring to your own item code when keying in data — but print both your own code and the supplier item code on the printed version that the supplier receives.

✔ **Add your logo to all business forms.** If you have a logo, you may as well use it.

✔ **Add standardised text or disclaimers.** Many wholesalers include a standard blurb that says something like 'All goods remain our property until they're paid for in full'. My lawyer has a very long and convoluted disclaimer on his QuickBooks invoice. Myself, I like to include warm and fuzzy messages on my invoices, but then, I'm just a particularly warm and fuzzy kind of person.

✔ **Move things around on printed forms to give them great visibility.** For example, if you want to make your website address more prominent, you could centre your website address at the top of the form, using a large font size and maybe even a different colour.

To get an idea of just how versatile templates are, hop online to `http://community.intuit.com/library/forms` (or, if this link is a dud by the time you try it, as is the way with so many website links, do a Google search on 'QuickBooks online template gallery'). This gallery includes over 100 pre-designed templates, all of which you can download for free. See 'Taking on pre-designed templates' later in this chapter for more details on the practicalities of this process.

Working with Templates

QuickBooks already comes with a swag of standard templates, the selection of which varies a little depending on which version of the software you're working with, and how you've selected your preferences (for example, unless you switch on the preference to work with sales estimates, the Custom Sales Estimate template won't show). The idea is to use these templates as your starting point, and then adapt them to work for you.

Customising your first template

Ready to customise your first template? Here goes:

1. **Go to Lists⇨Templates and select the template that you want to customise.**

   The standard templates include invoices, adjustment notes, sales receipts, purchase orders, statements, estimates and sales orders.

2. **Double-click the template that's closest to the style you're looking for.**

   For example, with invoices you can choose between a Professional, Service or Product template. Choose the template description you think will suit you best. QuickBooks takes you to the Basic Customisation window shown in Figure 11-3.

3. **Experiment with the settings in the Basic Customisation window, clicking Print Preview from time to time to see how your selections are shaping up.**

   I won't explain each itsy bit, because with a little common sense you can figure out how everything works. Have a go at changing the fonts and sizes of things such as your Company Name and Company Address, and decide what contact information you want to include on the template. If any of your company information is wrong, click the Update Information button to fix it on the fly.

4. **Click the Additional Customisation button to review what information is going to print on the final form, and what you want to view when you enter data.**

   You may receive a prompt to make a copy of this template (this message appears if you try to customise a default QuickBooks template). If this happens, click Make a Copy to proceed.

   When you arrive at the Additional Customisation window, you can choose what information you'd like to display or print in your headers, columns and footers. For example, you could choose to display Item Descriptions when you're creating a customer invoice, but decide not to print this information on the final form. For more details on tweaking columns, check out 'Deciding which columns to display and which columns to print' later in this chapter.

5. **Click the Layout Designer button and play with your design, dragging and dropping to move text around, or double-clicking text boxes to change fonts and colours.**

   Follow your nose and experiment (you can always hit the Cancel button when you're done so that your changes aren't saved). For more design tips, see 'Working with the Layout Designer' later in this chapter.

6. **Click OK to leave the Layout Designer, then OK again to return to the list of templates.**

   I haven't shared everything there is to know about customising templates in these six brief points — after all, that's what the rest of this chapter is about. By now, though, you should have an idea of how QuickBooks templates work.

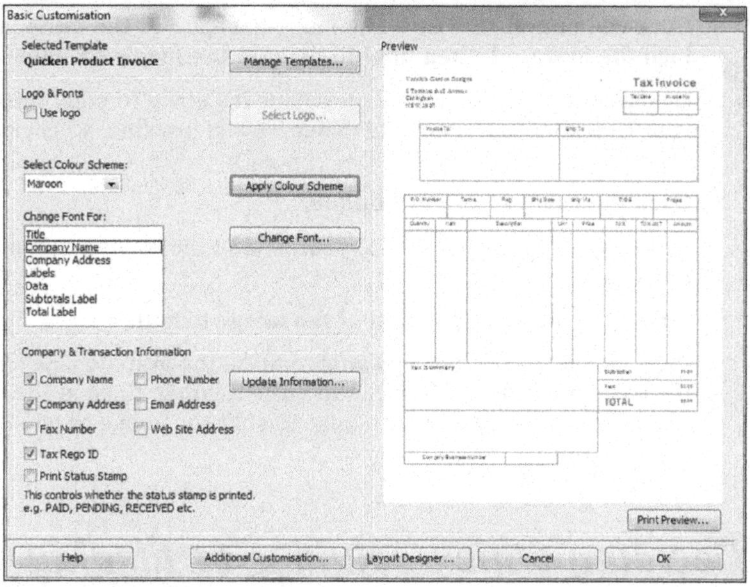

Figure 11-3:
Customising
an invoice
template.

Adding logos

If you've got it, flaunt it. There's no good reason not to have your company logo printing on every invoice, purchase order or other bit of correspondence that you send into the outside world.

Here's how to insert a logo in any of your business templates:

1. **Scan the logo and save the file using an appropriate size and format.**

   Your logo file can be in any image format, such as jpeg, gif, tif or bitmap. I usually find that jpeg or tif files work best, because they're smaller than bitmap files (taking less time to load). Whatever the format, make sure the file is no bigger than 2,000 kilobytes — you may have to lower the resolution or greyscale the image (make it black and white) in order to meet this condition.

   You can change file formats or edit images using any simple graphics program. If in doubt, try Microsoft Paint, which normally sits in the Accessories section of the Program folder on your PC.

2. **Copy the logo into a folder where you can find it.**

3. **Open the template that you want to add the logo to.**

   Go to Lists⇨Templates and double-click the template where this logo is going to go.

4. **Click the button that says Use Logo, navigate to the folder where the logo file is stored, then double-click on the logo's filename.**

QuickBooks displays a message saying it's going to copy this file into your QuickBooks documents folder. This is just fine, so click OK to proceed.

5. **Click the Layout Designer button.**

All being well, you should see your logo in the top-left corner of the form.

6. **Adjust the size and position of the image to suit.**

Drag the bottom corner upwards to make the graphic smaller, or drag the bottom corner downwards to make it larger. Click in the middle of the image and drag your mouse to shift the image to wherever you want it to sit on the form.

Deciding which columns to display and which columns to print

The next step in customising a template is deciding what you want QuickBooks to display when you record transactions, and what you want QuickBooks to print. You make these decisions by first selecting a template from your templates list, then clicking the Additional Customisation window.

Depending on the template or the version of QuickBooks you're using, QuickBooks displays four or five tabs along the top of the Additional Customisation window:

✔ **The Header tab.** For each item, click in either the Screen or the Print column, or both. If you've already defined custom fields for either customers or suppliers, these fields show up on the header tab as well.

✔ **The Columns tab (on all forms) and the Prog Cols tab (on some forms only).** The Columns tab works the same way as the Header tab — click in either the Screen or the Print column for each item. A further refinement with columns is that you can tell QuickBooks what order you want these columns to be in. The same principle applies to the Prog Cols tab, which relates to progress invoicing (available in QuickBooks Pro, QuickBooks Contract Edition and QuickBooks Premier only).

✔ **The Footer tab.** This area tends to get a bit crowded, so if you ask to display or print extra fields, QuickBooks usually displays a warning saying that this field overlaps existing fields. Click OK to ignore this message and then when you're ready, go to the Layout Designer and tweak the position of your footer fields so that they don't overlap. (I talk more about moving stuff around in 'Working with the Layout Designer' later in this chapter.)

✔ **The Print tab.** Here's where you tell QuickBooks whether to print Portrait (tall and elegant) or Landscape (wide and magnificent), and whether you want page numbers on forms when they run over two pages.

Newbies to QuickBooks often get confused about where custom fields appear on templates. To select display or print options on custom fields for customers or suppliers, go to the Header tab of the Additional Customisation window. To select display or print options on custom fields for items, go to the Columns tab of the Additional Customisation window. (One more thing: Custom fields won't appear anywhere unless you've already defined them in your customer, supplier and item lists. Refer to Chapter 2 to read about custom fields for customer and suppliers, or refer to Chapter 8 for more information on custom fields in items.)

With every field that appears under the Header, Columns, Prog Cols or Footer tabs, not only you can you choose whether it displays or prints, but you can also change the title. For example, you can change the title of the Ship To field to become Conference Address Details, or change Ship Date to become Conference Start Date. Take a look at Figure 11-4 to see how this can work.

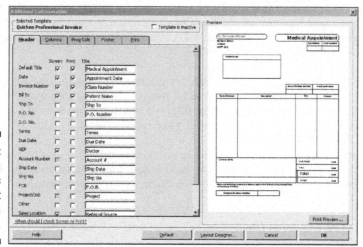

Figure 11-4: Changing the titles of what appears on your forms.

Working with the Layout Designer

If your layout gets a bit crowded, you're best to open up the Layout Designer (simply click the button called Layout Designer in the Basic Customisation window). Now you can move fields around, add or delete fields, tweak sizes, modify fonts and, if you're really ambitious, cook a five-course banquet.

Fooling around with fonts

Although the Layout Designer allows you to change the font size and colour on every single column, row or line of text, you're best to start by selecting default fonts in the Basic Customisation window (that's the first window you see when you double-click on a template from the templates list).

In this first window, can you see that you have the option to select a colour scheme? Before email communications became so established, I used to avoid selecting snazzy colour schemes because I didn't want the additional expense of printing in colour. However, these days I tend to email pretty much everything, so I go the whole hog with colour, producing documents in all colours of the rainbow.

Similarly, you can change the fonts and font sizes for the entire form by clicking any one of the headings on the left (Title, Company Name, Company Address and so on), then clicking Change Font on the right to select the actual font (Arial, Helvetica or whatever) and the size.

With these broad brushstrokes in place, you're ready to open up the Layout Designer and hone in on the fine detail. To change the font of a particular bit of data or text, double-click on it. From here, you can click the Text tab to choose different fonts or font sizes.

To make things a little more glam, try clicking the Border or Background tabs. I find the backgrounds are a bit heavy — strong colours sitting behind text tends to detract from readability — but adding borders is a simple enough way to add that extra edge (excuse the pun).

If you choose a font larger than the one you had before, the text may end up too tall or too wide to fit into the field. If this happens to you, simply enlarge the field by dragging out the bottom corner with your mouse.

Adding borders and lines

Try adding borders, boxes and lines to your invoices, receipts and purchase orders to make them look lean, mean and hungry. (For all of the pointers that follow, I assume you've already made your way to the Layout Designer.)

✔ **Borders.** To add a border around some text, either double-click the text or, alternatively, highlight the text and click the Properties button. In the Properties window, click the Border tab and decide whether you want the new border along the Top, Bottom, Left or Right, or on all four (you can see what these options look like in Figure 11-5). Decide whether you want rounded corners (the more curvy the better, in my book), and whether you want the line to be dotted or dashed, thin or thick. Click OK when you're done.

(To add a border to every single bit of text that prints on your form, quit the Layout Designer completely and close the template that you're working on. Then go to Printer Setup, select the Form Name from the top menu — invoice, receipt or whatever — and then unclick the option Do Not Print Lines Around Each Field. To remove the borders that print around every bit of text, do the opposite.)

To add a border around a section of text — maybe you want to group a whole lot of stuff together by drawing a box around it all — add a new text box to the form, drag out the corners until it's the right size, then add a border to the text box (which, of course, doesn't have any text in it).

Figure 11-5: Use borders to add that spark of pizazz to your invoices.

✔ **Lines — horizontal.** To add a horizontal line that isn't related to any particular field — maybe you want a line that runs right across the page, dividing it in two — select Text Box from the Add menu, and as the Border for this text box, select Top only (leaving Bottom, Left and Right unclicked). Then drag the bottom corner of the text box to change the size of the field so that it extends to exactly how far you want your line to run.

✔ **Lines — vertical.** To add a vertical line to your form, follow the same principles used for a horizontal line, except this time select only a Left border, and leave the Bottom, Top and Right unclicked.

✔ **Underlined text.** To add a line under some text, double-click on the text, then on the Text tab click the Font button. From here, click Underline as your choice of Effect.

Deleting stuff you don't need

One of the things you'll probably find when using the templates in QuickBooks is that they include a fair bit of information you don't need. Maybe you don't need salesperson details or shipping information; maybe you don't want to show purchase order numbers or tax breakdowns.

When you spot a field you don't need, simply get rid of it. To do this, click once on the field to highlight it and then press the Remove button. Or, if you want to delete an entire column and the Remove button is greyed out, close the Layout Designer and go to the Additional Customisation window. From here, remove the tick that appears in the Screen and/or Print column for the unwanted field.

Midnight Express

If you want, you can use pre-printed stationery (as opposed to plain paper stationery) for customer invoices, employee payslips or customer statements. Quicken has a special relationship with a company called Forms Express, which provides a range of stationery designed to fit with all QuickBooks products. Forms Express can also supply you with printed cheques that comply with Australian banking regulations.

The easiest way to order stationery from Forms Express is via the company's website at www.formsexpress.com.au. Alternatively, you can phone 1300 301 166.

Inserting new text

If you want to insert text into a template — maybe you want to insert a standard message at the bottom of each invoice or insert your bank account details on the bottom of customer statements — here's what to do (I'm assuming you're already in the Layout Designer at this point):

1. **Click the Add button on the toolbar and select Text Box from the drop-down menu.**

   The Text Properties window appears on-screen.

2. **Type the words you want to include as text in your template.**

   Don't worry about running out of room when typing in the Text box. Although it may seem that you can't add much here, you can actually write your entire life history in this box because the text wraps around.

3. **Click the Border or Background tabs, or the Font button, to adjust the appearance of your new text, then click OK.**

   You can change the font, size or colour of your text, add any kind of border, and even make the text bold, underlined or italicised. If you want to get really tricky, you can even add a background colour.

   When you click OK, a text box appears bang in the middle of your form.

4. **Drag the text to wherever you want it to sit on your template.**

   Position your mouse over the text box and click once so that a box appears around it. Hold your mouse button down, drag the text box to the correct spot on your form and then release the mouse button.

   If necessary, drag out the bottom corner to adjust the size or shape of the text.

5. **Click OK to save your changes.**

Adding extra information

I find that when my templates have evolved somewhat, I often end up wanting to undelete something I deleted earlier. Or, I decide that I want to make use of a field that doesn't normally print, such as a customer's credit limit or alternative contact details.

To add a new field, go to the top toolbar (I'm assuming you're still slaving away in the Layout Designer) and click the Add button followed by Data Field. A long list of available fields appears (similar to what you can see in Figure 11-6) covering everything from alternative customer contact details to customer credit limits, payment terms and so on. Double-click to the left of any name to insert the field you want into your template, dragging and dropping it into position when you're done.

Keep in mind that QuickBooks doesn't list all possible options in the list of available fields. If you close the Layout Designer and return to the Header, Columns and Footer tabs in the Additional Customisation window, you see a whole load more columns and fields that you can choose to include.

If you add custom fields to customer or suppliers, you can select to view or print these custom fields by choosing them on the Header tab of the Additional Customisation window. If you add custom fields to items in your Item List, you can select to view or print these custom fields by choosing them on the Columns tab of the Additional Customisation window.

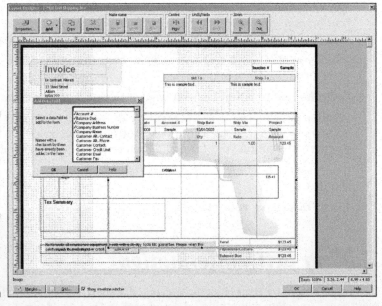

Figure 11-6: Using the data fields tool to select from a whole range of possible fields to insert in a template.

Lining everything up

Remember that every sales invoice you send to customers is a subtle piece of advertising in its own right. So make sure your forms look elegant and suave:

- ✔ **Move fields around so they line up with others.** To move a field or some text to somewhere else on your form, use your mouse to grab the object by the scruff of its neck, dump it wherever you want it to end up, and then fiddle with the size to make it match everything else on the form.

- ✔ **Match the height of similar fields.** Hold down the Shift key and then single-click on each of the objects you want to change. Still holding the Shift key, single-click the object that has the height you want to match. Next, click the Height button and QuickBooks instantly adjusts the height of all the objects you selected. (Lining up text is easiest if you get QuickBooks to automatically match the height and width of each, because it's much easier to arrange things if they all have similar dimensions.)

- ✔ **Match the width of similar fields.** Do the same as for matching the height, except click the Width or the Size button.

- ✔ **Snap to the grid.** Click the Grid button at the bottom of the Layout Designer and click the options to Show Grid and Snap to Grid. As the Grid spacing, select 1/16th inch, the smallest setting possible. With this Snap to Grid setting in place, QuickBooks automatically lines up fields to the nearest gridline, maintaining a microscopic accuracy that would be impossible to achieve by eye.

- ✔ **Line up your amounts.** If you're a wholesaler or manufacturer, you may show more than two decimal points on some of your pricing. If so, go to the Additional Customisation window, click the Print tab and modify your Trailing Zeros preference. This forces QuickBooks to align all amounts on the decimal point.

To select all objects within an area, first click an object that is in the bottom corner of this area. Then, while holding down the mouse button, drag the mouse diagonally to the opposite corner.

Setting up printers

If you work in an office that has more than one printer, and you tend to print stuff on different printers depending on what you're doing, then take a moment to select a default printer for each form.

Go to File⇨Printer Setup, select the form you want to configure, then select the Printer name and Printer Type. With this in place, QuickBooks always selects that printer when you print that particular form.

By the way, if you then click the Options button and select printing options specific to your printer (maybe choosing print quality or paper type), remember that this isn't a QuickBooks setting and QuickBooks won't remember these printing options next time you go to print that

form. If you want to make your printing options permanent, you need to head to Windows and fix the setting in the Printers folder in the Control Panel.

With some forms, QuickBooks offers the choice between Quicken pre-printed forms, blank paper or letterhead. The only difference between the blank paper and the letterhead setting is that for a letterhead QuickBooks doesn't print the company name and address info at the top.

Additional print options are available from the Print tab of the Additional Customisation window. These options vary, depending on the template you're working on.

Copying, Creating and Importing Templates

One of the things I love about customising templates is that the possibilities are endless. Clubs adapt invoices to become annual subscription reminders, colleges adapt invoices to become course enrolment templates and factories change purchase orders into production run lists.

One of the tricks in QuickBooks is that you can customise templates more than once. With one standard invoice and one company file, you can create lots of different templates for different situations.

Creating a new template from scratch

The quickest way to create a brand new template is to browse through the existing templates, find the one that's closest to what you want to create, then copy it. To do this, go to your templates list, highlight the template you want to copy and then from the Templates menu select Duplicate. Specify the kind of template you're creating, then click OK. The duplicate template then appears in your list of templates, with the words Copy Of in front of the template name.

Next, double-click this duplicate template to open it, then click the Manage Templates button. Change the Template Name to something a little more meaningful and then click OK.

Taking on pre-designed templates

Probably the fastest and easiest way to create a professional-looking document is to download a predesigned template from the QuickBooks template gallery, and then use this template as your starting point. Go to `http://community.intuit.com/library/forms` to find hundreds of different forms for estimates, invoices, purchase orders, sales receipts and so on, many with special finishing touches such as watermarks and remittance slips.

To work with a predesigned template, here's what to do:

1. **Visit** `http://community.intuit.com/library/forms`.

   Figure 11-7 shows the website's library page. If this link is a dud by the time you're reading this page — I know how quickly links change — simply Google 'QuickBooks library forms' and you should get to the right page.

2. **Find the form that you want and click Download, followed by Save.**

   When QuickBooks asks whether you want to open or save this file, select Save. Navigate to your QuickBooks program folder and save the form there.

3. **Back in QuickBooks, select Templates from the Lists menu.**

   You're back at the familiar templates list you've grown to love.

4. **From the Templates menu at the bottom, select Import.**

5. **Select the form template that you just downloaded, then click Open.**

   In a flash, QuickBooks imports the template and takes you to the Basic Customisation window.

6. **Click either the Additional Customisation or Layout Designer buttons to personalise the template for your business.**

   Because these templates are already set up for different businesses with different graphics and colours, you can use them as is, or customise them even more.

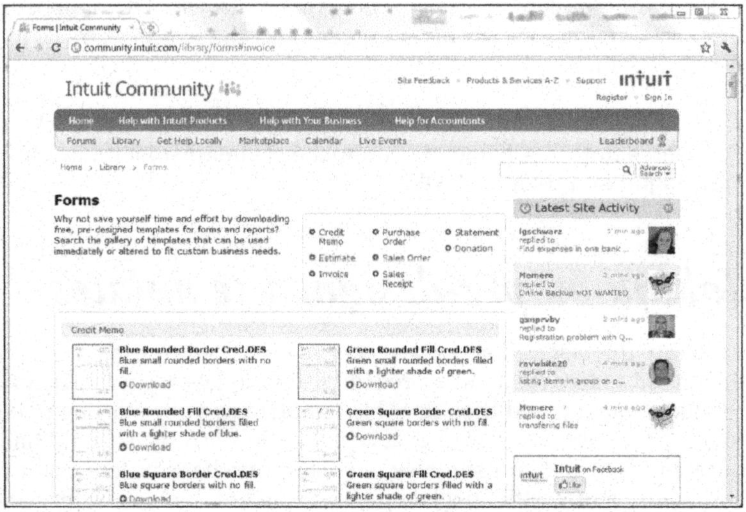

Figure 11-7:
The
QuickBooks
Forms
library is an
excellent
resource for
professional-
looking
forms.

Deleting or hiding templates

Over time, you often accumulate a few different templates. You may find that as your business grows and changes, you don't need all of these templates anymore. If so, I recommend you give your templates list a bit of a spring-clean.

To delete a template, first go to your Lists menu and click Templates. Click the template you want to delete, then click Templates at the bottom of the list. From here, select Delete Template. If you can't delete the template because it's already being used in transactions, QuickBooks suggests that you make it inactive instead. Click Make Inactive to do the deed.

If a template is inactive, it still shows in your list of templates, but with an 'x' to the left of its name. To hide inactive templates altogether from this list, untick Include Inactive (this checkbox appears at the bottom of the Templates window).

Sharing templates

So you've designed a whiz-bang template and you want to share it with a friend or colleague. No problem. Open up your templates list, select Export from the Templates menu at the bottom, then save the template somewhere so that you can find it later. As the filename, QuickBooks saves the template using the template name and adds the letters 'des' as the file extension.

Where QuickBooks stores your forms

The moment you import a form, it becomes part of your QuickBooks company file. The good thing about this is if you move your company file from one computer to another, or upgrade your company file, all your customised forms carry across automatically.

However, if for some reason you download custom forms from somewhere and haven't yet imported them into your QuickBooks file, remember that if you shift computers you'll need to copy these forms across separately.

From here, the easiest way to send a template to someone else is usually to email it. At the other end, the person receiving the template needs to save the file to a relevant folder (such as My Documents), then in QuickBooks open it by selecting Import from the Templates menu. Easy stuff when you know how.

Troubleshooting Blues

So, things aren't working out as they should? Nobody is perfect, and nor is life ...

- ✔ **The cents from dollar amounts are cut off.** This happens because QuickBooks is printing the amounts too far to the right on the form. The solution is to increase the Left and Right form margins (click the Margins button in the Layout Designer).

- ✔ **Only the first few letters or first few words of a text field print.** This happens because the field isn't big enough for the text. Go to the Layout Designer and drag out the bottom corner of this field to make it bigger.

- ✔ **Not all text prints, even though field sizes are clearly big enough.** Check the Font selected in the Printer Setup menu. Select the form in questions, click the Font button, then try a different font (try a really common font, such as Times New Roman).

- ✔ **The margins seem too wide.** If margins print out wider than you expected, it could be something to do with the minimum margin settings on your printer. Try adjusting the margins by clicking the Margins button in the Layout Designer.

✔ **When you create a PDF of a form, it comes up blank.** You may be able to solve the problem by using a different font. For the form (such as an invoice) that's affected by this problem, choose a standard font such as Arial or Times New Roman.

✔ **The form doesn't automatically come up with sequential numbers.** In other words, you change an invoice number from 1234 to 2345, but when you create a new invoice, QuickBooks comes up with 1235 as the number, not 2346. The reason this happens is that QuickBooks first sorts invoices by date, then by invoice number. If you click Save & New (rather than Save & Close) when recording an invoice that doesn't have the most recent date, QuickBooks keeps the old invoice numbering.

✔ **Estimates print out blank.** This sometimes happens if you create an estimate that's descriptive, or if you write the estimated price in the Description field of an estimate, rather than the amount. The solution? Go to Jobs & Estimates in your Preferences menu, and unclick Don't Print Items That Have Zero Amount.

✔ **The form takes a wet week to print.** A few things can cause printing to be slow, but try freeing up available memory by closing other Windows applications and making sure you have the latest printer driver. If you have a logo on your form, reduce the file size as much as possible, and if you have lots of lines and borders on your form, pare these down to the bare minimum.

By the way, it's a good idea to test that all of your customised forms look okay when QuickBooks converts them to PDF files (when you email a customer an invoice or monthly statement, or email a supplier a purchase order, QuickBooks creates PDF files to do so). To preview what your form will look like, first display the form (for example, opening up an invoice that you've already recorded) and then select Save as PDF from the File menu. Save the file on your desktop, and then open it up to check it out.

Chapter 12

Managing Payroll

In This Chapter

▶ Steaming through the Payroll Setup Interview

▶ Slogging through the boring stuff: Payroll items, tax, super and much more

▶ Setting up employee pay details

▶ Paying employees

▶ Taking leave, but not of your senses

▶ Reporting for different kinds of superannuation

▶ Paying taxes and other unavoidable facts of life

▶ Meeting your legal obligations with the help of the Employee Organiser

▶ Printing payment summaries when the year is done

*E*mployers often ask me whether it's worth converting to QuickBooks payroll. My answer is an unequivocal yes: If done by hand, managing payroll is one of the most time-consuming and difficult parts of running a business. Done with QuickBooks, payroll becomes blindingly swift. For this reason, if you have any more than two employees and you're still using QuickBooks EasyStart or QuickBooks Accounting, I suggest you switch to a more senior member of the QuickBooks family that includes payroll features (such as QuickBooks Plus or QuickBooks Pro).

In this chapter, I talk about setting up payroll for your business and cover fascinating topics such as superannuation, PAYG and leave entitlements. Reading this chapter may not be the most enthralling way to spend a sunny afternoon, I admit, but without pain there's no gain.

Heading for the Centre

So you're ready to abandon those fiddly Excel wages spreadsheets, or worse, those beastly handwritten wages books, and get QuickBooks to do all the dirty work? No problem.

Getting the ball rolling

The first step is to decide on a start date. Although you can start payroll at any time, I recommend waiting until 1 July, so you can enter a whole year using one method, making it easy to balance tax and print payment summaries. If you can't start on 1 July, at least try to start on the first day of a quarter — for example, 1 October, 1 January or 1 April. (Never start payroll transactions in the middle of the month, because you'll throw your super calculations out of whack.)

After you decide on a start date, carve yourself out some quiet time and assemble all your pay records. You need your wages books, employee details, employment declarations and so on. With these treasured but now archaic items at hand, you're ready to begin.

Turning payroll on

To explore QuickBooks' payroll, click the Employee Centre icon on your icon bar. Figure 12-1 shows what you'll find, although in this screenshot I've already added details on some employees.

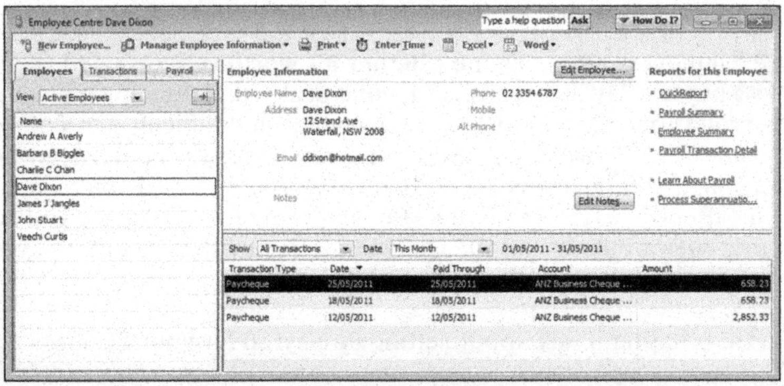

Figure 12-1:
Viewing the
Employee
Centre.

If you can't see a Payroll tab (rather, you see only one tab for Employees and another for Transactions), then you need to turn on your payroll preferences. Head to your Preferences menu, open the Payroll section, then select Full Payroll. (The No Payroll option is only relevant if you don't have any employees or you plan to use an independent payroll program.)

Sweating through the interview

Setting up payroll can be time-consuming, but the Payroll Setup Interview attempts to make doing so as easy as possible. Go to Employees on the top menu bar and select Payroll Setup. Then click the Next button to continue, as shown in Figure 12-2.

I could write a tedious step-by-step description of this setup interview, but I know you don't need that level of detail. Instead, here are a few tricks of the trade:

- ✔ **Payroll additions.** QuickBooks lists two payroll items for each payroll addition (more commonly known as *employee allowances):* One that's tax free and another that's taxable. Ask your accountant or visit www.ato.gov.au to find out whether the allowances that you pay employees are taxable (sadly, tax-free perks are few and far between these days), then select the items that apply to you. (Of course, if you don't pay any allowances for laundry, telephone, tools or motor vehicles, you can skip this section.)

- ✔ **Company contributions.** This section doesn't apply to most businesses. Even if your business does pay fringe benefits tax (FBT), most accountants prefer not to track FBT liabilities using payroll.

- ✔ **Holiday and personal leave.** QuickBooks offers three different ways to track leave. If you're not sure which one to choose, skip to 'Setting up leave' later in this chapter. (Unless you want to be hideously unpopular with employees, don't ask QuickBooks to reset leave each year, and don't set a maximum number of hours.)

- ✔ **Employee details.** After you enter an employee's name and address, QuickBooks asks if you want to set up the employee's payroll information. I suggest you fix up your Payroll Item List first, then return to add employees' details later. See 'Getting Acquainted with Payroll Items' later in this chapter.

- ✔ **Year-to-date totals.** The step most likely to cause trouble is completing the year-to-date totals for each employee (this only applies if you're starting Payroll after 1 July). Don't enter figures here unless you're sure they're 100 per cent perfect. (In the meantime, I repeat my earlier recommendation that the best time to start using payroll is from 1 July, rather than jumping in mid-year.)

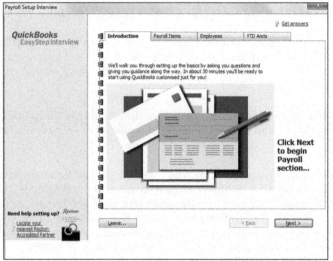

Figure 12-2: Getting started using the Payroll Setup Interview.

Tweaking accounts to make things easy

Like the proverbial black sheep, I stray from the fold in recommending that you modify your Chart of Accounts so you can report for payroll expenses and liabilities in more detail. Here's what I recommend:

- If you pay employees electronically, create a new Bank account called Electronic Clearing. (For the method in my madness, see Chapter 16.)

- Create two new liability accounts to track super and tax: One called Superannuation Payable; the other called PAYG Tax Payable. Make both of these two accounts subaccounts of your existing Payroll Liabilities account.

- If you deduct stuff from employee pays such as union fees, child support or garnishee orders, create a new account for each one (selecting Other Current Liability as the account Type). Make these accounts subaccounts of Payroll Liabilities as well.

- If you pay any allowances, create a new expense account called Employee Allowances. Make this account a subaccount of Payroll Expenses.

- One more thing: Create a new expense account called Superannuation Expense. Make this a subaccount of Payroll Expenses.

All done? Now you're ready to progress from the fairly boring-and-tedious stuff to the mind-blowing, how-did-I-get-myself-involved-in-this kind of stuff. Read on . . .

Getting Acquainted with Payroll Items

Whenever you record any kind of payroll transaction, QuickBooks expresses this transaction in terms of *payroll items* — for example, wages, deductions and super. Payroll items form the guts of everything you do in payroll.

Although QuickBooks comes prepared with a heap of standard payroll items, I recommend you give your payroll items a swift once-over, changing or adding them as necessary. So don't delay: Head to Employees⇨Manage Payroll Items⇨View/Edit Payroll Items.

Wages, holiday pay, sick pay and more

For every category of wages that you pay your employees, you require a different payroll item. Depending on the answers you selected in the setup interview, you may even find that QuickBooks creates all the wages payroll items that you need.

As a minimum, you need the following: Salary, Holiday Salary and Personal Salary for all salaried employees, as well as Hourly Pay for all hourly employees. (Personal Salary includes both carer's leave and sick leave.) If hourly employees are entitled to leave — in other words, they're not just casuals — you also need both Holiday Hourly and Personal Hourly, as well as items for any overtime or shift loadings that apply to your workplace.

Allowances, reimbursements and holiday loading

If you pay any extra stuff to employees, such as allowances, holiday loading or reimbursements, you need a payroll item for each one. Although you probably selected these items during the Payroll Setup Interview, I like to tweak the settings for both allowances and reimbursements by linking them to a different account from the default Payroll Expenses account.

For example, in Figure 12-3, after setting up a new payroll item for motor vehicles, I select an account called Motor Vehicle Allowance to track the expense. Working this way allows me to see allowances separately on my Profit & Loss reports.

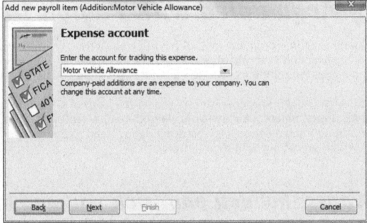

Figure 12-3:
Linking
allowances
to unique
expense
accounts
so that they
appear
separately
on Profit
& Loss
reports.

If you know for sure that an allowance is exempt from tax, untick the boxes for PAYG Tax and state payroll tax. Check with your accountant or visit www.ato.gov.au if you're unsure. (As a rule, most allowances are taxable, but most reimbursements are not.)

The last step when setting up allowances or reimbursements is to choose the calculation method: For things such as motor vehicle reimbursements, where you're reimbursing a certain number of cents per kilometre, ask for the item to be calculated based on quantity. For any allowance that's a fixed amount per pay period, click the Neither button.

One other thing that stumps non-accountants is the Tax Tracking question, which appears as the third window along when you create a new payroll item. The decision you make in regards to Tax Tracking affects where additional payments such as employee allowances appear on employee payment summaries. Here's how to decide which Tax Tracking option to use:

✔ Select Gross Payments for Holiday Loading or any other loadings in which the associated expenses are not tax deductible, such as crib loadings, home-to-work travel expenses or shift loadings.

✔ Choose Allowances for items that have tax-deductible expenses associated with them, such as Motor Vehicle Allowance or Tool Allowance.

✔ Pick None for anything that's purely a reimbursement or within the reasonable allowances amount for meals and travel.

Union fees, donations and other deductions

Whether QuickBooks has already set up deductions in your Payroll Item List or whether you're creating one from scratch, there are a couple of things to look out for.

I like to create a separate liability account for every different kind of employee deduction. For example, if you deduct child support from an employee's pay, create an employee deduction item called Child Support and select Child Support Payable as the liability account for this payroll item. The same idea goes for union fees, employee purchases and so on.

As the Tax Tracking type, select None if this deduction doesn't need to show on a payment summary. Usually, the only deductions you show on payment summaries — meaning you select Deductions as the Tax Tracking type — are union fees and workplace giving.

You don't need a separate payroll item for each amount that you deduct from employees. For example, if you deduct $20 from one employee for child support and $30 from another, you only need one payroll item called Child Support. As the calculation method, select Neither (meaning you can enter a flat amount per pay), leaving the default rate and limit blank. Then, when you pay this employee, specify the amount. When QuickBooks asks if you want to add this deduction to the employee's permanent record, click Yes to do so.

Tax, in every flavour possible

QuickBooks automatically creates an item called PAYG Tax in your Payroll Item List. Make the Agency for this item Australian Taxation Office and select PAYG Tax Payable as the liability account. (Create a new account by this name if you don't already have one.)

When checking the settings for PAYG Tax, you need to decide which payroll items this tax applies to. Generally, QuickBooks makes the correct selections, because you've already specified what's taxable and what isn't during the setup interview. However, if you know something shouldn't be taxed but for some reason it's ticked, then deselect it.

The courageous Madame QuickBooks also caters for state payroll tax, one of the most convoluted taxes known to man. I don't have scope here to explain the ins and outs of this tax, but chances are you're not affected by it in any case. State payroll tax kicks in at different thresholds, depending on the state you're in, but unless your wages bill exceeds half a million dollars a year, you don't have to give it a second thought.

Superannuation, guaranteed

If you're working with QuickBooks for the first time, you need to make sure super is set up correctly. You also need to create a separate payroll item for each fund that your employees belong to.

Alternatively, if you recently upgraded to the latest version of QuickBooks, you may need to update the way payroll calculates super (the new payroll item for super works slightly differently to earlier versions).

Here's how to add a new super fund to your payroll item list:

1. **From your Payroll Item List, select New from the Payroll Item menu.**

   Can't find the Payroll Item List? Head to the Lists menu.

2. **As the payroll item type, select Super Contribution. Then click Next.**

3. **Enter the name of the fund.**

   If your employees belong to more than one fund, you need to create a separate payroll item for each one. Right now, pick any old fund as your starting point.

4. **Check that the type of superannuation is Super Guarantee Act (SA).**

5. **Click Next.**

   QuickBooks displays the Agency for Company-Paid Liability window. Boy, this is gripping stuff.

6. **Complete the details for the super agency and change the liability and expense accounts to Superannuation Payable and Superannuation Expense.**

   As the agency, enter the name of the superannuation fund. If your employees don't all belong to the same fund, you need to create a separate payroll item for each fund.

   The most important thing to remember here is to change the liability account to Superannuation Payable, and the Expense account to Superannuation Expense. If you don't see either of these accounts, go to your Chart of Accounts and add them (for more information, refer to 'Tweaking accounts to make things easy' earlier in this chapter).

7. **Click Next.**

8. **As the Tax Tracking type, select None.**

   Why none? Because you don't need to show super on payment summaries.

9. **Click Next, ignore the Taxes window, then click Next twice more.**

   You ignore the Taxes window because superannuation doesn't affect PAYG Tax or state payroll tax.

10. **Choose to calculate super on gross pay, and click that Next button one more time.**

    If you calculate super on net pay, then you end up not paying enough super. So please choose to calculate super on gross pay instead (you're far too nice to go to jail).

11. **Enter 9% as the default rate, and leave the limit blank. Click Next.**

    Unless you promised an employee more, the percentage is 9 per cent. (I'm writing this in the year 2011, so if the years have since ticked by and this book is now of antiquarian interest, do remember to check the current rate.)

12. **Enter $450 as the Monthly Minimum Threshold. Click Next.**

    Unless you have an award with a lower threshold, you don't have to pay super if an employee earns less than $450 a month.

13. **Unmark any payroll items that are exempt from super.**

    Don't forget to mark off all payroll items that are exempt from superannuation, such as certain kinds of bonuses or overtime, in the same way as I do in Figure 12-4. See the sidebar 'Make sure you don't pay too much!' to find out more.

14. **Click Finish.**

    Holey moley! I don't know about you, but I'm exhausted.

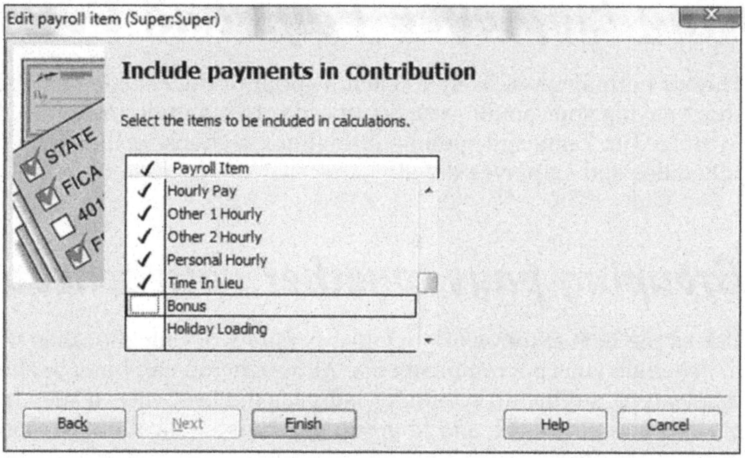

Figure 12-4: Avoid paying more than you have to: Deselect all wages categories that are exempt from super-annuation.

Make sure you don't pay too much!

Maybe it's my Scottish blood, but I hate paying more than I have to, or seeing clients do the same. However, it's surprising how often I come across clients who pay too much super on behalf of their employees.

The trick is to remember this: Superannuation is only due on what is termed *ordinary time earnings* (OTE). OTE includes things like basic pay, casual loadings and holiday pay, but doesn't include things like holiday leave loading, overtime and termination payments. (To view a handy help document that details

exactly what's what, select Superannuation Information from your Employees menu.)

To make sure that you're not paying too much super, go to your Payroll Item List (found under your Lists menu). Double-click every payroll item that relates to superannuation (you have to edit each item separately) and click Next a few times until QuickBooks asks you to select which payments should be included when it calculates super. Browse through this list and unclick any payroll items that don't attract super.

One more thing. This section explains how to set up the standard superannuation that every employer in Australia has to pay. However, if you have employees under a *salary sacrifice super arrangement* (in other words, they pay extra super out of their own pay and receive concessional tax treatment) then you have set this up separately. Skip ahead to 'Reporting Super Contributions (RESC)' later in this chapter.

Finalising Employee Pays and Details

There's nothing more likely to elicit a spout of thinly-veiled antagonism than short paying your employees. So, in order to maintain the peace, buy up big with the Tim Tams and spend a little time on checking the setup of payroll schedules and employee details.

Grouping pays together with schedules

One of the neat features of the latest versions of QuickBooks is the ability to schedule your payroll payments. Although you can bumble along without this feature, setting up schedules is by far the best way to keep track of pay periods and pay dates, and to group pay runs by location, payment method or pay frequency.

Here's the one-stop, no fuss, oh-so-brilliant guide to creating your first payroll schedule:

1. **Go to Employees⇨Add or Edit Payroll Schedules.**

2. **Click the Payroll Schedule button at the bottom of the window and then click New.**

3. **Dream up a name for this payroll schedule.**

   I suggest something pragmatic like Fortnightly Salaries or Casuals Cash Payments.

4. **Select the pay frequency for this mob of employees.**

5. **Choose when the next pay period ends and when you plan to pay.**

   For example, if your pay week runs from Thursday to Wednesday, but you pay employees every Thursday, then pick next Wednesday as the end date for the pay period, and next Thursday as the pay date. (To process pays retrospectively — maybe you're well into August but you want to go back and record pays from 1 July — choose dates that apply to the first pay period of the payroll year.)

6. **Click OK.**

   QuickBooks automatically detects any employees who have the same frequency as your new schedule and asks if you want to assign them to this schedule. Click OK if you do. (Otherwise, you can assign pay schedules to each employee by going to the Payroll & Compensation Info tab on each record.)

7. **Click the Payroll tab in the Employee Centre, as if you're about to process pays.**

   On the right-hand side, QuickBooks now displays your new payroll schedule, as shown in Figure 12-5 (although in my screen, I've already set up some different schedules). Check that the pay period dates and projected payment dates look okay. If there are any hiccups, return to Employees⇨Add or Edit Payroll Schedules to fix things up.

 Setting up pay schedules doesn't mean you can't process one-off pays for employees (such as pay adjustments, bonuses or terminations pays). To record a one-off pay, don't select a schedule. Instead, click the Unscheduled Payroll button.

Figure 12-5:
Setting
up pay
schedules
helps to
keep pay
periods
accurate
and group
employee
pays.

Checking the setup for each employee

So far in this chapter I've given you the lowdown on setting up QuickBooks payroll: Picking a start date, working through the setup interview, reviewing payroll items and setting up pay schedules. The last part of the setup process involves checking that each employee's record is set up correctly.

1. **Click the Employee Centre icon and check that the list of employees is complete.**

   If an employee is missing from this list, click New Employee to add name and address details now.

2. **Make sure address details are complete for each employee.**

   To view this info, double-click each employee's name and click the Address and Contact tab. (When the time comes to print payment summaries, a complete address is vital.)

3. **From the Change tabs menu, select Payroll and Compensation Info.**

   Things are hotting up now — this is where most of the action takes place.

4. **Select all payroll items that apply regularly to this employee, such as Hourly Pay or Salary, and record the Hourly or Annual Rate against each one.**

   Figure 12-6 shows the typical payroll items for a salaried employee. Note that you can express pays either as Salary or Hourly (Hourly tends to work best if the employee's hours vary from week to week or the employee receives any kind of loadings or penalties).

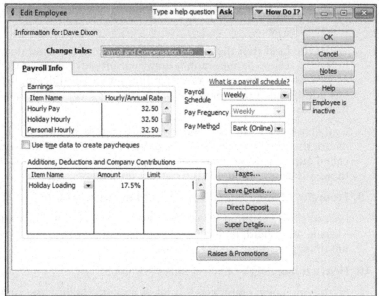

Figure 12-6:
Completing
payroll
details
for each
employee.

5. Select a Payroll Schedule and Pay Method.

If you haven't set up payroll schedules and you don't want to, then leave the Payroll Schedule blank and select a Frequency instead. If you select Bank (Online) as the Pay Method, don't forget to click the Direct Deposit button and enter the employee's banking details.

6. Click the Taxes button and set up the employee's tax scale and rebates.

No mortal is immune from taxes, in Australia at least. Enter the employee's Tax File Number (which QuickBooks calls the Employee Tax Reference Number) and select an appropriate tax scale (if an employee doesn't have any HECS or HELP debts and is an Aussie resident, select 2-TFT if the employee receives 17.5 per cent annual leave loading, or 7-No LL if leave loading doesn't apply).

For an illuminating explanation of tax scales, select Tax Table Information from the Employees menu, then click the Tax Table Info button.

7. Click the Leave Details button and figure out what you're going to do.

Yep, I know I'm being vague here. If in doubt, skip to the section 'Taking a Break' later this chapter, where I rave on in detail about leave.

8. **Click the Super Details button and set up superannuation details for this employee.**

   Select the fund that the employee belongs to (if the fund doesn't appear in the list, refer to 'Superannuation, guaranteed' earlier in this chapter), as well as the employee's membership number. If this employee also has additional superannuation or salary sacrifice, select these payroll items too.

   If an employee hasn't supplied you with details of their fund yet, don't ignore the employee's super setup, but select the default payroll item called Super instead. That way QuickBooks still accrues super, even though it won't fall under the correct fund name.

9. **From the Change tabs menu, select Employment Info.**

   Record the award that this employee is employed under in the Classification field, and tell QuickBooks whether the employee is full-time, part-time, casual or whatever.

10. **Heave a huge sigh of relief and click OK.**

    Setting up a new employee is a bit of an undertaking first time around, isn't it? But, like riding a bike, after you master it, you never forget.

My step-by-step guide explains how to set up individual employees. After you update one employee, you're well on your way to understanding how everything works. At this point, if most of your employees have similar pay or leave conditions, I suggest you save time by updating the New Employee Default Settings from the Manage Payroll Information menu first (you access this menu from the Employee Centre).

Processing Employee Pays

So, you reckon you've completed all the setup and you're ready to pay a few folk? The proof of the pudding — with the pudding being all the work you've done to get to this point — is whether employee pays calculate correctly. Happily, processing pays is as easy as having a second helping of dessert, so there's no need to be anxious.

Doing your first pay run

When I describe how to record your first pay run, I assume that you've already set up employee details, your payroll items list and payroll schedules (all explained earlier in this chapter). You're ready to roll:

1. **From your home page, click Payroll Centre.**

   Alternatively, click the Payroll tab from the Employee Centre.

2. **Assuming you've set up pay schedules already, double-click the schedule you want to process.**

   I talk about pay schedules earlier in this chapter, in the section 'Grouping pays together with schedules'. Alternatively, if you haven't set up pay schedules, click the Pay Employees button (the name of this button changes to become Unscheduled Payroll after you set up schedules).

   After you set up pay schedules, the only reason to record an unscheduled pay is if you process a pay adjustment or termination pay.

3. **Check the Pay Period end date and the Payment Date.**

   These dates usually come up correctly if you're running on track with pay periods, but you can always change them if you're doing something out of the norm.

4. **Check which bank account these pays will be paid from, and change it if necessary.**

   If you're paying electronically, select your regular business bank account or your Electronic Payments account. If you're paying cash (oh-glorious-cash) from the till, a bank account called Undeposited Funds is probably the go.

5. **Make sure everyone you want to pay shows on this list, and anyone who has resigned or been given the chop isn't on this list.**

   By now your Payroll Information window shows a summary of all the employees in this pay run. If an employee is missing, it's probably because you set up the employee's Pay Schedule incorrectly (for example, selecting Monthly instead of Weekly). On the other hand, if an ex-employee is listed, zap them from the list by going to the Employees tab in the Employee Centre, double-clicking the employee's name, then going to the employee's Personal Info tab and clicking Employee is Inactive.

6. **Click on each employee's name, one by one, to review or change pays.**

   When you click on an employee's name, you arrive at the Review Or Change Payments window, similar to Figure 12-7. The top half of this window shows Earnings and it's here that you change any hours that deviated from the norm (maybe an employee worked overtime, took annual leave or chucked a sickie).

   The second section is for Other Payroll Items, such as superannuation, deductions, loading or allowances. If you've set up payroll items properly, both sections calculate automatically.

7. **For each employee, check that superannuation appears in both Other Payroll Items and the Company Summary.**

   Unless an employee is under 16 or over 70, superannuation should *always* appear as a category in Other Payroll Items. Even if this employee hasn't earned $450 yet this month, meaning that super calculates at zero, the category itself should still appear. If super doesn't appear, add it now — the fines for underpaying super on employees are humungous, so you don't want to risk any mistakes.

8. **Click Next.**

   You arrive at the Review and Create Paycheques window, which shows a summary of each employee's gross pay, tax, deductions and so on.

9. **If you plan to pay any of these employees electronically, click in the Direct Deposit column against the employee's name.**

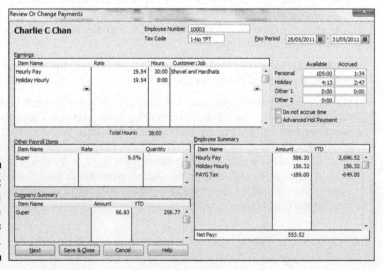

Figure 12-7: Reviewing an employee's pay.

10. **Click Create Payment and choose either to Print Pay Cheques or Print Pay Slips.**

    You're almost there. Unless you use printed cheques — and few businesses still do — click Print Pay Slips. You can also choose to send payments to each employee's super fund at this point — see the sidebar 'Solving a super headache (multiple funds)' for details.

11. **Click Close.**

    Congratulations. Your first pay run is now complete.

Viewing pay transactions and payslips

To view all pay transactions for someone, go to your list of employees, highlight the employee's name and click the QuickReport link on the right of the screen (or for a shortcut, press Ctrl-Q). You may also need to change the date range of this report.

To view payslips for someone, go to the Employee Centre, click Print, then click Print Pay Slips. Or, to email payslips, go to the Employee Centre, click Print, then click Email Pay Slips. Select the payslips that you want to email, click OK and then Send Now. (In order for payslips to appear in the Email Pay Slips window, first ensure that Email is selected as the Preferred Send Form Method under the Address and Contact details of the employee's information.)

Working with timesheets

Want to account for every second, minute and hour of employee time? No problem. Head to your home page and click Enter Time. From here, you can either enter a weekly timesheet, like mine shown in Figure 12-8, or log a single activity — check out both options to see which one suits you best. After you record time in a timesheet, it flows automatically through to the employee's pay for that period.

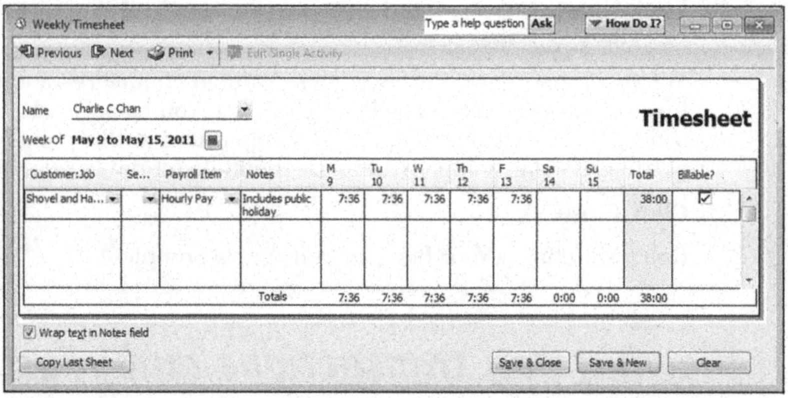

Figure 12-8:
Timesheets
work well if
you employ
lots of
casuals.

Follow your nose to make it all work, but bear in mind these points while you're at it:

✔ If the pay week on employee timesheets is defaulting to the wrong day (say a Monday rather than a Tuesday), head to the Time Tracking section in Preferences, click Company Preferences and select the first day of your work week.

✔ After you record a timesheet for someone, next time around click the Copy Last Sheet button, bottom left in the Timesheet window. This ensures all payroll items come up automatically. All you have to do is change the number of hours against each one.

✔ You can use timesheets to adjust regular pays for salaried employees. For example, if a salaried employee takes 8 hours' personal leave one pay period, you can record a timesheet that shows how many hours' leave was taken and when. This info then carries across to the employee's pay (you still need to manually adjust the employee's Salary, however).

✔ Remember to enter hours as decimals, not minutes. For example, if an employee works 8 hours and 15 minutes, this actually means they worked eight and a quarter hours, so key in 8.25 hours, not 8.15 hours. In true brilliance, QuickBooks instantly converts your decimal entry into minutes. (Maybe now you'll regret all those times you went surfing instead of going to maths class.)

Avoiding payroll hiccups

If you're having problems getting someone's pay to calculate correctly, here are some tricks:

- ✔ **Check the tax.** If the tax doesn't come up right, check the tax scale. Go to the employee's Payroll and Compensation Info tab and click the Taxes button.

- ✔ **Remember to record entitlements.** When you pay annual leave, reduce the number of hours listed against Hourly Pay and insert hours against Holiday Hourly (or reduce Salary and insert hours against Holiday Salary). The same principle applies for personal leave.

- ✔ **Check super is calculating correctly.** Make sure that superannuation appears on every pay (even if the amount next to this category is zero). However, don't worry if super calculates as zero in the first or second pay period of the month. That's because QuickBooks (ah, wonderful QuickBooks) doesn't calculate super until employees hit the $450 monthly threshold.

- ✔ **Switch off the preference that recalls hours if you employ lots of casuals.** The preferences in QuickBooks (go to Edit⇨Preferences⇨Payroll & Employees) include an option to recall the hour field on pays. Switch off this preference if you employ lots of casuals, because you don't want to pay someone the wrong number of hours because the hours came up automatically.

Deleting or changing pays

You can delete an employee's pay the same way you can delete any other transaction in QuickBooks: Find the pay transaction in your bank register, double-click, then select Delete Paycheque from the Edit menu.

To change an employee's pay, find the pay transaction in your bank register and double-click. From here, click the Paycheque Detail button to open the Review Paycheque window, which shows the original information behind that employee's pay (hours worked, leave accrued and so on).

If you want to make a change that *doesn't* affect the employee's net pay — for example, editing superannuation or pay period dates — then go right ahead. However, if you want to make a change that *does* affect net pay — changing rates or number of hours worked — you first need to click the Unlock Net Pay radio button at the bottom of the Review Paycheque window.

But wait — think before you jump! The only time I reckon it's okay to change the net amount of a pay is if the employee hasn't received the payment yet. Why? Because the moment money leaves your bank account to pay this employee, this pay transaction is set in stone.

If you delete or change the net amount of a pay transaction for an employee who has already been paid, then you're likely to muck up your payroll records, not to mention contravene your reporting obligations as an employer. The correct way to fix up a mistake with a previous pay is to fix it on the next pay by deducting overpayments or making up any shortfalls.

Taking a Break

I reckon that tracking holidays and personal leave is the trickiest part of managing payroll. (By *personal leave*, I'm referring to what most people used to call sick leave. However, the name has changed because employees can now take sick leave not only for themselves, but also to look after family members if they get sick.)

Don't forget that you need to accrue annual leave and personal leave for all part-time or full-time employees. For more info, visit the Fair Work Australia website at www.fwa.gov.au.

Setting up leave

Your success rate when tracking employee leave entitlements relies on how you set up your leave categories, something that you need to do before recording any pays. So catch your breath, slow down and read on carefully.

1. **Go to the General section of your Preferences menu, click the Company Preferences tab and select Decimal as the Time Format.**

   You may want to change the Time Format setting back to Minutes later on, if this works best for you for other activities in QuickBooks, but for the purposes of setting up leave and making sense of my instructions, Decimal is going to work best.

2. **Go to the Employee Centre, make sure the you're on the Employees tab, click the Manage Employee Information button and select Change New Employee Default Settings.**

3. **Click the Leave Details button.**

   You arrive at a window that looks uncannily like Figure 12-9. (The third and fourth tabs are simply labelled Other 1 and Other 2 at first, but you can customise these tabs later via your payroll preferences.)

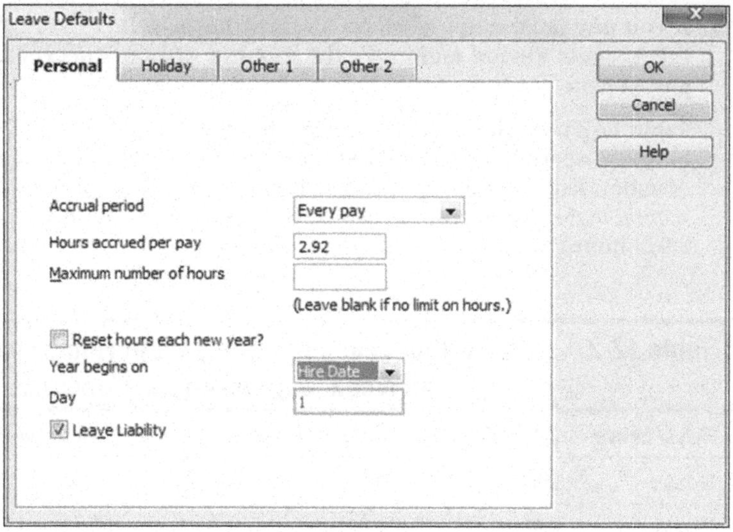

Leave Defaults

Personal	Holiday	Other 1	Other 2

OK
Cancel
Help

Accrual period   Every pay

Hours accrued per pay   2.92

Maximum number of hours

(Leave blank if no limit on hours.)

☐ Reset hours each new year?

Year begins on   Hire Date

Day   1

☑ Leave Liability

Figure 12-9:
Setting
defaults for
annual and
personal
leave.

4. **If you pay most employees on an hourly basis, select Every Hour as the Accrual Period and enter the number of hours accrued per hour paid.**

   If you're not sure about how many hours to enter here, see Table 12-1. For example, if you give employees 10 days' personal leave per year, this equates to 0.03846 of an hour for every hour paid, which is equal to just a tad over 2 minutes.

   When you set up leave to calculate for every hour paid, you must take care that leave doesn't calculate on things like overtime. See the sidebar 'Hey, don't overpay' later in this chapter for more details.

Table 12-1	Converting Leave Entitlements to Time Accrued Per Hour Paid	
Amount of Leave Per Year	**Hours Accrued Per Hour Paid (as a Decimal)**	**Hours Accrued Per Hour Paid (in Minutes and Seconds)**
5 days	0.01921	1 min 9 secs
8 days	0.03078	1 min 50 secs
10 days	0.03846	2 mins 18 secs
20 days	0.07692	4 mins 36 secs

5. **If you pay most employees on a salary basis, select Every Pay as the Accrual Period and enter the number of hours accrued per pay period.**

    Table 12-2 provides a quick guide to help you figure out how many hours to accrue per pay period for standard working weeks and common leave amounts. For example, if you give employees 20 days' annual leave per year and they work a 38-hour week, this equates to 2.923 hours (which equals 2 hours 55 minutes) per week.

Table 12-2	Converting Leave Entitlements to Hours Accrued Per Week, expressed as a Decimal			
Days/Leave	*28-hour Week*	*35-hour Week*	*38-hour Week*	*40-hour Week*
5 days	0.54	0.67	0.73	0.77
8 days	0.86	1.08	1.17	1.23
10 days	1.08	1.35	1.46	1.54
20 days	2.15	2.69	2.92	3.08

Don't forget to multiply these figures by two if you pay fortnightly, rather than weekly.

6. **Leave the Maximum Number of Hours setting blank and ignore the year settings.**

    In particular, don't click the option to Reset Hours each New Year. (You won't be popular if you do!)

7. **Tick the Leave Liability checkbox in the bottom-left corner.**

    By ticking this checkbox, QuickBooks automatically calculates the dollar value of all employee leave owing in your Leave Liability Report.

8. **Repeat for each kind of leave that your employees receive.**

    The other kind of leave that businesses often like to account for — especially in the non-profit sector — is long service leave. To define different types of leave, go to the Payroll & Employees section of your Preferences menu, click the Company Preferences tab, then edit the Other Leave Names for Other 1 and Other 2.

If your employees are under different awards or agreements — maybe some get 10 days' personal leave a year, but others get 15 days — then you can edit the leave settings for individual employees. From the Employee Centre, go to the employee's details, select the Payroll and Compensation Info tab and then click the Leave Details button. You can then edit this employee's individual leave settings.

Mum's the word

Payroll information is very sensitive. There's no better way to create friction between your employees than have them compare wages with one another (this occurs especially in family businesses where the children of the employers so often end up with a sweetheart deal). However, not only is payroll information sensitive, some of it is actually protected by the Privacy Act and, in particular, you're obliged to keep employee tax file numbers secure.

The only sure way to do this is to add a password to either the whole of your company file or, at the very least, the payroll section of your file. I tell you all about passwords in Chapter 15.

Catching up on ancient history

When you first set up leave entitlements, don't forget to let QuickBooks know about the amount of leave your hard-working employees already have owing to them.

1. **Go to the Employee Centre and double-click on the employee's name.**

2. **Choose the Payroll and Compensation Info tab and then click the Leave Details button.**

3. **Enter the hours currently available to this employee.**

   QuickBooks asks you to enter the hours as at the current date. For example, if you're fixing up employee entitlements in QuickBooks in the middle of a year then you don't worry about what the employee's entitlements were at the beginning of the year. Instead, calculate how much leave the employee was owed right up to the end of the most recent pay period.

4. **Leave the Hours Used This Year blank.**

   Because you're telling QuickBooks what entitlements this employee is currently owed, it's irrelevant how much leave they used in the year leading up to this point. The only reason you would enter historical leave data is if you wanted to produce retrospective employee leave reports that showed this information.

5. **While you're here, check that all other settings for this employee are correct.**

   Don't know how? Refer to 'Setting up leave' earlier in this chapter for more details.

6. **Repeat this process for each kind of leave this employee is owed.**

7. **Finally, repeat this process for each employee.**

When you're done, check your work by printing a Leave Liability report (found in your Reports menu in the Employees & Payroll section). This very nifty little report summarises leave available for each employee and, if you click the Modify Report button, can be customised to include lots of additional information about leave accrued and leave taken.

Recording leave taken

Dawn breaks to the sight of blue skies, a touch of wind and the perfect surf. Time to chuck a sickie? So survives another great Australian institution (if you're not an employer, that is).

To record personal leave taken (I'm talking about sick pay here), go to record pays as normal, but when you get to the Enter Payroll Information window, double-click on the employee concerned. From here, reduce the number of hours in Hourly Pay or Salary and instead enter these hours or the amount of pay against Personal Hourly or Personal Salary. For example, if someone who is paid hourly normally works a 38-hour week and takes two days' sick leave, type 22.8 against Hourly Pay and 15.2 against Personal Hourly.

Hey, don't overpay

If you calculate leave on an hourly basis, make sure that QuickBooks doesn't accrue leave on things like overtime: Go to your Payroll Item List, identify an item where leave shouldn't accrue, then double-click. Click Next and, in the definition window, click against the box called 'Do Not Include Hours In Leave Accruals'.

QuickBooks only offers the option not to include hours in leave accruals for payroll items that are an Hourly Wage, with Overtime selected as the type. For this reason, if you have any other kinds of wage payments that shouldn't attract leave — such as payments made at casual rates for part-timers who work additional hours — then set up these payments with Overtime as the type.

The same principle applies for annual leave, with the only difference being that you need to substitute Holiday Hourly or Holiday Salary for regular hours. You must also add holiday leave loading if relevant. You can see how I record a pay transaction that includes holiday pay and leave loading in Figure 12-10.

The other tactic for smart players, relevant if you pay for holidays in advance, is that you can tick the Advanced Hol Payment checkbox when editing a pay, and tell QuickBooks if you're paying leave in advance. This way QuickBooks averages out the tax across the correct number of weeks' pay.

By the way, if you're trying to troubleshoot employee leave balances — how much they're due, how much they've taken, how much they've accrued and so on — the tool for the job is the Paid Time Off List report (found in the Reports Centre under Employees & Payroll). This dream report tells you everything you ever need to know, and more.

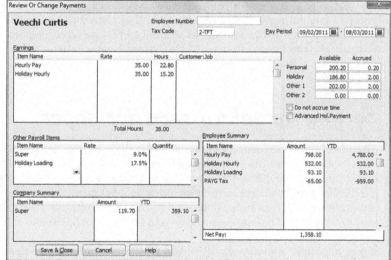

Figure 12-10: Recording holiday leave loading and holiday pay.

Reporting Super Contributions (RESC)

The Australian Taxation Office recently announced changes to the way employers report employee superannuation, defining a new category of super called *Reportable Super Contributions (RESC)*. Any super that an employer is obliged to report on an employee's payment summary is defined as RESC.

So what does RESC include? Put very simply (have sympathy for me here, I'm trying to condense 48 pages of government-tax-speak into two simple bullet points), RESC includes:

✔ Super that you deduct from an employee's pay under a salary sacrifice arrangement.

✔ Any super over the 9 per cent minimum that you pay to the employee as part of their employment offer. (If a business or organisation offers all employees more than 9 per cent, and the employee isn't able to influence this decision, then the amount over 9 per cent doesn't count as part of RESC.)

The good news? If, like 98 per cent of employers, you simply pay your employees 9 per cent super (in other words, the legal minimum), then you don't have to do anything. You don't need to change any QuickBooks settings, and you don't need to report employee super on your next batch of payment summaries. Yippee.

Alternatively, if any employees have a salary sacrifice arrangement, or you pay any employees at a rate that's higher than 9 per cent, then you *may* have to report the additional amount of this payment separately. Fortunately, the latest versions of QuickBooks cater most elegantly for this situation. Read on for more details ...

Setting up salary sacrifice super

The idea behind superannuation salary sacrifice is that the employee 'sacrifices' some of his or her wage in exchange for additional superannuation and less PAYG tax. For example, you may offer an employee a $70,000 salary package, which includes $65,000 gross wages and $5,000 superannuation (this super is in addition to the minimum 9 per cent that the employer pays). The employee only gets taxed on $65,000 and not $70,000.

If you negotiate a salary sacrifice deal with an employee, you need to make sure that the employee's settings are correct in QuickBooks. Here's the deal:

1. **Go to your Lists menu and select Payroll Item List.**

2. **Double-click on the Payroll Item called Salary Sacrifice.**

   This item is standard to QuickBooks and should appear in your list. If it doesn't, click New now to create a new payroll item with this name and choose Super Contribution as the Item Type.

3. **Click Next to proceed to the Super Contribution window. Check that the contribution type is Salary Sacrifice (SS).**

4. **Click Next and then Next again to proceed to the Tax Tracking Type window. Check that the tax classification is Gross Payments.**

   This setting means that the salary sacrifice super amount will appear in the employee's payment summary as reportable super, and will also be deducted from Gross Wages.

   When it comes to payment summaries and super salary sacrifice, you report the gross wage after salary sacrifice is taken out. For example, if an employee receives a $70,000 package of which $5,000 is salary sacrifice super, then you show $65,000 as the gross wage on the employee's payment summary.

5. **Click Next to progress to the Taxes window. Double-check that PAYG Tax is checked.**

   The idea with salary sacrifice super is that by sacrificing wages for super, the employee's tax is reduced. Your part of the deal is to click the PAYG Tax payroll item when you get to the Taxes window. This way, QuickBooks knows to get smart and adjust the tax.

6. **Leave all other settings blank, clicking Next a couple more times and then Finish to save your changes.**

7. **Go to the Payroll and Compensation Info menu of the employee's record and click the Super Details button. Decide whether to click the option to reduce employer contributions, or not.**

   I can't tell you the correct answer to this option. Some employers choose to pay the 9 per cent super guarantee on the grossed-up value of an employee's pay (which in my example would be $70,000), others choose to pay the super guarantee on the net value (which would be $65,000). Check with your accountant if you're not sure which rule applies.

Figuring out what to do with additional super paid by the employer

Whether or not you have to report additional super separately depends on whether the additional super is a deal that you've cut with an employee individually, or whether your business or organisation has a collective agreement that involves all employees getting more than the minimum 9 per cent. I'm not even going to try and delve into the technicalities of collective agreement stuff here, but if you want to check whether you need to include additional employee super as a RESC amount, then either ask your accountant for advice, or contact the Australian Taxation Office.

Please be careful here: In this section I'm talking about additional super an employer pays on behalf of an employee; for example, paying 12 per cent rather than 9 per cent. I'm not talking about any additional super that an employee chooses to have deducted from his or her pay on a voluntary basis, because this type of super isn't included in the government's definition of RESC.

If you do need to report additional super as RESC, then your first job is to check QuickBooks is set up correctly:

1. **Select Payroll Item List from your Lists menu.**

2. **Unless an item for additional super already exists, click New to create a new Payroll Item and when prompted, enter a name for this item.**

   I recommend you call this item something catchy like 'Additional Employee Superannuation'. Oh yes, and ensure that you select Super Contribution as the Payroll Item Type.

3. **Click Next to proceed to the Super Contribution window. Select Employer Additional (EA) as the type.**

   With Employer Additional (EA) superannuation, QuickBooks knows to print this total on the employee's payment summary. Perfect.

4. **Click Next and then Next again to proceed to the Tax Tracking Type window. Check that the tax classification is none.**

   This setting means that the additional employee super amount will appear in the employee's payment summary as reportable super, but won't be included in Gross Wages. Just right.

5. **Click Next to progress to the Taxes window. Double-check that PAYG Tax isn't checked.**

   You don't tax an employee extra just because you pay them super, so don't click this box.

6. **Click Next until you arrive at the Default Rate and Limit window. As the Rate, enter the percentage of extra super that you pay.**

   For example, if you pay an employee 12 per cent super, then enter 3 per cent as the Rate here (that's because 12 per cent less the minimum rate of 9 per cent equals 3 per cent).

7. **Click Next and then Finish to save your changes.**

And that's it! If you're as neurotic as I am, I suggest you process one pay for any employee who gets more than 9 per cent super, and then preview a payment summary for this person (go to the Employees menu and click Process Payment Summaries, then follow the prompts). Check that the amount you think should appear in the RESC box on the payment summary is what's actually printing. It is? Then all is well.

Paying Your Dues

You can't deduct money willy-nilly from employee pays without handing it over to someone else, sooner or later. Here's where I explain how to settle things like tax, superannuation and employee deductions.

Paying employee liabilities

1. **Go to the Employees menu, choose Payroll Taxes and Liabilities and then click Create Custom Liability Payment.**

   In previous versions of QuickBooks, this function was simply called Process Payroll Liabilities.

2. **Click the Dates drop-down list and choose the date range for paying payroll taxes, then click OK.**

   Pick your date range carefully. For example, if you're in July 2011 and you're paying superannuation for the last quarter of the payroll year, the date range needs to be 01/04/11 to 30/06/11, as shown in Figure 12-11.

   I have two date warnings to add here. First, don't include dates from the current month (why pay things before they're due?). Second, if you've underpaid a previous period, be aware that left-over balances won't show up. For more information, see 'Balancing employee liabilities' later in this chapter.

Figure 12-11:
Recording a payment for super-annuation.

3. **Click the Bank Account drop-down list arrow, choose the bank account that you'll make this payment from and enter the payment date.**

4. **Choose whether to review each payment individually, or not.**

   Akin to most members of the male sex (even though I'm not one), I snatch any opportunity to prevaricate before committing. So yes, choose to review each payment.

5. **Select the liability you want to pay now.**

   If, when you go to pay a liability, QuickBooks asks to associate an agency with this liability, it's referring to whom you're going to pay the money. For example, the agency for PAYG tax is the Australian Taxation Office, the agency for Child Support is the Child Support Agency and the agency for superannuation is the name of the individual fund. (That's why you need a separate payroll item for each super fund to which your employees belong.)

6. **To pay less than the full amount due for a selected liability, enter the amount to pay in the Amt. To Pay field.**

   If you want to pay less than QuickBooks tells you that you should pay, you better have a good reason.

7. **Click Create.**

   QuickBooks displays the payment. All you have to do is review this payment, checking that it all looks okay, and add a memo if you feel moved to do so.

8. **Click Save & Close.**

9. **Balance your payroll liability account.**

   They don't call me 'the dragon' for nothing. You can't be sure a payment is correct until you balance the account. See the next section to find out more.

Balancing employee liabilities

In theory, if you settle payroll liabilities in the way I describe in the preceding section, then they should always balance. However, because I'm a pernickety kind of person, I like to make sure.

The quick and dirty way to do this is to display your Balance Sheet for the month or quarter you just paid and look at the balance of your payroll liability account or accounts. (You may have a single account called Payroll Liabilities, or you may have separate accounts called PAYG Tax Payable and

Superannuation Payable — see 'Tweaking accounts to make things easy' earlier in this chapter for more details.) The balance of this liability account (or accounts) should be the amount you actually paid. For example, if you paid $2,010 superannuation in October for the months July, August and September, then you would expect the balance of Superannuation Payable in your September Balance Sheet to be $2,010 as well.

If super *doesn't* seem to balance, then return to the Create Custom Liability Payment window. This time, enter 1 July as the From Date (that's July from the beginning of last financial year, not this financial year), then as the through to date enter the date up to which you've just paid. See if any old super payments for previous months pop up. If they do, chances are you missed these payments and that's why your superannuation isn't balancing.

By the way, if you do all this and you *still* can't get super to balance, it's probably time to call in the cavalry. Your accountant or a Reckon Accredited Professional Partner is your best bet.

Recording tax payments

If you're registered for GST, then your PAYG tax payment is now part of your monthly or quarterly tax payment that you submit with each Business Activity Statement. I explain how to record this tax payment in Chapter 10.

Solving a super headache (multiple funds)

Reckon Tools Superlink is a nifty little service that hooks up with QuickBooks, helping you to manage your employees' super payments. Using QuickBooks, you can display a report to see how much super you owe, export this report to a special file and then upload this file to a secure website using the SuperLink service. SuperLink then completes the process that electronically transfers funds from your bank account to the bank accounts of the various superannuation funds to which your employees belong, and sends electronic remittance advices to each fund advising them of payment details for each one. Swish stuff.

Whether or not SuperLink works for your business depends partly on how many employees you have and how many different funds you have to make payments to. Currently, the cost of this service ranges between $110 and $825 per year, depending on how many employees you have. To find out more about this service, go to your Employees menu, choose Superannuation Information and follow the links for Super Choice and SuperLink.

Checking your tax tables

Tax tables are special formulas for calculating how much tax to deduct from employee wages. In recent years, the rates for personal tax have been changing every July, and so keeping up with tax tables is a big deal. (To view whether your tax tables are current, go to your Employees menu and select Tax Table Information.)

If you subscribe to Reckon Advantage, you receive tax table updates or product upgrades automatically every time tax tables change. To load new tax tables, head to your home page,

select Audit Company, click Next and then click Get Latest Tax Tables. Make sure you have your ID and PIN numbers at hand, and follow the prompts to proceed.

If you don't subscribe to Reckon Advantage, the only option is to upgrade to the latest version of QuickBooks. This costs pretty much the same as a year's subscription to Reckon Advantage, so you're probably best subscribing and getting the benefit of a year's technical support while you're at it.

Keeping Everything Shipshape

If you're an employer, you'll already be aware that staying on the right side of the law in regards to your employees is trickier than it looks. However, the recent release of QuickBooks makes many aspects of payroll management a tad easier with the QuickBooks Employee Organiser.

To explore the new Employee Organiser feature, select Employee Organiser from the Employees menu, and then browse through the sub-menus: Hiring, Raises and Promotions, Leave of Absence and Terminate Employee (is it just me or does the word 'terminate' make you think of Arnold Schwarzenegger too?).

I reckon that you'll be fine navigating your way through these screens as and when you need 'em, but here are a couple of points worth knowing about now:

✔ The Hiring wizard makes an employee's Tax File Number a compulsory field, and you can't proceed any further than Step 1 of the wizard without this info. Trouble is, sometimes you want to get an employee's details entered into payroll while you're still waiting for the employee to provide a Tax File Number. The solution? Enter '333 333 333' as the number for the time being. Just don't forget to return to the employee's record and fix up this info as soon as you get it.

✔ You may be concerned that your changes in the Raises and Promotions wizard won't flow through to the employee's Payroll and Compensation Info. Don't worry — every change you make here flows through to the employee automatically.

✔ The Terminate Employee wizard prompts you to complete important info about the circumstances of an employee's termination. However, remember that tax on termination pays almost always has different calculation rules, and that you often don't have to pay superannuation on unused leave payouts. Always check this info with your accountant before finalising a termination pay.

Printing Payment Summaries

It may seem pretty radical the first time you do it, but by far the easiest and quickest way to produce payment summaries (called *group certificates* in times gone by) is to print them on plain paper and then send a CD to the Australian Taxation Office.

1. **Check that all employees have a valid Employee Tax Reference Number.**

   You must enter an Employee Tax Reference Number (otherwise known as a Tax File Number) for each employee before you can generate payment summaries. To record this information, go to the Employee Centre, double-click the employee's name, select the Payroll and Compensation Info tab and click the Taxes button. (If the employee is under 18 and earns less than $112 per week, you can get away with using 333 333 333 as the number.)

2. **Go to your Employees menu and select Process Payment Summaries, followed by Select Payment Summaries to Print.**

   QuickBooks also offers an option to email payment summaries, but I always like to print them first.

3. **Select the Tax Year.**

   For example, if you're doing payment summaries for 30 June 2012, then select 2011/2012 as the tax year.

4. **Ensure the Payment Summary type is INB Payment Summaries.**

   The other type is an ETP Payment Summary, which you only use when giving an employee an Employee Termination Payment.

5. **Click OK and then Print.**

   QuickBooks obligingly prints a payment summary for each employee.

6. **Engage your brain, read through the payment summaries and think long and hard.**

   There's nothing like a bit of grey matter to help you get things right. Check that the figures on the payment summaries seem reasonable, and in particular ask yourself whether the figures for reportable super (RESC) is correct. Refer to 'Reporting Super Contributions (RESC)' earlier in this chapter if you're not sure.

   RESC only includes additional super, such as super that you pay over and above the 9 per cent minimum, or employee sacrifice super. You don't include the regular 9 per cent super guarantee charge anywhere on payment summaries.

7. **Ask your employer or the business accountant whether any employees have reportable fringe benefits.**

   I don't have enough scope in this book to cover the reporting of fringe benefits on your payment summaries. However, if the answer is 'yes' — you do need to show fringe benefits — then refer to the QuickBooks online help for more info.

8. **Add up total Gross Payments on the payment summaries. Check that this total equals total wages for the year in your Profit & Loss report.**

   Admittedly, this is a gruesome accounting task, but someone has to do it. Here's the lowdown: Total Gross Payments on payment summaries must match Wages Expense in your Profit & Loss (employee allowances could create a difference if they're reported in a separate expense account, but that's okay). If the two totals *don't* match, you may need to ask a Reckon Accredited Professional Partner or your accountant for assistance.

9. **Go to Employees⇨Process Payment Summaries⇨ATO Magnetic Media.**

   A window appears that's almost identical to the previous payment summary window, except this time it shows an extra button called Electronic File.

10. **Click Select All followed by the Electronic File button. When prompted, save this file to your QuickBooks folder and then to a CD.**

    Don't worry — this electronic file doesn't contain any confidential business information, other than what's already on your payment summaries.

11. **Hop onto the ATO website at** www.ato.gov.au **and print a Magnetic Media Information form.**

    This is the form you have to submit along with the CD. Either do a search on 'magnetic media' or 'NAT 8106' to locate the form.

    Alternatively, if you have an AUSkey and ECI software from the ATO, you can skip this step. Instead, go to the Business Payment Summary report menu within your ECI software and follow the prompts to send your electronic file direct.

12. **Photocopy your payment summaries, hand out or post the originals to all employees, then post the CD and Magnetic Media Information form to the ATO.**

    Just in case nobody's expressed their appreciation lately, let me assure you that you're a miracle of efficiency.

13. **Make a special backup of your QuickBooks company file.**

    Chapter 15 explains everything you ever needed to know about backing up. The idea this time is you make a special backup, never to be used again, that you store in a safe place for at least seven years. (At which point, a handsome prince appears.)

Chapter 13

Reporting on the Situation

In This Chapter

▶ Exploring all the reports in QuickBooks

▶ Making reports look good

▶ Saving reports so you can use them more than once

▶ Sending reports to Excel, and emailing them to the outside world

▶ Printing QuickBooks reports

Want to know how your business is going? Then mosey on down to the QuickBooks Report Centre. Here you find a whole heap of reports, everything from what time Julia ate lunch on Monday to how much tax you owe your beloved federal government.

Of course, clicking a button to view a report is only the first step. In this chapter, I explain how to go one step further, refining the information you need, getting your report to look good and saving your settings so you can use this report again later on.

You may also be wondering what to do if the standard fare that QuickBooks provides doesn't quite fit the bill. No worries. In this chapter, I also explain how to persuade QuickBooks to have a conversation with Excel, thereby creating your very own custom reports.

Creating Different Kinds of Reports

The first sections in this chapter cover finding the report you want and changing the information so that you get what you need.

For example, although the information on a regular Profit & Loss report is pretty handy, I like to view my Profit & Loss reports quarter by quarter. Sometimes, I condense the results to display only main headings, and sometimes I expand the results to show every detail. I also sometimes prefer to view Profit & Loss reports sorted by sales rep, item type or even shipping method. By changing the settings in QuickBooks, I get all the information I need in order to face up to the startling reality of my financial situation.

Heading to the centre

If you go to the Reports menu and click Report Centre, you arrive at the screen shown in Figure 13-1. From the category list on the left, click the type of report you need, such as Sales, Employees & Payroll or Company & Financial. QuickBooks displays a whole list of reports that belong to that category.

Browse through the report list to find the report you need. If you're not sure by looking at the names which one is going to give you the information you need, rest your mouse over the report icon to the left of the report. No, you're not instantly transported to the South Seas — more's the pity — but obligingly enough, QuickBooks displays an example of the report. Alternatively, click the More hyperlink that appears to the right of each report description to go straight to QuickBooks help, which gives you more details on the report's content, dates and ways to customise the report.

When you've found the report you need, click the report name to display it. From here, you can select the date range and, depending on the report, vary the column display (for example, with a Profit & Loss report, you can select Quarter from the column menu to display a separate column for each quarter's results).

Figure 13-1:
The Reports
Centre
offers more
than 100
standard
reports.

Creating your first report

I find it a little difficult to be prescriptive about generating QuickBooks reports, because what works best depends so much on the report itself. However, here I explain how to generate a Sales by Customer Summary report. Try to follow what I do step by step, even if you don't need this particular report right now. That way, you get a general idea of how the reports in QuickBooks work.

1. **From the Reports menu select Reports Centre, then click the Sales tab on the left-hand side.**

2. **Click the Sales by Customer Summary report.**

   QuickBooks displays this report for the current month.

3. **Select a date range that makes sense for you.**

   You can either type in start and finish dates, or select a period such as This Week or This Month-to-Date from the Dates menu. Suit yourself.

4. **Decide which columns you want to display.**

   With a Sales report, QuickBooks offers a whole swag of options. You can select separate columns for each day, week or fortnight, or separate columns for item types, shipping methods or sales reps. Experiment with the column settings and see what appears before your very eyes.

5. **Click the Modify button and explore the four different tabs: Display, Filters, Header/Footer and Fonts & Numbers.**

   For some reports, you can click the Display tab to add extra columns, or delete columns you don't need. In this sales report, you can add columns for previous periods and years.

   To restrict the information QuickBooks displays, click the Filters tab (I talk more about this feature later, in the section 'Narrowing things down'). I also suggest that you explore the Header/Footer and Fonts & Numbers tabs and experiment with the formatting of your report (for help tweaking the format, see 'Bringing out the artist within' later in this chapter).

6. **Click OK to return to the report display.**

   By now, your Sales by Customer Summary report probably looks similar to mine, shown in Figure 13-2 — assuming, of course, that all your customers are characters from *The Wind in the Willows*.

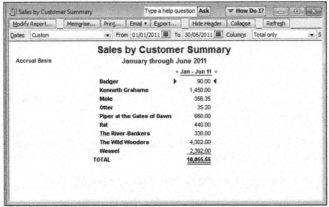

Figure 13-2:
Viewing a
modified
Sales by
Customer
Report.

7. **Decide whether you want to sort the information in a different way.**

   For example, you can sort the Sales by Customer Summary report by the Default sort (listing customers in alphabetical order) or by Total (listing the customer with the top sales first).

8. **Decide whether to save, print or memorise the report, and whether you'd also like to send the report to someone else.**

   I talk heaps more about these decisions later in this chapter, in the section 'Saving and Sharing'.

9. **Read the results of your fine efforts.**

   Yep, I know I'm stating the obvious, but it's amazing how many reams of reports lie around offices, lonely and unloved, without anybody giving them as much as a second glance.

Querying individual accounts, customers or suppliers

Sometimes you probably don't want to trek all the way over to the Reports menu, but instead you want a quick report that gives you a little more detail on what you're currently working on. For example, you may be right in the middle of invoicing a customer and, as part of deciding how much discount to offer, you need to generate a report showing how much this customer bought during the previous six months.

Chances are you can rustle up this information without leaving the Customer or Supplier Centre. Check out the right-hand side of both centres to find these handy reports:

- ✔ **QuickReport.** Highlight a customer or supplier name and then click QuickReport to see a list of transactions in date order, including estimates, invoices, statement charges, credits and payments received. I show an example QuickReport in Figure 13-3.

- ✔ **Open Balance report.** Highlight a customer or supplier name and then click Open Balance to see a list of all outstanding customer invoices or supplier bills, detailing due dates, total amounts and the open balance due.

- ✔ **Estimates by Job report (Customer Centre only).** Click Show Estimates to view the amount and status of estimates for each customer and job.

If you want to view all transactions by account, rather than by customer or supplier — maybe you want to view all transactions allocated to Telephone Expense, rather than all transactions allocated to Telstra — the quickest approach is to scoot over to your Chart of Accounts (that's Ctrl-A if you fancy using a shortcut key), single-click on the account you want a report on, then from the Reports menu select QuickReport.

Figure 13-3:
A QuickReport is usually the quickest way to glean information from QuickBooks.

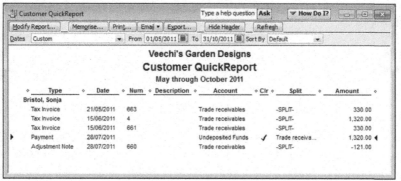

Narrowing things down

When you create a report, QuickBooks often gives you more information than you need. For example, if you want to check out all sales to a particular customer and you generate a Sales by Customer Summary report, QuickBooks starts by showing *all* sales to *all* customers.

To narrow information in QuickBooks so that you get just what you're looking for, you need to apply what's called a *report filter*. Click the Modify button followed by the Filters tab, shown in Figure 13-4. You can see heaps of options here, including Account, Amount, Date, Name and so on. You can select any filter to restrict the information that QuickBooks displays — for example, filtering a report so it only shows sales for a particular customer.

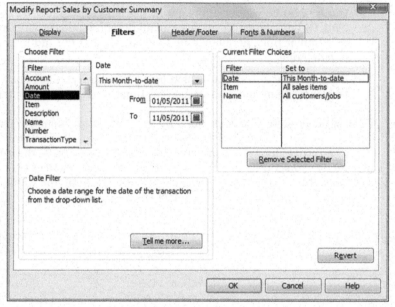

Figure 13-4:
Modifying a report using filters.

Here are some extra tips and tricks when working with filters:

REMEMBER

✔ **Don't limit yourself to one.** You can apply filters either one at a time or in combination with each other. The idea is that each additional filter further restricts the content of the report.

✔ **Select more than one name, or more than one account.** To choose two or more specific accounts or names, click Multiple Accounts or Multiple Names. Then simply click against each account or name that you want to include.

✔ **Filter by amount.** If you want to stick to the main game and hide from view all those piddly little transactions that can be distracting, select Amount as the filter and restrict transactions so that QuickBooks only shows amounts over $100 or $1,000, or whatever you specify as the amount.

✔ **Think outside the square.** When you filter by Item, not only can you select individual items or multiple items, but also filter by item type. For example, sometimes it's handy to filter by All Tax and view tax amounts only. Alternatively, you can filter by All Discounts and view the amounts of discounts given to different customers.

Getting Reports to Look Good

I find the standard reports in QuickBooks are often close to what I'm looking for, but not quite perfect. I sometimes need to delete, move or resize columns so the information fits on the page, and if I have time, I change fonts and add colours so that my reports look suitably elegant and well-dressed.

Before you plunge into formatting a report, take note of one thing: The moment you close a report, QuickBooks loses all your settings. The only way to retain these settings for the future is to memorise the report — for help doing so, see 'Saving reports for next time around' later in this chapter.

Mucking around with columns

If a report has more than one column, in the way that heaps of standard QuickBooks reports do, I often like to shift columns around and, if necessary, resize them.

To move a report column, place your mouse over the column header until it changes to a cute little hand. Hold down the left button on your mouse and drag the column to the left or to the right. (By the way, you can only move report columns on *list* and *detail* reports.)

To widen or narrow a column, rest your mouse on the small diamond that appears to the right of the column title, then drag to the right, or drag to the left.

To delete a column, the easiest method is simply to narrow it so much that it disappears. (To resuscitate a column that has been given the chop in this way, click Modify Report and then select the column from the list that appears under the Display tab.)

When you click Modify, you see a list of all the columns displayed on your report. I frequently deselect the first column labelled Left Margin — which QuickBooks always selects automatically — so I can fit that bit more information on a printed page.

Fitting everything in

Sometimes a report won't fit on a single page width and spreads itself across a couple of pages. It's time to impose some slimming measures:

✔ **Reduce the font size.** Right-click on the text in any column and reduce the font size (8 point or 9 point works pretty well for most reports).

✔ **Change the orientation.** Change the way the report prints on the paper. To do this, go to your File menu and click Printer Setup and change the orientation of the paper from Portrait to Landscape.

✔ **Scale down the report.** Click the Print button at the top of the report and choose to make the report fit on one page wide.

✔ **Trim unnecessary data.** Get rid of any columns you don't need by narrowing them so much that they disappear. (Rest your mouse on the diamond to the right of the column title, and drag to the left.)

To check how the report will look before you sacrifice any trees to the cause, first click the Print button, then select Preview.

Bringing out the artist within

After you've figured out what you want to include on a report, take a few moments to make it look really good:

✔ **Change the font (including colour, size and format).** First display the report, then rest your mouse on whatever you want to change. Click your right mouse button and select the font, style, size and colour you want. (Remember that although colours look funky and everything, if you tend to print out reports and want to save on colour cartridges, it's probably best to avoiding choosing colours and print office reports in greyscale — using black ink only.)

✔ **Change the header.** Display the report, click the Modify button and select the Header/Footer tab. Here you can change such niceties as the company name, report name, subtitle and so on. For example, one of my non-profit clients renames his Profit & Loss report to Income and Expenditure report by changing the header. Also, depending on your political preferences, you can choose whether to align your report headings to the left, the centre or the right.

✔ **Decide how you want to display numbers.** First display the report, then click the Modify button, followed by the Fonts & Numbers tab. Decide how you prefer to display negative numbers, decide whether you want dollar amounts without cents, and decide whether you want to hide 0.00 amounts on the report (usually, I prefer to hide 0.00 amounts, so I can focus on information that's important).

Figure 13-5 shows a report I've modified. I've added a few colours (not shown here — sorry), changed the header and footer and had a play with fonts. If you like what you come up with, and you want to make these settings the default for all your QuickBooks reports, head to your Preferences menu, select the Reports section, click the Company Preferences tab and select the Format button. Repeat your format settings here, and they'll carry across to all future reports.

Figure 13-5:
Experimenting with the formatting options to create eye-catching reports.

	Week of May 1, 11	May 8 - 21, 11	May 22 - 31, 11	TOTAL
Acmer Pty Ltd	3,500.00	0.00	0.00	3,500.00
Bristol, Sonja	0.00	300.00	0.00	300.00
Hadrians Wall Company	200.00	0.00	0.00	200.00
Olympic Park	1,925.00	0.00	0.00	1,925.00
Sunshine Seeds	0.00	180.00	0.00	180.00
TOTAL	5,625.00	480.00	0.00	6,105.00

Veechi's Garden Designs
Wholesale Sales for NSW
May 2011
Accrual Basis

By the way, if you think that all the fancy fonts and colours in the world can't make a report look interesting, or if you're sending a report to an audience whose eyes glaze over as soon as they see more than three rows of figures, then ask yourself whether you'd be better off creating a pie chart or bar graph. QuickBooks includes various graphs in the Report Centre, such as the Income and Expense Graph, the Net Worth Graph, the Sales Graph and the really scary Accounts Payable Graph. Alternatively, try sending the report to Excel — I show you the mechanics of how this is done in 'Sending reports to Excel' later in this chapter — and from there, convert your report data into a more pictorial representation.

Print screen, print!

Want to print exactly what you can see on the screen at the moment? You can. And it's easy!

Press the Print Screen key on your keyboard (often called PrtSc or Prnt Scrn). Then select Start➪Programs➪Accessories➪Paint. Go up to the Edit menu in your Paint program and click Paste. Aha! Your picture appears, ready to print.

Saving and Sharing

Have you ever spent heaps of time customising a report, but when you closed it to do something else, you lost all your work? The solution is easy: If you think you want to generate that report in a similar format sometime in the future, then you ask QuickBooks to *memorise* the report.

One good thing about memorising reports is that you can share them with others. Using the same principle, other people can share their memorised reports with you, which you import into your reports list.

Saving reports for next time around

Ready to memorise your report settings so that they're available next time you need them? Then read on:

1. **Create the report of your dreams.**

   For a run-down on creating your report, read through everything in this chapter up until this point. Never mind if your final report is tall, dark and handsome or if it's small, fair and intelligent (like yours truly, although the intelligent bit is always up for debate).

   One thing to remember. When memorising a report, try selecting a date range that's generic rather than specific. For example, if you want to memorise a Profit & Loss report for circulating to management every month, select Last Month-to-Date from the drop-down Dates menu, rather than typing specific dates into the From and To date fields.

2. **Click the Memorise button (or alternatively, Ctrl-M) and when prompted, name your new report.**

   Make the name something meaningful, so you know later why you created the report in the first place. If you have lots of custom reports, I also recommend that you click Save in Memorised Report Group, and store your report in whatever group make most sense.

   QuickBooks has groups such as Accountant, Banking and Company, but I often like to create new report groups, such as Daily Reports, End-of-Month Reports and End-of-Year Reports.

3. **Click OK to return to your report.**

4. **Select Memorised Reports from the Reports menu.**

   A list of all your memorised reports appears, as well as some memorised reports that QuickBooks provides as standard. Select the report you just memorised, click Display and note how all your formatting and report filters have been saved.

By the way, if you've got a report that you use heaps, a smart idea is to memorise the report, then add it to your icon bar. First display the report, selecting a date range that's generic rather than specific (for example, select Month-to-Date, rather than 1/4/11 to 30/4/11). Then choose View⇨Add Report to Icon Bar. Create a Label and Description for the icon bar button, then click OK.

Sharing memorised reports with others

My clients often find they want to share their memorised reports with other businesses or colleagues, or across different company files. For example, a client of mine has several QuickBooks company files, one for each of his property developments, and he likes to have the same set of memorised reports available in each company file.

Sharing memorised reports is a piece of cake:

1. **Go to Reports⇨Memorised Reports⇨Memorised Reports List and highlight the chosen report.**

2. **Select Export Template from the Memorised Report menu.**

   Don't click the Export button. All this does is send your report to Excel.

3. **Decide where you want to store this template, then click Save.**

   I often create a folder called Memorised Reports inside my QuickBooks folder, and store all my templates there. QuickBooks uses the report name as the filename and adds the letters QBR as the file extension.

Now that you've saved your memorised report, you're ready to send it anywhere. To open up a memorised report in a different QuickBooks company file, whether it's on the same computer or in the frozen wilds of Lapland, the principle is the same. Read on . . .

Downloading reports from other sources

In this next set of instructions I assume you have a memorised report that you want to import into your QuickBooks company file — maybe you've exported this report from another company file, maybe a colleague has sent you a report template, or maybe you've downloaded a report template from the QuickBooks website. Here's what to do:

1. **Go to Reports⇨Memorised Reports⇨Memorised Reports List.**

2. **Select Import Template from the Memorised Reports menu.**

Now you see 'em, now you don't

The moment you import a report template it becomes part of your QuickBooks company file. What this means is if you move your company file from one computer to another, or upgrade your company file, all your report templates carry across automatically.

However, if for some reason you've downloaded custom reports from somewhere and haven't yet imported them into your QuickBooks file, remember that if you shift computers you'll need to copy these report templates across separately.

3. **Navigate to wherever you stored the template that you're trying to import, highlight the template, then click Open.**

   QuickBooks displays the Memorise Report window.

4. **Give the report a name.**

   Personally, I like the name Genevieve for a girl, Lloyd for a boy.

5. **QuickBooks makes a subtle *kerplunk* sound as it imports your report.**

   Listen carefully. True, it's not Paul Kelly but still, it's music to my ears.

Now that you're a dab hand at importing reports, why not make your way to http://community.intuit.com/library and then click the link to the Reports page. Herein lies a treasure trove of report templates, all of which you can download for free. (Who said there was no such thing as a free lunch?)

Reporting to the Outside World

Imagine that you're working in an office and the receptionist speaks German, the bookkeeper speaks Turkish and the manager speaks Japanese. They struggle along doing their separate jobs and then one day a translator, who speaks all three languages, arrives at the office. Suddenly, everyone can communicate with one another and work goes along much more efficiently.

Think of the business software in your office as being a group of individuals, all trying to communicate with one another. Your job is to get them talking to one another — for example, generating reports in Excel using QuickBooks data, sending emails directly from QuickBooks with reports attached, generating PDF files direct from QuickBooks, and much, much more.

Sending reports to Excel

If you have a report that does almost everything you want, but not quite, then the solution is to send the report from QuickBooks into Excel. Sending reports to Excel is child's play. First display the report, then click the Export button that appears along the top. You arrive at the Export Report window. Click Export and watch as Excel opens automatically, displaying your report in all its finery, as shown in Figure 13-6. After the report is in Excel, you can change headings, cut and paste columns, convert figures into graphs and lots more.

Figure 13-6:
A QuickBooks report imported into Microsoft Excel.

You probably don't need to know much more, but here are some tricks I've picked up along the way:

- ✔ In order to send a report to Excel, you don't need to open Excel first. QuickBooks automatically tells Excel what to do, and unbelievably enough, Excel follows suit.

- ✔ One neat tip I love — and only discovered recently — is this: When the Export Report window opens, I click the Advanced tab and from there, I click the Auto Filtering button. What this does is set up a whole load of drop-down menus in Excel, allowing me to filter my Excel report in lots of different ways. Refer to Figure 13-6 — note that the drop-down field automatically appears in the Name column (or any column that I select). Very handy stuff.

- ✔ If you want to get rid of the spacer columns and rows that QuickBooks inserts when it sends a report to Excel, click the Export Report button and then select the option to export a comma-separated-values (CSV) file. Click Export, save the file on your desktop, then open Excel and import this file.

✔ If you export to an existing Excel workbook, the new worksheet is placed in front of the last active sheet and named 'Sheet2' or whatever the next available number in the series is. I find this feature handy for copying across actual results from QuickBooks as a separate sheet in cashflow or budget workbooks.

Emailing reports around the globe

Did you know that you can email reports directly from QuickBooks, in either Excel or PDF format? Harking back to my save-the-trees theme, what this means is that I can email reports to colleagues or clients rather than printing them. Even better, if I email reports in Excel format, whoever receives my report can manipulate the data, search for information, create bar charts or whatever. (Remember, not everyone has QuickBooks, but almost everyone has Excel.)

Emailing reports is a walk in the park. First display the report, then click the Email button. Next, choose between Send Report as Excel or Send Report as PDF. (Excel is better if you want the person receiving the email to be able to modify the report.) Enter the email address when QuickBooks provides the prompt, click OK and you're done.

Creating a silk purse from a sow's ear

Sometimes, customising standard reports within QuickBooks or sending standard reports to Excel isn't enough. You need a report that gets a bit of information from one place, a bit of information from another place, multiplies one column by another and so on. It's time to improvise:

✔ Start by browsing the QuickBooks community library at http://community.intuit.com/library to see if anyone has already created the kind of report you're looking for. (Go to the Reports page that sits within the Library page.) Refer to 'Downloading reports from other sources' earlier in this chapter for more information on importing reports.

✔ Alternatively, get a report custom-written. For a list of independent system developers, all of whom develop software or reports that integrate with QuickBooks, visit www.veechicurtis.com.au/quickbooks-add-ons.html or visit www.quicken.com.au and search the software developer's catalogue found on the Partners page.

Exporting data, not reports

In this chapter, I talk about sending reports to Microsoft Excel direct from QuickBooks. However, sometimes you may want to extract data out of your company file without using Excel — maybe you want to send data into a different program altogether, or maybe you want to send information into Excel in a different format than what's available in the Reports menu.

In this case, a better approach is often to export data itself, rather than reports. In both

the QuickBooks Customer Centre and Supplier Centre, if you click the Excel button, you can choose to export customer or supplier lists, as well as customer or supplier transactions. When the Export Report window appears, you can choose between creating an Excel file or a CSV (comma-separated-values) file. Either works fine, depending on how you intend to use the data.

Battling those Printing Blues

I know how it is. It's 6 pm on a Friday evening and you promised your partner/girlfriend/boyfriend/spouse that you would be on time for the latest exciting social engagement. You have to print a report before leaving work and at the crucial moment the printer plays possum.

What should you do next? Read on and (hopefully) you'll get a life.

- ✔ **Connection.** Is the cable connecting the computer to the printer plugged in at both ends? Wiggle each end of the cable a little to make sure both are secure.

- ✔ **Power.** Switch off your computer and your printer and wait a couple of minutes. Read a short novel. Then switch everything back on and try again.

- ✔ **Printer driver.** Reinstall your printer driver, using the original CD that came with the printer.

✔ **Reinstall your QuickBooks program.** If you can print from your word processor but you can't print from your QuickBooks company file, then reinstall your QuickBooks program from your CD. (Don't worry, doing this reinstalls the program only; you won't lose any of your precious data.)

✔ **Printer cable.** If your printer is toying with you, being good some of the time but garbled the rest of the time, then you may have a faulty printer cable. Try using another one.

If all else fails, employ psychological warfare. Close the door, then go enjoy your Friday night. Maybe by Monday morning the printer will be feeling contrite and ready to talk to you again.

Chapter 14

Managing Profit and Growing Your Business

. . . .

In This Chapter

▶ Finding out what's profitable in your business (and what isn't)

▶ Generating reports for different locations, branches or cost centres

▶ Reviewing your Profit & Loss, your Balance Sheet and Company Snapshot

▶ Setting up budgets and planning for the future

. . . .

*W*hat if your Profit & Loss report always comes up with surprises and you find it hard to predict results? What projects or business strategies are the real stars, and what's a complete waste of time?

One of the best things about QuickBooks is that it can analyse where you make money, and where you don't. In this chapter, I show you how to track jobs to see how much profit you make on individual jobs or projects, and also how to allocate classes to each transaction so that you can analyse cost centres or locations.

With this analysis in place, you can then step back a little and look at your Profit & Loss as a whole, deciding where you plan to head in the future. From here, you're ready to set up budgets and start driving your business, rather than have your business driving you.

Distinguishing Fool's Gold from the Real Thing

One of the fascinating facts about many self-employed people is that they're actually running more than one business. Take myself as an example: I write books (that's my authoring business) but I also do consulting work (that's my consulting business). The lady who does my PR is more eclectic: She has her publicity work (her publicity business) but then she has her real passion (her horse-training business).

One of the secrets to success in business is to know what's profitable and what isn't. Too often, I come across clients who believe they're making most of their profit from a certain aspect of their business. When we do the analysis, however, they often discover that although that part of their business generates the most *income*, it generates scarcely a cent of profit.

That's why I talk about differentiating between fool's gold and the real thing. What I explain in this chapter is how to use QuickBooks to see which parts of your business are profitable, and which parts are dragging it down.

Analysing transactions, reporting on profit

In this section, I talk about the *class system* in QuickBooks, showing you how you can code every transaction in several different ways. For example, in the Write Cheques transaction in Figure 14-1, the Pay to the Order of field shows the name of the company that I'm paying, the Account column shows the type of the expense and the Customer:Job column shows the customer and the project name. In addition, the Class column shows the branch of the business that incurred the expense.

If you record all transactions in this way, you can call up Profit & Loss reports on every job or project you undertake, as well as track profitability for each class (which could be a branch, location or cost centre) of your business. By analysing how much money you're making (or losing!) you could be driving a fancy sports car before you know it.

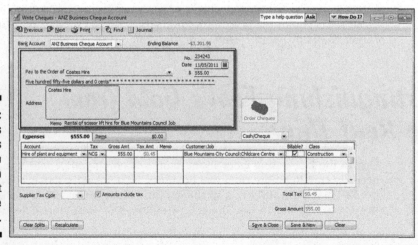

Figure 14-1:
Use jobs and classes on each transaction to see just where the profit lies.

Imposing a class system

To take advantage of the class feature, you first need to switch on class tracking. To do this, go to Edit⟶Preferences⟶Accounting. Under the Company Preferences tab, click the option to Use Class Tracking and, if you want to be reminded to select a class on every transaction, tick the option for QuickBooks to prompt you to assign classes.

Next, go to your Lists menu, select Class List, and from the Class menu, select New. You know the drill; it's the same as creating all lists in QuickBooks. Enter a Class Name, click OK to save it, then repeat the process for every class you want to create.

The main obstacle for most people is not the mechanics of how to create a Class List in QuickBooks; rather it's figuring out how to divide their business into classes.

Browse through the following scenarios and see if any are similar to your own business:

- A client of mine runs a guesthouse with both accommodation and dining facilities. She allocates all accommodation income and expenses to a class called Accommodation, and allocates all dining income and expenses to a class called Dining. She loves how she can print Profit & Loss reports for her accommodation business, Profit & Loss reports for the restaurant and a Profit & Loss for everything combined.

- A hairdresser friend has two salons in different suburbs of Sydney. She has two classes in her Class List (Paddington and Rose Bay) and codes all income and expenses to either one class or the other. By doing so, she can print a Profit & Loss on each salon separately, as well as a Profit & Loss on the two salons combined.

- An architect client has two main income streams: One is design and planning, the other is project management. By creating a class for each income stream and allocating expenses to each class, he can see how much profit he makes from each.

- A real estate client separates all income and expenses into two classes: One for property management, the other for sales.

Allocating classes to transactions

After you decide how you want to use classes and you've switched on class tracking in your preferences, allocating classes to transactions is simple. Here are a few pointers to help you along the way:

- ✔ **Try it and see.** Have a look at the Write Cheques transaction in Figure 14-1. The expense account is Hire of Plant and Equipment and the Class, way over in the last right-hand column, is for the construction arm of the business. Experiment in the same way with your data — after all, there's nothing that you can't undo.

- ✔ **Use the Class field at the top of the form whenever possible.** On some forms, such as sales and purchases, there's a Class field at the top next to the customer or supplier name, as well as a class column in the body of the transaction itself. If you know that you're going to allocate every line of a transaction to the same class, it's quicker to select the class at the top. That way, QuickBooks automatically completes the class on every line below.

- ✔ **Decide whether you want to allocate a class for each paycheque, or for each earnings item.** If you want to split paycheques across more than one class, then change your preferences (under Payroll & Employees in your Preferences menu) so that you assign class by earnings item, not by paycheque.

- ✔ **Create a class for administration costs.** Sooner or later, when you're working with jobs, you'll come across expenses that are difficult to allocate to any one particular class. Things such as accounting fees, bank charges, legal fees, merchant fees and even telephone bills are often hard to pigeonhole. I have a neat solution to this dilemma: Create an additional class called Admin and use this class for any income or expenses that don't belong to a particular class.

Generating reports by class (or cost centre)

Organising your business into different cost centres or classes is one thing, but pulling reports out of QuickBooks is another. Here are some of the class reports you can create, and how:

- ✔ **Class QuickReport.** To generate this report, go to your Class List, highlight the class you want a report on, then select QuickReport from the bottom Reports menu. Up comes a report listing every transaction allocated to that class. The default format for this report sorts in date order, but you can sort this report in almost any way you like.

✔ **Profit & Loss Class report.** To access this report, go to your Class List, click the Reports button, followed by Reports on all Classes, followed by Profit & Loss by Class. This report shows a standard Profit & Loss report, with a separate column for each class, similar to Figure 14-2. (The interesting thing about these results is that although the Leichardt branch generates more income, it's actually less profitable.) If you have many different classes in your Class List, or just want to report on one class at a time, go to Modify Report, click the Filters tab, and after choosing Class as your filter, select the class or classes you want to report on.

✔ **Profit & Loss Class report, with only some accounts showing.** If you want to summarise key information on each class, showing only income and expense accounts that are relevant, you can. Go to Modify Report, click the Filters tab, and after choosing Account as your filter, select the accounts you want to report on.

With any of these reports, if you modify the filters — perhaps by choosing to report on one class only — QuickBooks does its stuff obligingly enough, but doesn't state anywhere on the report header which class it's reporting on. In this kind of situation, I usually modify the Header of the report to include the name of the class or classes that I'm reporting on.

Figure 14-2:
Generating a Profit & Loss report for each 'class' or cost centre in your business.

Profit & Loss by Class			
Modify Report... Memorise... Print... Email ▼ Export... Hide Header Collapse Refresh			
Dates Custom ▼ From 01/08/2011 To 15/09/2011 Columns Class ▼ Sort By Default			

Vogue Hair
Profit & Loss by Class

Accrual Basis

	Haberfield Branch	Leichardt Branch	TOTAL
Ordinary Income/Expense			
Income			
Hairdressing Income			
Colours and styling	▶ 3,500.00	◀ 7,200.00	10,700.00
Cuts	12,000.00	10,400.00	22,400.00
Products	520.00	890.00	1,410.00
Total Hairdressing Income	16,020.00	18,490.00	34,510.00
Total Income	16,020.00	18,490.00	34,510.00
Cost of Goods Sold			
Cost of Goods Sold	320.00	520.00	840.00
Total COGS	320.00	520.00	840.00
Gross Profit	15,700.00	17,970.00	33,670.00
Expense			
Books and Publications	37.00	52.00	89.00
Consulting Expenses	0.00	890.00	890.00
Office Supplies	320.00	90.00	410.00
Rent	2,900.00	3,200.00	6,100.00
Repairs	0.00	3,200.00	3,200.00
Wages	4,200.00	4,800.00	9,000.00
Total Expense	7,457.00	12,232.00	19,689.00
Net Ordinary Income	8,243.00	5,738.00	13,981.00
Net Income	**8,243.00**	**5,738.00**	**13,981.00**

Managing Projects and Individual Jobs

By now you've probably noticed that every single transaction in QuickBooks includes a field or column labelled Customer:Job. For example, if you make a sale in QuickBooks, the Customer:Job field appears in the top-left corner. If you make a purchase or record a cheque transaction in QuickBooks, a Customer:Job column appears on each line.

What this means is that you can track not only income for each customer, but also expenses for each customer. You can even mark expenses as billable so that QuickBooks prompts you to onbill these expenses when you're next ready to bill that customer.

Adding jobs to your Customer List

For some businesses, each distinct job or project belongs to a different customer. In this case, you don't need to add jobs to your customer list — you simply have one customer name for each job.

When a class action makes no sense

One thing that almost everyone finds hard to get their head around in QuickBooks is when to use classes, when to use customer types and when to use jobs.

My rule of thumb is to use classes if distinct expenses are associated with a stream of income. For example, most real estate agents have an entirely different set of expenses, including different staff, between their property management division and their sales division, and for this reason they use class tracking to report on each division.

However, if income comes from distinctly different types of customers, but expenses are shared across the board, then customer types probably work better. For example, a client of mine doesn't use the classes feature in QuickBooks at all, but divides her customers into three types: Wholesale, Retail and Mail Order. (You configure the customer type by going to the Additional Info tab for each customer.) However, although you can filter most QuickBooks reports according to customer type, you can't always get the customer type to display on the report itself, which can be a real pain.

On the other hand, if you want to analyse income according to a particular project, then using job reporting makes most sense. Most builders work in this way, setting up each building project as a separate customer, or as a separate job, in the Customer Centre.

Other businesses may have several jobs or projects attached to a single customer name. For example, a carpenter friend of mine does lots of work for the local council. The local council is a customer in his Customers & Jobs List, with each individual project for the council a different job within that customer file. To see how this pans out, he checks out the Job Profitability Summary report, shown in Figure 14-3.

To create a new job within a customer, simply highlight the customer, then select Add Job from the New Customer & Job menu (alternatively, right-clicking with your mouse and selecting Add Job does the same thing). From here, add details for each job in exactly the same way you do when creating a new customer. If you like, you can record job details such as Job Status and Description on the Job Info tab of each record.

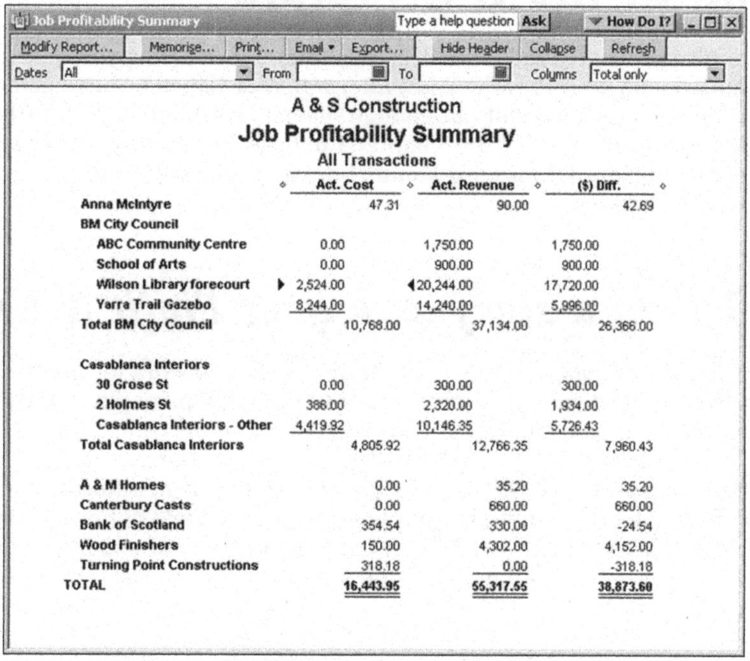

Figure 14-3: Incorporating jobs within your customer list to track income and expenses specific to single projects, jobs or cases.

A & S Construction
Job Profitability Summary
All Transactions

	Act. Cost	Act. Revenue	($) Diff.
Anna McIntyre	47.31	90.00	42.69
BM City Council			
ABC Community Centre	0.00	1,750.00	1,750.00
School of Arts	0.00	900.00	900.00
Wilson Library forecourt	2,524.00	20,244.00	17,720.00
Yarra Trail Gazebo	8,244.00	14,240.00	5,996.00
Total BM City Council	10,768.00	37,134.00	26,366.00
Casablanca Interiors			
30 Grose St	0.00	300.00	300.00
2 Holmes St	386.00	2,320.00	1,934.00
Casablanca Interiors - Other	4,419.92	10,146.35	5,726.43
Total Casablanca Interiors	4,805.92	12,766.35	7,960.43
A & M Homes	0.00	35.20	35.20
Canterbury Casts	0.00	660.00	660.00
Bank of Scotland	354.54	330.00	-24.54
Wood Finishers	150.00	4,302.00	4,152.00
Turning Point Constructions	318.18	0.00	-318.18
TOTAL	**16,443.95**	**55,317.55**	**38,873.60**

Reporting on the profitability of every job

When it comes to reporting, there are a few different reports that you can pull out of the QuickBooks hat:

✔ The Profit & Loss by Job report shows all income and expenses allocated to a particular job, with each job showing as a separate column. I often like to modify this report, clicking the Filters tab and filtering by Name to view one job at a time.

✔ The Job Profitability Summary report is similar to the Profit & Loss report, but shows all costs, including those associated with Balance Sheet items. The information here is in a more summarised format, with one column for costs, one for revenue and another for the difference (namely the profit). I find this report handy, but often end up printing a Job Profitability Detail report at the same time so that I can see what makes up the figures in the summary report.

✔ The Sales by Customer Summary report is yet another way of viewing the same information, although this report only shows income for each customer or job, rather than income and expenses.

Looking at the Big Picture

You've probably read a hundred business books telling you how to understand your Profit & Loss, interpret your Balance Sheet, go crazy with ratio analysis and print out enough budget reports to sink a battleship. In the following pages of this chapter, I put this heavy-duty theory into the context of QuickBooks, explaining how to produce these reports and ensure they make sense.

Telling a story with your Profit & Loss

I'm always amazed by the number of clients who work for hours and hours every week, punching information into their company file, without taking the time to generate any reports and look at them.

Now that you have QuickBooks up and running, generating a Profit & Loss report is as easy (quite literally) as clicking a couple of buttons. Did you make a profit? If not, why? What happened with your expenses? Can you save money on anything? How did sales compare to last month, last year or the year before that? What trends can you see in these figures?

Because my Profit & Loss is such an important report, I like to add it to my icon bar. To do this, first display your Profit & Loss, choosing This Month-to-Date in the Date menu. Then go to your View menu and select Add Profit & Loss to Icon Bar. Choose an icon, click OK and there you have it — your Profit & Loss report is on tap at all times, just a single button-click away.

Dare to be gross!

Gross profit isn't a way of referring to the excesses of capitalism. Rather, gross profit is the profit you make after allowing for costs of goods sold, such as raw materials, subcontractors or commissions. For businesses that buy and then resell things, the gross profit margin — in other words, gross profit as a percentage of sales — is like a litmus test for business health.

Gross profit generally goes up when sales go up and down when sales decline. You can verify this ratio by modifying your standard Profit & Loss report to include a % of Income subcolumn (to see what this looks like, refer to Figure 14-4). The Profit & Loss report can then show income month by month and, although income may fluctuate every month, you can see whether the cost of goods sold as a percentage of income is constant.

If you do get a fluctuation in your gross profit margin, then you need to investigate why. Common causes include bookkeeping mistakes, pricing errors or employee theft.

If you're new to QuickBooks, I recommend you start with the standard Profit & Loss report and experiment with the following settings, using different report formats to gain insights into your business:

- ✔ Click Modify Report and then, on the Display tab, add a % of Income subcolumn. If you do this, you end up with a report similar to mine, shown in Figure 14-4. I find the % of Income column is the best way to monitor my gross profit margin, as well as the percentage of expenses against income (see the related sidebar 'Dare to be gross!' in this chapter to find out more).

- ✔ Select a broad date range (say, the last 6 or 12 months) and from the Columns drop-down menu, select Month or Quarter. Viewing your results in columns side by side helps you see trends and sometimes helps you spot mistakes.

- ✔ Click the Collapse button to condense your Profit & Loss report to headings only, then click Expand to make the details magically re-appear.

- ✔ If you're a non-profit or community organisation, click Modify Report and then, on the Header/Footer tab, change the header to Income and Expenditure report.

- If you're stumped as to why your Profit & Loss says you've made a profit, yet you've got no cash in the bank, try clicking Modify Report and on the Display tab select Cash as the Report Basis. If you display a Profit & Loss report on a cash basis, income only shows up on this report when you get paid and, similarly, expenses only appear when you part with the cash.

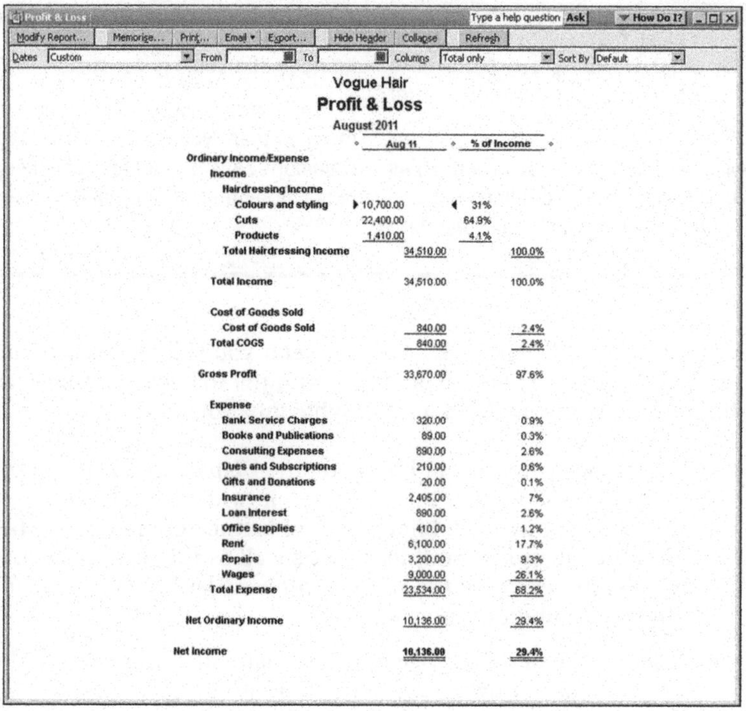

Vogue Hair
Profit & Loss
August 2011

	Aug 11		% of Income	
Ordinary Income/Expense				
Income				
Hairdressing Income				
Colours and styling	10,700.00		31%	
Cuts	22,400.00		64.9%	
Products	1,410.00		4.1%	
Total Hairdressing Income		34,510.00		100.0%
Total Income		34,510.00		100.0%
Cost of Goods Sold				
Cost of Goods Sold		840.00		2.4%
Total COGS		840.00		2.4%
Gross Profit		33,670.00		97.6%
Expense				
Bank Service Charges		320.00		0.9%
Books and Publications		89.00		0.3%
Consulting Expenses		890.00		2.6%
Dues and Subscriptions		210.00		0.6%
Gifts and Donations		20.00		0.1%
Insurance		2,405.00		7%
Loan Interest		890.00		2.6%
Office Supplies		410.00		1.2%
Rent		6,100.00		17.7%
Repairs		3,200.00		9.3%
Wages		9,000.00		26.1%
Total Expense		23,534.00		68.2%
Net Ordinary Income		10,136.00		29.4%
Net Income		10,136.00		29.4%

Figure 14-4: Adding a percentage of income column to Profit & Loss reports.

Taking a photo with your Balance Sheet

Think of your Profit & Loss as the story of what goes on in your business over any period of time, whereas your Balance Sheet is more like a photograph. A Balance Sheet is really a picture of how much you own and how much you owe at any point in time, and the difference between how much you own and how much you owe is your stake in the business. For a picture of a very simple Balance Sheet, see Figure 14-5.

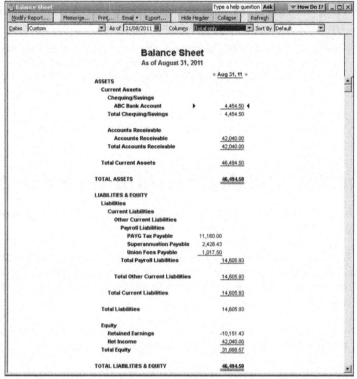

Figure 14-5:
Under-
standing
your
Balance
Sheet is a
vital part
of good
business
practice.

Even though most people find Balance Sheets hard to understand, that doesn't mean they're not really important. A Balance Sheet is the first report I look at when I want to check if the Profit & Loss reports are accurate, because this is where mistakes are easiest to spot. In other words, if you want to be able to rely on your Profit & Loss reports, you have to ensure your Balance Sheet is correct.

✔ **Read every line.** Ask yourself whether every single line on your Balance Sheet makes sense. A simple idea, but it works.

✔ **Check that every bank account shows the right balance.** Savings and investment accounts are the most prone to neglect, so check the amount showing on the Balance Sheet against the latest bank statements.

✔ **Consider the balances of your fixed assets.** Do they make sense? Perhaps you have an old bomb that barely scrapes through rego, but Motor Vehicles shows up as a $50,000 asset in your Balance Sheet. If you're at all unsure of any amount in your fixed assets, compare the end-of-year values for each asset group against your most recent Depreciation Schedule.

✔ **Make sure all accumulated depreciation accounts are minus figures.** They're not? Something is definitely crook.

✔ **Check that all liability accounts are positive figures (not minus).** If a liability shows up as a minus figure on your Balance Sheet, then something is almost certainly amiss. (GST Paid on Purchases, if you have an account by this name, is an exception to this rule.)

✔ **Ensure that Opening Balance Equity is equal to zero.** Go on, check your figures (if the balance isn't zero, refer to Chapter 9).

Checking business health with one click

Are business worries keeping you awake at night? Then I recommend you get acquainted with your personal Company Snapshot.

The Company Snapshot is a feature new to recent versions of QuickBooks. Similar to what I show in Figure 14-6, this snapshot displays an instant summary of your income and expense results, reminders, account balances, receivables and payables.

To view this feature, simply select Company Snapshot from the Company menu. You can customise this view in two different ways.

Figure 14-6:
Check your
vital signs
with the
Company
Snapshot.

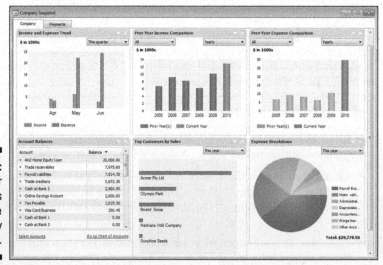

The first way you can transform your Company Snapshot is to hide certain graphs from view, or add other graphs that don't show up in the default settings.

✔ To add a new graph or table, click the Add Content link that appears in blue just below the Company tab. This gives you a choice of 12 different graphs and tables (some of which are already included in the default settings). Simply click Add to add a new graph or table.

✔ To delete a graph or table, click the little 'x' that appears in the top-right corner of each one.

The second way you can customise your Company Snapshot is to tweak the settings of the individual displays. For example:

✔ To change the reporting period on your Income and Expense Trend, just change the month or year in the drop-down box to the right of the chart.

✔ To view different account balances, click Select Accounts in the left-hand corner and click against the accounts you want to view.

✔ To change the Reminders display, click Set Preferences and for each kind of reminder, click whether you want to see summary info, all the gory details or nothing at all.

By the way, when you change your Company Snapshot settings, QuickBooks remembers which graphs or tables you prefer to display, but doesn't remember the individual tweaks that you make to each graph (such as the choice of reporting period). You have to make these selections every time you open the Company Snapshot.

One more thing: If a user doesn't have permission to access a particular function in QuickBooks, then that person won't be able to add any company snapshots that relate to that function. For example, if you want to prevent employees from knowing the full guts and glory of your company's profitability, you can set access restrictions so that they can't view sensitive financial reports. (I talk more about password settings in Chapter 15.) With this restriction in place, employees won't be able to view the company snapshot analysing Income and Expense trends.

Customising financial reports

Unless your business has very specific requirements, you'll probably find that the standard financial reports in QuickBooks provide everything you need, especially considering how much you're able to modify and filter the information in each report.

However, if you're still hungry for additional financial reports, try the reports library at `http://community.intuit.com/library`. (Chapter 13 explains how to download reports from this website and import them into your company file.)

Alternatively, the Accountant Edition of QuickBooks includes a Financial Statement Designer which has a whole heap of additional financial statements, including multiple balance sheets, income statements and statements of cashflows. You may want to ask your accountant to open your company file in their Accountant Edition and generate some additional reports at the end of each quarter or financial year.

Working to a Budget

When you're a businessperson, the daily recipe of life is a concoction of hope, dreams and hours of hard work. The secret ingredients that make this recipe work are a generous pinch of realism and forward planning. That's where budgets come into their own.

Budgeting as if you mean it

Part of getting intimate with your financials is deciding what you *want* the figures to be (as opposed to just looking at what they are) and figuring out how you're going to achieve your goals. In order to do this, you need to draw up a few serious budgets.

1. **Go to your Company menu, select Planning & Budgeting, followed by Set Up Budgets.**

   You arrive at the Create New Budget window or, if you've already set up a budget in the past, another window appears. In this case, you need to click the Create New Budget button to create another budget.

2. **Select a year for your budget, and whether you want to create a Profit & Loss budget or a Balance Sheet budget.**

   Unless you're a particularly technical accountant-nerdy-type, chances are you're creating a Profit & Loss budget.

3. **Click Next and decide whether you want to create separate subbudgets within your main budget.**

   For the really masochistic folk out there, you can create budgets not only for your overall Profit & Loss, but for each job and class as well. QuickBooks is smart the way it does this. For example, you can view actual versus budget reports for each job, as well as actual versus budget reports that consolidate all the individual job budgets into one big budget. The same principle applies to class reports.

   If this is the first budget you've ever done, I recommend you keep things nice and simple, and select the No Additional Criteria button.

4. **Click Next and decide whether you want to build budgets from scratch, or start with data from the previous year.**

   Why journey off to cuckoo-land when you could be firmly grounded in reality? If you have data from the last financial year, I suggest you use it. And, if you increase the budget for an income account or decrease the budget for an expense account by more than 10 per cent when compared to last year, you'd better have a really good reason!

5. **Click Finish.**

   QuickBooks lists your new budget in the Set Up Budgets window, as shown in Figure 14-7. Here you can toggle between all the budgets you've created so far, using the Budget drop-down menu.

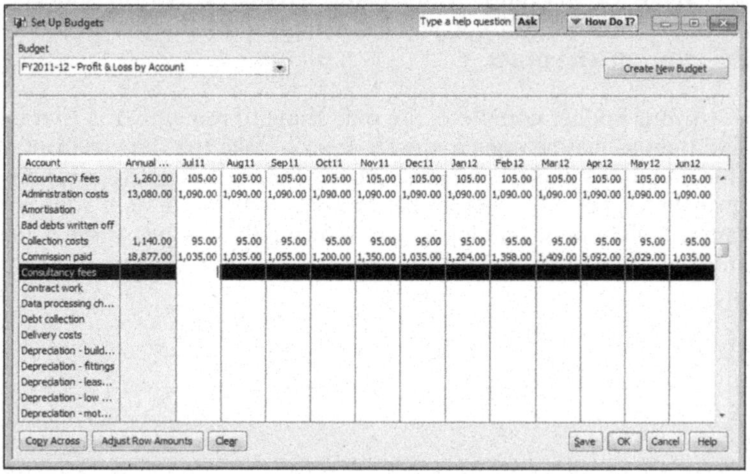

Figure 14-7: Setting up budgets in your accounts.

6. **Enter or revise your budgets, line by line.**

   Now's the time to forget about the purchase of that sports car and think about buying gruel in bulk. By the way, if an expense is going to be the same every month (like rent or insurance), save time and enter one column only. Then click the Copy Across button to complete the other 11 columns.

   When setting up budgets, remember that some expenses are irregular, such as quarterly electricity bills or one-off annual payments. Also, keep an eye out for months with five pay weeks, rather than four, and always make some allowance for unforeseen expenses, especially if you're doing a budget for a new business. Things always cost more than you think.

7. **Click OK to save and close your budget.**

   Actually, if you're going to continue working on budget figures for a while, keep clicking the Save button as you work.

8. **Make your way to the Reports Centre and print out the Budget Overview report.**

   A budget isn't worth a piece of parrot poo unless you read it, communicate it to others and create a business plan that ensures your budget is achievable. Also, if you have a few people working in the business, ask for input on the budget figures. The more involved everyone is, the more realistic the budget.

9. **At some point in the not too distant future, return to your budget and update figures as necessary.**

   I'm assuming here that you've printed your budget, thought long and deeply about it, and now you're ready to tweak a few figures here and there. Go to Company⇨Planning & Budgets⇨Set Up Budgets, then select the budget you just created from the Budget drop-down list in the top-left corner.

With your budget complete, the only thing to remember is that every now and then — maybe once a month or so — take the time to print a report that compares budgets against actuals (all the budget reports are tucked away in Reports⇨Budgets & Forecasts). And of course, if your colleagues or family members or employees are blowing the budget, there's nobody better than you to pull them back in line.

Gazing into the future

When you go to the Set Up Budgets menu (Company⇨Planning & Budgets⇨Set Up Budgets), you may notice another two options: Set Up Forecast and Cash Flow Projector.

When you explore Set Up Forecast, you discover that forecasts work in just the same way as budgets. In fact, if QuickBooks didn't call it a forecast in the top-left corner, you could imagine you're still creating a budget.

Lots of clients ask me about the difference between a budget and a forecast. For most people, a *budget* is a statement of how a business — or department within a business — intends to spend available funds. In some cases, budgets even include contingency plans that show alternative sources of funds in the event of a shortfall in income. By contrast, a *forecast* predicts future income and expenditure. Often, businesses make lots of different forecasts, using scenario planning to ask 'what if' questions. What if sales decreased by 10 per cent but expenses increased by 15 per cent? What if the opposite happened?

Despite being the QuickBooks advocate that I am, I admit that I'm not a great fan of the forecasting tools. I find the budget features handy, especially because I'm able to compare actuals to budgets every month and nip excess spending in the bud, before it creates problems. However, I prefer to create forecasts in Excel, usually by first creating a budget in QuickBooks, then exporting it to Excel. That way, I can set up smart formulae to generate lots of different what-if scenarios without having to re-key figures for each scenario.

I'm of the same opinion when it comes to using the cashflow feature in QuickBooks (Company⇨Planning & Budgets⇨Cash Flow Projector). This feature is okay for short-term insights — I find it handy for projecting how much money I'll receive from customers and how much I'll have to pay suppliers over the next few weeks — but this format isn't nearly as flexible as creating a cashflow using a spreadsheet program (such as Excel). Again, in this situation I tend to export a budget report from QuickBooks into Excel, and then modify the Excel workbook to create a cashflow report.

Chapter 15

Looking After Your Company File

In This Chapter

▶ Understanding file types

▶ Backing up, backing up, backing up

▶ Restoring data (and what to do if it doesn't work)

▶ Looking after your data

▶ Ensuring Windows 7 and QuickBooks are on speaking terms

▶ Restricting employee access to those private parts of QuickBooks

*Y*our average chapter about backing up and restoring files should start with a doom and gloom story. You know, the one about a business being brought to its knees because it didn't back up. Yeah, yeah. You've heard it all before.

Instead, in this chapter I'm going to wax lyrical about how, if you back up on a regular basis, you can rescue yourself from the very jaws of death, wriggling out to freedom at the 11th hour.

I also explain how to set up users and password protection on your company file, safeguarding your financial information from curious eyes.

Getting Your Bearings

In order to sail through this chapter without a glitch, it helps to understand the jargon. So here's a list of QuickBooks file types, along with the file extension used by each one. (A *file extension* is the letters Windows adds to every filename to indicate what type of file it is. Sometimes the display in Windows hides these letters, but the description in the file type column tells you much the same thing.)

✔ **A company file.** The QuickBooks file you work in, day in, day out. The file type is QuickBooks Company File and the file extension is QBW.

✔ **A backup file.** This is a file you create when you use the Backup command in QuickBooks. This file contains not only your company file, but also supporting files, such as printer settings, logos and spellcheck data. The file type is QuickBooks Company Backup File and the file extension is QBB.

✔ **A portable file.** This is a compressed file that squashes your QuickBooks company file down to about one-tenth of its original size. Portable files don't include any supporting files. The file type is QuickBooks Portable Company File and the file extension is QBM.

✔ **A transaction log file.** This file logs all transactions since your most recent backup, and in the event of disaster, can be used to reconstruct transactions in your company file. The file type is called tlgFile and the file extension is QBW.TLG (note the double extension).

Backing Up to Save Yourself from Doom

What does all this talk about backing up mean? Put simply, a *backup* is when you make an extra copy of your business data and store this copy somewhere other than on your computer, usually on a CD, DVD or external hard drive. The reason why this extra copy is so important is that it can save your bacon if anything ever happens to your computer, such as hard disk failure, virus invasion, theft or fire.

Your business is more than QuickBooks

While you're considering what type of backup system to put in place, have a think about all the files on your computer that need backing up. For most businesses, a bare minimum includes everything in your My Documents folder, everything to do with your emails (including all Inbox and Sent mail folders), plus any data belonging to software specific to your business. If your office computers are networked, you often need to make a backup that includes both local data on each workstation, plus data on the server.

Draw up a list of the types of files you should be backing up, as well as how much storage space is required to back up these files. If these files live in several different places on your computer, try to automate the process either by using the Reckon Online Backup service (see the section 'Backing up your company file online' in this chapter), or by installing automated backup software.

Deciding how often to back up

The irony of backing up is that the busier you are, the more often you need to do it. If you work on your accounts every day, then back up QuickBooks daily. If you work on your accounts every week, then back up QuickBooks weekly.

You need to make archival backups as well as ordinary backups because if your company file gets damaged and it takes a while before you discover it, you can go back to the previous month's backup. For this reason, I recommend you make an extra backup once a month, and keep this separate from your normal backups. Similarly, make an extra backup at the end of each financial year.

Don't forget that many networks are configured so that only information stored on the main server is backed up. If your QuickBooks company file is located on a local workstation, remember to devise special backup procedures for your vital accounting information.

Backing up your company file on a local drive

Okay, are you ready to party? Here goes:

1. **Insert a CD or DVD into the relevant drive, or plug your external flash drive or hard drive into the USB port.**

   In order to back up onto a CD or DVD, you need a CD or DVD burner (which is a bit different from a regular CD or DVD drive). If you're not sure what you've got, ask the nearest propeller-head.

   Also, when buying CDs, you have the choice between CD-RWs and CD-Rs. CD-RWs allow you to write to them again and again, meaning that you can delete or add more data to the CD as often as you like. CD-Rs let you write to them once only, which means you can't delete or update the CD after you're done.

   If you back up locally and your hard disk has more than one drive, you can back up onto a different drive from the one where you keep your working data, or back up to a network drive. However, you'll need to combine this local backup with regular off-site backups, in order to protect against fire and theft.

2. **Choose File from the top menu bar and then select Save Copy or Backup.**

   I'm assuming you have your company file open at this point. Oh yes, and if anybody else is working on your QuickBooks file at the moment, politely boot them off. (To back up company files, you need to be in single-user mode.)

3. **Choose either to create a Backup copy or a Portable company file, then click Next.**

   For regular backups, always ask to create a backup copy. (For more information on portable files, see 'Creating a portable file instead' later in this chapter.)

4. **Choose whether you want to save your backup locally or online.**

   If you're backing up onto a CD, DVD or external drive, click Local Backup. (For more about backing up online, see 'Backing up your company file online' later in this chapter.)

5. **Remember to click the Options button (that's *before* you click Next), check all the various settings, then click OK.**

   The Options button, hidden away and so innocuous looking, is crucial. First, specify where you want to save your backup (QuickBooks defaults to a local folder on your hard drive, which is *not* what you want). Instead, you need to select an external drive, as I do in Figure 15-1. For example, if you're backing up onto CD or DVD, that's usually the D: or E: drive. External hard drives could be listed as the E: drive or F: drive.

   All the other settings are fairly self-explanatory: Always add the date and time to the backup name; set a limit to the number of saved on-demand backup copies only if you're going to run short of space (when you reach your limit, the oldest file is removed and the newest one is saved); ask for a reminder to back up every single time (change 4 to 1); and ask QuickBooks to do a Complete Verification every time it saves.

6. **Click Next.**

7. **Decide whether you want to save your backup right now, or whether you want to schedule future backups while you're at it.**

   If you choose to save right now and schedule future backups, you can choose to schedule backups at particular times each week. Whether this works for you depends on how regularly you work in your QuickBooks file. If you have a password to log into Windows, remember to click Set Password and store your details there. This provides you with permission to run the scheduled backup.

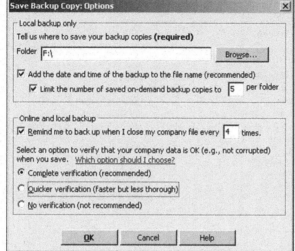

Figure 15-1:
Checking
your Options
settings is a
vital part of
the backup
process.

The danger with scheduling backups is that you can be lulled into a false sense of security. Remember, QuickBooks won't run a scheduled backup if the company file is open, so you need to schedule a time when the computer is on, but nobody is working in QuickBooks. If such a time is difficult to determine, I suggest that you schedule backups to run every time you close your company file instead.

8. Click Next.

9. Check the filename, location and then click Save.

The filename that appears automatically is your company name followed by — if you asked for a date stamp when selecting your options — the date and time. Usually, this filename is fine and you can leave it as is. However, the important thing to check at this point is that you're definitely saving to the correct location, as I do in Figure 15-2.

If you're backing up to a CD or DVD, Windows may also prompt you to burn the file after clicking Save.

10. Check that the file actually copied onto your backup, before you remove the disc or external device.

I know I'm neurotic, but I always like to go into My Computer in Windows, navigate to my backup drive, and check that the file is sitting on my backup.

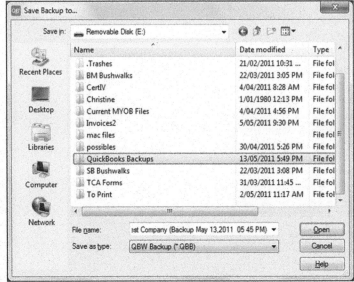

Figure 15-2:
Ensuring
you back
up to an
external
drive.

11. **Label your backup and store it in a cool, dry place away from the office.**

   If you want your backup to live a full and healthy life, don't store it on the dashboard of your car, underneath the rabbit cage or, worse still, on top of the computer. Take it away from the office and put it somewhere where it won't be disturbed.

If you're making an archival backup (such as an end-of-year backup), consider writing your password on the backup's label. That way, if you need to restore this backup several years later, maybe in the event of an audit, you won't be scratching your head trying to remember what password you used all those years ago.

Backing up your company file online

Reckon Tools Backup enables you to backup important files automatically, storing these files at secure, remote locations on the internet. To find out more about this service, go to File➪Save Copy or Backup, and when prompted, ask to make an online backup. After registering, you're prompted to first select all important files that live on your computer — the service automatically selects your company file — and second, to set up a regular scheduled backup.

I think the service offered by Reckon Tools Backup is the ant's pants. The simple fact that backups are automatic helps me to achieve a peace of mind normally associated with much more exotic activities. I don't have to worry about taking backups off-site, and because this service is internet-based, I can access my files from anywhere.

That's not to say that backing up online works well for everybody. Other solutions, such as removable hard drives, are quicker and provide more storage (both speed and storage capacity are essential considerations if you're operating on a network and need to back up the entire server, plus data on local machines).

Reckon Tools Backup offers a few storage plans ranging from 100MB storage to 10GB storage (and a corresponding price tag that ranges from $29.95 per year to $375.00 per year). (GB is short for *gigabyte*, just in case you're wondering, which is the equivalent of 1,024 megabytes, or MB, of data.) If you have data on more than one machine, bear in mind that the online backup software can't run on more than one machine using the same account number.

Creating a portable file instead

When you go to create a backup copy of your file, QuickBooks actually offers two options: You can either create a backup file or a portable file.

A portable file is just another way of backing up your company file, except that portable files don't contain supporting files such as printer settings, logos and spellcheck data, and that QuickBooks compresses information so that the file takes up a fraction of the space. For example, if your company file is 50MB, chances are that after compression the portable file will be somewhere between 5MB and 10MB. The real boon of portable files is that, unless your company file is unusually large, they're small enough to send via email. (Most email services don't accept attachments of more than 10MB or so.)

To create a portable file, go to File⇨Save Copy or Backup. Tell QuickBooks you want to create a portable company file and then click Next, saving this file to a folder on your computer when you're ready. QuickBooks closes and reopens your company file before creating a portable company file. (Portable files save with a QBM extension, meaning Windows adds these three letters to the filename.)

At the other end, whoever receives the portable file needs to fire up QuickBooks, select Open or Restore Company from the File menu, point to wherever the portable file is, and select a location to save the portable file to. I always add the current date to the filename when restoring a portable file, so that I don't overwrite any existing company files sitting in this location.

Backup blues

Okay, tell me truthfully: Where do you store your backups? If your answer is that you store them in the office somewhere (or if you work from home, at home somewhere), then my reply to you is that unless these backups are stored in a fire-proof safe, you may as well not bother making a backup.

Why? Because if you store your backup anywhere near the computer, you're not protected

against fire or theft. The only other solution is to take your backups off-site, away from where you work. If you work from home, ask a close relative or friend to look after your backups at their home. If you work in an office, take your backups home, ideally every night. If you know that you won't ever become this efficient, delegate the job to someone else.

Whatever you do, don't get confused between making a portable file and making an accountant's copy. The purpose of an accountant's copy is that your accountant can open the file, work on it and send it back to you, then you merge the accountant's changes with your current file (Chapter 18 talks more about this process). This means that you can keep working on your file at the same time as your accountant is doing so. By contrast, if your accountant or anyone else restores a portable file and makes changes to it, these changes can't be merged with any other company file.

By the way, when you restore a portable company file, the restored company file often ends up being a tad smaller than your original company file before you went through the whole shenanigans of creating the portable file. This is because the process of creating a portable company file removes blank records from the file, such as deleted transactions.

You need the administrator password in order to create a portable company file. Bear this in mind if you send someone a portable file and you intend for them to later create a new portable file to return to you. If you don't want this person to have access to the administrator password, you're best to ask them to back up the file in a regular way, maybe saving it onto a CD in order to return it to you, rather than creating a portable file.

Redeeming Yourself in the Nick of Time

Few situations are as stressful as thinking that all of your QuickBooks data has been lost or damaged. Here I try to provide a few first-aid solutions to soothe your shattered nerves.

Restoring your file

When you make a backup, QuickBooks not only backs up and compresses your company file, but also backs up several other important files that exist separately from your company file, such as images, letter templates and printer settings. QuickBooks stores these files together in a single file (you can always identify backup files, because they have QuickBooks Company Backup File as the Windows file type, as well as the letters QBB attached to the filename).

 Because a backup is a special kind of file, you can't just copy a QuickBooks backup file into your QuickBooks folder and start working. Instead, you need to use the Restore command from within QuickBooks to bring your data back to life.

To begin the restore process, start by telling anyone else who's currently logged into QuickBooks to quit, because you need to be in single-user mode to restore a file.

Then, with your fingers crossed, follow these instructions:

1. **Insert your backup CD or DVD into the computer's drive, or plug in your removable hard drive or flash drive.**

2. **Open up your company file or a sample company file.**

   You can open your normal company file or any QuickBooks sample file. Any file will do.

3. **Select Open or Restore Company from the File menu.**

4. **Choose to restore a backup copy or to restore a portable copy, then click Next.**

5. **Locate your backup company file and click Open.**

   In the Look In menu, double-click on the drive's name where your backup is stored (QuickBooks may select this drive automatically). Select your backup file and click Open.

6. **Select a destination folder for your restored company file.**

   If any part of restoring a file is going to confuse you, this is it. When the Restore To window appears, you have to decide where you want your restored company file to live. In 99 out of 100 cases, you restore your company file into the actual folder where you normally store your QuickBooks company files (see 'Locating your company file' later in this chapter if you're unsure). You may need to change the drive name or the folder name that appears in the Save In menu to navigate to this folder.

7. **Change the suggested filename to include the date, then click Save.**

   If you don't change the suggested filename in some way — I suggest simply adding the current date to the name, as shown in Figure 15-3 — then you run the risk of restoring your backup file on top of the most recent company file. You don't want to take this chance! If you accidentally select an old file to restore, then you risk wiping out the most current file that's sitting on your hard drive, making your situation even gloomier.

8. **Click OK after QuickBooks completes the restoration process and check that everything is where you want it.**

   Whenever you restore a backup file, it's worth browsing through the transaction journals and checking that you've restored the right file.

9. **Decide if you need to restore any of the supporting files (images, customised letters, spellcheck files and so on) and if so, follow the QuickBooks guidelines to copy these files to their correct locations.**

   For more information about this process, see the sidebar 'Restoring everything, not just the file'.

Figure 15-3: When restoring your company file, select the destination folder and name with care.

Restoring everything, not just the file

When you restore a backup, QuickBooks creates an additional folder called Restored Files that sits in the restored location. This folder stores all the supporting files (other than your company file) that QuickBooks needs to run, such as images, customised letters, printer settings, spellcheck files and designer financial statements.

If you're restoring a recent backup onto the same machine that you'd already been working on, you don't have to worry about the files sitting in this additional folder, because all these supporting files will still be in their original locations. However, if you're moving your QuickBooks company file onto a new computer, you need to figure out which of these supporting files you need and copy them into their correct locations. These locations are listed in detail in the readme document called HowToRestoreExternalFiles.txt, which is located in the Restored Files folder.

Running a rescue mission

You can tell I'm a realist, because not only do I explain how to restore a backup file, but I address the possibility that you've tried to run a restore, and it hasn't worked or worse still, you never had a backup in the first place.

Stay cool, there's no need to flee into exile quite yet. There are a few things you can try before packing your suitcase:

- **Dig deeper.** Even if you think you have no other backups, dig around for one that you or someone else may have made in the past. Even if a backup is a couple of months old, this may be better than nothing. It's also possible that you or someone else has backed up onto your hard disk sometime in the past. See 'Locating your company file' later in this chapter to find out how to search for QuickBooks files.

- **Change the file attributes.** Sometimes when you back up onto CD or DVD, the attributes of your file automatically change to read-only status, meaning that you can't open or restore the file. The solution is to copy the backup from your CD onto your hard disk, and then, from My Computer, select the backup file, go to your File menu in QuickBooks and select Properties. Untick the Read Only box and everything should be sweet.

TIP

✔ **Ensure the file is a Company Backup File, not a Company File.** Backup files end with the letters QBB, whereas regular company files end with the letters QBW. (See if you can spot the difference in Figure 15-4.) If the file you're trying to restore doesn't end with the letters QBB, this means that you've copied your company file instead of running a backup using the QuickBooks backup command. The solution is to copy the file from the backup drive into your QuickBooks directory and then open it (you may also need to change the file attributes, as described in the preceding paragraph).

✔ **Fix the backup data.** If your backup media is damaged (maybe the CD has scratches on it, or the disk has bad sectors), and you can't copy the backup onto your local hard drive, it's possible that the Reckon Data Services team can resurrect your file (visit www.quicken. com.au and search for Data Services on the Support page). Avoid using disk repair utilities — because your QuickBooks backup is a compressed file, repair utilities can cause further problems, preventing data from restoring at all.

✔ **Recover data since the last backup using the transaction log.** QuickBooks uses a transaction log file to track all changes to your data since the last time you backed up your company file (this transaction log file has the same name as your company file, but uses the QBW. TLG file extension). If your most recent backup was a depressingly long time ago, the Reckon Data Services team may be able to use your transaction log file in conjunction with your most recent backup to recover your data.

Figure 15-4:
Spotting the difference between a Company Backup File and a regular Company File.

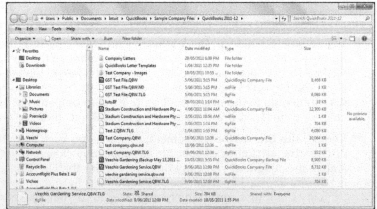

Taking Care of Your Data

Your company file is a sensitive and impressionable creature. It needs a stable home life, occasional counselling and a lot of love and affection.

Dealing with a file that's too big for its boots

Sometimes your QuickBooks company file grows so big, slow and lumbering, it's like living with an elephant (not that I've ever lived with an elephant). You have a few ways of dealing with this dilemma.

Older versions of QuickBooks used to have limits, both in regards to the number of transactions you could have in a file, and the number of records you could have in a list. With recent versions of QuickBooks, these limits no longer apply. So, the solution to your problem could be as simple as upgrading.

Otherwise, the easiest way to make your file smaller is to purge transactions from previous financial years. See 'Cleaning up your company file' next in this chapter.

If you've already purged transactions from previous financial years and your company file is still pretty huge, you can reduce the size a little by creating a portable file, restoring this portable file and using the restored file in place of your original company file. (Refer also to 'Creating a portable file instead' earlier in this chapter.)

Finally, if you can't get your file any smaller but it's still running slowly, head to http://community.intuit.com/quickbooks and browse the 'QuickBooks Performance Issues & Program Errors' forum board.

Cleaning up your company file

One of the new features in QuickBooks 2010/11 is the ability to 'clean up' your company file. This procedure gets the vacuum cleaner out and summarises transactions from prior years, leaving your company file lean, mean and (hopefully) a fair bit faster.

While QuickBooks is cleaning up your data, you can't use other applications (well, you can, but everything runs as slow as a wet week, and you may as well not bother). Because of this restriction, and also because cleaning up QuickBooks data can take several hours, you may want to run this process at the end of the afternoon, so QuickBooks can do its stuff while the foxes prowl and the owls hoot.

1. **From the File menu, select Utilities and then click Clean Up Company Data.**

   By the way, you must be in single-user mode to use the clean up command, so kick your colleagues out of QuickBooks if need be.

2. **Click the option to Remove Transactions as of a Specific Date and enter the date you want to go up to.**

   I usually run this procedure at the end of a financial year, and unless a company file is really huge, I like to keep at least two years' worth of data on tap. Therefore, if I'm doing a cleanup in July 2011, I select 30/6/2009 as the date. This date means that QuickBooks is going to clean up and then summarise all transactions up to 30 June 2009.

   By the way, don't even think about doing a cleanup for a period that you or your accountant is still working on. Why? After you do a cleanup, you can't update or add any transactions that fall within the period you selected to clean up.

3. **Click Next and then Next again, clicking when prompted against any transaction types or items that you don't want to be removed.**

   If in doubt about what any of these options mean, stay on the safe side and leave that option unchecked.

4. **Ready to do the deed? Then click Begin Cleanup.**

   The cleanup process can take anywhere from a few minutes to several hours, depending on the size of your company file and the speed of your computer. So don't start this process unless the time is right.

5. **When prompted to make a backup, select a suitable location and click Save.**

   This backup keeps a vital record of any transactions that QuickBooks deletes from your company file. Immediately following the backup, QuickBooks also creates an archive copy of your data and then verifies the integrity of your data.

6. **Be patient.**

   Because backing up, archiving, cleaning and verifying takes a fair while, you may start wondering if anything is still happening. Be patient — if your hard disk shows activity, then the process is still happening.

7. **When you get a message saying that QuickBooks has successfully removed your old data, click OK.**

   Well done! You can now keep working as normal, but with a company file that's free of cobwebs and as sprightly as a spring lamb.

Are you struck with remorse for the deed you have just done? To restore your company file to the state it was in before you cleaned up your data, use your backup copy, and not the archive copy (the archive is a read-only file, and not useable for data entry).

Locating your company file

In recent versions, QuickBooks installs your company files into your Documents and Settings folder (look in C:\Documents and Settings\ All Users\(Shared) Documents\Intuit\QuickBooks\Company Files). This change in location makes sense, because your company file now lives in a more logical place for backup purposes, and you won't strike hiccups with permission requirements and the very territorial Microsoft Windows.

If you're looking for your company file, or maybe a previous backup file, and you don't know where it's gone, here's what to do:

- ✔ **On a PC, using Windows Vista or Windows 7.** Go to your Start menu. If you're looking for your company file, type any part of your filename in the Search box that appears. If you're looking for a backup file, type the word QBB to display all backup files. When you see what you're looking for, click on the item to view where this file is located on your computer.

- ✔ **On a PC, Windows XP or earlier.** Go to My Computer. Click the Search button (the magnifying glass icon). Choose to search for all files or folders. If you're looking for your company file, type any part of your filename in the Search box that appears; if you're looking for a backup file, type *.QBB as the filename that you're looking for (the asterisk means all files, and backup files always end with QBB).

  Under the Look In drop-down box, select My Computer. Click Search. The results are displayed in a list, but you may need to widen the In Folder column so that you can view the full description outlining where this file is located on your computer.

If a few files crop up in your search results, you need to figure out which company file is the one you're looking for. To do so, view the Size and Date columns (you may need to select Details from the View menu in order to see this info). Usually the largest file size is the most current, and the Date column tells you the last time the file was touched.

If your company file is currently open, you can find out where it's stored by pressing the F2 function key on your keyboard. QuickBooks displays a Product Information window, shown in Figure 15-5, displaying not only your current file location, but a whole lot of other (very nerdy) information.

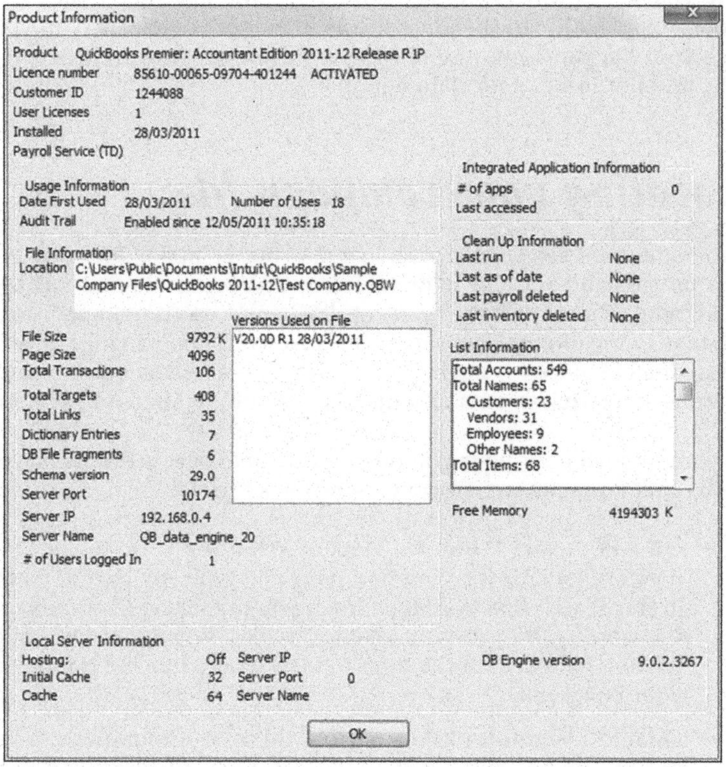

Product Information

Product   QuickBooks Premier: Accountant Edition 2011-12 Release R1P
Licence number   85610-00065-09704-401244   ACTIVATED
Customer ID   1244088
User Licenses   1
Installed   28/03/2011
Payroll Service (TD)

Usage Information
Date First Used   28/03/2011   Number of Uses   18
Audit Trail   Enabled since 12/05/2011 10:35:18

File Information
Location   C:\Users\Public\Documents\Intuit\QuickBooks\Sample Company Files\QuickBooks 2011-12\Test Company.QBW

Versions Used on File
File Size   9792 K   V20.0D R1 28/03/2011
Page Size   4096
Total Transactions   106

Total Targets   408
Total Links   35
Dictionary Entries   7
DB File Fragments   6
Schema version   29.0
Server Port   10174
Server IP   192.168.0.4
Server Name   QB_data_engine_20
# of Users Logged In   1

Integrated Application Information
# of apps   0
Last accessed

Clean Up Information
Last run   None
Last as of date   None
Last payroll deleted   None
Last inventory deleted   None

List Information
Total Accounts: 549
Total Names: 65
    Customers: 23
    Vendors: 31
    Employees: 9
    Other Names: 2
Total Items: 68

Free Memory   4194303 K

Local Server Information
Hosting: Off   Server IP
Initial Cache   32   Server Port   0
Cache   64   Server Name

DB Engine version   9.0.2.3267

OK

Figure 15-5: Pressing F2 to view product information on your company file.

Staying honest, keeping clean

The Verify Data utility is a special tool in QuickBooks that detects if your company file is damaged. Like brushing your teeth, verifying your file is one of the best kinds of preventive medicine. To run the Verify utility, go to File⇨Utilities⇨Verify Data. Close all open windows when prompted and wait a couple of minutes while QuickBooks does it stuff. If you get a message saying the coast is clear, you can sleep easy. However, if you get a more sombre message declaring that your data has lost integrity, you'll need to address the problem.

Chapter 15: Looking After Your Company File

QuickBooks logs any errors it finds in a Qbwin.log file. This log file accumulates over time, documenting every time you verify or rebuild your data, and over time can become very large. One easy way to identify current errors in the data file is to rename the Qbwin.log file, located in your QuickBooks directory, to Qbwin.old. If you do this, QuickBooks automatically creates a new Qbwin.log file next time you open your company file. You can then run the Verify Data utility and view the latest results in isolation in the new log file.

Sometimes the log shows up a particular transaction as being damaged. In this situation, you're best to back up your company file, note down the transaction details, delete the transaction from your company file altogether, then finally, run the verify utility again to ensure you've pinpointed the error.

If you still get a verification error, or if the log didn't show up with any particular transaction that was damaged, you need to rebuild your file. Read on for the gruesome details ...

Rebuilding your file

The rebuild utility provides a way for ordinary mortals — namely you and me — to try to repair any damage that's found in a QuickBooks company file. Here's how it's done:

1. **If you're running on a network, copy the company file onto a local drive.**

   Never run the rebuild data across a network, because it can cause irreparable damage to the file.

2. **Go to File⇨Utilities⇨Rebuild Data.**

3. **Click Yes to make a backup of your company file.**

   I explain how to back up earlier in this chapter, in the section 'Backing up your company file on a local drive'. Backing up first is essential, because on occasion, the rebuild data process can actually make your problem worse.

4. **When the rebuild is complete, close your company file and then re-open it.**

5. **Go to File⇨Utilities⇨Verify Data.**

   Hopefully, the verification process now runs without a hitch. However, if you still receive a message saying that your data is damaged, your only choice is to restore your most recent backup. After you've restored this backup file, run the Verify Data utility again. If you still get a verification error, work your way backwards through your backups until you find the most recent clean file.

Sometimes, the whole process of verifying, rebuilding and restoring data is to no avail. If all your restored files come up with data verification errors, or if the most recent clean file is too long ago and it's impractical to re-enter so much data, you can try sending your damaged file to the Reckon Data Services team for repair: Visit www.quicken.com.au and search for Data Services on the Support page. A fee applies for data recovery services.

Avoiding data hiccups in the first place

Why sweat away with all the nightmares of rebuilding and restoring data if you can avoid the problem in the first place? Here's some food for thought:

- ✔ **Be careful with that power-off switch.** If you work on the host machine (in other words, the machine where your QuickBooks company file lives) don't turn off the power on your machine while your colleagues are still working on the company file.

- ✔ **Keep the power clean.** If you live in an area that experiences lots of storms or you work in a factory environment where heavy equipment makes for a dirty power supply, get an uninterruptible power supply (UPS), a device or powerboard that provides protection from power surges and outages for computers.

- ✔ **Ensure you have enough storage space.** Make sure that you've got ample hard disk space free (say, 100MB). Files are much more likely to fall over if they don't have enough room to 'breathe'.

- ✔ **Get an IT tech person to give your network the once-over.** Things that cause problems include electrical cables running over network cables, fluoro lights next to network cables, faulty network adaptor cards, poor network connections, out-of-date network drivers, fast machines with slow network cards and slow machines with fast network cards.

- ✔ **Regularly verify your company file.** Refer to 'Staying honest, keeping clean' earlier in this chapter.

Upgrading to Windows 7

Have you just purchased a new computer that has Windows 7 as the operating system? The good news is that QuickBooks 2010/11 is compatible with all recent versions of Windows, including Windows 7. The bad news? Although you can still install and run earlier versions of QuickBooks on Windows 7, you may well encounter problems. (Some known issues include printing errors, the crashing of Google Desktop and problems opening the QuickBooks program.)

If you intend upgrading to Windows 7, upgrade your version of QuickBooks first. One more thing: I haven't experienced this problem myself, but I've read on QuickBooks blogs that some users have problems with QuickBooks when they upgrade from Vista to Windows 7, rather than simply installing the latest version of QuickBooks onto a computer that already has Windows 7. You may find you need to uninstall and re-install QuickBooks if you upgrade your operating system.

Also, if you currently send email messages with Microsoft Outlook Express (as opposed to the full version of Microsoft Outlook), then check carefully before upgrading to Quickbooks 2010/11. At the time of writing, QuickBooks can't send email messages via Windows Live Mail, which is the replacement for Microsoft Outlook Express in Windows 7.

Protecting Private Information

I don't know about you, but I like to keep my financial situation private. And just as I wouldn't leave my tax return lying around on the coffee table when friends are visiting, I like to protect my company file from uninvited inspection.

Protecting the privacy of your company file is easy because all you have to do is create an administrator password.

Creating an administrator password

Your main password is called the *administrator password*. If you haven't already created a password for your QuickBooks company file, here's how to set this up the first time:

1. **With your company file open, go to Company⇨Set Up Users.**

    QuickBooks displays a message saying you need to set up a password for the QuickBooks administrator first. (The administrator automatically has unlimited access to the company file and is the only person who can create new user IDs and set restrictions for other users.)

2. **Think of a password and enter this in the Adminstrator's Password and Confirm Password fields.**

    Try to avoid using the names of your pets or children — they're too obvious.

3. **Click OK.**

QuickBooks takes you to your User List, from where you can add, edit or delete users.

4. **Remember your password!**

Next time you open up your company file, you'll need this password. So guess what? Don't forget it! Also, if you're going to manage security effectively, only the business owner or manager should know the password that's associated with the Administrator ID.

Restricting employee access

Whenever you open your company file using your Administrator password, you gain unlimited access to all areas, including the ability to set up new users and specify what areas of QuickBooks they can access.

1. **Go to Company⇨Setup Users and log in with your Administrator password.**

If you don't have an Administrator password, then add one now.

2. **Click Add User and enter a User Name and Password for this employee.**

Every employee needs their own User Name and Password. Don't let employees log on as Administrator, and ask them not to share their password with anyone else.

3. **Click Next.**

4. **Tell QuickBooks you want this employee to have access to selected areas of QuickBooks only.**

5. **For each area of QuickBooks, specify whether you want this employee to have No Access, Full Access or Selective Access, clicking Next to progress through the QuickBooks functions.**

Kind of like movie censorship, except you get to set the ratings. Unless an employee is responsible for payroll transactions, I suggest you select No Access when you arrive at Payroll and Employees.

Two steps further on, you arrive at the option where you must decide whether to grant access to sensitive financial reports (see Figure 15-6). If you allow full access here, then employees will be able to view payroll information on reports, even if you've selected No Access for payroll.

6. Click Finish to save the new User Name and restrictions.

After you save your changes, tell the employee why you're giving them a password and, if you've restricted them from some areas in your company file, explain why. People can become curious (and sometimes even resentful) if they think you're trying to hide something from them, so it helps to explain your reasoning.

If you find that this level of password control isn't sophisticated enough for your needs, consider upgrading to QuickBooks Enterprise. This version enables you to assign roles to each employee, and the access rights for each role can be defined with a very high degree of detail.

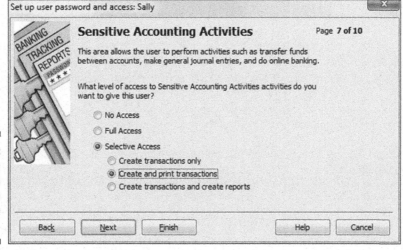

Figure 15-6:
Restricting
employee
access to
sensitive
data.

Part IV
The Part of Tens

Glenn Lumsden

'Poor guy obviously doesn't use QuickBooks.'

In this part ...

Grab a pen and paper, find yourself a quiet spot and make a few lists: As a starting point, may I suggest the ten most stupid things you've ever done, your ten most disastrous relationships and the ten times you drank far, far too much.

A rather gloomy document? Don't worry. Tear up this catalogue of sins and read through my lists instead.

I offer tips for paying suppliers electronically (and why not, it's so much faster), speed-merchant tips for getting your work done in record time and tips for working with your accountant.

Hot on the heels of these three chapters comes a handy Appendix, cataloguing the different members of the QuickBooks software family.

Chapter 16

Ten Tips for Electronic Payments

In This Chapter

▶ Sending payments straight from QuickBooks to your bank

▶ Setting up electronic payments for both suppliers and employees

▶ Letting suppliers and employees know you've paid 'em

▶ Practising senseless acts of random kindness — at 10 cents a pop

▶ Protecting yourself against employee fraud

*W*hy travel by carthorse when a BMW is waiting to go? Paying people electronically is *sooo* much quicker than writing cheques or messing around with cash.

QuickBooks makes online payments a cinch: All you do is flag payments that you plan to pay online, make your way to the Online Banking Centre, then generate a file that you can import into your banking software. A few clicks of the mouse, a couple of pirouettes, and both employees and suppliers are paid. Want to know more? In this chapter I provide ten tips for processing electronic payments with elegance and grace.

Go the Whole Hog

You can pay your employees and suppliers electronically in two different ways.

> ✔ **Recording electronic payments using an electronic payment file generated from QuickBooks:** With this method, you record employee or supplier payments in your QuickBooks company file, create an electronic payment file, open this file using your bank's internet banking service and then send your payment to suppliers and employees. Banks often refer to this file as a *direct entry batch file*.

Although most Aussie banks let you import batch files as part of their regular Internet banking service, at the time of writing, ANZ and Westpac only offer this service if you subscribe to business transaction banking services.

✔ **Recording transactions both in internet banking and in QuickBooks:** With this method, you record the payment using internet banking, paying one employee or supplier at a time. Later on, you re-key this transaction into QuickBooks. Alternatively, you record transactions first in QuickBooks, then open up your internet banking and re-key the payment details there.

Obviously, the first method is heaps more efficient that the second method, because you only enter data once, not twice. (This is why I devote the rest of this chapter to making electronic payments using this brilliant technique.)

Be Prepared (Before Diving In)

Ready to launch online banking in QuickBooks? From your Chart of Accounts, double-click your bank account and click the Online Bank Details tab. Here are some tips:

✔ The Branch Code required by QuickBooks is your BSB number. You find this six-digit number on any bank statement or cheque book.

✔ You only need to tick Include Balance Record if your bank requires a self-balancing transaction for each electronic payment (your bank will let you know if that's the case).

✔ Your APCA number (also sometimes referred to by banks as a Direct Entry User ID or a Bank ID) is a special number that your bank requires for creating batch entry files. Simply ring your bank's Customer Service line (don't you just love call centres?), give them your account details, and ask them what your APCA number is.

Get Employees and Suppliers Up to Speed

You can't pay your employees or suppliers electronically unless you tell QuickBooks their innermost secrets:

1. **Double-click the employee's or supplier's name.**

   I assume you know to go to the Customer Centre or Employee Centre first.

2. **Head for their banking details.**

   With employees, you select the Payroll and Compensation Info tab, followed by the Direct Deposit button. With suppliers, simply select the Bank Details tab.

3. **If this person is an employee, specify how many accounts you want to send their pay to.**

   Some employees like to split their pay across a couple of accounts, maybe paying half into a regular account and half into a tax haven in the Bahamas.

4. **Complete the account details — you know the drill.**

5. **What do you want this person to see on their statement? Enter these words into the Lodgement Ref field.**

   For suppliers, your business name is probably best. For employees, the word Pay is elegant efficiency.

6. **If this person is an employee, return to the Payroll and Compensation Info tab and select Bank (Online) as the Pay Method.**

Use a Clearing Account

When you pay a batch of employees or suppliers online, your bank normally shows this batch as a single debit on your bank statement. However, QuickBooks shows these transactions individually in your bank account register.

If you want to group payments in the same way as your bank does, making it easier to match QuickBooks with your bank statement, create a new bank account in your Chart of Accounts called Electronic Clearing or something similar. Then, whenever you record electronic payments in QuickBooks, select this account as the bank account.

Later, when you send payments to the bank for processing, you record a Transfer Funds transaction that shifts the total value of electronic payments out of your business bank account and into your electronic clearing account. That way, the balance of your electronic clearing account always starts with zero and returns to zero, and your QuickBooks bank register matches perfectly with your bank statement. Figure 16-1 shows how it's done.

Figure 16-1: Tracking employee payments using a clearing account.

Figure shows: Account QuickReport window

Willow Wind and Dreams
Clearing Account QuickReport

Type	Date	Num	Source Name	Memo	Split	Amount	Balance
Electronic Clearing							0.00
Bill Pmt -Cheque	11/05/2011		ABC Supplies		Accounts Pa...	-987.60	-987.60
Bill Pmt -Cheque	11/05/2011		Caltex (Fuel)		Accounts Pa...	-53.00	-1,040.60
Bill Pmt -Cheque	11/05/2011		Customs Clearing	Bill for GST ...	Accounts Pa...	-1,000.00	-2,040.60
Bill Pmt -Cheque	11/05/2011		Telstra		Accounts Pa...	-330.00	-2,370.60
Transfer	11/05/2011			Funds Trans...	Cheque Acco...	2,370.60	0.00
Total Electronic Clearing						0.00	0.00
TOTAL						**0.00**	**0.00**

Group Payments Together

After you set up your bank account details in QuickBooks, as well as the account details of employees and suppliers, you're ready to make payments online. I know that you're no dummy — despite the title of this book — but here are few pointers to help you on your way:

✔ Record Write Cheques and Pay Bills as you normally do. The only difference is you select Bank Online as the Payment Method.

✔ Remember that selecting Bank Online as the Payment Method doesn't actually mean that QuickBooks makes an electronic payment. The next step is to go to the Online Banking Centre and create an electronic payment file.

✔ Record electronic payments in groups and only head for the Online Banking Centre when you have a few payments ready to process. The good thing about making payments in batches, rather than one by one, is you save time and bank fees.

✔ The first time around, pick two or three people and pay them (electronically) ten cents each. Why? Because if this payment fails, no damage is done. Much better than attempting your first electronic payment on payday, and having to explain to all the staff why their pays didn't go through on time.

Keep Track of ABA Files

To generate an electronic payment file, click the Online Banking icon on your icon bar. You arrive at the Online Banking Centre, as shown in Figure 16-2.

The top section shows all bank accounts that have been configured for online access, the middle section shows a history of any electronic statements you've downloaded direct from your bank, and the bottom section shows all transactions that you've marked for online payment that haven't been processed yet. This bottom section is where all the action takes place.

Start by clicking the Preview ABA File button. (An *ABA file* is a special file that summarises the electronic payments, ready for your bank to process.) If you like, you can print this page and file it, so that you maintain a separate record of all electronic payments (I find this handy if the person responsible for reconciling the bank accounts doesn't have access to the online banking features).

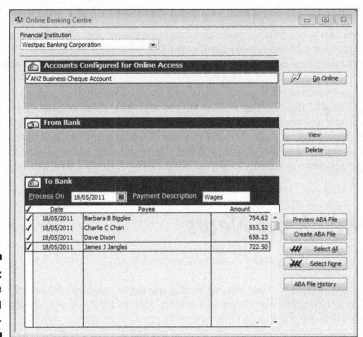

Figure 16-2:
The Online Banking Centre.

If you're happy with the payments as they appear, simply click the Create ABA File button, saving the file when prompted. But wait — see the processing date? If it's already after banking cut-off times (usually 4 pm), enter the next day's date instead so that your payment won't be rejected.

Never Enter Anything Twice

After you create an electronic payment (ABA) file, you're ready to open this file in your banking software. The symmetry of this line dance depends on which bank you're with, but the essential idea is always the same:

1. **Fire up internet banking.**

   Earlier in this chapter, I explain that some internet banking services don't allow you to import electronic payment files, and you may need to subscribe to specific business banking services instead.

2. **Open your electronic payment file.**

   If it's not obvious how to open this file, ask your bank for help.

3. **Check your payments and send them off into the wild unknown.**

   When you open up your electronic payment file, you should see each payment listed one by one, complete with banking details. Check these payments one last time and then send the file. The deed is done!

Can you see how this process doesn't involve re-keying a single date, name or amount? I hate seeing clients go through the shenanigans of recording electronic payments in QuickBooks, and then re-keying every detail into their banking software. Not only is this doubling up, but could introduce mistakes. So, if you find yourself entering anything twice, chances are you're doing something wrong, and you need to re-read my instructions.

Share the Good News

Remember to let people know you've paid them.

To notify suppliers that you've sent a payment, go to File⇨Select Forms to Email⇨Supplier Remittance Advices. Alternatively, if you'd rather print remittance advices, go to File⇨Print Forms⇨Remittance Advice.

The same principle applies to employee payments. To print payslips, go to File⇨Print Forms⇨Pay Slips. To email payslips, go to File⇨Select Forms to Email⇨Pay Slips. If there's a hiccup, you may need to go the Address and Contact tab for this employee and complete their Email address and select Email as the Preferred Send Method first.

Clean Out the Dead Wood

Sometimes when you first try to prepare electronic payments, you find that a whole bunch of transactions appear, dating months or even years back. The most common cause for this problem is that you've made the mistake of selecting Bank (Online) as the payment method for payments that have already been processed online, and for which you're never going to create an ABA file for sending to internet banking.

The solution is easy. In the Online Banking Centre, simply click Select All to mark off every single unprocessed payment, and then scroll to the bottom and, if necessary, deselect any recent payments that you do still need to process. Then to get rid of the payments that you've highlighted, click Create ABA File. You can name this ABA file anything you like, because you're never going to do anything with it.

If QuickBooks comes up with an error message saying that you need to complete account details for certain employees or suppliers, and there are so many missing details this would take hours to complete, then I suggest another approach. Create a new account called Electronic Clearing and process all future online payments out of this account. (For more details, refer to 'Use a Clearing Account' earlier in chapter.)

Guard Yourself against Online Fraud

If you're a business owner, I want to ask you a question: Would you be happy to give your bookkeeper the key to a safe in your office with $10,000 cash inside? If your answer is 'no', then I'm going to suggest that you pause for breath before allowing your bookkeeper to generate electronic payments out of QuickBooks.

The most common way a bookkeeper commits fraud is by recording electronic payments that substitute a supplier's banking details with their own. (Although banks ask for an account name, the only thing the bank matches when making a transfer is the account number and branch.) In other words, your blue-eyed innocent-looking bookkeeper may prepare a payment ready for you to authorise, and although at first glance this payment looks as if it's going to a known supplier, the banking details have actually been changed.

Even if you authorise all the electronic payments your bookkeeper prepares for you, you certainly won't have time to check the bank account details for every person or company listed on every payment. However, what you can do is spot-check account details on a regular basis (and ever-so-casually let the bookkeeper know you do so).

For more info about guarding against fraud, check out the illustrious *Bookkeeping For Dummies*, Australian & New Zealand edition, published by Wiley Publishing Australia and written by yours truly.

Chapter 17

Ten Tricks for Speed

In This Chapter

▶ Committing shortcut keys to memory

▶ Searching for stuff the smart way

▶ Learning to type, without delay

▶ Automating anything you can

Although I've been slogging away for many months writing this book, even I realise there's much more to life than QuickBooks. Sure, I want to go to work, run my business and make money. But I like to have fun too, especially if good food, fine wine and exotic adventures to far-flung islands are involved.

If you also like to live life to the full and spend as little time as possible doing the books, then this chapter is for you.

Take the Short Way Home

Want to record a payment to someone? You don't have to quit out of wherever you are, navigate to your home page and then click Write Cheques. No, you're much more intelligent than that. Instead, you simply type Ctrl-W and, in two shakes of a lamb's tail, you arrive at the Write Cheques window.

Using this shortcut means finding the Ctrl key (usually at the bottom left of your keyboard) and holding it down. Keep holding it down and then press the letter W. Let go and you're there.

Write Cheques isn't the only place you can go to using shortcuts. Ctrl-J takes you to the Customer Centre, Ctrl-I to Create Invoices, Ctrl-A to your Chart of Accounts and so on. I summarise these shortcut keys (plus many more) on the Cheat Sheet for this book available at www.dummies.com/cheatsheet/quickbooksau.

Forget That Furry Mouse

Want to move faster? Then grab your mouse, kiss it a fond farewell and hurl it out of the window.

This may sound radical but you can do just about every transaction without using your mouse. To see how this works, press the Alt key on your keyboard — next to the space bar. See how all the commands along the top menu suddenly have one letter underlined? (For example, Customers becomes Customers.) Now, instead of clicking the Customers menu with your mouse, you can press down the Alt button, followed by the letter U.

After you arrive where you want to go, continue working without your mouse. Press the Tab key to go forwards, or the Shift key plus the Tab key to go backwards.

Get Smart When Searching

Looking for something? Don't waste time trawling through the registers. Instead, cut straight to the chase and do an Advanced Find.

1. **From your home page, head up to the Edit menu and click Find.**

2. **See the two tabs at the top? (One labelled Simple, the other Advanced.) Click the Advanced tab.**

3. **Choose a Filter — in other words, click on the type of filter that you want to search by.**

   If you want to search for an amount, click the Amount filter (see Figure 17-1). To search for a word that's part of a transaction's memo, select the Description filter. To search for an invoice or bill number, click the Number filter.

   Don't forget that you can run multiple filters on a single search — for example, searching for all transactions within the current month that have $10,000 as the amount, and the words 'Lotto win' in the memo. (Optimism never dies.)

4. **Enter some details of what you're searching on.**

   For example, enter the amount, word or invoice number you're searching for. Or, if you're searching by name, either select a single name from the list or click Multiple Names and then select whatever names you want from the list.

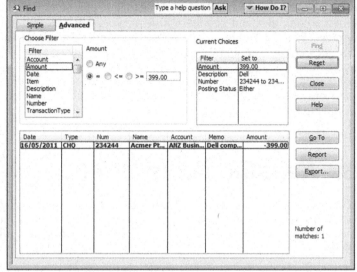

Figure 17-1:
Using
Advanced
Find in
QuickBooks
to track
down a
transaction.

5. **Click Find.**

   All transactions that match your criteria flash up on the screen. Isn't QuickBooks the ant's pants? To print a report showing the transactions found, click Report.

6. **To open a transaction, select the transaction you want to see and click Go To.**

   Alternatively, to start again and search for different transactions, click Reset.

Work Those Fingers

I doubt there's any other activity that people spend so much time doing quite so badly. The average person wouldn't consider using a Swiss army knife to chop down a tree, but yet may persist in using a computer, hour after hour, without learning how to type.

It's basic. If you spend more than half an hour a day working on a computer, then you should know how to type. The average speed of a non-typist is about 15 words a minute — and that's for a pretty hot two-fingered typist — but by touch-typing, you can easily expect 60 words a minute. That's four times faster!

Consider this: If you're a non-typist who usually spends four hours a day in front of the computer and you learn how to type, you'll save about 15 hours a week, every week. And learning how to type only takes about an hour a day for six weeks.

Even if *you* can type properly, consider your employees. If they're spending time in front of the computer every day and they can't touch-type, think about paying for them to learn.

Memorise Regular Transactions

Most businesses have a number of transactions that happen every week or every month. Regular lease payments, loan repayments, rent payments and repeating sales are common examples of transactions that are made over and over.

Don't put yourself through the agony and toil of writing the details afresh each time. Instead, memorise these transactions: With the transaction open, select Memorise from the Edit menu and give this transaction a name. For transactions that are the same every month, tell QuickBooks to record the transaction automatically by making it a Standing Order. For transactions that vary, ask for QuickBooks to display a pop-up reminder when they're due.

To call up a memorised transaction, either go to Lists⇨Memorised Transactions or type Ctrl-T if you're feeling clever, then double-click the memorised transaction.

Become a Copycat

Why type details again and again, when QuickBooks can do the legwork for you? If your business has any transactions that are repetitive, it's time to tweak your preferences:

✔ **Banking preferences, Company tab.** If you click the option Autofill Payee Account Number in Cheque Memo, then QuickBooks automatically displays the relevant supplier account number in the Memo field of Write Cheques transactions.

- ✔ **General preferences, My Preferences tab.** If you click the option Automatically Remember Account or Transaction Information, QuickBooks offers two choices: You can either choose for QuickBooks to recall all details of the last transaction on any name, or you can choose for QuickBooks to pre-fill accounts based on past entries. (I prefer QuickBooks to recall the Account only, because transaction amounts normally change.)

- ✔ **General preferences, My Preferences tab.** The default date for new transactions can be either today's date or the last entered date. I find that if a client is doing a backlog of bookwork, then setting the default date to the last entered date works best.

Get Columns Just Where You Want 'Em

Don't waste time scrolling up and down lists. Sort them any which way simply by clicking on the column header. To see what I mean, call up your Item List. Want to sort by Description, rather than by Name? Click on the Description column once and the deed is done. Apply the same principle to sort by item Type, Account or Price.

The other trick is to change the columns themselves. If the columns that QuickBooks shows as a default don't provide the info you need, go to View➪Customise Columns and choose the columns you want to see, the columns to hide and the order you want to view them in. All lists in QuickBooks can be customised this way.

Stop Printing

If you can avoid printing, then rest assured that not only will you save a few trees, but you'll save time as well. As long as you keep good backups of your QuickBooks company file (as I explain in Chapter 15), you don't need to hang on to paper records. Consider the following:

- ✔ **Customer invoices.** Why print a customer invoice? Email it instead. (Certainly, don't bother printing copies of customer invoices just to file in the office — electronic copies are just as valid.) To email a customer invoice, click the To Be Emailed checkbox in the bottom-left of the invoice, then select Email Tax Invoice.

- ✔ **Purchase orders.** Why on earth would you print a purchase order when you can email it directly from your QuickBooks company file? Click the To Be Emailed checkbox in the bottom-left of the purchase order, then click Send from the Email menu at the top.

- **Profit & Loss reports.** So management wants a monthly Profit & Loss report? Display the report and select Send Report as PDF from the Email menu.

- **Customer statements.** No need for all that printing and posting. Just email 'em. Go to Create Statements from your home page and click the Email button.

- **Remittance advices for suppliers.** Forget about printed cheques and remittance advices. Pay electronically instead, then email remittance advices direct (refer to Chapters 6 and 16 for more details).

Give QuickBooks a Boost

Is your QuickBooks company file running as slow as a wet week? One of the easiest ways to give QuickBooks back some bounce is to increase the RAM. (I've found that RAM has more impact than other things such as processor speed or available hard disk space.)

By RAM, I'm not talking sheep, I'm talking Random Access Memory. So long as your computer isn't too old to accept the change, upgrading available RAM for your computer is normally relatively cheap.

Alternatively, a really simple way of making more RAM available to QuickBooks is to close any memory-hungry programs that you have running. For example, I find QuickBooks runs noticeably slower if I forget to close Photoshop before I start working on my accounts.

Add Key Reports to Your Icon Bar

Do you have certain reports that you refer to all the time? Then a neat tip is to add these reports to your icon bar. (I'm assuming here that you've configured QuickBooks so that your icon bar is displayed. If you can't see this handy helper, go to your View menu and click against Icon Bar.)

Now display a report that you use regularly and once displayed, select Add to Icon Bar from the View menu. Think up a Label (that's the text that's going to appear below the icon), a Description and a graphic.

All done? Seems almost too easy to be true.

Chapter 18

Ten Tips for Working with Your Accountant

In This Chapter

▶ Becoming an irritating pedant (if you're not already)

▶ Putting yourself through a mini-audit

▶ Using the accountant's copy features

▶ Sharing the love — tell your accountant about QuickBooks

▶ Closing off the year when everything's done

▶ Building a different kind of relationship with your accountant

*W*ith QuickBooks, there's no formal process for closing off a financial year. Instead, you can hold onto your business information year after year, without needing to purge data and lose precious historical records.

When tax time comes around, you keep working as normal, creating a special copy of your QuickBooks company file so that your accountant can make adjustments and return them to you. You then import your accountant's adjustments into your company file and before you know it, the last financial year is complete. Sounds too good to be true? That's QuickBooks.

In this chapter, I share ten handy tips for working with your accountant and for starting a new financial year.

Cultivate Your Inner Pedant

Ready to send year-end information to your accountant? Here goes:

1. **Complete every transaction up to 30 June.**

   You don't have to finish recording transactions on the last day of June. In fact, it may be months later by the time you've finished recording everything for the previous year.

2. **Go to your home page and give your company file an audit.**

   Sounds thrilling? For more information on this process, see 'Audit Yourself (Better You than Someone Else)' later in this chapter.

3. **Check that your Profit & Loss and Balance Sheet reports for last year make sense.**

   For chapter and verse about financial statements, head back to Chapter 14.

4. **Make a backup.**

   Don't know how? Refer to Chapter 15.

5. **Create an Accountant's Copy of your company file.**

   See 'Create an Accountant Copy' later in this chapter.

6. **Wait a few weeks … La di da. When your accountant sends the changes back, merge the accountant's file with yours.**

   Skip to the section 'Review Changes before Merging' for details.

7. **Do a final backup and label it Final End of Year.**

   The only difference between end-of-year backups and regular backups is that you store end-of-year backups separately, never to be used again. If you change passwords regularly, consider writing your current password on the front of the backup itself.

8. **Set a closing date so you can't make any more changes to the year just gone.**

   For this last thrilling instalment, make your way to 'Set a Closing Date' later in this chapter.

9. **Pop the champagne bottle — you're done!**

Audit Yourself (Better You than Someone Else)

Want to make sure your company file is squeaky clean before handing it over to your accountant? Then head to your home page and click Audit Company. So long as you've backed up and verified recently (and if not, refer to Chapter 15), and you've reconciled all bank accounts (Chapter 7), the Data Auditor is where you spend most of your time.

Enter the first date of the financial year as the start date and the current date as the end date, then click the Audit Company File button. QuickBooks displays a window with a column of green ticks and red question marks, similar to the rather sobering outlook shown in Figure 18-1.

With the following reviews, your aim is to get a green tick and not to give up until you do.

✔ **Reconcile invoices with linked receivables.** The idea here is that the total of your receivables report matches with the balance of Accounts Receivable in your Balance Sheet. If it doesn't, then you need to find out why not!

✔ **Reconcile purchases with linked payables.** Similar to receivables, the total of your payables report should match the balance of Accounts Payable in your Balance Sheet.

✔ **Scan for post-dated transactions.** This review identifies transactions that are dated beyond the current date, such as a transaction dated June 2018, rather than June 2011. Post-dated transactions are almost always mistakes and need to be fixed up.

✔ **Scan for prepaid transactions.** This review highlights any transactions where the payment for a sale falls earlier than the date of the sale itself, or where the payment for a purchase falls earlier than the date of the purchase.

✔ **Check item value with linked asset account.** If you don't get a green tick for this one, refer to the information on balancing your inventory account in Chapter 8 to find out what to do.

The next four reviews relate to GST, and although a red cross doesn't necessarily indicate a problem, you need to display the exception report and investigate why you're getting an error message (Chapter 10 goes into lots more detail about these four reviews and what to do).

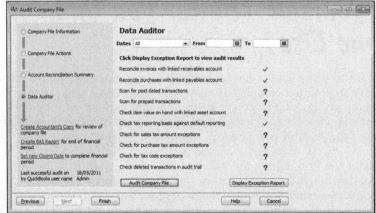

Figure 18-1:
Auditing
your
company
file.

The last review identifies deleted transactions in the audit trail, and again, a red cross doesn't necessarily indicate a problem — after all, it's often fine to delete a transaction. However, it's worth scanning this report and checking that everything looks okay.

Create an Accountant Copy

QuickBooks has a clever feature that enables you to create a special accountant's copy of your company file. Your accountant can use this copy at the same time as you keep working on your original company file. When the accountant sends their copy back to you, complete with adjustments, you then merge the accountant's file with yours.

To create an accountant copy, go to File➪Accountant's Copy➪Create Accountant's Copy and then click Next. QuickBooks asks for a dividing date (usually 30 June) to separate the part of your company file you're going to work on from the part your accountant's going to work on. Save the file when prompted (you can change the name if you like, but the file must have a .QBX extension) and then send the file to your accountant. Figure 18-2 shows a neat snapshot of this process.

While you have an accountant's copy running, the title bar in QuickBooks displays the message Accountant's Changes Pending. This message only disappears after you merge the file that your accountant returns to you.

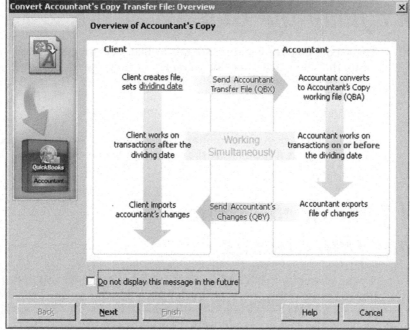

Figure 18-2:
An overview
of the
Accountant
Copy
process.

Review Changes before Merging

When your accountant returns the Accountant's Copy to you, you're
ready to merge the file with yours. No sweat. Go to File➪Accountant's
Copy➪Import Accountant's Changes. Locate the accountant's file (it will
have a .QBY extension), and click Open.

At this point, don't click Import to incorporate the accountant's file without
taking a look at it. Before you doing anything, click Print and have a careful
read through all the changes your accountant has made. (This document
can make pretty interesting reading — at last you'll find out just what your
accountant does to earn those fees!)

After you click Import, QuickBooks displays the import results (click Print
if any warning messages are shown here). From here, follow the prompts to
back up, then click Close.

Don't Jump the Gun

The accountant copy feature sounds brilliant — and indeed it is — but be aware that during the time an accountant's copy exists, you won't be able to edit or delete accounts, nor reconcile bank accounts. This restriction isn't too bad if your accountant processes adjustments within a few weeks, but can be a nightmare if the accountant is on a go-slow.

The solution? Ask your accountant to let you know when he or she is ready to work on your file, and only then create an accountant's copy.

Tell Your Accountant about QuickBooks

If your accountant isn't a QuickBooks convert yet, then you're just the one to spread the word. In true evangelical fervour, suggest that your accountant become a Reckon Professional Partner (for $579, membership includes all QuickBooks software, plus unlimited technical support). This fee also includes the QuickBooks Accountant Edition, which enables your accountant to make adjustments to your work in a format that you can then import automatically into your company file.

Despite your entreaties, occasionally accountants prefer to work on their clients' accounts using their own practice management software. That's okay, but if you've already created an accountant's copy in QuickBooks, then you need to do two things. First, you need to cancel the accountant's copy: Go to File⇨Accountant's Copy⇨Cancel Accountant's Changes, then click Yes. Second, ask your accountant for a record of adjustments made and then record these adjustments in your company file. This way, your end-of-financial-year statements in QuickBooks will match with the financial statements that your accountant provides.

Set a Closing Date

At Step 8 in the section 'Cultivate Your Inner Pedant' earlier in this chapter, I talk about setting a closing date. When you set a closing date, you lock your company file so that no one can accidentally create or edit transactions in the period that you've just completed. Closing dates are a vital part of working with your accountant — the last thing you want to do is inadvertently make changes to last year's figures after your accountant has already finalised everything and lodged your tax return.

To set a closing date, first make sure you're in single-user mode, then go to Edit⇨Preferences⇨Accounting. Select the Company Preferences tab. In the Closing Date section, enter the date up to which you want to close off accounts, and then enter a password (passwords aren't compulsory here, but without a password it's so easy to make changes that you lose any benefits from setting a closing date).

I don't reserve the closing date feature for financial year-ends only. I often suggest clients set a closing date each time they lodge their Business Activity Statement, so that they can't inadvertently make changes to an accounting period which has already been finalised.

Communicate

The biggest key to any relationship, whether it's with your accountant, your spouse or your cat, is communication. With QuickBooks, communicating with your accountant is easier than ever, so long as you know a few tricks of the trade:

- ✔ **Plan ahead for tax.** Don't wait until June has come and gone before worrying about your tax bill. Get your accountant to give your company file the once-over in April or May and ask for advice to help you minimise your tax, before it's too late.

- ✔ **Ask for advice instead of bookkeeping.** Have you ever heard of an accountant who lowered annual fees? No, me neither. So, if you've recently switched to QuickBooks and you're doing 90 per cent more of the work, harbour no illusions that your labours will save money. Instead, be realistic and get your pound of flesh by asking for business advice in place of the bookkeeping services your accountant used to provide.

- ✔ **Become more informed.** With QuickBooks, you can produce your own Profit & Loss and Balance Sheet reports whenever you want, at the click of a button. Ask your accountant to look through these statements with you, explain what they mean and analyse what you could be doing better.

Keep Track of Your Assets

Did you know that QuickBooks has a fixed asset register tucked away in the Company menu? To check out this secret feature, go to Lists⇨Fixed Asset Item List. The first time you look at this list it's empty, of course, but adding an asset is easy: Click New on the Item menu and follow your nose to complete the details, such as a description, purchase price and serial number.

I'm always one to sing the praises of QuickBooks, but the fixed asset register is a feature that transports me to the edge of evangelical fervour. Having somewhere logical to keep track of assets makes good business sense, and in the event of an insurance claim — those insurance companies will do almost anything not to cough up — having a detailed record of asset purchase dates, serial numbers and warranty expiry dates is a godsend.

The other reason I'm so keen on the fixed asset register is this: Because depreciation is such an important tax deduction, you need to take all the measures you can to ensure you don't miss out. Provide your beloved bean-counter with a copy of your asset register at the end of each financial year, sorting this register by purchase date. When your tax return is complete, match up this register against your Depreciation Schedule and check that all is well.

Anticipate the Obvious

Make things easy for your accountant by anticipating some questions:

- ✔ **Your motor vehicle percentage.** If you use a motor vehicle for part-business, part-personal use, you need to tell your accountant the percentage split. (You also need to do one of those mind-numbingly bureaucratic log books at least once every five years.)

- ✔ **Your home office percentage.** If you claim home office expenses such as rent, rates, mortgage interest or dog food for that vicious guard-dog poodle, provide your accountant with a record of how you've calculated your home office percentages. Also, tell your accountant how you've dealt with these expenses in your company file (Chapter 5 shows one way of splitting transactions to separate the personal amount from the business amount).

- ✔ **Interest or dividend income.** You need to tell your accountant about any interest or dividend income that you didn't bank in your business account (and therefore isn't showing in your QuickBooks company file).

Appendix

The QuickBooks Family

The QuickBooks software family is one of those old-fashioned prolific dynasties spanning several generations, with lots of offspring and a wide network of in-laws and out-laws. Not only does this include the standard QuickBooks accounting software family, ranging from QuickBooks EasyStart to QuickBooks Enterprise, but there's also an extended family of products that includes Reckon's Retail Point of Sale, Reckon Payroll Premier and Quicken Personal. In this appendix I talk about each one.

Choosing the One that's Right for You

'Choosing the One that's Right for You' makes me think of those hapless relationships earlier in my life that flourished and then floundered, blossomed then withered. Life could have been quite different, if only choosing the right one had been a little easier.

Fortunately, choosing accounting software is much easier than choosing husbands. Have a read through the summary of the different versions of QuickBooks in this chapter, and ask yourself whether you've made the best choice.

It's not a problem if you've got extra features that you don't need (after all, a man who's happy to shop as well as cook suits me just fine), but if you start off without the features that your business needs, then you'll be cramping your style.

I can't give you a definitive explanation of which version is best, because the decision varies according to the size and nature of your business. However, here's my rough guide to finding the perfect QuickBooks partner:

✔ **QuickBooks EasyStart.** For a small service business just getting started and running from home, QuickBooks EasyStart is the best bet. Businesses using this product include architects, gardeners, home-based consultants and musicians.

Although QuickBooks EasyStart has fewer features than its bigger brothers and sisters, if you simply require small business basics this version's simplicity can work to your advantage: Because you have less to master, your chances of making a mess are massively reduced!

✔ **QuickBooks Accounting.** For an established service business that requires solid accounting, streamlined bank reconciliations or cost centre analysis, QuickBooks Accounting is an excellent choice. Examples of businesses using this product include graphic designers, journalists and sales consultants.

✔ **QuickBooks Plus.** For any business requiring payroll management or inventory, QuickBooks Plus is the go. QuickBooks Plus is the core small business product in the QuickBooks range.

✔ **QuickBooks Pro.** This version has all the features of QuickBooks Plus, but also allows you to create quotes and generate progress invoices. QuickBooks Pro also offers foreign currency and importing of bank statements.

✔ **QuickBooks Contractor.** Similar to QuickBooks Pro, QuickBooks Contractor enables businesses to draw up quotes or bill customers progressively, and is ideal for tradespeople or builders. The main distinction between QuickBooks Contractor and QuickBooks Pro is that QuickBooks Contractor offers time billing.

✔ **QuickBooks Premier.** QuickBooks Premier provides multi-user access, advanced financial forecasting and multiple price levels.

When I say that QuickBooks Premier has *multi-user access*, what I mean is that more than one person can log onto QuickBooks Premier at the same time, enabling several employees to work simultaneously on accounts. For example, someone can raise invoices, another person can record expenses, a bookkeeper can reconcile the bank account and a manager can browse through financials — all at the same time.

QuickBooks Premier comes with three licences, with additional licences required for up to five users. (By contrast, you can use QuickBooks Pro in a multi-user environment, but you have to purchase a separate copy of the software for each additional user.)

✔ **QuickBooks Premier, industry-specific versions.** QuickBooks Premier also comes in five industry-specific flavours: Premier Contractor Edition, Premier Manufacturing & Wholesale Edition, Premier Nonprofit Edition, Premier Professional Service Edition and Premier Retail Edition.

Although the features in each industry-specific version are virtually identical to QuickBooks Premier itself, the strength of industry-specific versions is that they include customised reports and business templates specific to that industry.

✔ **QuickBooks, hosted by Reckon Online.** This online version of QuickBooks offers all the features of QuickBooks Premier, but as an annual subscription. Your data (and the QuickBooks software itself) is hosted online by Reckon and you access your accounts via a remote desktop connection.

What are the upsides of working this way? First, you can access your data from anywhere in the world using any computer. Second, depending on how many users you have, the online subscription service often works out a bit cheaper than buying QuickBooks Premier outright.

✔ **QuickBooks Enterprise.** Available as an annual licence fee, QuickBooks Enterprise is the matriarch of the QuickBooks family, offering multi-user capacity for up to 30 employees, multi-company reporting across subsidiaries and remote access from multiple locations.

I strongly recommend you get a version of QuickBooks that includes payroll if you have two or more employees, simply because you'll save so much time. All products from QuickBooks Plus upwards (in other words QuickBooks Plus, QuickBooks Pro, QuickBooks Premier and QuickBooks Enterprise) include payroll.

Moving Up the Family Tree

So, you've outgrown your current version of QuickBooks software and want to move up a level? Hey, it's time to upgrade.

Many people don't realise that when upgrading QuickBooks software, you don't have to go out and buy a whole new package. Instead, you can pay a smaller fee to purchase a *family upgrade*. For example, if you initially purchased QuickBooks EasyStart and now want to upgrade to QuickBooks Plus, you only have to pay for a family upgrade, which is a lot cheaper than going out and buying a whole new copy of QuickBooks Plus.

The other piece of good news is that you don't lose any of your work when you upgrade. You simply install the new software and ask it to do its stuff. It whizzes, groans, moans and grunts, but only for a few minutes until the job is done. Every bit of information you had in your earlier version of QuickBooks software is carried across into the new format, without missing a beat.

The easiest way to upgrade your software is to phone QuickBooks Customer Service on 1300 784 253.

Other QuickBooks Products

After you've chosen your core QuickBooks accounting software, consider whether any other QuickBooks products may come in handy for your business.

Retail Point of Sale

Reckon's Retail Point of Sale is the main product in this range, but if you're opening a new retail business for the first time and you haven't purchased any QuickBooks software yet, then the Retail Starter Kit is probably the better deal, because it includes not only QuickBooks Plus and Retail Point of Sale, but a cash drawer, thermal receipt printer and barcode scanner as well.

For stores with items that don't have barcodes such as bakeries, bars and cafes, Retail Point of Sale Touch Screen gives you the ability to manage front of store operations with greater ease. You can also adapt Retail Point of Sale to the hospitality industry, using in-built features to track table orders, send orders to the kitchen, recall orders from any terminal and track order numbers.

One of the best things about Reckon's Retail Point of Sale product is that it speaks the same language as QuickBooks. At the end of each day or week, Retail Point of Sale automatically sends the details of every transaction into your QuickBooks company file, so that you maintain a complete record of sales, purchases and movements in inventory in your accounting system. To find out more about Reckon's point-of-sale products, visit `www.quicken.com.au` and follow the links for Point of Sale.

Reckon Payroll Premier

The Payroll that comes with QuickBooks Plus, QuickBooks Pro and QuickBooks Premier is excellent for most businesses, but it does have its limits. As a rule of thumb, if you have more than 30 employees, you're likely to need more sophisticated software in order to cope with multiple awards and payroll security concerns. The answer is Reckon Payroll Premier, a stand-alone payroll package that integrates seamlessly with QuickBooks Plus, QuickBooks Pro and QuickBooks Premier.

Included in Payroll Premier's list of can-dos is an Awards module, which stores relevant rates and details of allowances for full-time, part-time and casual employees. The timesheet component in this module lets you determine the pay rates that apply to hours worked at various times and days of the week. All you have to do is enter the start and finish time of each shift and Payroll Premier does the rest automatically.

Quicken Personal

Quicken Personal is the world's leading personal finance organiser and is the best way to keep track of your investment portfolio. Not only can you keep track of share prices, purchases, gains and losses, but you can track your spending and savings, optimise your investments, prepare for taxes and plan for your future.

Quicken Personal Plus is essentially the same software but with a few more bells and whistles. One neat feature is the ability to download your portfolio and trading history into Personal Plus when trading with the online trading service Reckon E*TRADE.

Index

· ·

• A •

A/P Ageing Summary report, 147, 150, 155–156, 206
A/R Ageing Detail Report, 106
A/R Ageing Summary report, 83–85, 206
ABA files
  generating, 150, 369
  previewing, 369
ABN
  entering, 219
  missing, 144
  recording, 14, 66
abnormal expenses, 33
access rights. *See* passwords
account balances on home page, 21
account numbers
  customers, 40
  versus names, 119
account types
  defined, 31–32
  selecting, 34
accountant's copy
  cancelling, 384
  creating, 382
  reviewing changes, 383
  versus portable files, 348
  working with, 384
accountants, 380, 385
Accounting Basis, 238
accounts. *See also* Chart of Accounts
  adding, 31
  clearing, 367
  customising for GST, 218–219
  deleting, 36, 37
  for credit cards, 123–124
  grouping, 36–38
  GST, 209–211, 228
  items, 178
  making inactive, 37
  merging, 37
  moving, 37
  opening balances, 209–214
  reconciling, 158
  reporting on, 310–311
  selecting, 116–117
  suspense accounts, 103, 117
  Uncleared Transactions account, 159
accounts payable
  defined, 32
  reporting for, 147, 156
accounts receivable
  defined, 32
  reporting for, 18, 156
accrual reporting
  for GST, 134, 156, 210–211, 234, 238
  for income tax, 225, 234, 235
accumulated depreciation, 334
activating QuickBooks software, 27
activities (billing for), 61
Additional Customisation window, 256, 258–259, 262
Additional Info tab, 40, 43
Adjust Quantity On Hand window, 188, 200
Adjustment Account (inventory), 188, 197, 200
Adjustment Date field, 188
adjustment notes. *See* credit notes
adjustments
  forced, 170
  payroll, 285
administrator password, 15, 359
Adobe Acrobat, 81
advance payments, 89, 97–98

Advanced Find feature, 374
ageing receivables reports, 85
ageing payable reports, 147
allocation accounts, 117
allowances
  on payment summaries, 275–276
  reporting on, 274
  setting up, 273, 275
  tax exemptions, 276
  Tax Tracking, 276
American dates, 26
amounts
  filtering by, 312
  searching by, 141
analysing
  expenses, 38
  income, 179
  production costs, 186
  profitability, 323–332
  sales, 179
annual leave. *See* entitlements
APCA number, 366
applying payments automatically, 88
archival backups, 343
archiving data, 353–355
assets
  asset register, 386
  checking, 333
  purchasing, 144–145
asterisk symbol, 165
ATM withdrawals, 111, 112
Audit Company window, 233, 381
audit integrity, 56
audit trail, 382
AUSkey
  configuring QuickBooks for,
    241, 243
  payment summaries, 305
Australian Taxation Office, 219
Auto Filtering button, 319
average cost
  adjusting, 198–199
  calculating, 194
  opening, 189
awards (employee), 284

• B •

backing up. *See also* backups
  archival, 343, 346
  data other than QuickBooks, 342
  end-of-financial year, 380
  end-of-payroll year, 305
  frequency, 343
  how to, 343–344
  importance of, 342
  off-site, 343
  on a network, 343
  online, 346–347
  onto CD, DVD, 343–346
  scheduling, 344–345
  storage, 348
  templates, 269
  troubleshooting, 351–352
backorders, 63, 137
backups
  finding, 351, 355
  repairing, 352
bad debts, 108–109
Balance Sheet report
  account types, 31
  budgets, 336
  displaying, 212
  matching with accountant, 214
  understanding, 333–334
balancing. *See* reconciling
bank accounts
  multiple, 114–116
  opening balances, 16,
    159–160
  preparing for online, 366
  reconciling, 157–174
  selecting, 112
  transferring funds between, 120
  viewing transactions, 121
bank deposits, grouping,
  85–86
bank fees
  GST on, 229
  recording, 117, 131, 163
Bank Reconciliation report, 174

bank reconciliations. *See* reconciling bank accounts
Banking Register window, 121
barcode scanners, 187
BAS. *See* Business Activity Statements
Base Unit of Measure, 181
batch payment files, 365–366, 368
batch printing, 79
beginning balance
  checking, 169
  matching, 161, 162
  troubleshooting, 167, 170–173
billing for time, 61
bills
  duplicate, 156
  entering, 137
  for services, 139–140
  getting GST right, 145
bills of materials, 186
bonuses, 279, 281
borders, adding to forms, 261
boxes, adding to forms, 261
branch billing, 62
BSB number, 366
Budget Overview report, 338
budgets
  consolidating, 337
  for tax, 385
  setting up, 336–339
  using Excel, 320
  versus forecast, 339
builders, 328, 388
Business Activity Statements. *See also* GST
  adjusting previous periods, 72
  closing dates, 385
  configuring, 220, 236–240
  getting right, 227
  lodging, 240–244
  maintaining integrity of, 72
  PAYG withholding, 239
  preparing for, 236
  printing, 240, 242
  receiving a refund for, 246–247
  recording payment of, 245
  saving, 240, 242
  wages, 236

• *C* •

CAG tax code, 145, 223, 224, 230
CAG tax item, 221
CAI tax item, 222
capital acquisitions
  allocation accounts, 117
  on BAS, 239
  tax codes for, 145, 223
  tax items for, 221
capital contributions, 102
capital losses, 33
Cash Back menu, 91
Cash Flow Projector, 339
cash
  generating, 104–109
  payments, 89
  reporting for GST, 225
  reporting for profit, 235
  sales, 73
cashflow reports, 320, 339
casuals, 289
CDs, 343, 351
cents
  hiding, 314
  missing, 269
Chart of Accounts. *See also* accounts
  adding accounts, 34
  bank accounts, 115
  customising columns, 35
  customising for GST, 115
  mapping tax codes, 227
  reports, 311
  setting up payroll accounts, 274
  understanding, 29–38
chasing overdue accounts, 104–109
checklist, end-of-year, 381
Cheque No. field, 112
cheques. *See also* Write Cheques window
  deleting, 122
  uncleared, 158
child support, 274, 277, 300

classes
  adding, 325
  allocating expenses, 326
  generating QuickReports, 326
  how they work, 324
  on pays, 326
  switching on, 325
  when to use, 325, 328
Classification field, 284
classroom training, 24
Clean Up data command, 354
Cleared Balance, 169
cleared transactions, 123, 155, 165
clearing accounts, 245, 247, 367
closing dates, 380, 384
closing your company file, 25
collection letters, 106
collective agreements, 297
colours
  adding to forms, 260
  changing schemes, 20
  home page, 22
columns
  adding, 252, 254, 258
  changing on reports, 309, 313
  customising, 35, 59, 191, 377
  deleting, 262
  for dates, 74
  hiding, 252, 254, 258
  sorting by, 42, 377
commissions, 33
community forum, 24
company contributions, 273
company details, 13
company file
  accountant's copy, 382–383
  closing, 25
  creating, 13–15
  locating, 15, 355
  looking after, 353–358
  naming, 15
  opening, 25
Company Snapshot, 22–23, 334–335
condensing data, 353–355
confidentiality. *See* passwords
Config button, 237, 241

consultants, accredited, 23
Contractor Edition, 388
conversion date, 12–13
converting data, 13
corruption, avoiding, 358
cost centres. *See* profitability
cost of goods sold, 33, 331
costs
  adjusting, 198–199
  calculating, 194
  opening inventory, 177, 189
  viewing, 194
Create Custom Liability Payments
    window, 247, 299
Create Invoices window, 57–58, 252
Create Sales Receipt window, 89–90
credit cards
  accepting payment by, 89
  opening balances, 123–124
  paying off, 126
  paying suppliers using, 150
  personal expenses, 126
  reconciling, 158, 170, 173
  recording debits, 124–126
  setting up, 123–124
credit limits, setting, 84
credit notes
  applying to invoices, 72
  creating, 71
  dating, 71
  from suppliers, 156
  printing, 79, 80
creditors. *See* accounts payable
credits
  applying against invoices, 72,
    96, 106
  applying against purchases, 156
  applying to debits, 153–154
  from suppliers, 153
  holding against accounts, 95
CSV files, 319
Ctrl keys, how to use, 373
custom fields
  customers, 40, 258, 259, 264
  defining, 47
  items, 186, 259

printing, 254, 259
suppliers, 258, 259, 264
custom pricing, 62
custom reports
  creating, 320
  importing, 317–318
  QuickBooks community, 318
  saving, 316–317
Customer:Job column, 328
Customer & Supplier Profile List, 46
Customer Centre, 39
customer deposits, 97
Customer Lists, 39–48
Customer Message field, 58, 62
customer payments
  applying automatically, 88
  by credit card, 89
  deleting, 93–95, 165
  depositing, 90
  finding, 92–93, 166
  grouping, 85–86
  in advance, 97–98
  overpayments, 95
  part-payments, 73
  troubleshooting, 92–97
  undeposited funds, 85–86
  viewing history, 93
customer statements
  customising, 62
  generating, 104–105
  emailing, 378
Customer Total Balance field, 105
Customer Type List, 46
customers. *See also* receivables
  account numbers, 40
  adding custom info, 40, 48
  addresses, 40
  applying credits, 96
  billing, 55, 81
  changing details, 44
  creating, 39–40
  grouping, 46, 47
  keeping notes, 107
  managing credits, 72
  merging, 45
  opening balances, 11, 40, 204–207

overseas, 231
payment details, 88
payment terms, 60
refunds, 72
reports, 311
types, 46, 89
viewing details for, 42
customising
  chart of accounts, 29–34
  colour schemes, 20
  columns in lists, 42
  home page, 21
  QuickBooks, 252–259
  reports, 313, 320
  templates, 251–270

● **D** ●

data
  exporting, 321
  importing, 179
  rebuilding, 357–358
  repairing, 352, 358
  verifying, 25, 356
Data Auditor, 234, 381
database features in QuickBooks, 47
data-entry, facilitating, 253
date-driven payment terms, 154
dates
  back to front, 26
  defaults, 377
  inserting on invoices, 74
  memorised transactions, 77
  on memorised reports, 316
  payroll, 272, 285
  stocktakes, 201
  when to begin, 10, 12–13
debits and credits
  GST, 240
  on BAS, 240
debt collection
  improving, 84
  keeping notes, 107
  reports, 83–84
  techniques, 104–109
deciding when to begin, 12–13

decimal points (displaying), 265
deductions, tracking using payroll, 277
defaults
  date, 377
  entitlements, 290
  fonts, 260
  payroll, 284
  reporting basis, 234
  reports, 315
  tax codes, 34, 231
  templates, 58
  text on emails, 143
deleting
  accounts, 36, 37
  customers, 45
  expense transactions, 123
  items on forms, 262
  sales, 70
  suppliers, 45
demographics, recording, 46
deposits
  choosing tax codes, 103
  from customers, 97
  transferring funds, 90–91
  uncleared, 158
depreciation
  checking, 333
  claiming, 386
  opening balance, 213
desktop, 19–21
direct debits, 111, 112, 118, 163
direct entry files, 365
direct funds transfer, 370
director loan accounts, 103, 116
disappearing transactions, 163
disclaimers, 255
discounts
  adding to invoices, 64
  as item type, 51
  GST on, 62, 151
  suppliers, 151
  understanding, 64
  versus price levels, 62, 195
downloading templates, 267
drawings. *See* personal expenses
duplicate entries, 72

• E •

EasyStep Interview, 10, 13–16
EFTPOS
  merchant fees, 163
  payments from customers, 85–86
  payments to suppliers, 111–114
Electronic Clearing account, 367, 371
electronic payments
  getting rid of, 371
  safeguarding against fraud, 371–372
  sending, 370
  testing, 368
  tips for, 365–372
  to employees, 274, 285, 286
  to suppliers, 112, 148, 150
  two methods, 365
  using clearing accounts, 367, 371
emailing
  changing default text, 81
  company files, 347
  customer statements, 105
  in batches, 81
  pay slips, 287, 370
  purchase orders, 143
  reports, 320
  sales invoices, 80–81
  testing, 81
  to multiple addresses, 40
emails, backing up, 342
Employee Centre, 272, 282
Employee Organiser, 302
employee termination payments, 303
employees. *See also* payroll
  banking details, 367
  classification, 284
  inactive, 285
  liabilities, 299–300
  paying electronically, 366–368
  processing pays, 286
  recording time, 287
  setting up, 273, 282
  tax file numbers, 283, 303
  tax scales, 283, 289
  terminating, 303

Employment Info tab, 284
Ending Date, 163
end-of-year
  backing up, 346, 380
  closing dates, 379, 384
  matching statements, 384
  reports, 174
  tax tables, 302
Enter Bills window, 138, 140, 153
entitlements
  calculating, 292
  carried forward, 293
  defaults, 290
  not overpaying, 294
  overview, 290–295
  recording when taken, 294
  resetting, 273
  setting up, 275, 290, 293
  troubleshooting, 295
equity, defined, 32
errors, logging, 357
estimates
  accounting for, 77
  adapting, 252
  converting to sales, 78
  creating, 77–78
  invoicing progressively, 78
  printing, 78, 270
  reports, 311
Excel
  creating cashflows, 339
  creating graphs using QuickBooks
    data, 315
  deleting spacer columns, 319
  importing from QuickBooks, 47,
    321
  sending reports to, 319
exemptions (tax), 276
EXP tax code, 225
EXP tax item, 222
expenses
  analysing, 38
  claiming, 127
  defined, 33
  deleting, 122
  finding, 121

input-taxed, 114
onbilling, 56, 114, 328
recording, 111–119, 131
selecting accounts for, 113, 116
splitting, 117–118
versus cost of goods, 33
what tax code to pick, 114
Export Report window, 319
export sales, 67, 238
exporting
  data, 321
  lists, 47
  reports, 317

● *F* ●

F1 command, 23
F2 command, 27, 356
FBT, tracking via payroll, 273
fields, overlapping, 259
file size, reducing, 353–355
files. *See also* backing up
  attributes, 351, 352
  extensions, 341
  growing too big, 353
  naming, 341, 345, 350
  PDF, 81
filtering
  by account, 312
  by amount, 312, 374
  by class, 327
  by item, 313
  by number, 374
  in Excel, 319
  on reports, 309, 311
Financial Statement Designer, 336
financial statements, 330–334
financial year. *See* end-of-year
finding
  any transaction, 374
  customer payments, 92–93
  info in lists, 45
  supplier payments, 154
  supplier transactions, 122
  your company file, 355
fixed assets, 32, 386

floats, 129
FOB, defined, 56
fonts
  changing, 256, 260
  default, 260
  on reports, 314, 315
footers, customising, 252
forced adjustments,
    170, 215
forecasts, 339
foreign currency, 388
forms. *See also* templates
  adding boxes, 261
  adding lines, 261
  customising, 251–270
  defined, 18
Forms Express, 262
fraud, safeguarding against,
    371–372
FRE tax code, 223, 224, 227
freight, recording, 138
frequently asked questions, 23
fringe benefits, 304

• *G* •

garnishee orders, 274
getting started
  deciding when, 12–13
  general, 10–16
  GST, 209–211
  opening balances, 203–214
  payroll, 272–284
  reconciling, 158–162
goodwill, 32
Google Desktop, 358
government charges, 228
graphs, printing, 315
Gross Payments
  payroll items, 276
  reconciling, 304
gross profit margin, 331
group certificates. *See* payment
    summaries
group item type, 51

grouping
  accounts, 38
  customers, 46, 47
  items, 183–185, 191
GST. *See also* Business Activity
    Statements
  accruals basis, 134, 235
  bank fees, 163
  calculating, 68, 145
  cash basis, 235
  creating accounts for, 218
  fixing mistakes, 72, 156
  not 10 per cent, 145, 231–232
  not registered for, 67, 104, 114,
    145, 229
  on bad debts, 109
  on deposits, 91, 103
  on discounts, 62, 64, 151
  on expenses, 113
  on items, 180
  on petty cash, 130
  on private drawings, 232
  on sales invoices, 65–68, 177
  on supplier bills, 144–145
  opening balances, 204, 209–211, 213
  overview, 217–248
  preferences, 225
  reconciling, 242
  Record Deposits window, 104
  switching tracking on, 16
  Tax Code List, 222–225
  Tax Items List, 221–222
  what code to use, 229–230
GST-free sales, 238
GST-free supplies, 218

• *H* •

head office billing, 62
header accounts, 38
headers on reports, 314
health check, 22–23, 234, 381
help options, 23–24
historical transactions,
    204–205, 207

holiday leave. *See* entitlements
holiday leave loading, 275, 295
holiday pay
  in advance, 295
  paying, 289, 295
  setting up, 275
home office expenses, 229, 386
home page
  colour of, 22
  customising, 21
  defined, 17
  hiding account balances, 21
hours worked, recording, 288
housekeeping, 92

• I •

icon bar
  adding reports, 317, 330, 378
  customising, 20
  defined, 18
  hiding, 19, 20
importing
  accountant's changes, 383
  electronic payments, 370
  lists, 47, 179
  reports, 317
  templates, 269
imprest system (petty cash), 129
improving speed, 353
inactive
  accounts, 37
  customers, 45
  items, 192
  templates, 268
income. *See also* customer payments
  analysing, 30–31, 179, 325, 328, 333
  choosing tax codes, 103
  defined, 33
  interest, 100–102, 104
industry, choice of, 14, 30
industry-specific editions, 388
INP tax code, 104, 145, 223, 224
INP tax item, 221
input-taxed expenses, 114

input-taxed purchases, 114, 145, 218
insurance
  claiming, 103, 386
  GST on, 229, 231
integrating other applications, 318
interest
  expense, 117
  income, 100–102, 104, 163, 223
internet banking, 366
inventory. *See also* items
  accounts, 179
  adjustments, 197
  assemblies, 51
  checking, 189–190
  item types, 51
  opening balances, 187–190, 208
  preferences, 180
  receiving items, 136–137
  reconciling, 201, 381
  reports, 190, 200, 201
  selecting accounts, 177
  switching on, 176
Inventory Assembly items, 185
Inventory Valuation Summary report, 190, 201
investment income, 100–102, 391
invoice numbers
  avoiding duplicates, 56
  changing, 57, 270
invoices. *See also* bills, sales
  adding standard messages, 62
  adjusting columns, 59
  cash, 73
  emailing, 58, 80–81
  finding, 69
  fixing mistakes, 69–72
  GST, 65, 72
  including balance outstanding, 105
  inserting date column, 74
  monthly, 74
  over $1,000, 66
  pending, 63
  printing, 79
  tips, 68, 73–77

Item List. *See also* items
  defined, 48
  organising, 184
  spring-cleaning, 192
  viewing, 191
  working with, 48–51, 176–178
items. *See also* inventory, Item List
  adjusting, 197
  assemblies, 185
  categorising, 186
  creating, 48–50, 57, 176–178
  custom fields, 186
  deleting, 191–192
  duplicate, 193
  finding, 191
  grouping, 179, 183–185, 191
  how they work in QuickBooks, 48
  importing from other software, 179
  merging, 193
  naming, 49, 177
  non-inventory, 136–137
  parent items, 183
  pricing, 180, 193–197
  reports, 199–201
  selecting accounts, 50, 178–179
  sorting, 191
  subitems, 183
  supplier codes, 176
  tax codes for, 180
  types, 50–51

• J •

jobs, 39, 328–330
juniors, tax file numbers, 303

• K •

knowledge browser, 23

• L •

land tax, GST on, 229
Layout Designer
  overview, 260–265
  working with, 256

lease payments
  GST on, 229
  recording, 119, 376
leave. *See* entitlements
legal structure, choosing, 14
letters, chasing money, 106
licences (for QuickBooks)
  additional, 388
  locating, 26
  registering multiple, 26
limits on transactions, 353
lines
  adding to forms, 261–262
  adding to invoices, 70
  deleting from invoices, 70
lists. *See also* Chart of Accounts
  defined, 18
  limits on size, 40, 353
  memorised transactions, 75
  searching within, 45
  understanding, 29–51
loadings, 280
loans
  from banks, 103
  from directors, 103
  reconciling, 158
  recording, 32, 102–103
Locate Discrepancies button, 171
locating company files, 355
locations
  analysing profitability, 325
  grouping customers by, 46
Lodgement Ref field, 367
log books, 386
logos, adding, 255, 257–258
long service leave, 292
long-term liabilities, 32
lost QuickBooks files, 355

• M •

magnetic media form, 304
management reporting, 134
manufacturers
  assembly items, 185
  cost of goods sold, 33, 179

industry edition of QuickBooks, 388
   part numbers, 176
   price levels, 195
   using inventory, 176
margins, fixing, 269
Memo field, 58, 62, 112
memorised reports, 316–317
memorised transactions
   changing, 76
   date problems, 77
   grouping, 76
   recalling, 76
   sales, 74, 90, 376
   standing orders 75, 118–119, 376
menu bar, 17
merchant fees
   GST on, 163, 228–229
   recording, 117, 131
merging
   accounts, 37
   customers, 45
   items, 193
   suppliers, 45
messages, adding to invoices, 62
Microsoft Excel. *See* Excel
minutes as decimals, 288, 291
missing transactions, 163–165
mistakes
   finding, 157, 333
   fixing, 69–72, 93, 165
   GST, 72, 156
   purchases, 146
monthly retainers, 74
monthly threshold, 279
motor vehicle
   allowances, 273, 275, 276
   classifying expenses, 34, 38
   purchase of, 32, 221, 223, 333
   private use, 229, 232, 386
   registration, 228, 229
mouse, doing without, 63
moving accounts, 37
moving around QuickBooks, 63, 374
MPN, defined, 142
multiple bank accounts, 114

multiple price levels, 56, 62
multi-user access, 26, 388

● *N* ●

navigating
   around QuickBooks, 17–22
   to Centres, 39
   using navigation bar, 17, 19
NCF tax code, 220, 224
NCF tax item, 222
NCG tax code, 224, 226
NCG tax item, 222
NCI tax code, 224
NCI tax item, 222
net reporting, 235
networks
   backing up, 343, 347
   best practice, 358
   corruption, 358
New Item window, 176
non-inventory parts, 51
non-posting accounts, 77
non-profit organisations, 331
non-taxable transactions, 224
Notepad window, 107
NR tax code, 114, 145, 224, 228, 230
numbering
   invoices, 270
   items, 49, 176
numbers, hiding cents, 314

● *O* ●

odd amounts, 156
On Hand field, 177
one-off sales, 73
online payments. *See* electronic payments
Open Balance report, 311
Open Window List, 19
Opening Balance Equity
   bank reconciliation adjustments, 166,
      170, 214
   explained, 215
   general ledger balances, 204, 213, 334

opening balances
  accounts, 209–214
  bank accounts, 16, 160–161
  credit cards, 123–124
  customers, 11, 40, 204–206
  GST, 209–211
  inventory, 187–190, 208
  suppliers, 11, 44, 207–208
  troubleshooting, 214
  uncleared transactions, 158–159
  what not to do, 207
opening your company file, 25
orders. *See* purchase orders, sales orders
Ordinary Time Earnings, 280
other charges, 51
other current assets, 32
other current liabilities, 32
other expenses, 33
other income, 33
out of balance
  bank reconciliations, 160–161, 168
  inventory, 201
  opening balances, 214
out-of-pocket expenses, 56, 127–128
overcharges, 70
overdraft accounts, 115, 168
overdue accounts. *See* debt collection
overheads. *See* expenses
overpayments
  from customers, 95
  to suppliers, 99–100
overseas
  customers, 67, 231
  travel, 229
overtime, 275, 294
owner's contributions, 103
owner's expenses, 56, 127–128

● *P* ●

Paid Time Off report, 294–295
parent items, 183
part-payments, 73, 151
passwords
  assigning roles, 361
  company snapshot, 335
  creating, 15, 359–360
  linking restrictions to, 360
  on backups, 346
  on portable files, 348
  payroll, 293
  Windows, 344
Pay Bills window, 134, 148–150
pay slips, 287, 371
payables, reconciling, 381
PAYG Instalment tax, 239
PAYG Withholding tax
  exempt from, 276
  paying, 299–301
  setting up, 239, 277
  tax tables, 302
  tracking, 274
payment (as item type), 51
Payment Info tab, 40
payment methods
  adding, 86
  online, 368
  selecting, 112
payment summaries
  additional super, 298
  lodging via AUSkey, 305
  printing, 303–305
  reconciling, 304
  RESC, 304
  salary sacrifice super, 297
  what to include, 276–277
payment terms
  customers, 59–60
  suppliers, 150
  understanding, 154
payments, 121–123. *See also* expenses,
    customer payments
payroll. *See also* employees,
    entitlements
  additions, 273
  adjustments, 281
  confidentiality, 293
  deductions, 277
  defaults, 284
  getting started, 11, 272–284
  liability accounts, 274
  processing pays, 285–287

restricting access to, 360–361
schedules, 280–282, 285
software versions, 389
switching on, 272
tax tables, 302
timesheets, 287–288
transaction recall, 289
troubleshooting, 289
version of QuickBooks, 271
viewing pays, 287
Payroll Centre, 285–290
Payroll Clearing account, 245, 247
payroll items
defined, 275
selecting, 282
superannuation, 280
Payroll Setup Interview, 273
Payroll Summary report, 236
payroll tax, 277
pays
changing, 289
classes, 326
deleting, 289
splitting, 367
PDFs
blank, 270
invoices, 81
previewing, 270
pending sales, 63
performance, improving, 353, 378
permissions. *See* passwords
personal expenses
allocating, 116
credit cards, 126
deposits, 103
GST on, 145, 229, 232
splitting business and private, 117
tax codes on, 114, 228
personal leave. *See* entitlements
petty cash
floats, 129
GST, 130, 229
overview, 126–130
recording, 91
running a tin, 128–129
sole operators, 127–128

pictures, adding to forms,
257–258
point-of-sale software, 187
portable files
file type, 342
in order to reduce file size, 353
restoring, 348
versus backup files, 347
post-dated transactions, 381
preferences
account numbers, 119
ageing reports, 85
bank accounts, 89, 115, 148, 376
classes, 325
closing dates, 384–385
estimates, 77–78
inventory, 176–178, 180
payroll, 272, 289
price levels, 196
relationship with home page, 21
sales, 56, 89
supplier bill numbers, 150
tax, 225, 234
tweaking for speed, 376
work week, 288
prepaid transactions, 381
pre-printed stationery, 262
price levels
preferences, 56
versus discounts, 62
prices
changing, 194, 196
custom, 62
different levels, 195–197
displaying ex-tax, 68, 180
including GST, 177, 180
items, 193
printer drivers, 321
printing
avoiding, 377–378
credit notes, 80
defaults for each form, 266
estimates, 79
in reverse, 80
invoices, 79
orientation, 314

printing *(continued)*
  purchase orders, 143
  reports, 314–315
  screen dumps, 315
  slow, 270
  troubleshooting, 80, 321–322
privacy. *See* passwords
Privacy Act, 293
private expenses. *See* personal
    expenses
product groups, 179
Product Information window, 27
Professional Partner scheme, 384
Profit & Loss report
  account types, 31–33
  accrual, 134
  adding to icon bar, 330
  budgets, 336–339
  by class, 324, 327
  by Job, 329
  by project, 324
  cash basis, 332
  checking, 331–332
  customising, 331–332, 336
  design, 29, 37, 178
  emailing, 378
  historical, 212
  modifying columns, 331
  viewing differently, 38,
    307–308
profitability
  analysing, 324–332
  by job or profit centre, 329
progress invoicing, 16, 78, 258
projects, reporting on, 328
purchase orders. *See also*
    purchases
  adding comments, 142
  and workflow, 137
  closing, 146
  customising, 142
  emailing, 143
  printing, 143, 377–378
  recording, 134–137, 141
  searching for, 141

purchases. *See also* bills, purchase
    orders, suppliers
  benefits and downsides, 133–134
  credit notes, 156
  deleting, 146
  finding, 141
  fixing mistakes, 146
  overview, 133
  recording bills, 138
purging transactions, 354

• Q •

QBB file type, 342, 349, 352
QBM file type, 342
QBW file type, 15, 342, 352
Qbwin.log file, 357
QBX file type, 382
quantities, adjusting, 197–198
Quantity Available field, 181
QUE tax code, 229, 230
QuickBooks
  Accountant Edition, 336, 384
  activating, 27
  as your database, 47
  choosing what version, 271, 387–389
  community forum, 24, 318, 320
  customising, 259
  navigating around, 16–21
  product family, 3, 387–391
  registering, 26–27
  speeding up, 378
  template gallery, 255, 267
  upgrading, 15, 389
QuickBooks Accounting, 388
QuickBooks EasyStart, 388
QuickBooks Enterprise, 361, 389
QuickBooks industry editions, 388
QuickBooks online version, 389
QuickBooks Plus, 388
QuickBooks Premier, 388
QuickBooks Pro, 388
QuickBooks Retail Point of Sale, 390
Quicken Accredited Partners, 23
Quicken Personal, 391

QuickReports, 310–311
quotes. *See* estimates

• *R* •

RAM, upgrading, 378
rates, GST on, 229
rebuilding data, 357–358
recalling accounts, 377
receipts, customising, 253
receivables, 83–85, 381
Receive Inventory window,
    136–137
Receive Payments, 86–87
Reckon Advantage, 24, 302
Reckon Data Services, 352, 358
Reckon GovConnect, 243–244
Reckon Online, 389
Reckon Online Backup, 346
Reckon Payroll Premier, 390
Reckon Point-of-Sale, 187
Reckon Superlink, 301
Reckon Tools, 89, 301, 346
Reconciliation Discrepancy Report,
    171–173
reconciling
  GST, 242
  inventory, 190, 201, 381
  opening balances, 206
  payables, 381
  payment summaries, 304
  receivables, 381
  superannuation, 299–300
reconciling bank accounts
  credit cards, 170, 173
  forcing adjustments, 170
  missing transactions, 164, 166
  overview, 157–158
  reports, 174
  shortcut keys, 167
  sorting by cheque number, 164
  the first time, 158–160
  tips, 168
  troubleshooting, 162–173
  undoing, 172–173

Record Deposits window
  and GST, 103
  overview, 90–91
  receiving loans, 102
  selecting accounts, 103
  supplier refunds, 99
recurring sales. *See* memorised
    transactions
Ref No field, 125
referral source, tracking, 46
refunds
  from BAS, 245, 246–247
  from suppliers, 99–100
  to customers, 72, 95–96, 117
registering QuickBooks, 26–27
registers, defined, 18
regular payments, 118–119
reimbursements
  claiming from customers, 56
  paying to employees, 275, 276
reminders, 107, 119
remittance advices
  customising, 152
  sending, 151–152, 370–371
remote access, 389
rent payments, 376
rental income, 104
repairing data, 352, 357–358
Report Centre. *See* reports
reportable super. *See* RESC
reports
  adding to icon bar, 20, 317, 378
  Bank Reconciliation report, 174
  by account, 311
  creating graphs, 315
  custom, 320, 336
  customers, 311
  displaying, 308–309
  emailing, 320
  exporting, 317, 318–320
  filters, 309, 311
  formatting, 313, 314
  importing, 317
  memorising, 316–317
  modifying, 309, 320
  narrowing information, 311–312

reports *(continued)*
  overview, 307–322
  printing, 314, 321–322
  profitability, 329–330
  QuickBooks community library, 320
  Report Centre, 308
  saving, 316–317
  scaling, 314
  sending to Excel, 319–320
  sensitive, 360–361
  sharing, 317
  suppliers, 310–311
re-registering QuickBooks, 27
RESC, 295–298
residential real estate, 222
restoring data
  how to, 349–351
  portable files, 347–348
  supporting files, 351
  troubleshooting, 351–352
  using transaction log, 352
restrictions. *See* passwords
Retail Point of Sale, 390
retailers
  cost of goods sold, 33
  point-of-sale, 187, 390
  recording sales, 86–88
Retained Earnings, 215
revenue, analysing, 30–31
reversals of numbers, 168
right-click commands, 73
rounding of GST, 246

• *S* •

salary packages, 296
salary sacrifice super, 280, 296–297
sales. *See also* bills, invoices
  changing, 70
  deleting, 70
  emailing, 80–81
  export, 67
  GST-free, 66–67
  preferences, 56
  reporting, 225

taxable, 66
trends, 179
Sales by Customer Summary report,
    309–310, 330
sales orders
  creating, 63, 77–78
  receiving payments against, 88
Sales Price, changing, 194
Sales Receipts
  recording interest, 101
  when to use, 73, 88–90
sales territories, 46
savings accounts, 158
schedules. *See* payroll
scheduling backups, 344–345
screen dumps, 315
screens, customising, 59–60
searching, 45, 141
self-balancing transactions, 366
serial numbers, 186
service businesses, 388
service items, 51, 57
Set Credits button, 154
Shares, 391
shift loadings, 275
shipping direct to customers, 136
shortcut keys
  alt key, 374
  how to use, 2, 63, 373
  Pay Bills, 150
  sales, 59
sick leave. *See* entitlements
Simplified BAS/IAS, 237–238, 240–242
Snap to Grid command, 265
software, registering, 26–27
sorting
  accounts, 36–37
  by cheque number, 164
  customers by amount owing, 84
  info on reports, 310
  items, 191
  lists, 69
  payables report, 148
  supplier bills, 148
  transaction registers, 121

speed (of QuickBooks), 353
speeding up your work, 373–378
splitting expenses, 117–118
stamp duty, 229
standard payment terms, 154
standing orders, 75, 77, 119, 376
starting date, 12–13
state payroll tax, 277
Statement Date, choosing, 160
statements. *See* customer statements
stocktakes, 199–201
storing
  backups, 348
  information in QuickBooks, 18
subaccounts, 34, 36, 38
subcontract labour, 33
subitems, 183–184
subtotals, 51, 64
superannuation. *See also* RESC
  accounts, 274, 278–280
  additional, 297–298
  age limits, 286
  balancing, 300–301
  checking, 289
  exemptions, 279
  funds, 278, 284
  linking to employees, 284
  missing fund details, 284
  more than 9 per cent, 296
  not overpaying, 280
  on payment summaries, 304
  paying, 117, 299–300
  salary sacrifice, 296–297
  setting up, 278–280
  Superlink service, 301
  tax code for, 228
  tax tracking, 274, 278
  threshold, 279, 286, 289
  what to pay, 280
supplier bills. *See* bills
Supplier Centre, 39, 154
supplier item codes, 142, 176, 254
Supplier List, 39–48
supplier payments
  amount owing, 147–148

by credit card, 150
credits from, 153–154, 156
deleting, 155
finding, 154–155
electronic, 150, 366–367, 368
payment terms, 43–44, 147, 150,
  154
prepayments, 32
recording, 148–149
suppliers. *See also* purchases,
  supplier payments
adding new, 43–44
addresses, 43
changing details, 44–45
merging, 45
not registered for GST, 229
opening balances, 11, 44, 207
receiving refunds, 99–100
reports, 311
searching by name, 141
support, 23–24
suspense account, 103, 117

● *T* ●

T2, 239
Tab key, 63
tax, planning for, 385
Tax Agency field, 221
tax amount exceptions, 235
Tax Code Exceptions report,
  235
Tax Code List, 222–225
tax codes. *See also* GST
  choosing, 66–67
  default, 231
  defined, 220
  income accounts, 227
  on expenses, 114, 228
  on purchases, 144–145
  selecting, 113, 115
  versus tax items, 220, 226
tax file numbers, 283, 302, 303
Tax ID, 14
tax-inclusive prices, 180

Tax Invoices
  customising, 252–255
  printing, 65, 377
  requirements, 66
Tax Item List, 221–222
tax items, 220, 226
Tax Payable account, 218–219, 220, 245
Tax Rego ID field, 66
tax reporting basis, 234–235
tax scales, 283, 289
Tax Summary report, 236
tax tables, updating, 302
tax tracking (GST), 16
Tax Tracking (payroll)
  payroll items, 276
  salary sacrifice, 297
  superannuation, 278
  what to select, 276, 277
taxable supplies, 217
tax-free sales, 222
technical support, 23–24
templates. *See also* forms
  adding new fields, 264
  adding text, 255, 263
  backing up, 269
  converting to PDF, 270
  copying, 256, 267–268
  customising, 59–60, 251–270
  deleting, 268
  downloading, 267–268
  finetuning, 265
  importing, 267–268
  logos, 257–258
  moving items, 263
  multiple versions, 254
  online gallery, 255, 267–268
  printing, 266, 269–270
  sharing, 268–269
  storing, 269
  troubleshooting, 269–270
  undoing deletions, 263–264
templates (reports)
  exporting, 317
  importing, 317
  location of, 318

termination pays, 281, 285, 303
text (on forms)
  adding, 263
  lining up, 265
  truncated, 269
time, billing for, 61, 388
timesheets
  employees, 287–288
  Payroll Premier, 390–391
  work week, 288
tlg file type, 342, 352
To Do List, 107
toggling between files, 25
Total Value field, 177
trade creditors, 208
trade debtors, 206
tradespeople, 388
trailing zeros, 265
training, 23–24
transaction banking software, 366
transaction limits, 353
transaction log file, 342, 352
transactions
  editing, 123
  memorising, 118–119
  not reportable, 224, 230–231
  post-dated, 381
  prepaid, 381
  recalling, 377
  recording automatically, 76
  searching by supplier, 122
  sorting, 69
transferring funds
  between accounts, 90–91, 120
  electronically, 367
  to credit card, 126
travel expenses
  GST on, 229
  recording, 117
trends, analysing, 330–332
troubleshooting
  entitlements, 295
  inventory balances, 202
  opening balances, 214

payroll, 289
printing, 321–322
restoring data, 351–352
templates, 269–270
viewing tips, 19–20
typing, learning how, 375–376

• *U* •

unapplying payments, 87
uncleared transactions
  creating account for, 159
  listing, 158–159
  reconciling, 161
undeposited funds
  explained, 85
  preferences, 56
  reconciling, 166
  selecting, 89
  when to use, 86
  working with, 90–92
undo last reconciliation, 172–173
union fees, 274, 277
units of measure
  recording, 177
  working with, 181–182
upgrading
  expanded list sizes, 40
  from older versions, 13, 15, 389
  to Windows 7, 358–359
users, setting up, 359
utilities, 354–355

• *V* •

Value Adjustment checkbox, 188
verifying data, 25, 356
views, customising, 19–20, 42
voiding sales, 70

• *W* •

W1, 236, 239
W2, 236, 239
W3, 239
W4, 239
wages. *See also* employees
  reporting for, 236
  showing on BAS, 239
  tax code, 228
WET tax, 222
wholesalers
  industry edition of QuickBooks, 388
  price levels, 195
windows, customising views, 19–20
Windows 7, 358–359
Windows Live Mail, 359
withholding tax, 144
workers comp claims, 103
workflow
  electronic payments, 370
  paying suppliers, 146
  purchases, 137
working capital, 104
workplace giving, 277
Write Cheques window
  GST, 112–113
  overview, 111–118
  petty cash, 129–130
  versus Pay Bills, 134
writing off bad debts, 108–109

• *Y* •

year-to-date totals, 273

FOR DUMMIES®

Business & Investing

Bookkeeping FOR DUMMIES

978-1-74216-971-2
$39.95

Small Business FOR DUMMIES

978-1-74216-853-1
$39.95

Marketing Your Small Business FOR DUMMIES

978-1-74216-853-1
$39.95

Buying Property FOR DUMMIES

978-0-73037-556-2
$29.95

Getting Started in Small Business IT FOR DUMMIES

978-0-73037-668-2
$19.95

Getting Started in Bookkeeping FOR DUMMIES

978-1-74246-874-7
$19.95

Getting Started in Small Business FOR DUMMIES

978-1-74216-962-0
$19.95

Tax for Australians FOR DUMMIES

978-1-74246-848-8
$34.95

Exchange-Traded Funds FOR DUMMIES

978-0-73037-695-8
$39.95

Managed Funds FOR DUMMIES

978-1-74216-942-2
$39.95

CFDs FOR DUMMIES

978-1-74216-939-2
$34.95

Share Investing FOR DUMMIES

978-1-74246-889-1
$39.95

FOR DUMMIES®

Reference

978-1-74216-999-6
$39.95

978-1-74216-982-8
$39.95

978-1-74216-983-5
$45.00

978-0-73140-909-9
$39.95

978-1-74216-945-3
$39.95

978-0-73140-722-4
$29.95

978-0-73140-784-2
$34.95

978-0-73140-752-1
$34.95

Technology

978-0-47049-743-2
$32.95

978-1-74216-998-9
$45.00

978-0-47048-998-7
$32.95

978-1-74031-159-5
$39.95

Health, Fitness & Pregnancy

978-0-73140-760-6
$34.95

978-0-73140-596-1
$34.95

978-0-73037-500-5
$39.95

978-0-73037-664-4
$39.95

978-0-73037-536-4
$39.95

978-1-74216-984-2
$39.95

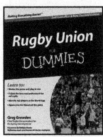

978-1-74031-073-4
$39.95

978-0-73037-660-6
$39.95

978-1-74216-972-9
$39.95

978-1-74216-946-0
$39.95

978-1-74031-103-8
$39.95

978-1-74031-042-0
$39.95

ed in Australia
r 2022
846